DEDICATED TO MY GRANDCHILDREN
WARREN LAMSON LOBDELL
RUTH LOBDELL
HARRISON LOBDELL.

CONTENTS

CHILDREN AND DESCENDANTS OF ISAAC (5) LOBDELL—MIRRIAM POMEROY AND JERUSHA LOBDELL. (JOSHUA [4], JOSHUA [3], JOSHUA [2], SIMON [1])

	PAGE		PAGE
Mirriam (6) .	64	Olive (6)	. 64
Lois (6) . .	64, 65, 66. 74	Princess (6) .	64, 70, 77
Anna (6) . .	64	Jerusha (6) .	. 65, 71
Isaac (Jr.)	65.	Lovisa (6)	65, 71, 72
66, 67 70, 74, 75, 76, 77, 78		James Hervey Sr (6)	72, 73, 74
Joshua Pomeroy (6)	64		

CHILDREN AND DESCENDANTS OF ISAAC (6) LOBDELL, JR.—NANCY UDELL, AND CLORINDA CHAPIN BABCOCK. (ISAAC [5], JOSHUA [4], JOSHUA [3], JOSHUA [2], SIMON [1])

Luman (7)	66, 74, 75, 76, 77, 78	Harriet (7)	67
Justus (7)	66, 75	Mirriam (7)	67
Jane (7) .	66	Isaac D M (7) 67, 68, 69, 70, 76, 77	
Nelson (7)	66, 75, 76	Mary Jane (7)	70
Hervey (7)	67	Emily M (7)	70
Loretta (7) .	67	Francis W (7) .	70
Margaret (7) .	67. 76	Victor B (7)	70
Joshua Tompkins (7)	67		

CHILDREN AND DESCENDANTS OF JAMES (5) LOBDELL AND MARY VENABLE. (JOSHUA [4], JOSHUA [3], JOSHUA [2], SIMON [1])

Elizabeth (6)	79	Sarah (6) .	79
Gilbert (6)	79	Mary (6)	79
John (6)	79, 80, 81, 82 83	James (6)	. 79, 80

CHILDREN AND DESCENDANTS OF SIMON (5) LOBDELL AND GRACE POMEROY. JOSHUA [4], JOSHUA [3], JOSHUA [2], SIMON [1])

Rebecca (6)	84, 85	Enos (6) .	85
Simon, Jr. (6)	85, 86, 87, 88, 89, 90	Lydia (6)	85
Jacob (6) .	85	James (6)	85
Gideon (6)	85	Grace (6)	85
James (6)	85	Mirriam (6)	85
Daniel (6) .	85		

CHILDREN AND DESCENDANTS OF ABRAHAM (5) LOBDELL AND SARAH KENNARD. JOSHUA [4], JOSHUA [3], JOSHUA [2], SIMON [1])

Mary (6)	91	James Alexander (6)	91, 92
Abraham, Jr (6)	91, 93	Wm Carter (6) .	91
Sarah P (6)	91	Lydia C. (6) . .	91
Alfred (6)	91		

CHILDREN AND DESCENDANTS OF ABIJAH (5) LOBDELL AND MARY LITTLE (JOSHUA [4], JOSHUA [3], JOSHUA [2], SIMON [1])

Finishes the line of descent of Joshua (4) and Sarah (Scott) Lobdell

---

CHILDREN AND DESCENDANTS OF EBENEZER (4) LOBDELL AND DEBORAH PALMER. (JOSHUA [3], JOSHUA [2], SIMON [1])

CHILDREN AND DESCENDANTS OF JACOB (5) LOBDELL— BETTY WHITNEY AND REBECCA MOREHOUSE. (EBENEZER [4], JOSHUA [3], JOSHUA [2], SIMON [1])

CHILDREN AND DESCENDANTS OF ANSON (6) LOBDELL— ELIZA PURDY AND SARAH TOWNSEND. JACOB [5], EBENEZER [4], JOSHUA [3], JOSHUA [2], SIMON [1])

CHILDREN AND DESCENDANTS OF NATHAN (6) LOBDELL AND ANN ELIZA LYON. (JACOB [5], EBENEZER [4], JOSHUA [3], JOSHUA [2], SIMON [1])

CHILDREN AND DESCENDANTS OF JOHN (4) LOBDELL AND ELIZABETH SHERWOOD. (JOSHUA [3], JOSHUA [2], SIMON [1])

Finishes the line of descent of John (4) and Elizabeth (Sherwood) Lobdell
Also finishes descendants of Joshua (2) Lobdell through Joshua (3) and
Mary (Reynolds) Lobdell

CHILDREN AND DESCENDANTS OF EBENEZER (3) LOBDELL AND REBECCA BENEDICT. (JOSHUA [2], SIMON [1])

Finishes the line of descent of Ebenezer and Rebecca (Benedict) Lobdell

---

CHILDREN AND DESCENDANTS OF CALEB (3) LOBDELL— ELIZABETH ———, BETHIA PADDOCK AND RUTH ———. (JOSHUA [2], SIMON [1])

Finishes the line of descent of Caleb (3) and wives, Elizabeth ——— Lobdell and Bethia Paddock Lobdell.

CHILDREN AND DESCENDANTS OF JOHN (3) LOBDELL AND RUTH SHERWOOD (JOSHUA [2], SIMON [1])

Finishes line of descent of John (3) and Ruth (Sherwood) Lobdell

LOBDELLS MENTIONED IN COUNCIL OF APPOINTMENT IN MILITARY RECORDS NEW YORK STATE, 1783-1821

Essex County

BOUGHTON LOBDELL—Appointed Second Lieutnant Artillery, July 3, 1804, and EBENEZER RICE appointed Second Lieutenant vice BOUGHTON LOBDELL, moved, 1806

JACOB LOBDELL—Ensign Riflemen Thirty-seventh Regiment, 1815

JACOB LOBDELL—Lieutenant, Riflemen Thirty-seventh Regiment vice HASCALL, moved, 1816

JACOB LOBDELL—Captain Riflemen, 1819

JOHN "LOBDEN"—First Lieutenant, vice TROOP, promoted, 1811

JOHN "LOBDEN"—Captain, vice GEO TROOP, 1812

SAMPSON SMITH—Seventh Regiment Cavalry, First Squadron, vice LOBDELL, resigned

SYLVANUS LOBDELL—Quartermaster vice ASA FORBES, re-signed, 1802

JARED REYNOLDS—Quartermaster, vice SYLVANUS LOBDELL, resigned, 1807

Dutchess County

EBENEZER LOBDELL—Lieutenant Sixty-first Regt Infantry, 1817

Ontario County

JACOB LOBDELL—Lieutenant, 1805

JACOB LOBDELL—Captain, vice ELISHA BRACE, 1806

JACOB LOBDELL—Captain, 1807

Oneida County

JOHN LOBDELL—Cornet in Captain (Theodorus) Ross troop (Essex Co.), Reg, First Brigade of Cavalry, First Squadron, 1808

Montgomery County

JOHN L LOBDELL—Ensign, Thirty-fourth Regiment Infantry, 1819

JOHN L LOBDELL—Captain, Light Infantry, 1820

STEPHENSON LIVINGSTON—Capt, vice LOBDELL, moved, 1822,

NATHAN B LOBDELL—Captain, 122d Regular Infantry, vice BROWN, moved, 1817

CALEB W. SLOCUM—Captain, 122d Regular Infantry, vice LOBDELL, resigned, 1820

Westchester County

JOSHUA LOBDELL—Lieutenant, Thirty-eighth Regular Infantry, vice STRATTON, promoted

EXPLANATIONS

b   stands for born

m   stands for married

bapt   stands for baptized.

d   stands for died

An interrogation point means uncertainty

The different generations are indicated by exponents placed after the Christian names—thus· JOSHUA (2) LOBDELL means JOSHUA LOBDELL of the second generation from the emigrant

In a parenthesis— as, John B, (6), Wm (5), Samuel (4), Samuel (3); Joshua (2), Simon (1)—means John B of the sixth generation was the son of Wm. (5), Wm (5) was the son of Samuel (4); Samuel (4) was the son of Samuel (3), Samuel (3) was the son of Joshua (2); Joshua (2) was the son of Simon (1) (the emigrant)

PREFACE

The present work is the result of eight years of labor by the compiler, and also embraces the researches of many who have kindly placed much valuable information in my hands. When commenced I never thought nor intended putting it before the public in the form of a family history, but started to trace the lineage of my husband that I might give to my grandchildren some knowledge of their Lobdell ancestors. After securing this, as no history of the family had been published, I undertook to put in a permanent form the genealogical history of its different members, taking Simon Lobdell (whose name, with others of the pioneer fathers, hangs in the Town Hall at Milford, Conn) as the root of this branch of the family. The tradition of the family is, that they came from Wales, but search made by a descendant fails to verify this. Every available source of information has been consulted. Letters of inquiry have been written to every Lobdell descendant to be found, and it seems impossible that any shall escape representation in the book. Although nearly every state in the Union is represented in this work by descendants, Connecticut was the birthplace and last resting place for the majority of the first three generations.

The leading occupation of the male descendants has been agriculture. Three towns in the United States have been named after descendants of Simon Lobdell—viz : Lobdell, La., a short distance above New Orleans, where, in close proximity, reside the descendants of Abraham, James, and John Little Lobdell, the pioneer Lobdell settlers of Louisiana and Mississippi, for whom the place was named; Lobdell, Clinton Co., N. Y., named after the descendants of Jared Lobdell. Lobdell, Lane Co., Kansas, after the Hon. Charles E. Lobdell, formerly Speaker of the Kansas House of Representatives, who is also a descendant of Jared Lobdell.

In my extensive search I have found an honest, industrious, sober people, many awaiting the revelations of the Lobdell genealogical history, and to me it is a matter of deep regret that so many who have faithfully assisted me have fallen by the wayside ere my work was completed

To each and every one who has in any way given me "the least bit" of assistance in gathering together the data for this work, I wish to gratefully thank, and I pray for God's blessing on themselves and their households.

That each one may enjoy the work's revelations and history in the same measure that I have in its compilation is the fervent wish of

Yours sincerely,
Julia Harrison Lobdell.
(Mrs. James H. Lobdell.)

FIRST GENERATION.

SIMON LOBDELL.

The name of "Simon Lobdell" appears among the 'after-planters" names of Milford, Conn.—about forty—a framed list of which is now hanging in the Town Clerk's office at Milford, Conn.

My supposition—after much study—is, that Simon came as a young lad with one of a party from Hereford, England (a shire in West of England, bordering on Wales) in 1645, at which time history tells us the second party came—that his sisters Ann and Elizabeth came at same time but remained in Boston.

From public records at Milford it appears that Simon Lobdell, in 1646, had given him by the "first planters" of the town, for a house lot, a triangular shaped half-acre of ground.*

A. In 1655 we find his name given as a resident of Milford. He took the freeman's oath at Hartford. Conn. May 21, 1657 and was a tax-payer of that place in 1667. A. He went to Springfield, Mass., probably through the influence of his brother-in-laws (his sisters both having married prosperous men of Springfield.) There he was prison-keeper from 1666 to 1674, and there he must have accumulated considerable property. B.

In 1681 Simon purchased 60 acres (but was not a settler) at Stony River, between Springfield and Windsor, and had interests in Hull, Mass., in 1682. No proof of his marriage nor birth of Mary, his first child, has been found, but I assume without proof

---

* These first planters formed a general court under whose direction and authority land was distributed among the so-called after-planters. The deeds from the original planters are short and have an informal tone, simply stating as in Simon's case.

A. Persons were made Freemen by the General Court of the Colony, and also by quarterly courts of the Counties. None but Freemen could hold offices or vote for rulers. This regulation was so far regulated by Royal order in 1664, as to allow individuals to be made Freemen, who could obtain certificates of their being correct in doctrine and conduct, from clergymen acquainted with them.

B. Burt's First Century of Springfield tells us that on 3 Dec, 1670, he is granted 3 acres of land near by Goodman Thomas, 28 Aug, 1671, 5 acres, beyond Cornelius Williams, 13 Dec, 1671, 5 acres, and in 1673, 20 acres, on the west side of the great river, next to Lieut Cooper's. From records, he appears to have given liberally to the church at Springfield, although not a member.

that he married Persis Pierce, dau. of Thomas and Elizabeth Pierce of Charlestown. Mass., and that the families were members of the same party on their way to the new home in New England.

Simon returned to Milford, Conn., where his wife Persis was admitted to the First Church of Milford, 7 January, 1677, and on 9 April, 1710, Simon united with the same church.

At Milford, his children married and there Simon died, previous to 4 Oct., 1717. as on that date, at Probate Court held at New Haven. Conn., his son Joshua Lobdell of Ridgefield. Conn., moved for administration on the estate of Simon Lobdell of Milford, lately deceased, which was granted on his bond. The same administrator exhibited a jointure made between the deceased and the widow, of full satisfaction.

Names given: Joshua Lobdell, son of Simon; Wm. Roberts, Deliverance Downs; David Wooster (All in right of their wives.) Anna Lobdell; Joseph Benedict of Ridgefield; a debt of John Sheppard and a bill for funeral expenses.

In the will of Simon Lobdell, he calls himself Lieut., but as the records kept are very imperfect, I fail to find the proof.

WILL OF SIMON LOBDELL.

"To all Christian people to whom these presents shall come, I, Simon Lobdell, send greeting in the Lord God everlasting

Know ye, that I, Simon Lobdell (Lieut.), of Milford in the colony of Connecticut and county of New Haven in New England, for and in consideration of my fatherly affection unto my only son Joshua Lobdell, have given, granted and confirmed and by these presents do freely, clearly and absolutely give, grant, endorse and confirm unto the said Joshua Lobdell, his heirs and assigns forever, all my lands, rights in lands, housing, out-housing, orchards and whatsoever freehold estate or leases or interests in or of any lands or orchards lying within the bounds of Milford aforesaid, viz.: my house-lot containing about one acre, be it more or less, bounded with Walter Smith, his lot north, with all the buildings, orchards and whatever privileges and appurtenances thereunto belongeth; also one parcel of land containing twenty-seven acres, be it more or less, lying partly on the west side of the road and partly across the westerly part of the Mill River and being bounded with a highway or New Haven line eastward, and Capt. Sam'l Ells' land southward and a highway westward and John Terrill's land northward, with all the privileges and appurtenances thereunto belonging.

Likewise all my rights in the two last Indian purchases of lands within the bounds of Milford made by the inhabitants of Milford, and all other leases, rights, interests and privileges I have in other lands or orchards the said Joshua Lobdell is to have and to hold to him, his heirs and assigns forever.

And further, I, the said Simon Lobdell, do covenant and promise for myself, my heirs and assigns that those who so possess, hold and enjoy the premises without any lett or molestation from any person or persons whatsoever that shall lay any legal claim thereunto.

In witness whereof, I have hereunto set my hand and seal this nineteenth day of January, 1703-4."

SIMON LOBDELL (Seal)

SISTERS OF SIMON LOBDELL.

Ann and Elizabeth Lobdell.

Ann Lobdell, of Boston, Mass., married 3 Jan., 1660, Samuel Terry of Springfield, Mass.

Children:

1 Samuel Terry, Jr., b. 1661, m. a dau of Miles Morgan of Enfield, Mass It is on record that a child of Samuel Terry, Jr, was the first white child born in Enfield.

2. Ephraim Terry; b. 1663, d young

3 Thomas Terry, b. '65.

4 Mary Terry b. 1667.

5. Rebecca Terry, b 1669; d young

6 Ephraim Terry, b. 1672.

7. Rebecca Terry; b 1673.

8 Elizabeth Terry, b 1675; d. young

9. Anna Terry.

Elizabeth Lobdell, of Boston. Mass, m 20 Oct., 1651, Jonathan Burt of Springfield, Mass.

The only child of this union of whom I have found record, is Sarah Burt, b. 4 Sept 1656, m. 14 Sept. 1676, Luke Hitchcock;

their dau., Mercy Hitchcock, b. 1 Feb., 1681, m. 18 April, 1700, Ebenezer Day ; their son, Luke Day, b. 2 July 1706, m. 9 Nov , 1734, Jerusha Skinner; their dau., b 4 Feb., 1747, m. 29 Nov., 1770, Nathaniel Gaylord; their son, Nathaniel Gaylord, Jr., b. ——, m. 26 Feb , 1807, Bathsheba Carter; their dau., Ann M Gaylord, b. 16 Sept., 1824, m. 10 June 1848, Cyrus Lang, their dau., Ada M. Lang, b. ——, m. 25 Aug. 1886, Mr. A O. McGarret of East Orange, N. J. who kindly gives this record for those interested.

———

"Henry Burt, whose wife's given name was Ulalia, d 30 April 1662. His wife d. 29 Aug. 1690 Three of their sons were Jonathan, David and Nathaniel. Jonathan Burt, the oldest son, b. in England, was m. at Boston in 1651 to Elizabeth Lobdell. He removed to Springfield. He is called 'a man of note.' He was a church deacon. Henry Morris, in his early history of Springfield, mentioned him as being in 1675 one of the leading men of the town, ' wise and sagacious,' but ' well advanced in life,' says he was 'for a time town clerk' He d in Oct. 1715 One of his daughters, Sarah, m (in that memorial year for Springfield when on Tuesday, 5 Oct 1675, out of 45 houses in Springfield 32 were burned by the Indians) Benjamin Dorchester of Springfield, who dying in 1676, she m in 1677 Luke Hitchcock."—(From the West Springfield Ball Family)

SECOND GENERATION.

CHILDREN OF SIMON AND PERSIS LOBDELL.

1. Mary. 2. Elizabeth. 3. Joshua. 4. Anna. 5. Rebecca.

i. Mary, b. about 1667, not knowing where. She m. David Wooster, b. 1666, eldest son of Edward Wooster of Milford, Conn.

* David Wooster d. 29 March, 1711 and left his wife Mary to administer his estate.

ii Elizabeth, b at Springfield, Mass., 7 Oct., 1669, m Wm. Roberts, whose parentage and descendants I am unable to find.

iii. Joshua, an only son, b. at Springfield, Mass., 23 Dec, 1671, m. for his first wife at Milford, Conn., 11 Aug., 1695—Gov. Robert Treat performing the ceremony—Mary, dau of John and Alice Burwell, early settlers of Milford, Upon one of the stones of "Memorial Bridge" at Milford, is carved the name of the father of Mary. No record can be found of her death, but perhaps it occurred soon after the birth of her dau , Susannah, who was bapt. 5 March, 1710, and on 9 April, 1710, Simon Lobdell, then an old man, was admitted to the First Church of Milford.

I have often wondered if this did not immediately follow the burial of Mary,

(The following item of Joshua is contributed by Mr Henry Lobdell of Salem Center, who is now living on part of the original farm in the manor of Cortland, Westchester Co., N. Y., leased by his great grandfather—Ebenezer Lobdell before the Revolution—of Stephen De Lancey, and afterward purchased by him at sheriff's sale.)

"After the death of Mary, Joshua, with his children moved to the town of Ridgefield, Conn., "in 1712, in which year on 3 March, he bought of James Brown of Norwalk, Conn., one twenty-ninth part of the town of Ridgefield. (The above James Brown was one of the original proprietors who purchased of the Indians, in

---

* The will of Simon Lobdell was drawn 19 January, 1703 or 4, at which time David Wooster was alive. Simon's estate was administered 4 Oct., 1717, and mention is made of David Wooster as son-in-law.

13

1708, all that land, now called Ridgefield.) During the succeeding twenty or thirty years Joshua was continually adding to his estate by purchase from the proprietors or their grantors. The date of the death of Joshua cannot be determined from Ridgefield records but it must have occurred before 31 Oct. 1743, as on that date, Caleb agrees to assume the support of his mother, Eunice, widow of Joshua Lobdell (deceased), late of Ridgefield."

———

From Burt's first century of Springfield, Mass.

"In 1743 a deed in Book S. Springfield records mentions—

"Samuel Lobdell; Caleb and John Lobdell; Jabez Northrup and wife Sarah; Seaborn Burt and wife Susannah—all of Ridgefield, Conn. Samuel Plum and wife Mary, of Derby, Conn., and Joshua Lobdell of Cortlandt Manor, N. Y., to Ebenezer Lobdell of Ridgefield. Conn., all interest in estate of our father Joshua—and land that formerly belonged to Simon Lobdell, formerly of Springfield, Mass."

*About 1713 Joshua m. for his second wife, Eunice, dau. of Lieut. John Olmstead and his wife, Mary Benedict of Norwalk, Conn.

Eunice was b. about 1689, and was aunt of Rebecca St. John, who m Samuel, eldest child of Joshua and Mary (Burwell) Lobdell.

iv. Anna Lobdell, b. at Springfield, 1 Dec. 1674, was at the time of her father's death, unmarried and residing at Milford

v. Rebecca Lobdell, b. at Springfield in 1677, m. Deliverance Downs, b. 1669, son of John and Mary Downs of New Haven, Conn. Rebecca d at Milford, 2 Feb. 1740

———

* Lieut. John Olmstead, bapt at Hartford, Conn., 20 Sept., 1649, d. at Norwalk, Conn., 1704-5; m. 11 Nov., 1670, Mary Benedict, dau. of Thomas and Mary (Bridgum) Benedict. The inventory of his estate was taken 22 Dec. 1704-5, at which time Eunice was fifteen years old

From Norwalk Land Records —

"Joshua Lobdell of Ridgefield sells land in Norwalk, in 1718, his right—that was one of the daughters of Lieut. John Olmstead of Norwalk, (deceased). She had it by distribution from Lieut. Olmstead's estate, March 23, 1722-3."

14

THIRD GENERATION.

CHILDREN OF MARY LOBDELL AND DAVID WOOSTER.

1 Jerusha 2 Persis 3. Tamar

ı   Jerusha Wooster, b. 1702 at Derby, Conn. m. —— McFarland (no record.)

ıı.   Persis Wooster, b. 1704, m. 2 April. 1724. Ephraim Gillett, son of Eliphalet and Mary Gillett, of Milford.

ııı   Tamar Wooster, b 1707, m Enos Brooks

From Beers Commemorative Biography of New Haven Co., Conn :—

"Capt Enos Brooks, b. 15 Feb , 1708. at Cheshire, Conn., spent his entire life in Cheshire, where he owned a large amount of land. The present Brooks' homestead stands upon the original spot where in 1732 Enos and his wife lived He d 22 Sept., 1771. Tamar d. 7 Oct., 1775 Both are buried in the family burial ground at Cheshire.

"He was Capt. of a company of militia ; was a liberal supporter and an active member of the church Rev. David Brooks his son, m Elizabeth Doolittle."

Daughters of American Revolution Lineage Book, Vol. 19, gives the following —

"Enos Brooks, wife Tamar Wooster."

CHILDREN OF REBECCA LOBDELL AND DELIVERANCE DOWNS.

1. Rebecca 2 John. 3 Mary 4 Elizabeth.

ı   Rebecca Downs, bapt at Milford. Conn 26 June. 1709 ; m. David Northrup, b Aug. 1701. at Milford David was a brother of Jabez Northrup who m Sarah Lobdell, a niece of Rebecca (Lobdell) Downs.

ıı   John Downs, bapt. 1709.

ııı   Mary Downs, bapt. 1709.

ıv   Elizabeth Downs, bapt 5 March, 1710

15

FOURTH GENERATION.

CHILDREN OF PERSIS WOOSTER AND EPHRAIM GILLETT

1. Ephraim 2 David Wooster 3 Freelove 4 Mary
5 Joseph 6 Benjamin.

i. Ephraim Gillett, b 1725
ii. David Wooster Gillett. b. 1727 at Derby, Conn , 6 July, 1748.
iii Freelove Gillett. b 10 Aug. 1729, m to Eden Sperry b.
27 June, 1725.
iv. Mary Gillett, 1732.
v. and vi Twins Joseph and Benj Gillett, b 1744

CHILDREN OF REBECCA DOWNS AND DAVID NORTHRUP.

All bapt. 1734-35-38.
Northrup by name —
1. David. 2 Isaac. 3 Rebecca. 4 Eunice. 5 Sarah. 6.
Elizabeth. 7 Joshua

Children and Descendants of
Joshua[2] Lobdell, (Simon[1])

(1) Wife, Mary Burwell
(2) Wife, Eunice Olmstead

THIRD GENERATION.

CHILDREN OF JOSHUA AND MARY (BURWELL) LOBDELL.

1 Samuel, 2. Joshua, 3. Sarah, 4 Mary, 5 Ebenezer, 6. Susanna; all born in Milford, Conn

I Samuel, b. 2 Feby . 1699. m. 26 Dec., 1722. Rebecca, dau, of Samuel and Rebecca (Olmstead) St. John. While a young lad he moved to Ridgefield. Conn , with his father and probably resided there during his life, altho I find no record of his death. On 28 May, 1721. Joshua conveys to his beloved son Samuel, three acres of land in that town (Ridgefield records). Samuel Lobdell, Caleb and Ebenezer paid church rates to St. Stephen's church 24 Oct., 1744. (Ridgefield history) Sam'l., John, Caleb and Ebenezer were of Ridgefield, 1746. (Fairfield Co. History.) Of Samuel and his wife, I can find nothing further.

II. Joshua, ii, b. 16 March, 1703; m. Mary, dau. of Joseph Reynolds of Ridgefield. They resided in Ridgefield, for several years after marriage, presumably after 1730 they moved over the line—from Ridgefield, into Courtland Manor—North Salem, Westchester Co., N Y. state. Joshua was Capt of Westchester Co. Militia Company for several years, and many of his Company with Joshua as their Capt. volunteered for the French and Indian wars of 1755-60

History records the death of Capt. Joshua, as before 1769,—probably in 1767—as on that date his son, Joshua, third, was appointed administrator of his estate. His widow survived him, residing in Courtland Manor in 1768 at which time a deed is recorded at Ridgefield in which she joins with her children in selling land in Ridgefield to John Whitlock of Ridgefield.

A rare historical document—through the courtesy of the late Philip Verplank of Yonkers—has been placed before the public, being accurate copies of muster rolls from the Verplank family papers, containing the names of Westchester County Volunteers who fought in the famous French and Indian Wars of 1755-60 Among the names given are those of Capt Joshua Lobdell and his five sons—viz , Sergeant Joshua Lobdell; corporal Ebenezer Lobdell, privates Daniel, Jacob and John Lobdell

III. Sarah Lobdell, b 1 Feby , 1702; d. young

IV Mary Lobdell, b. 30 Oct.. 1704; m. Samuel, son of John Jr and Rachel (Bunnell) Plum of Milford, Conn. Samuel Plum bought

18

land in Derby. Conn.; in 1728, d there March, 1790, aged 87 years
I have no record of the death of Mary.

V. Ebenezer, b. 24 Feby., 1707; m. 28 Dec.. 1732. Rebecca Benedict, b. 1713, dau of Thomas and Elizabeth (Barnum) Benedict.

Ebenezer was evidently a man of property.

History says that he was one of the principal inhabitants of
Ridgefield, 1784. In 1743 he bought from the heirs of his father the
property that was formerly the property of Simon Lobdell.

In 1751 Ridgefield court granted him license to keep public house
and sell strong drinks. (Fairfield Co. court records).

Husband and wife died where they had lived, he, in 1801; she, 1
Aug. 1798, aged 85 years.

VI. Susannah, b. 27 Feby., 1709; m. Seaborn Burt; b. 4 July,
1706, son of Benj. and Sarah (Belding) Burt of Ridgefield. From
Burt's History I copy the following, which I know will be of interest to descendants· "Benjamin Burt, (David's youngest son), with
his wife, was captured by the Indians at the burning of Deerfield,
Mass., and taken to Canada. Ensign John Sheldon of Deerfield,
made four expeditions to Canada, to redeem his fellow-townsmen
and finally on 30 May, 1706, left Quebec with over forty of them,
among whom was Mr Burt, his wife and child. They went down
the St. Lawrence and thence by sea to Boston, where they arrived
on Aug 2." On the voyage Mrs. Burt gave birth to a son, who was
named "Seaborn," from the place of his birth An old deed is in
the hands of a descendant with Seaborn Burt's signature dated 12
March, 1749-50, deeding land in Ridgefield to his brother, Daniel
Burt,* who m. Hannah Benedict Burt's historian says: "After
disposing of his land, he removed to place unknown to the compiler."

CHLDREN OF JOSHUA 1, AND EUNICE (OLMSTEAD) LOBDELL (Second Wife)

1 Sarah, 2 Caleb, 3 John, 4 Darius, 5. Elizabeth.
6 Simon, 7. David; all born in Ridgefield, Conn.

I. Sarah, b 27 Sept., 1714; m. 6 March, 1734; Jabez Northrup
b at Milford, Conn, 1710, son of Daniel and Sarah ——? Northrop.

They resided at Ridgefield, where their four children were born.

II Caleb, b 1 Feby., 1716, m. for his first wife, 27 June, 1749.
Elizabeth ——? who d. Nov., 1752. He m. (2), 19 July, 1758,
Bethia Paddock, b. 22 Jan.. 1729-30, who d. after 1761. dau of
Zachariah F and Elizabeth (Howes) Paddock,

He m for his third wife, Ruth ——? who survived him, and m
Mr. ——? Smith

---

* Dan'l Burt's dau Phebe, m David Lobdell (Joshua?)

19

Caleb resided at Ridgefield, where he probably was a store-keeper. He was identified in the Episcopal church during the ministry of Rev. John Beach and Rev. Richard Caner, both itinerant ministers, whose circuit included Ridgefield. Caleb d at Ridgefield, 17 Jan'y., 1802.

One, Dr Chichester, was among the early residents of Wilton. Fairfield Co., Conn,—his residence was very near the center of the town. His old account books have been kept by one of his descendants, and the following is copied—just as it is found in one of his books:

June the 8th Day	Calop Lobdon, Cr.			
In the year 1754	to 8 pare of Stockings at			
	New York Prise	£	S	D.
	Stocking clears 13 shillings			
	9 D New York money	0	13	09
Jan'y the 30th Day				
In 1756	to 1£ old tenor which			
	makes 2 shillings New			
	York Money	00	02	00
	to 2 Shillings 7 D Prock			
	money which makes			
	3 S 5 D New York money	00	03	05
		£00	19	04
Feby the 10 Day				
In 1756	to Cash, 5 S 1 D			
	New York Money	00	05	05
	A ballance in full of all accounts			
(Dr Chichester)		1	04	03
	to a 33 yards of Camblet tes			
	16 shillings pur yard	03	16	00
	to 1 Quarter of Tee 15 Shillings	00	15	00
		09	11	00
	Brought In to N Y. money			
	9 Pounds 11 Shillings old Tenor			
	which makes 1 £. 4 S 3 D.	01	04	03
	N Y Money			

III John, b 21 Aug.. 1721. m. 25 June. 1744; Ruth, Sherwood, b. in Ridgefield, 29 March, 1723. dau of Daniel and Ruth (Bradley)

* "Old tenor"—that is, in the bills of credit issued by the Colony

Sherwood—dau of John and Hannah (Sherwood) Bradley of Ridgefield They resided in Brookfield, Conn, where John d. in 1778, and his sons John and Caleb were the administrators on his estate. Ruth d 4 May, 1787

*The following, of great interest, is kindly contributed by Mrs. Eliza (Alvord) Millaux of Waterbury, Conn, granddaughter of Dennis Barlow Lobdell

"In 1729, Joshua Lobdell bought for $340 a tract of land lying in that part of Connecticut now known as Brookfield

In 1742 John Lobdell, Joshua's son, received from Daniel Sherwood, his father-in-law, various sums of money and tracts of land on his wife Ruth's account. In 1746 John being very sick and thinking himself near to death, made his will, giving all his possessions to his wife Ruth and an unborn child, and of this will he says: "I appoint my trusty brother **Samuel Lobdell**, Executor," but strange to relate, John recovered and lived until 1778, having nine children in all

In 1778 we read the division of his property among these children as follows

    John Lobdell, Jr
    Caleb Lobdell.
    Lewis Lobdell
    Ormand Lobdell
    Sarah Lobdell Peck.
    Orpah Lobdell Dunning
    Hannah Lobdell Hepburn
    Chloe Lobdell
    Married, Ruth Lobdell Bradley.

All these children and their property we lost sight of—Grandfather (Dennis B Lobdell) having only possessed his father's papers

In 1775 the British raided through Brookfield and Caleb's losses were great by their marauding of various flowered coverlets linen sheets, tankards, etc

In 1776 Lewis was taken into the Federal Army

John Lobdell married a Miss Barlow and lived to have five children * Abigail, Orpha, Ruphine and Dennis; Clark, the youngest, dying at the age of two years.

"This I have copied word for word as it was given me some twenty years ago. Several papers were found after Grandma Northrop Lobdell Barnum died, she having been married twice; Dennis Lobdell being her first husband"

IV. Darius, b 18 Oct, 1729, m Mary, (dau of Jerjah and Mary (Ingersol) Baldwin of Litchfield, Conn), 16 Jany, 1751. She

* The dates and names of children of the above do not accord with mine, but I give it as given by the descendant

21

was b. 30 July, 1730, bapt, 17 Oct., 1743. She had a sister Ann, to whom in 1752 Darius Lobdell of Litchfield was appointed guardian.

Darius, d. 29 Nov., 1796; aged 67.

Mary, d 6 March, 1825, aged 95.

From records I find that on 4 Dec., 1744,—after the death of his father,—Darius chose his brother Caleb as his guardian. In 1754 he removed to Derby, Conn., where his half-sister Mary lived, but in 1756 returned to Ridgefield, and in 1759 migrated to Filkinton or Philipstown—9 Partners, Dutchess Co. History of Danbury, Vt., tells us. "In Fall of 1763 or Spring of 1764 a road was laid out by Darius Lobdell and Samuel Rose—formerly of Nine Partners, N. Y.—from Bennington to Danby, Vt. Darius Lobdell settled in Danby, about the time of the revolution,—was an active, industrious and energetic pioneer, progressive and closely connected with town affairs He was a blacksmith by trade,—a member of the Legislature in 1784 " Was a Revolutionary soldier, having participated in "Battle of Bennington" His energetic business methods have been transmitted to his descendants instanced, by a family record being kept —from the time of the birth of children of Darius,—until the present day.

V Elizabeth, b 14 Nov., 1732 m., as his second wife, Isaac Northrup, 16 Jany., 1752 His first wife was Harriet Gunn.

Isaac, b 10 Nov., 1725 at Ridgefield, was son (*) of Joseph and Susannah (Roberts) Northrup Isaac and Elizabeth lived in Ridgefield then moved in 1773 to South Salem, Westchester Co., N Y., where Elizabeth d about 1790, Isaac d 9 July, 1810

VI Simon; b 1739. I have no proof that Simon was a son of Joshua, but among the names found in second annual report of N. Y. State Historian, we find the name of Simon Lobdell. He enlisted for the war against Canada on 8 April 1758—aged 19 years. Born in Conn

He, perhaps, died, as I find no further mention of him and no other Simon until the fifth generation.

VII David, b about 1739. (I find no record of the birth of this David, but according to dates, given later, he must have been either the son of said Joshua I, or—of Samuel, the eldest son of said Joshua, and as David gave to his only son the name of Joshua, I think, without doubt, that he was Joshua's son.)

David m Phoebe, dau of Daniel and Hannah (Benedict) Burt of Ridgefield, where Phoebe was b 15 July, 1738. They resided in Warwick, Orange Co., N. Y., until 1791, when David received a letter of dismissal from the church of which both himself and wife were charter members, organized at Warwick in 1765. Mr

---

* I assume—without proof—that Susannah (Roberts) Northrup, "mother of Isaac", was dau. of Wm and Elizabeth (Lobdell) Roberts, and grand dau of Simon and Persis Lobdell

Thomas Burt of Warwick kindly made search of Baptist church records and tells us that David was a loyal member of said church, appointed on committees to look after the poor; to maintain order during service and reconcile members to each other when they were at variance. On the whole, his church life appears influential and honorable." I find no record of his wife's taking a letter of dismissal, nor any record of her death. David was road master of the town of Warwick in 1789. He later was residing in McConnellstown, Penn., and in 1808 he went with his son Joshua to St. Albans township, Licking Co., Ohio, where he d. in 1809, aged 70 years, his being the first death, and burial in the township. He was buried on the Drake farm, nearly a mile west of Alexandria. David and his son Joshua were among the number that organized the Baptist church on the Welsh Hills in above township in Sept., 1808.

As regarding Simon and David being twins and sons of Joshua, first, I have submitted the facts, and leave the solution to the opinion and judgment of Lobdell descendants.

Children and Descendants of
Samuel $^{(3)}$ Lobdell, (Joshua $^{(2)}$, Simon $^{(1)}$)
Wife, Rebecca St. John

FOURTH GENERATION.

CHILDREN OF SAMUEL AND REBECCA (ST. JOHN) LOBDELL.

1. Rebecca, 2 Mary, 3. Abigail, 4. Samuel; all born in Ridgefield, Conn.

I. Rebecca, b. 1 Oct., 1723.
II. Mary, b. 8 April, 1725.
III. Abigail, b. 26 Oct , 1726.
IV. Samuel ii, b. 10 Sept., 1728, migrated to Warwick, Orange Co., N. Y., where he m. Elizabeth, dau of Thomas and Katherine (Weesner) Blain of Florida, Orange Co. At Warwick, their children were b and Samuel d. about 1792, as his will was recorded in Surrogate's office, 11 Sept, 1792.) He evidently was an able, patriotic citizen. Under date of 14 Sept., 1775, we find him as a Second Lieutenant of Warwick Company; and 5th Sept., 1778, as an exempt of Orange Co., possibly at that time too old to be in the service.

On page 73 of a manuscript volume entitled "Military Returns, 1775, Vol 26, in the custody of the regents of the University of the State of New York, in the State Library at Albany, the name of Samuel Lobdell is recorded, under date of 14 Sept., 1775, as a Second Lieutenant in Capt Charles Bardsley's Company, belonging to the Florida and Warwick Regiment of Orange Co. Militia, commanded by Col. John Hathorn, and that the above record shows that the said Lieutenant Samuel Lobdell performed active service in the Revolutionary War

---

Last will and testament of Samuel Lobdell, of town of Warwick, Orange Co., N. Y.

(Recorded in Surrogate's Office, 11 Sept., 1792)

"Give to son, Wm. Lobdell, all lands that belong to me at my death, consisting of mountain lands, &c.

Give to daughter, Anna Lobdell, and to dau. Mary Lobdell. 1 good cow & calf, 1 feather bed, bedstead, &c.

JOHN BLAIN LOBDELL (6)
(Wm. [5])   (1804-1861)
(Page 28)

Give to dau. Elizabeth Wilson, wife of
                    Joseph Wilson.
    "   "   " Rebecca, wife of
                    Nathaniel DeKay.
    "   "   " Catherine, wife of
                    Cornelius Lezere,
    "   "   " Sarah. wife of
                    Peter Alyea.
each,—the sum of two pounds.
    Appoint Wm. Lobdell and Cornelius Lezere, ex's.
    David Lobdell, Tives Heywood, John Hathhorn, witnesses.

FIFTH GENERATION

CHILDREN OF SAMUEL II. AND ELIZABETH (BLAIN) LOBDELL.

    I. William an only son. b. about 1769, m Elizabeth Todd.
They resided at Goshen, Orange Co. N Y., during the first part of
their married life, then joined the exodus of many families for
Seneca Co, N Y. settling at Romulus. The daughters.
    III. Mary and Anna unmarried at the time of their father's
death, 1792.
    IV. Elizabeth; m Joseph Wilson
    V. Rebecca, m Nathaniel DeKay.
    VI Catherine, m Cornelius Lezere
    VII Sarah; m Peter Alyea

SIXTH GENERATION.

CHILDREN OF WILLIAM AND ELIZABETH (TODD) LOBDELL.

    1. Peggy. 2 Sally. 3 Polly. 4. Samuel iii, 5. John B.
6. Wm. Hickey.

    I Peggy, m. Mr. Tompkins, d. at Williamston, Ingham Co.,
Mich
    II Sally, m. Mr. Hibbard, d at Palmyra or Auburn, N. Y
    III Polly, m Mr Newberry, d. in Mich not knowing at what
place
    IV The oldest son was
    Samuel iii, b. 26 March, 1799, at Goshen, Orange Co., N. Y He
removed to Romulus, Seneca Co, N Y. probably as a young boy,

27

with his parents. He m. as his first wife, Susannah, dau. of Wm. Stout, d. 1833-4

He then remarried, at Romulus 3 Nov., 1836, to widow, Mary Ann (Wyckoff) Lyon, b. 14 Jan., 1808, at Romulus; d. same place, 25 April, 1889, dau. of Peter and Anna (Pruden) Wyckoff.

Mr. Lobdell was a successful farmer. In Seneca Co., Probate is a record of deed from Samuel Lobdell and wife to Elizabeth Lobdell, presumably his unmarried dau., dated 1889. He lived to a ripe old age, dying 7 Aug., 1891, aged 92 years.

V. John B. (probably John Blain), was b. 4 Sept., 1804, d. 8 Nov., 1861, at Grand Rapids, Mich., aged 57 years; m. 22 Feby., 1822; Charity Daken, b. 20 June, 1804, at Romulus, d. 22 July, 1874. Mr. Lobdell was the proprietor and landlord of the Lobdell house at Williamston, Ingham Co., Mich., before 1860, was a Democrat, and himself and family of eleven children, all Methodists.

VI. Wm. Hickey, lived in Romulus, with his wife Laura ——? had no children. During the gold excitement he went to California, where he died. His widow d. soon after.

SEVENTH GENERATION.

CHILDREN AND DESCENDANTS OF SAMUEL (6) LOBDELL.

(1) wife, Susanna Stout
(2) wife, widow, Mary Ann Lyon

By (1) wife, Susanna (Stout) Lobdell
1. Mary Ann, 2. Wm. S., 3. Samuel A., 4. Elizabeth, 5. Abel H.

I. Mary Ann, b. 8 Jany., 1822, d. 20 May, 1842.

II. Wm. S., b. 21 June, 1824, d. 8 Nov., 1894, at Stanley or Flint, Ontario Co., N. Y., m. 3 Dec., 1856; Elizabeth Woods, dau. of James and Elizabeth (McKnight) Woods of Flint. The widow (1903) is living with her son-in-law, Mr. W. E. Cook at Flint. Wm. S. had two children, (1) James W. (8), d. 5 April, 1891. (2.) Mary E. (8) b. 28 May, 1867, d. 3 Sept., 1898, m. Wm. E. Cook, b. 11 Feb., 1865, son of Wm. F. and Elizabeth (Richardson) Cook of Flint, N. Y.

III. Samuel A., no record.

IV. Elizabeth, b. 19 Sept., 1829. Is (1907) living with Miss Ann E. Lyon at Romulus, N. Y. (her step sister).

V. Abel H., b. 8 Aug., 1832, m. Emily Harding; has two sons.

28

SAMUEL LOBDELL (6)
(William [5])   (1799-1891)
of Romulus, N. Y.
(Page 27)

ELIZABETH LOBDELL WALLACE (7)
(John B. [6])
of Grinnell, Iowa
(Page 30)

SARAH LOBDELL (7) CONNELLY
(John B. [6])   (1832-189?)
of Muskegon, Mich.
(Page 31)

JOHN B. LOBDELL (7) JR.
(John B. [6])   (1836-1897)
of Georgetown, Mich.
(Page 31)

1. Samuel H. (8), of Pontiac, Mich
2. Eugene (8), of Holly, Mich. No answer from either

By second wife, Mary A W L. Lobdell
1. Gilbert, 2. Augustus

VI. Gilbert Randolph; b. 23 July, 1837. In 1858 resided in town of Varick, Seneca Co., d 23 Nov.. 1895, at Belleview Hospital, N Y. City; m Mary Carr, at West Troy, N. Y., 1891.

CHILDREN
1 Bertie (8), dead
2. Genevra (8), dead.
3 Blanch (8); b. 23 July, 1873, m Otto Fischer, living at Troy, N Y
4. Roy Fred (8); b 22 Oct, 1876
5. Marion (8).
6 Sidney (8); living at Troy, N Y.
7 Gerald (8)
VII. Augustus C. (7), b. 9 May, 1843, living. No record.

CHILDREN AND DESCENDANTS OF JOHN B. 1, AND CHARITY (DAKIN) LOBDELL.

1. Anderson. 2. Fanny Jane. 3 Wm Hickey. 4 Elizabeth, 5 Sarah Hibbard. 6 John B 11. 7 Abraham Dakin, 8. Polly Lucinda. 9 Charity, 10. Annette, 11 Henry L.

I. Anderson S. b 28 Jany. 1823 m Mrs Charity M Leroy, and had one son (8) The only record I have is taken from a local paper of Muskegon, Mich.

"W. H. Lobdell received a dispatch Sunday announcing the death of Anderson S. Lobdell, his brother, at the Soldiers' Home, Grand Rapids, that morning, May, 1895. He attended the funeral Monday afternoon. Deceased was over 72 years old and never recovered from the hardships of war. His relatives deemed best to have him among his old comrades where every care and attention was given him. Sometime since the surgeons decided that amputation of both legs was necessary, but the old veteran replied that he had but one death to die, and he purposed to die that with his legs on He was born in the town of Friendship, Alleghany Co, N Y., and came to Michigan in '36 when the present State was a territory engaging in sawmilling and farming and afterwards prospected several years among the Black Hills. He was an uncle of the editor, and we visited the Home Monday with W. H Lobdell. although unable to remain to attend the funeral. It is one of the grandest of our State institutions and its roof is a canopy of heaven to the army of old vets, who hobble about among its halls and partake of its generous messes. Deceased leaves many relatives scattered throughout Michigan and some who remained back on the old New York homestead."

II. Fanny Jane; b. 18 April, 1824, m. Jonas Kent; d. at Sand Lake. Mich., Oct., 1893. Had three children.

III. Wm. Hickey, a lumber inspector of Muskegon, Mich., was b. 27 Jany., 1826, at Friendship, Alegheny Co., N. Y.; m. 8 Nov., 1855, Mary Hallett, b. 1830, July 14, at Aurilius, Cayuga Co., N. Y. His only son (8), b. 20 April, 1863; d. 26 Dec., 1894, a dau. Carrie V (8), b. 9 Oct., 1857 is the wife of H. L. Bourdon, 339 Lake St., Muskegon, Mich. They have one son, W. H. Bourdon, engaged in business in Chicago, Ills.

IV. Elizabeth, b. 4 Nov., 1829, at Friendship, N. Y.; m. Warren P. Wallace, b. 10 Sept., 1825, in Steuben Co., N. Y., son of James and Margaret (Aulls) Wallace of Cohocton, Steuben Co., N. Y. Mr. and Mrs. Wallace resided at Grinnell, Iowa.

As the following copy of a clipping from their local paper tells you of his sickness and passing away. I will add he so longed to see his family all together, before his summons came. On the last day of May, children and grandchildren met at the old homestead and made glad the parents' hearts. One son, Scott, who had not visited the old home in twenty-nine years, came and with him his wife, and the days passed all too quickly, for they were happy and joyous days.

"Warren P. Wallace, who died at his home on South Park street on August 16, 1905, was born at Cohocton, N. Y., on September 10, 1825, and so was nearly eighty years old. In 1855 he was married to Miss Elizabeth Lobdell and in the same year came to this struggling little town out on the Iowa prairies. To this union were born eight children. The mother, seven children and four grandchildren remain to mourn the loss of a kind and loving husband, parent and grandfather.

He passed away last Wednesday afternoon after a lingering illness. The funeral services were held from the late residence and his own sons acted as pallbearers.

Mr. Wallace has for many years been a familiar figure on the streets of this city, having been one of the early settlers in Grinnell. Indeed if he had lived until October he would have celebrated the fiftieth anniversary both of his marriage and of his coming to this city. In all these years he has borne a spotless reputation and has led a good life. In the dark days of the early sixties he joined the Union forces to fight for the country he loved; his health was undermined and during after life he never fully recovered from the effects

ABRAHAM D. LOBDELL (7)
(John B. [6])
of Hudsonville, Mich.
(Page 32)

LUCINDA LOBDELL BURDICK (7)
(John B. [6])
of Wirt Center, N. Y.
(Page 32)

ANNETTE LOBDELL LOCKWOOD (7)
(John B. [6])
of Williamston, Mich.
(Page 33)

of his army experience Consequently he led a quiet life but one which left only an honored name and a loving memory to his children.

His comrades in the G. A. R. and his many friends will miss the sight of his familiar form on our streets, but those who were near and dear to him and who cherish his memory will rest in the knowledge that in answering the last muster he has joined the better and brighter army of eternal peace."

V. Sarah Hibbard, b 9 Sept, 1832; m. James Smith, who d leaving three children, viz Dolly Smith (8), Fred Smith (8) and Edwin J. Smith. She remarried to Mr. Patrick J Connoly, who d in 1894 The following tribute from her home paper testifies to her worth:

"Mrs. P J Connolly died at her home, 181 W Western Ave., at noon, 30 March. 1893 She had been a long and patient sufferer, bearing her misfortunes in a most patient manner The first serious apprehension of her condition was felt last Monday night, when she suddenly became worse and continued to fail until death came to her relief. Mrs. Connolly was born in Wirt Center, N. Y., Sept. 22, 1833, moving to Grand Rapids, from where she came to Muskegon in 1869 She has been an active worker in the cause of temperance and was a member of the Woman's Relief Corps and the Lady Garfield Union at the time of her death. She was a woman of warm heart and tender sympathies and possesed of a disposition that gained for her the admiration of all who knew her. Her husband, Patrick J Connolly, was summoned from Chicago shortly before her death. Her son, Edwin J Smith, postmaster at Whitehall, and a daughter, Mrs M W. Decker, of 56 Unity street, were at her bedside at the time of her death. The funeral will be held Sunday afternoon at 2:30 at the Central M. E. Church, Rev. W A Hunsberger officiating."—Muskegon News.

VI John B., Jr., b. 13 May, 1836, at Wirt, Allegany Co, N. Y., d 6 July, 1897, at Georgetown, Ottawa Co, Mich, m. Katie Wilson, dau of Ebenezer Wilson of Georgetown. Mrs Lobdell d at Jenison (Georgetown), 29 Aug, 1871, leaving one son about four years of age, named

Frank Eben (8), b. 11 Oct, 1867 at Georgetown, m at Wirt Center, Allegany Co, N. Y., 23 Jan, 1890, Elizabeth Fanny Burdick, b. 6 Dec. 1872, at Titusville, Pa., dau. of Willett Francis and Polly Lucinda (Lobdell) Burdick of Wirt Center N. Y. Mr. Lobdell resides upon a farm in Farowe, Mich., is a Democrat, and in religion, a Baptist Has two children:
1   Reba Esta (9), b. 22 June 1893
2   Frank Ivan (9), b. 7 Sept., 1895

After the death of his first wife, John B re-married, 21 Oct, 1873, to Mara Anna Ellsworth, who having had no children of her

31

own, has faithfully supplied the place of mother to Frank and his family. Mrs. L. resides at Farowe and to her we are indebted for the following·

J. B. Lobdell was born in the state of New York in 1836 and was one of a family of eleven children, seven of whom are still among the living. My husband's parents came to Michigan when he was a year old and settled in Ingham county, and town of Dexter, if I remember right. having been a resident of Jenison for a number of years, and lastly removed to his farm in Georgetown, where he has since resided. He was a man of very quiet demeanor and gentle manners. but underneath that great self-possession lay a warm heart that wakened to the touch of friendship and love, and those who knew him will long remember him as a valued friend. His health has not been good for some years, and a short illness this summer was followed by a convalescence which his friends hoped would terminate in a recovery. He assisted his son Frank one day in haying, and at eventide took his milk pails and went to the barn to milk. His wife becoming alarmed at his long absence went to see the cause, and found him lying where he had fallen, nearly or quite dead. Thus had the messenger come, silently and without a moment's warning, and wafted his soul to the realms above. The physician pronounced his death due to dropsy of the heart. Mr. Lobdell was united in marriage to his present wife, Miss Mary Ellsworth, in Greenville, Montcalm county. Mich., October 21, 1873. His death occurred July 6, at the age of 61 years. He leaves a wife, a son, Frank, by his first wife, his son's wife, and two grandchildren to mourn his departure, with the sympathy of friends on every hand and the promise of a meeting beyond earth's tears and sorrow.

VII. Abraham Dakin, b. 13 Feb., 1839, in Ingham Co., Mich., is living with his family on a beautiful old farm on the town line between Georgetown and Blendon. He m. at Muskegon, 1 Jan., 1874, Marion Scott, b. 19 Feb., 1852, at Hamilton, Canada, dau. of John and Catherine (Seeber) Scott. Mr. Lobdell has resided in different cities of Michigan, viz: Dexter, Lansing, Muskegon, Grand Rapids, Manistee.

Mr. A. D. Lobdell served all through the Civil War; was sergeant of Company A, Sixth Michigan Corps.

He has two sons unmarried, at the home farm.

Charles Wesley (8), b. 3 Feb., 1876.

Scott Earl (8), b. 6 Sept., 1881.

And one daughter. Grace Alice (8). b 15 Jan, 1878; m. John Nibbelnik, and living near.

VIII. Polly Lucinda, b 12 Jan., 1842, in Ingham Co., Mich.; m. 18 June, 1870, at Belmont, Allegany Co., N. Y., Willett Franklin Burdick, b. 18 July, 1844, at Wirt, N. Y., son of Wm. and Avis L. (Thurston) Burdick.

Mr Burdick is a farmer, a Democrat, and in religion a Seventh

WM. HICKEY LOBDELL (7)
(John B. [6])
His wife; daughter; her husband and son
of Muskegon, Mich.
(Page 30)

Day Baptist They reside at Wirt Center, N Y Have one son.
Corda Abram Burdick (8) b 26 March, 1871; m Nellie Victoria Burdick

IX Charity M , b. 12 Feb., 1844, m Eli P. Loranger. She d. in Lansing, Mich , 13 Nov , 1899, leaving three children one dau. (8) living in California and one (8) living at Montcalm, Mich. Mrs. Loranger was identified with Ingham township nearly fifty years, and was sincerely mourned by many

"Since the death of her son Fred, about two years ago, mother has gradually been nearing the valley of the shadow. Her suffering in her last illness was intense, but the final passing away was like unto sleep conquering the drooping eyelids of a child. Of ten brothers and sisters, seven responded to the call of death as follows: A D. Lobdell and John Lobdell, South Blendon; Wm. Lobdell, Montague , Anson Lobdell, Grand Rapids, Henry Lobdell, North Muskegon , Mrs Chas. Lockwood and Mrs E P. Loranger, Williamston, Mich Mrs Elizabeth Wallace, Grinnell, Ia ; Mrs. Willett Burdick, Wirt Center, N Y , and Mrs Jane Kent, Sand Lake, Mich , were prevented from coming by sickness There were many kind friends who lent willing hands, and the victory of the silent Harvester was softened by their sweet ministrations A woman in whose heart there was no room for thought of self, but whose life was filled with yearning and sacrifice for the welfare of others, she passed away, strong in the faith and with a benediction for those left behind."—(A local papér)

X Annette, b 2 Sept , 1847, at Danville, Ingham Co., Mich ; m. 19 Sept , 1876, at Friendship, N Y , Charles E. Lockwood, b 15 Dec , 1838, at Barre, Orleans Co., N Y , son of Ebenezer and Eunice (Angevine) Lockwood Mr Lockwood and family reside at Williamstown, Ingham Co , Mich , where he is engaged in business as merchant and produce dealer. Is a Republican and a Methodist Children

1 Fred S Lockwood (8), b 25 Feb , 1878.
2 J B. Lockwood (8), b. 2 Oct , 1880
3 Ada Grace Lockwood (8), b 6 July, 1882
4 Effie C Lockwood (8), b 5 June, 1885
5 Neta Lockwood (8), b 18 Aug , 1887

XI Henry L (7), b. 26 Oct , 1850; m. Elizabeth McMann No further record, as my letter of inquiry was never answered

EIGHTH AND NINTH GENERATIONS

Children of Elizabeth Lobdell and Warren P Wallace

1   Mayo Charles
2. Scott Henry
3. Margaret Eliza.
4. Frank Otto.
5   Carrie L.
6. Fred Sheridan.
7   Lottie Lenora
8   Etta May
All born at Grinnell, Iowa.

I.   Mayo Charles Wallace, b 13 Aug, 1856, m. 9 Jan., 1890, at Omaha, Neb, to Nellie Theresa Kelly, who d. 10 Jan, 1894 Resides at Omaha Is conductor on U P. R R.

II   Scott Henry Wallace, b. 7 April, 1858; m 1894 at Little Rock, Ark., ———— Is depot agent at the City of Old Mexico, Mexico.

III. Margaret Eliza Wallace, b. 29 Jan., 1860, m. 29 Nov. 1881, Angus McDonald, b 12 Sept., 1843, at Goodrich, Canada, who d 6 Dec, 1890, leaving a widow and two daughters:

1   Nellie May McDonald (9), b at Winterset, Madison Co., Iowa, 10 Aug, 1886 At this time (1903) is attending college at College View, Neb.

2. Sadie Elizabeth McDonald (9), b 24 Jan, 1888.

IV   Frank Otto Wallace, b 8 Feb, 1862; m 1891 to Mary L Schultz

V   Carrie L. Wallace died in infancy, 1864

VI. Fred Sheridan Wallace, b. 31 March, 1866; m. Maggie A. McMurray Resides at Junction City, Kan

VII Lottie Lenora Wallace, b 26 Oct., 1868, m 17 Nov, 1892, Henry C. Boggie

VIII. Etta May Wallace, b. 13 Oct, 1870; m Edward Ellsworth Craver, a grocer of Harvey, Ill, 1901 No children Later moved on to a farm three miles out of Marshalltown, Iowa.

34

CARRIE LOBDELL BOURDON (8)
(Wm. Hickey [7])
of Muskegon, Mich.
(Page 30)

FRANK E. LOBDELL (8)
(John B. [7]. Jr.)
of Wirt Center, N. Y.
(Page 31)

CORDAN A. BURDICK (8)
(Lucinda)
of Friendship, N. Y.
(Page 32)

Children and Descendants of
Joshua[3] Lobdell (Joshua[2], Simon[1])
Wife, Mary Reynolds

FOURTH GENERATION

Children of Joshua (II) and Mary (Reynolds) Lobdell.

1 Mary   2 Joshua (III).   3 Ebenezer.   4 Jacob   5. Rachel.
6 Daniel.   7 John.

1, 2 and 3 were b in Ridgefield, Conn , 4, 5, 6 and 7 were b in Cortlandt Manor (Salem), Westchester Co , N Y.

1   Mary, b 6 Dec , 1725; m. Robert Pedrick, Jr , bapt. 22 Jan , 1727 (b. 30 June, 1726), son of Robert and Hannah Pedrick of Oyster Bay.   No further record.

The name of her husband, Robert Pedrick, Jr , is among the list of Westchester Co Volunteers who fought in the famous French and Indian Wars of 1755-1760

→ II.   Joshua (III) b 13 April, 1727; m , about 1750, Sarah, dau. of David Scott of Ridgefield, Conn   They resided in Cortlandt Manor until after 1767, when the family moved to Rensselaerwyck, Albany Co , N. Y , and settled in that part of the colony that on 29 March, 1784, was formed Stephenstown   When the boundary line between New York and Massachusetts was settled in 1786, I assume that the farm land of Joshua (III) lay in Berkshire Co , Mass. (in Lanesboro) across the line from Stephenstown, N Y   There his three youngest children were bapt by Rev Bostwick, and there Joshua probably died.

His widow remarried to James Wiley of Stephenstown   No date of her husband's death, but as Widow Sarah Wiley she was a charter member of the Presbyterian Church at Stephenstown Flats 19 July, 1794   In her extreme old age she made her home with her sons, Isaac and Simon Lobdell, at Westerlo, Albany Co , N Y , where she died 3 Feb , 1823, aged 103½ years   Is buried in Chesterville burying ground

The following is copied from Ridgefield, Conn , deeds, but the year was not sent me.   (1765-6?)

"Joshua Lobdell, Jr , and wife Sarah of Cortlandt Manor ; John Rockwell, Jr , and wife Hannah ; Joshua Rockwell and wife Mary of Ridgfield, James and Daniel Scott of Ridgefield, sells land formerly belonging to David Scott of Ridgefield (deceased, 1765).

36

Joshua was corporal in his father's company in the war against Canada (1755-60), and is also recorded under date of 21 May, 1783, as a private in Capt. Cornelius Wiltse's company, under Col. Thaddeus Crane. Westchester Co. militia, and performed active service in the Revolutionary War

III. Ebenezer, b 1 Dec., 1730. m Deborah Palmer, b 29 Dec., 1734, at Greenwich, Conn., dau. of Jonathan Palmer b. 1699. She probably was of Westchester Co., as Jonathan Palmer—evidently her brother—b 6 Dec., 1724 was in same company as her husband in the wars of 1755-60. I have been unable to find maiden name of her mother, but Deborah was granddaughter of James Palmer (of Greenwich) and Sarah, dau. of Rev. Thomas Derham of Rye. N Y.

(The family of Jonathan Palmer consisted of 13 children. viz: James, Sarah, Jonathan, Anna. Sarah, Robert. Samuel. Deborah. Winans. Hannah. Gideon. Nathaniel and Elizabeth.)

During the Revolutionary War, in 1783, Ebenezer and his son, Ebenezer, Jr., provided substitutes to fill their places.

This is to certify that the names of Ebenezer Lobdell and Ebenezer Lobdell, Jr., appear in "Manuscripts of the Colony and State of New York in the Revolutionary War." Volume 25, folio 148, as follows:

"To all to whom these presents shall come, We the Major Part of a Class in the Regiment of militia of the State of New York, Commanded by Lieutenant Colonel Thaddeus Crane in the County of Westchester, having, under an Act entitled 'An Act for raising Troops to complete the Line of this State in the Service of the United States and the two Regiments to be Raised on Bounties of Unappropriated Lands and for the further Defense of the frontiers of this State passed the 23rd Day of March last, engaged John Edwards to serve in the Company Commanded By Captain Thomas Hunt untill the first day of January Last Past in the Ridgment of Levies Commanded by Lieutenant Colonel Weisenfels, his heirs asines Do hereby grant, transfer, assign and Set over unto Nathaniel Delivan. Esquire, all our estate, right, title and Intrust to any Lands we are or may Become intitled to for engaging the said John Edwards to serve as aforesaid By or in virtue of the said Act. to have and to hold the Estate, right, title and Intrust aforesaid of in and to the said Lands unto the said Nathaniel Delivan, Esquire. his Heirs assigns for Ever, in witness whereof we have hereunto

37

Set our hands and Seals the Sixth Day of February in the year of our Lord one thousand seven hundred and eighty-three.

"Ebenezer Lobdell.

"Ebenezer Lobdell, Jr

"Sealed and Delivered in the presence of Stephen Delivan, Peter Crane"

Ebenezer d. between 23 Feb , 1799. and 12 June, 1799, as on the former date his will is dated. and probated on the latter. "He resided on a farm at North Salem, of nearly 200 acres, leased by him from Stephen Delancey—before the Revolution, and afterward purchased by him at sheriff's sale."

At the Register's office at White Plains, N. Y , we find deed from "Epenetus Ward to Ebenezer Lobdell," dated 15 April, 1771: 10 acres near the "house that Jacob Lobdell formerly lived in " Also "Samuel Lyon to Ebenezer Lobdell, 6 Sept , 1788, 160 acres in Cortlandt Manor." now in possession of Ebenezer Lobdell—"adjoining lands of John Lobdell."

Ebenezer was closely identified with St James Episcopal Church. I think one of its first trustees, after its incorporation, 3 June, 1786

Ebenezer was corporal in His Majesty's Seventh Company of Militia in the upper battalion, in Westchester Co , in the French and Indian wars of 1755-60, in his father's (Joshua II) Co., under Col. Wm. Willett

Copy of the will of Ebenezer Lobdell:

In the Name of God, Amen I, Ebenezer Lobdell, of North Salem, in the County of Westchester and State of New York, being at present under considerable indisposition of body, though sound in mind and memory—blessed be God therefor—and calling to mind my own mortality and knowing that it is appointed for all men once to die, I make and ordain this my last will and testament And first I recommend my soul to God, who gave it, and my body to the earth, to be buried in a decent and Christian-like manner at the discretion of my executors And as touching my worldly things wherewith it hath pleased God to bless me with, I dispose of in the following manner First, it is my will that all my just debts and funeral charges should be paid by my executors out of movable estate Secondly, I give unto my loving wife Deborah the improvement of all my real and personal estate during her natural life after my just debts and funeral charges are paid Thirdly, I give

38

unto my son, Jacob Lobdell, my dwelling house and orchard, bounded on my son Ebenezer on the west, and down south by said Ebenezer so far that a due east line to the highway will include the orchard, thence north by said highway and west to the beginning at the land of the said Ebenezer Lobdell to be taken by my son Jacob after the decease of my said wife, Deborah. Fourthly, I give unto my sons, Jacob Lobdell and Ebenezer Lobdell, and to my daughters, Deborah Field, wife of Isaac Field; Cloe Brown, wife of Nathan Brown, and Ann Reynolds, wife of Benjamin Reynolds, the Remainder of my real and personal estate, to be equally divided between them after the decease of my said wife Deborah, excepting one equal share with one of the above mentioned to be equally divided between my two grandchildren, namely, Jacob Bailey and Deborah Bailey, heirs to my daughter, Mary Bailey, deceased. And I hereby appoint my son, Jacob Lobdell, to be my executor to this my last will and testament In testimony whereof I hereunto set my hand and affix my seal this twenty-third day of February, in the year of our Lord one thousand seven hundred and ninety-nine Ebenezer Lobdell (X) (his mark) (Seal) Signed, sealed, published and pronounced to be the last will and testament of him the said Ebenezer Lobdell, in the presence of Daniel Lobdell, Nathan Rundell, Joseph Cable

IV Jacob, Sr., b about 1732, m 28 Aug, 1757, Ruth Boughton, b 16 July, 1737, at Stamford, Conn., dau. of Eleazer and Elizabeth (Seymour) Boughton

They resided on a farm in Cortlandt Manor, where most of their children were born We find in the deed of purchase by his brother Ebenezer that in 1771 he had left the farm He probably had moved with his family to Rensselaerwyck, where his brother Joshua was living (The Manor of Rensselaerwyck was formed into a "District" 24 March, 1772, and as Rensselaerwyck was the only colony which remained uninjured by the war, as a consequence many farms were taken up and the population generally prospered) His land, like his brother Joshua's, lay on soil that, after the boundary line between New York and Massachusetts was settled was in Berkshire Co, Mass Jacob's in West Stockbridge, adjoining Lanesboro, the home of Joshua

Jacob probably d in West Stockbridge, Mass. His wife, at the home of her son John in Westport, Essex Co, N. Y., 16 April, 1816

"This is to certify that on page 53 of a manuscript volume entitled 'Treasurer's Certificates' in the custody of the Regents of the University of the State of New York, in the State Library, the name of Jacob Lobdell is recorded as a private in November, 1781, in the company commanded by Captain Ephraim Lockwood, belonging to the Fourth Westchester Co. regiment of the New York State Militia, commanded by Col. Thaddeus Crane, also that this said regiment was employed in active service in the Revolutionary War."

V. Rachel, b ———? m Jacob Rundle. Can reach no descendant From a muster roll of Westchester men who passed muster for service

"Jacob Rundle, b. 1732, enlisted 14 April, 1758, age 26; born in Conn.; by trade, a weaver; 5 feet 8 inches high, grey eyes; a scar on his upper lip.

VI. Daniel Lobdell, b. about 1740, m 12 Jan., 1764, Elizabeth, b. 24 Aug., 1743, dau of Joseph (b. at Fairfield) and Agnes Money Lockwood

Daniel was a farmer, residing in Cortland Manor until 1774, when he sold his farm of 123 acres to Gershom Hanford, and with his family moved to "the Royal Grant,"* Herkimer Co., N. Y. They settled in a place called Salisbury, where they suffered privations such as we of the present day can scarcely realize From Revolutionary records I have secured the following, which will give us some idea of what they endured

I have no record of death of Daniel or wife. His children remained in Herkimer Co.

This is to certify that on page 79 of a manuscript volume entitled 'Assembly Papers,' volume 16, in the custody of the regents of the University of the State of New York, in the State Library, occurs the following affidavit:

Montgomery County.

To the Honourable Board of Commissioners appointed by the Legislature of the State of New York, etc.:

"This may certifie that Daniel Lobdell of Palentine Town in the County aforesaid did belong to Capt. John Cuizer's Company of

---

* "The Royal Grant" contained nearly 100,000 acres of choice land, mostly situated in the county of Herkimer, N Y Was formerly the property of Sir Wm. Johnson The title to this land was confirmed by the British government, hence called Royal Grant."

* Herkimer Co. was not organized till 1791 when it was taken from Montgomery Co, so that Daniel Lobdell served in a militia organization of the latter county

Molitia in my Ridgment in the year of our Lord one thousand Seven Hundred and Eighty, and was so fare in actual Service as to be held Ready for Service at a minute's warning, and being at home at his own house in the Royal grant on the third Day of April in the year afore said, was Taken prisoner by a party of Indians, himself and three sons, one of abought Sixteen years of age, the other two younger, and Carried prisoners to Canady and theire cept three years and a half stript of His property Sutch as they Could Carry away, and Left his wife with the Remainding part of his Children in Distressed Surcomstances

"February 12, 1793

"John Keyser

"Jacob Klock, Led. Corl."

VII.   John, b 10 March, 1743, m. 30 May, 1764, Elizabeth, b. at Ridgefield, 16 May, 1744, dau. of Daniel and Jerusha (Whitney) Sherwood. They resided on a farm in Cortlandt Manor, close by the farms of John's brothers, Daniel and Ebenezer. There his children were born, and it is thought that there John and Elizabeth died—Elizabeth, 22 July, 1804; John, 15 Oct., 1812

In register's office, White Plains, Westchester Co, N. Y., is copied a deed from Stephen De Lancey and others to John Lobdell, 15 Aug., 1774. 160 acres of land bounded east by the "Oblong" line and west by "Ebenezer and Daniel Lobdell's farms " Also—

"John in 1795 bought another piece of 27 acres, adjoining him on the southwest."

In 1787 John was sheriff of Salem, N. Y. In 1787 John sells the portion of the estate of Sarah Sherwood, who was a maiden sister of his wife, b 1751.

Nov., 1781, John Lobdell is recorded as a private in the company commanded by Capt. Ephraim Lockwood, belonging to Fourth Westchester Co Regiment of the State Militia, which regiment was under the command of Col. Thaddeus Crane; also, that said regiment was employed in active service in the Revolutionary War.

FIFTH GENERATION.

CHILDREN AND DESCENDANTS OF JOSHUA (4) AND SARAH (SCOTT) LOBDELL.

1, 2 and 3, b. at Ridgefield, Conn.

4, 5, 6, 7. 8 and 9 b at Salem, N. Y.

10, 11 and 12 bapt. at Lanesboro, Mass.

1 Joshua H̶.. 2. Isaac, 3 Sarah, 4 James, 5. Hannah, 6. Simon, 7. Huldah, 8 Abraham, 9 Abijah, 10. Mary, 11. Rachel, 12 Rebecca.

I. Joshua H̶., b. 1752, m. for first wife, Jane Pouce and for his second wife, Jane Yaw He d. in Westerlo, 13 May, 1813, aged 61 Here, he and his wives are buried.

II Isaac, b. 8 March, 1755 When a lad, his parents moved from Cortlandt Manor (Salem), Westchester Co. N Y, to Lanesboro, Berkshire Co., Mass., at which place Isaac m Mirriam Pomeroy of the same County for his first wife; she was b. 12 June, 1759. In about twelve years Isaac and Mirriam moved to Westerlo, Albany Co, where, on the Baptist church records, (church organized in 1800) we find the names of Isaac and Mirriam Lobdell among the charter members Mirriam d at Westerlo, 11 Sept., 1802 aged 43 y. 5 m

Isaac m for his second wife, Jerusha Lobdell (his cousin) dau of John (Joshua II), and Elizabeth (Sherwood) Lobdell of Salem, N Y. Jerusha d. at Westerlo 2 May, 1849, aged 80 y. 3 m Mr Orville Lobdell of Westerlo found the graves and copied the above from the two gravestones between the two, the body of Isaac lies, he having d 24 March, 1838, aged 83 y. 16 d.

The first mills in Albany Co. were erected in 1795, at Westerlo, by Isaac Lobdell and one Mr. Baker, sold afterward to his sons, —Isaac Jr., and James Hervey I

Isaac was a soldier in the Revolutionary War. He entered the service at Hancock, Mass, and was drafted in the month of August,

42

1778, for the term of 3 months and joined Capt. Joseph Barnes' Co and Col Simonds' regiment and immediately went to Pittsfield in Mass where he joined the said Co. and then with said Co marched down through Danbury and Reading, to New Fairfield and there joined the said regiment and went with said regiment to Kingsbridge and there joined General Washington's army He was then ordered to Valentine's Hill where he and the said company and regiment built a fort After this he marched to a place called Tuckahoe, and then to White Plains and engaged in the Battle at that place. He continued there until in the month of Nov., when he was dismissed and returned home, having served at this time three months.

In the month of Aug. of the next year, he again entered the said service at Hancock aforesaid, and joined Capt. Smith's Co. and was immediately marched to Lake George and was at the taking of Burgoyne Was at Saratoga, and other places at the northward until late in the fall when he was discharged and returned home

He made an application for pension on 25 July, 1832, at which time he was 77 years of age, and residing in Westerlo, N Y His pension was allowed for six months' actual service as a private in the Mass troops Witnesses Wm Wheaton, Simon Lobdell

III. Sarah was bapt. 28 Feb, 1752. Mr John Little Lobdell in his letter tells us "she m. for her first husband, Mr. Sprague and had children For her second husband, Daniel Hubbard of Lenox, Berkshire Co, Mass, and had 1 Daniel Hubbard (6) who m and settled on the Onondaga River, Broome Co, N Y, and 2 Sarah Hubbard (6) who m — Seymour, also settled in Broome Co., N. Y."

IV. James was bapt at Salem, N. Y. by Rev. Dr. Deblee, 13 July, 1757, resided with his parents at Lanesboro, Mass, and while there m Miss Mary Venable of Stephenstown, N. Y.

James was a Revolutionary soldier, having joined the army at Hancock, Mass

He afterward moved and settled in Warren Co, Miss.

V. Hannah, bapt at Salem, N. Y., 24 June, 1759, m. Jeremiah (son of Elijah, Sr, and Margaret (Gillett) Goodrich) b at Hancock Mass, 4 Aug 1757

"They resided at Hancock, had children, viz
    1 Jacob Goodrich (6), b 27 Jan, 1782.
    2 Lucy Goodrich (6), b 19 March, 1784.

3 Hannah Goodrich (6), b. 13 Sept. 1786, m. Thomas G. Hubbard.

4. Jeremiah Goodrich (6). b. 1 Feb.. 1789, m. Melared A. Watkins

5. Sarah Goodrich (6), b. 12 June, 1791

6 Abraham Goodrich (6). b. 8 Nov., 1793.

7. Abijah Goodrich (6), b. 15 Oct.. 1795, m. Miss Wallis.

8 Seymour Goodrich (6), b. 11 Dec.. 1797, d. single "— (Goodrich Genealogy)

VI. Simon was b. 25 Feb., 1762, resided with his parents, at Lanesborough, Mass., where he m. Grace Pomeroy of Berkshire Co (a sister of Mirriam, who m Isaac, the brother of Simon), b. probably at Lenox, Mass., 10 June, 1762 They moved to Westerlo where their children were born and where both Simon and Grace d and are buried. He, 19 Dec., 1850, aged 88 y., 9 m., 24 d. She, 12 Oct. 1845, in her 84th year

VII. Hulda was baptized at Salem, N. Y., 5 June, 1763. According to Mr John Little Lobdell, she m. John Hamlin and removed to the County of Chenango—or Otsego, N. Y. She had three children:

1 Gilbert Hamlin (6).

2. John Hamlin (6).

3 Marcia Hamlin (6).

VIII Abraham, bapt at Salem, N. Y., 25 Aug. 1765, migrated with his brother James to the State of Missisippi, there m. Sarah Kennard, b. 29 Aug., 1785, and removed to the Parish of East Baton Rouge, La., afterward to West Baton Rouge, La.

IX. Abijah, b. 30 April. 1767, was bapt. at Courtlandt Manor, (Salem) N. Y., by Rev. Dr. Deblee of Stamford Parish, Conn., 23 Aug., 1767. He was taken by his parents to Stephentown, Rensselaer Co., which part on which Joshua's land lay was afterward Lanesboro, Mass., where he resided until he made a start in life for himself at Johnstown, (then Montgomery Co., now, Fulton Co., where (he and) his wife both d. in the 40's. He m. Mary Little, b. 14 June, 1771, dau. of Major John Little and Leah Crawford of Corry's bush, Albany Co., (now Princeton, Schenectady Co., N. Y.) (The family of Capt John Little were for a time, inmates of Fort Plain, "which was situated on the brow of the hill about 2½ miles from Fort Plain village near Johnstown, and built as a fortress and place of retreat and safety for the inhabitants and families in case

44

of incursions from the Indians.") Maj. John Little d. 29 Sept., 1822, and is buried in the old cemetery in Johnstown.

The D. A. R. Society has placed a boulder to mark the spot where his (Capt. John Little) regiment stood during the battle at Johnstown. In 1802, Abijah was master of the Masonic lodge, instituted at Johnstown, by Sir Wm. Johnson. In 1806, he was 2nd. Lieut. 5th Reg Artillery—2nd Battalion—Montgomery Co., and on 24 May, 1809, was promoted to 1st Lieut The old home of Abijah —a double house—still stands in Johnstown. In one half Abijah lived, his children were born and he passed away—and it was afterward occupied until her death, by his grand daughter—Mrs. Lucian Bertrand.

In the other half lived James (5) Lobdell (Daniel, 4, John, 3, Joshua, 2, Simon, 1), until he moved to Troy, N. Y., where he was one of the principal dry goods merchants. The grandfathers of Abijah (5) and James (5) were half brothers, both sons of Joshua, 1.

X. Mary, bapt. at Lanesborough, Mass., by Rev Gideon Bostwick, 4 Nov., 1770. Mr. John Lobdell says, "m. Peleg Allyn, removed to Cayuga Co., N. Y., afterward to the State of Indiana."

XI. Rachel, b. at Lanesborough; m James Dixon; removed to Ontario Co., N. Y., had two sons

XII Rebecca, died an infant at Lanesborough 4 Sept., 1774.

SIXTH GENERATION.

CHILDREN AND DESCENDANTS OF JOSHUA (5) LOBDELL IV.

---

(1) wife, Jane Pouce
(2) wife, Jane Yaw

(By (1)wife, Jane (Pouce) Lobdell:
1. Joel (6). 2. Abraham (6) 3 Joshua (6).

I. Joel, a farmer, resided at South Westerlo, Albany, Co., N. Y., was b. in 1779 at Stephenstown, Rensselaer Co., N. Y., d. in 1835 at Stockport, Columbia Co., N. Y, m. at South Westerlo, where she was b., Hannah Udell. She d. at Stockport.

II. Abraham, a farmer, b. 20 Feb, 1789, at Westerlo, N. Y., d. 30 July, 1867-8, at East Worcester, Otsego Co., N. Y, m 10 March,

45

1810, to his first wife, Elizabeth Wilson, b 1785, at Chesterville, Albany Co , N. Y., d. 6 Nov , 1830, at Maryland, Otsego Co., dau. of Robert Wilson and ——? Wilsey. In youth, Mr. Lobdell was a Baptist in religion, but became a Methodist, was a devout Christian and his children's children revere his name, to the present generation Abraham, m. for his second wife (by whom he had no children), Lydia Wing, b 11 July, 1791, (widow of David Titus), dau. of James Wing and wife Hannah Bowerman "James Wing was a mariner, owned his own vessel and made trading voyages up the North River. He once passed the winter at Washington's headquarters at Newburg His sloop—the Unity, with a cargo of salt was captured by the British and confiscated In the early part of year 1800 he removed to the Little Nine Partners, since called Milan, Dutchess Co , N. Y., where he purchased a farm, and where he d. in 1842, aged 84." (Geo Dikeman Wing.)

III. Joshua V. No date of birth, he d. in the town of Sanford, Broome Co., N. Y.; m Cornelia Finch at Whitehall, Washington Co., N. Y. She d at Westford. Otsego Co., N Y.

By (2) wife, Jane (Yaw) Lobdell

---

1 Sarah, 2 Abigail. 3. Philip. 4 Hannah, 5 Daniel 6 Electa, 7 John.

I. Sarah, m. Geo. Smith. Removed to Oneonta

II Abigail, died unmarried Lived at Westerlo.

III Philip, a cooper, residing at Westerlo, where he was b 4 Oct., 1800, where he also m. 1 Oct., 1823, Harriet Lamb, b 20 Jan , 1807, at Westerlo, dau of Jehial Lamb and Mary Smith. The family were Methodists ; Philip d 30 June, 1872, at Westerlo, his wife, 12 Jan , 1888, at Rensselaerville, Albany Co

IV Hannah, d unmarried Lived at Westerlo

V Daniel b. 31 March, 1805, at Westerlo, N Y., d 30 May, 1882, at Sidney, Delaware Co , N Y ; m for his first wife, 24 Oct., 1830, Mary Youngs, b 10 Dec , 1804, at Oneanto, Otsego Co , N Y., where she d. 28 March, 1841, leaving a little dau only 10 days old who was taken and raised by a sister of her mother's. Soon after his marriage Daniel and his wife moved to Oncanto taking with him his mother, but probably she longed for her old home and friends for after a short stay she returned to Westerlo and made her home with her unmarried dau Hannah

46

DANIEL LOBDELL (6)
(Joshua [5])   (1805-1882)
of Sidney, N. Y.
(Page 46)

BRITTON LOBDELL (7)
(Joel [6])
of Afton, N. Y.
(Page 47)

LUCIUS LOBDELL (7)
(Abraham [6])   (1822-1898)
of Deposit, N. Y.

ROSANDER LOBDELL (7)
(Joshua [6])
of McGrawville, N. Y.

Daniel m his second wife, Eliza Martindale, on 2 June, 1841.

VI. Electa m James Crandall. Lived at Rensselaerville.

VII. John m. Mahala ——? I am told that they moved from Westerlo into Sullivan Co , but could find no trace of them ; and the only record is in Westerlo church, "Mahala Lobdell dismissed by letter 2 Dec., 1837 "

SEVENTH GENERATION.

CHILDREN AND DESCENDANTS OF JOEL LOBDELL (6) AND HIS WIFE, HANNAH UDELL.

1 Britton. 2 Theodosia. 3. Joshua. 4. Elizabeth. 5. Jane. 6 Sarah. 7 Abigail. 8 Julia Ann. 9 Hannah 10 Marion 11. Joel 12 Lucius 13 Lionel.

I Britton was b. 30 Oct , 1824, at Westerlo, N. Y. His father died while Britton was a mere lad, and his boyhood was a hard struggle, which developed a man of steady, industrious habits and sound and conservative judgment, always having held the respect and confidence of his neighbors and town people By his industry and thrift he has raised a large family of children to great credit to himself. He m. at Maryland, Otsego Co., N. Y., 12 July, 1825, Maria Lobdell—his cousin—dau of Joshua Lobdell and Cornelia Finch, and today (3 June, 1902), they are both living—at Afton, Chenango Co , N Y , enjoying the society of those of their children who remain near the old home and of their old time friends.

II Theadosia, m. Glen Van Valtenburg; had Caroline Van Valtenburg (8) and Wm Van Valtenburg (8).

III. Joshua, b. 16 Sept , 1809, at Westerlo, d. 4 Aug., 1886, at Kent, Ohio, m at Catskill, N Y., Eliza Ann Hoover, b 26 Nov , 1815, at Pleasantville, N. Y, dau of John Hoover and Margaret Sherwood

IV. Elizabeth, m Oliver Butler, no children.

V Jane, m Geo Judkins, no children

VI. Sarah, m Christopher Stickles, had sons Charles and Wm. (8).

VII. Abigail, m Hiram Decker, had dau. Elizabeth (8), m. Mr New and resides at Valatie, N Y, also had sons Geo., Jacob and John Decker (8).

47

VIII. Julia Ann, m. Wm. Clark, had 2 daus.
IX. Hannah, m Abel Butler.
X. Marion, m. (1) Wm Phillips, (2) Abram Van Alstyne.
XI. Joel, died in infancy
XII. Lucius, d. 1847, aged 19 years
XIII Lionel, m. Lydia Webb.

EIGHTH GENERATION.

CHILDREN AND DESCENDANTS OF BRITTON (7) LOB-DELL AND HIS WIFE, MARIA (7) LOBDELL.

1. Joel Britton. 2 Melvin Joshua. 3. Addison LaRoy 4 Cornelia Adelaide. 5. James Elon. 6. Ida May. 7. Flora Vernette 8. Geo. Lincoln. 9. Clara Maria

I. Joel Britton, b 14 March, 1847, at Stockport, Columbia Co., N. Y., m 18 Nov., 1875, at Hancock, Mass., Ida R Halstead, b 16 Nov., 1857, at Hancock,—dau. of Benj. Halstead and Sarah Bailey Mr. Lobdell is a farmer and Republican.

CHILDREN.
1 Alice Elizabeth (9), b 21 Feb., 1879.
2 Britton DeWitt (9), b 30 Aug., 1881
3 Frank (9), b 7 April, 1883.
4. Judson (9), b. 30 Oct , 1885
5 Bertha May (9), b 19 Sept , 1895

II. Melvin Joshua b. 10 March, 1849, at Stockport, Columbia Co., N. Y , is unmarried, residing at Afton.

III. Addison LeRoy, a farmer, residing at Valatie, Columbia Co., N. Y., was b. 29 April, 1851, at Sanford, Broome Co., N. Y., m. 4 Feby , 1877, at Fowler, Benton Co , Ind , to Josephine E Morris, b. 17 March, 1853, at Anderson. Madison Co , Ind , dau of John Morris and Mary Chenoweth

CHILDREN.
1 Clara Bell (9), b 2 Feb , 1878
2. Renetta Floy (9), 15 Sept , 1881.
3. Effie Vernette (9), b 21 March, 1883.
4 Jennie Florence (9), b 9 Aug , 1886.
5 Mary Josephine (9), b 4 Dec , 1884

48

IV. Cornelia Adelaide had no children. She was b. at Sandford, N. Y., 21 July, 1853, m. 3 July, 1870, at Sanford, Eugene Van Sternburg and d. at Sanford 15 Sept., 1870.

V. James Elon, a blacksmith, living at Wellington, Sumner Co., Kansas. Prohibition in politics, was b. 30 March, 1856. at North Sandford, Broome Co., N. Y., removed west and m. 7 Feby., 1880, at Geuda Springs, Kansas, Harriet Celia Ward, b. 14 June, 1858, at Bethel, Iowa, dau. of Orren James Ward and Caroline Celia Hapgood

CHILDREN.

1 Helen Celia (9), b. 31 Jan., 1883.
2. Asenath Maria (9), b. 2 March, 1885
3 Britton James (9), b. 11 Jan., 1888.
4. Llewellyn (9), b. 12 March, 1890; d. 23 March, 1890
5 Lemuel Hapgood (9), b. 21 Oct., 1891.
6 Geo. Lincoln, Jr., (9), b. 21 Jan., 1896.
7 Angie Ellen Harriet (9), b. 28 Nov., 1898

VI. Ida May, b. 30 July, 1858. at Sanford, N. Y., d. 11 Sept. 1891, at Sandford; m. 28 Feby., 1881, at Susquehanna, Penn. Charles E. Johnson, b. 5 Dec., 1851, at Carbondale, Penn., d. 7 Aug., 1891, at Danville, Penn. No descendants.

VII Flora Vernette, b. 11 Oct., 1862, at Sandford, unmarried. Resides at Afton.

VIII. Geo. Lincoln, a minister—at present at Divinity School, Eugene, Oregon—b. 10 March, 1866, at Sanford, m. 2 Sept., 1899, at Anthony, Kansas, to Lizzie Viola Harris, b. 4 Aug., 1873, d. 21 July, 1901, at Oxford, Kansas, leaving a little dau. Esther (9), b. 14 June, 1900, at Grenola, Kansas.

Mrs Lobdell was dau. of Whitsett Morrow Harris and Mary Ellen McMahon. Since writing the above I rec'd the cards of Mr. and Mrs. Geo. L. Lobdell and wish to insert the following from their local paper:

EUGENE REGISTER. Sept 17, 1902

Yesterday at 10 a. m. at the home of Dean E. C. Sanderson of the Divinity school, was celebrated in a quiet way, the marriage of Miss Eugenia O'Connor, of Grenold, Kansas, daughter of Dr. B. R. O'Connor, to Rev. Geo L. Lobdell.

Rev. Lobdell is a well known student of the Divinity school, now pastor of the Christian church at Junction. The bride is a graduate of the New England Conservatory of Music and for two years has been teacher of music in the Central Normal College at Danville, Indiana Mrs. Lobdell will take charge of the musical department of the Divinity school

The young couple will be welcomed to Eugene, where they will be at home to friends at 446 East Eleventh street, after October 1st.

IX Clara Maria, b. 25 June, 1868, at Sandford, m 12 Feby., 1886, Alnoon Russell Williams, b 18 Oct., 1861, at Friendship, son of Andrew Williams and Lucia Russell. They reside in Afton, and have two children.

 1 Claude Arleigh Williams (9), b. 31 June, 1887

 2 Harold Jennings Williams (9), b 9 July, 1896

CHILDREN OF JOSHUA (7) LOBDELL AND ELIZA ANN HOOVER.

1 Frances Cornelia 2 Elizabeth Jane. 3 Ira. 4 Mary Ann 5. Charles Britton. 6 Wm Henry

I. Frances Cornelia, b 14 Nov, 1833, at Westerlo, where she lived until about 18 years of age when she went to Norwalk, Ohio, to visit her uncle, C J Osborn Her father and family removed to Norwalk about 6 months later There, on 15 Feby., 1854, she m. Lucius Boughton, now living at Bowling Green, Ohio, who lovingly tells me· "She was a true wife and a noble woman." After their marriage they moved to Greenwich, Ohio, where she d 21 Feby, 1855, leaving an infant dau, Frances C (9), who d 18 months later

II. Elizabeth Jane, b 4 Feby, 1837, at Westerlo, N Y, m 8 Aug., 1860, at Stuyvesant Falls, Columbia Co, N. Y., Robert McKeon, a native of Ireland, b 5 Feby., 1835, son of James McKeon and Elizabeth Elder of Brooklyn, N Y.

To Robert and Elizabeth (Lobdell) McKeon were born

 1 Clara E McKeon (9), b 17 April, 1864.

 2 Alice Louise McKeon (9), b 6 July, 1866

 3 Minnie B McKeon (9), b. 12 April, 1879; m. Fred Siegle

 4 Nellie J McKeon, b 14 Dec, 1872

III. Ira, b 9 June, 1839, m Ann Jeffreys

IV Mary Ann, b 19 March 1842

V. Charles Britton, b 8 May, 1843

VI. Wm Henry, b 7 Aug., 1845, m Elizabeth Greggs.

SEVENTH GENERATION.

CHILDREN AND DESCENDANTS OF ABRAHAM 6 LOBDELL AND FIRST WIFE, ELIZABETH WILSON.

1. Aurilla. 2. Harriet 3 Jarvis 4 Jason. 5 Smith 6 Samantha 7 Richard 8 Lucius 9 Jane. 10. Charlotte. 11. Sarah. 12 George

I Aurilla, b 21 Aug 1812, at Coxsackie, Green Co., N Y., m 1833. Francis Jones, who d. at Otsego Co., N Y., 19 April, 1887 Mrs. Jones is living with her son-in-law and her dau. Mr and Mrs Jacob Pane (8), at East Worcester, N Y.

II. Harriet, b 29 Aug 1813 at Coxsackie, m. 1 June 1831, David Fellows, b 26 Aug 1810, d 9 March 1889. Children—

    1. Joseph Hiram Fellows, b 9 June 1832; lives at Belvidere, Ill

    2 Lydia Ann Fellows, b 21 Oct 1833; lives at Coldwater, Mich

    3 Emily Miranda Fellows, b. 27 Aug. 1835, d 27 June, 1900; m Lorenzo Dow Scisco, d 10 Aug 1870 One son, Lorenzo Dow Scisco, Jr, is a business man of Chicago, Ill.

    4 Isaac Clark Fellows, b 18 Sept. 1837, deceased

    5 Sabrina Jane Fellows, b 30 Nov. 1839, m. Sylvanus Hausen

    6. Rose Ellen Fellows. b. 28 June 1847, d 2 Nov 1856

    7 Wm Abram Fellows, b 8 Jan 1850; lives in Schenectady, N. Y.

III. Jarvis, b Feby., 1816, d 1817.

IV. Jason, b. 25 March, 1817, d 15 Dec., 1896, at Deposit. Broome Co, N. Y., m. Mary Ann Waterman who d at Deposit 15. Sept, 1894 Jason, with his wife and three children moved from Otsego Co, N Y, to Sandford, Broome Co., N. Y., in 1840. The country was new and heavily timbered and with the help of his children he cleared 300 acres of land; 14 children were born to himself and wife and all lived to grow to maturity. Two were in the "War of the Rebellion," one dying at Gettysburg. Both Jason and his wife lived to a ripe old age, though long invalids, cared for

51

with loving and gentle hands by their dau. Anna, who still resides in the old home

V. Smith, b. 2 May, 1818, at Maryland, Otsego Co., N. Y., m. 14 Oct., 1839, Eliza Delia Bailey b. 6 May, 1818, at Jefferson, Schoharie Co., N. Y., at which place Mr. Lobdell, as a young man settled and began life's work—as a farmer. His Religion was of the Baptist denomination, Mrs. Lobdell was dau. of Cornelius Bailey and Sarah Umery. In their old age Mr. and Mrs Lobdell both made their home with their son, Mr. Wm. Geo Lobdell (8) of Unadilla, Otsego Co., N. Y., who wrote me, a short time since, that both parents were well and active. How few are permitted to enjoy together for so long a period, life's happiness and sorrows.

VI. Samantha, b. 12 Oct. 1819, m. James Wing. I was given the name of her son, Valentine Wing (8), Poughkeepsie, N. Y., but received no reply to my letter, of inquiry.

VII. Richard, b. 5 May, 1821, d. 27 June, 1898, at Fowler, Benton Co., Ind., m. 1 Jany., 1845, at Worcester, N. Y. Mary Permelia Flint, b. 2 Dec., 1822, d. at Fowler, Ind., 1 Feb., 1884.

VIII. Lucius, a farmer, b. 2 Sept., 1822, at Westerlo, N. Y., d. 6 March, 1898, at Deposit, Broom Co., N. Y., m. in Jany., 1846 at Oneanto, Qtsego Co., N. Y., to first wife, Mary Ann Wakelee. b. 1823, (dau. of Noah and Huldah Wakelee), d. 17 March, 1847. at Oneanto, leaving an infant dau. Mary E. (8), b. 23 Feby., 1847.

Mr. Lobdell m. 7 Nov., 1847, for his second wife, Hannah M. Brownell b. 18 March, 1824, at Prattsville, N. Y., d. 7 Jany., 1881. at Deposit, dau. of David Brownell and —— Gore.

Mr. Lobdell's parents moved to Otsego Co., while he was a small boy and he lived in that County until April 1876, when he moved to Deposit, where he spent the remainder of his days. He was a devout Christian, honored by all. For many years was one of the foremost in the Methodist church, holding positions of trust, and at all times ready to befriend those to whom trouble and sorrow had come.

IX. Jane, b. 1 Dec. 1823, m. John Eaton.

X. Charlotte, b. 23 June, 1825, m. Robert Shaw. Has a son, Theodore Shaw (8), of Baldwinsville, N. Y.

XI. Sarah, b. 11 Oct. 1826, m. Wm. Smith.

XII. George W., b. 11 Jany., 1829, at Worcester, N. Y., lived at Schenevus, Otsego Co., N. Y., m. Angelica Crippen, dau. of Egbert Crippen and Ann Eliza Chase. He is now living at Kinderhook, Branch Co., Mich Is a miller I am told that he was a soldier in the Civil War.

CHILDREN.

1. Geo. E. (8), a farmer, residing at Bethel, Mich , was b 12 May, 1855, at Worcester, Otsego Co , N. Y.; m. 14 Aug., 1884, Minnie E Hillyer.

2. Clara (8), b. 11 Dec., 1857.

3. Florence (8), b. 21 April, 1858

4. Ann Eliza (8), b. 25 April, 1860

5. Kate (8), 26 July, 1862

6. Susan (8), b. 5 Dec., 1864

7. Fenton (8), b. 18 Nov., 1866.

8. Minnie (8), b 11 April, 1869.

9. Amos (8), b 9 May, 1873

EIGHTH GENERATION.

CHILDREN OF AURILLA (7) LOBDELL AND FRANCES JONES.

I. Elizabeth Jones, b. 1834, m. Jacob Pane. They reside at East Worcester, N. Y., and have one dau. (9).

II. Theodore Jones, b. 1835, d. 1840.

III. Luman Jones, b. 1840, died in infancy

IV. Amanda Jones, b. 31 Jany , 1841, m Martin Northrup. They reside at East Worcester, N Y , and have four sons, viz.:

Frank Northrup (9) and Wm Northrup (9), of East Worcester

Jacob (9), (called Jack Northrup). and Morris Northrup (9), living at Cobleskill, Schoharie Co , N. Y.

V. Louisa Jane Jones, b. 1843, d. 1851.

VI. Abigail Jones, b 28 Nov , 1852. d. 1860.

VII. Mary Jane Jones, b. 15 May, ——, m. Erskine Sullivan and resides at Binghamton. N Y.

CHILDREN AND DESCENDANTS OF JASON (7) LOBDELL AND WIFE, MARY ANN WATERMAN.

---

1. Abraham 2. John. 3. Smith. 4 Sarah. 5. Elizabeth. 6. Richard 7 Electa 8 Bertha 9 Geo D. 10. Isaiah S. 11 Jennie 12. Samuel. 13. Anna 14 Elijah

1 Abraham, a farmer, b. 23 June. 1837, m Abigail Huggins Reside at Sandford, N Y No children.

II. John, a twin to Abraham, m. Annie Merrill; have two sons (9), both m. All are farmers

III. Smith, a farmer, b 12 Dec. 1838; m 1st, Rachel Carpenter, by whom he had 5 children (9). By 2nd, Alice Simmons, had one child (9).

IV. Sarah, b 14 Sept , 1840, d. unmarried

V. Elizabeth, b 24. Oct , 1843 m. ——? McDonald.

VI. Richard, b. 13 April, 1844, d. in Civil War, at Gettysburg

VII Electa, residing at Springfield, Ills., b. 25 Nov., 1845, m. Alvah Peter Myers, had two boys and one girl

One son, Amos Melvin Myers (9), was b 13 Feby., 1876, at Quincy, Ills., was taken to Sanford, N. Y , when only four weeks old, and at the age of four years was adopted by his uncle Abraham (8). He took the name of Lobdell and there resided until he was 21 years old Was duly educated while with his uncle and became a school teacher, and later took to farming, m 13 Nov, 1898, at Sandford, Broome Co., N Y , Sarah Sabrina Tripp, b 12 Dec., 1879 at Sandford, dau of Julius Tripp and wife, Ida Augusta Gruzbeck

CHILDREN.

1. Irene Lillian Myers (10), b 1 Aug , 1899
2 Gladys Mae Myers (10), b 20 Nov , 1900

VIII Bertha, b. 15 Aug., 1847, at Sandford, N. Y , m. 1 Feby., 1876, Wm. Burton Hartley (of English descent), b 17 Sept , 1836, near Philadelphia, d 2 Jany., 1897, son of Benj. Hartley and wife, Margaret Burton. Bertha resides at Santa Rosa, Cal. Two of her heildren (9) are in Battle Creek, Mich , one (9) in Oakland, Cal , and one (9) in St. Helena

IX George D., b 10 March, 1849, m. but I cannot give name of his wife, she d in 1899, probably at Boulder, Colo , where Geo D., resides, who promised to send me a family record, but evidently has entirely forgotten it; his address is 2119 Spruce street, Boulder, Colo. Has 1 son, 2 daus. (I am sorry not to have heard further, for his letter was very interesting, but he could not remember dates and wanted time to collect, etc)

X. Isaiah S , b 2 Jany., 1851, m. Jennie Showers. Is proprietor of the "Lobdell House," at Little Cooley, Pa (No record.)

XI Jennie, b 1 Sept., 1853, m. Mr. Huyck Reside at Croton, Delaware Co., N. Y Have 2 sons, 1 dau.

XII. Samuel, b 2 July, 1855, m 1st, Millie Seely, had 3 children, 2nd., Chloe Seely. No children. (Reside at Sandford, N. Y)

XIII. Anna, b. 14 Nov., 1857, an estimable maiden lady living at the "old home," at Deposit, N. Y.

XIV Elijah, b. 7 June, 1860. Unmarried.

CHILDREN OF SMITH 7 LOBDELL AND WIFE, ELIZA DELIA BAILEY.

1. Mary Eliza. 2. Wm. Geo.

I Mary Eliza, b. 16 Sept., 1840, m Wm Hamilton Sowles, a carpenter, whose son William D. Sowles (9), b. 22 March, 1868, at Maryland, N. Y., m. Albertie (8) dau. of Lucius (7) Lobdell—a brother of Smith's.

II Wm. Geo , b 11 May, 1843, a farmer, residing at Unadilla, Otsego Co , N. Y , m 26 Dec., 1865, at Bainbridge, Chenango Co , N. Y., Mary Elizabeth, dau. of Daniel (6) Lobdell and Mary Young He enlisted in the "War of the Rebellion," Aug , 1862, was corporal of Co. F., 121st N. Y. Volunteers Served until close of the war. Children, all b at Unadilla, N. Y

1 Fannie May (9), b 18 Dec., 1868 , m. 29 Aug., 1888, to Lester O Frear, a farmer, residing at Unadilla, b. 9 March, 1866, at Franklin, Delaware Co , N. Y., son of Rufus S. Frear and Lucy Miranda Gilbert. They have one son, James Stanley Frear (10), b 18 Nov., 1889

2. Inez Eliza (9), b 19 March, 1871 , m 2 Oct , 1895, to Fred J. Fisk, a farmer residing at Unadilla, b 27 April, 1869, at Gilbertsville, Otsego Co , N Y (son of Amos Fisk and Mary Hallock). They have one dau., Edith Marion Fisk (10), b 28 March, 1899.

3. Daniel Smith (9), a mason of Unadilla, b 4 July, 1873; m. 11 Dec., 1895, to Bertha Spencer (dau. of Henry Spencer and Harriet Quimby). They have one son, Stewart Henry (10), b 8 April, 1899

4 Olive Mabel (9), b. 10 Feb., 1879; m. 11 Sept , 1900, at Oneanto, Otsego Co., N Y , to Frank Edward Randall, a machinist, b 17 Aug , 1876, at Unadilla, where he now re-

55

sides (son of Edward Payson Randall and Sally Ann Lyon).
Have—

    1. Frances Pauline Randall (10), b. 10 Aug., 1901.

CHILDREN AND DESCENDANTS OF RICHARD (7) LOBDELL AND WIFE, MARY PERMELIA FLINT.

1 Judson C. (8). 2. Geo J. (8). 3 Flint (8).

I. Judson C., residing at Fowler, Benton Co., Ind., was b. 5 July, 1846, at Worcester, Otsego Co., N. Y.; m. 16 Feb., 1868, at Coldwater, Branch Co., Mich., to (first wife) Sarah J. Cheney, b. 14 Feb., 1847, in State of Ohio, who d. 27 Dec., 1873, leaving two young children, the eldest, Lay (9), b. 2 Jan., 1870, died 7 July, 1888. The younger, Burr (9), b. 21 July, 1872; m. Minnie Dewey. I am told he is a resident of Detroit, Mich.

Mr Lobdell m. for his second wife, Mary J. Burnham, b. 29 March, 1848, a native of Ohio. Their children are:

    1. Anna (9), b. 16 Oct., 1876; d. 30 Oct., 1876.
    2. Frank (9), b. 30 June, 1878, d. 31 July. 1899.
    3. Mary Pamelia (9). b. 24 July, 1880.
    4. Olive (9), b. 1 May. 1882; d. 17 May, 1882.
    5. Eva (9), b. 21 Sept., 1885.

II. Geo. J., b. 12 June, 1849; m. Caroline Jacobs. Understand he is in furniture business at Fowler, Ind.

III. Flint, b. 26 April, 1852; m. Retta Murphy.

CHILD AND DESCENDANTS OF LUCIUS (7) LOBDELL AND FIRST WIFE, MARY ANN WAKELEE.

1. Mary E.

I. Mary E. (8), b. 23 Feb., 1847, at Oneonta; m 15 Aug., 1867, at Worcester, Otsego Co., N. Y., Briggs W. Waterman, b. 9 Sept., 1845, at Worcester, son of Ezra Waterman and wife, Rachel B. Wilber.

Mr. and Mrs. Briggs Waterman reside on a farm in Worcester. The family are Methodists. Mrs. Waterman has given much valuable assistance to this work—always willing to answer my letters of inquiry, and I think often driving miles to secure such information. We will all appreciate her kindness. Their children are:

SIDNEY LOBDELL (7)
(Daniel [6])
of Dryden, N. Y.
(Page 60)

MARY LOBDELL WATERMAN (8)
(Lucius [7])
of Oneanta, N. Y.
(Page 56)

ANNA LOBDELL (8)
(Jason [7])
of Deposit, N. Y.
(Page 55)

EZRA L. WATERMAN (9)
(Mary E.)
of Westfield, N. J.
(Page 57)

1. Ezra Lucius Waterman (9), b. 12 Oct., 1868, at Worcester, where he remained until his 20th year, when he went to New York City, where he engaged in the business of making iron fences and railings, m. 3 Feb, 1897, in New York City, Anna Walker, b. 6 Sept., 1872, at New York, dau. of Geo. Walker and his wife, Margaret McDonald. May 1, 1902, Mr. Waterman moved his family to Westfield, N. J., where they now reside, still doing business in New York. They have two daus.:
    1. Jennie Waterman (10), b 13 Oct., 1898.
    2. Ida May Waterman (10), b. 4 Dec., 1901.
  2 Albertie R. Waterman (9), b. 9 June, 1874; d. 22 July 1874.
    3. Ida May Waterman (9), b 26 April, 1886

CHILDREN AND DESCENDANTS OF LUCIUS (7) LOBDELL AND (SECOND WIFE) HANNAH M. BROWNELL.

1. Lucius Adelbert. 2. Duane. 3. Melvin 4. Birdsal. 5. Albertie. 6. Eugene.

I. Lucius Adelbert, b. 5 Feb, 1849, at Oneonta, Otsego Co., N. Y.; d. 20 Oct., 1882, m. Elizabeth Gile. b. 19 July, 1853, at Richmondville, Schoharie Co., N. Y., dau. of Stephen Gile and Sarah —— (?) Children all b. at Deposit, N. Y.
    1. Charles E. (9), b. 8 May, 1876; d. 5 Oct., 1876.
    2. Floyd A. (9), b. 17 Sept, 1877.
    3 Gile, b 23 July, 1882
Mr. Lobdell died when his children were very young. The mother re-married (name of husband not known). They all reside at McDonough, N. Y.
II. Duane, b. April, 1851; d. Sept., 1851.
III Melvin D, b. 5 Oct., 1854, at Schenevus, Otsego Co., N. Y.; m. 21 Nov., 1881, at Rensscaerville, Albany Co., N. Y., Harriet Lobdell, b. 28 Oct, 1854, at Rensselaerville, dau. of Joseph W. Lobdell and Nancy Lounsbury, his wife. Children.
    1. Mildred C., b. 20 Nov., 1882; m. LeRoy A Hale.
    2. Ivan H., b. 4 July, 1885.
    3. Edith E., b. 14 Nov., 1887.
    4. Ada E., b 30 July, 1895.

IV   Birdsal, b. 1856, d. 4 July, 1862.

V   Albertie, b 21 Nov, 1862, at Maryland, Otsego Co., N. Y., m, 5 April, 1888, for first husband, Daniel H. Nichols of Waterbury, Conn, who d. 18 March, 1890, leaving one son.

Harry H Nichols (9), b. at Waterbury, Conn, 13 May, 1889.

Mrs Nichols m. for second husband, on 30 Oct, 1892, at Unadilla, Otsego Co, N Y, William D Sowles, b 22 March, 1868, at Maryland, Otsego Co, N Y., son of W Hamilton Sowles and Mary Eliza Lobdell (dau of Smith Lobdell). Mr and Mrs W D. Sowles and son reside at 9 Valley View street, Oneonta, N Y.

VI   Eugene, b. 22 July, 1865; m Julia Sweeny

SEVENTH GENERATION.

CHILDREN AND DESCENDANTS OF PHILIP (6) LOBDELL AND WIFE, HARRIET LAMB.

1. Mary E   2. Evaline A   3. Joseph W   4. Carlton

I.   Mary E, b 30 July, 1824

II   Evaline A, b 26 Sept., 1826, at Westerlo, Albany Co, N. Y., m, 24 Jan., 1844, at Westerlo, to Joseph Addison Gardner, b. 9 May, 1821, at Westerlo, d 19 Feb., 1888, at Rensselaerville, Albany Co, N Y, son of Wm W Gardner and wife. Jane St John

CHILDREN.

1. Harriet Jerusha Gardner (8), b. 17 June, 1845, at Westerlo; m. 28 June, 1870, at Rensselaerville, Alexander Wm. Mackay, a farmer, b. 8 May, 1833, at Rensselaerville, son of Willett A Mackay and wife, Elizabeth Deane The family reside in town of Rensselaerville, P O. Medusa, Albany Co

CHILDREN.

1. Eudora J Mackay (9), b. 15 July, 1871; resides with her parents

2 Addison G. Mackay (9), b. 9 May, 1874; resides at Coxsackie, Green Co., N. Y

3 Elizabeth Mackay (9), b 15 Sept, 1877; d 4 Sept, 1897.

4 Frank B. Mackay (9), b 3 June, 1880, P O, Coxsackie, N. Y.

58

5   Evalyn G. Mackay (9), b. 29 July, 1882; m. Orson Makely of Medusa.

2. Susan Elizabeth Gardner (8), b. 24 Feb., 1848, at Westerlo; m. 7 Oct., 1874, at Rensselaerville, James Madison Finch, a farmer, b. 22 Oct., 1840, in Rennselaerville, d. in same town 14 Oct., 1888, son of Smith Finch and wife, Martha Knowles The families are Methodists

III   Joseph W., b. 29 Jan., 1829, at Westerlo, m. Nancy Lounsbury, dau. of Elisha Lounsbury and wife, Cecelia Mackey.

They settled in Rensselaerville, where he d. 14 Nov., 1901 He had poor health for the previous five years, a form of Bright's disease, and about a month before his death had a shock from which he never recovered In his younger days he was a shoemaker, but lived on and worked his farm many years Is buried at Medusa, Albany Co., N Y. I had considerable correspondence with Mr. Joseph W Lobdell and always valued his letters He was greatly interested in wishing to trace back his father's line of descent. How I wish that I had been able to have given it to him then as I now can.

CHILDREN.

1   Harriet (8), b. 28 Oct., 1854, at Rensselaerville, m. 21 Nov., 1881, Melvin D. Lobdell (8), a farmer, son of Lucius (7) and his wife, Hannah Brownell, b 5 Oct., 1855, at Schenevus, Otsego Co Their home was in Deposit, Broome Co, where their children were born, viz

1.   Mildred C (9), b 20 Nov., 1882, m LeRoy A. Hale

2   Ivan H (9), b 4 July, 1885

3   Edith E. (9), b. 14 Nov., 1887, d. 3 July, 1891

4.   Ada E (9), b 30 July, 1895.

2.   Judson Elisha, a farmer of Berne, b. 3 April, 1858, at Greenville, Greene Co, N. Y., m. 27 Nov., 1878, at Berne, Albany Co, Carrie L Smith, b. 12 July, 1860, at Berne, dau. of Harvey Smith and wife, Caroline Stewart Children:

1   Mabel E (9), b 17 June, 1883

2   Perry J (9), b 16 Feb., 1885

IV.   Carlton S, a carpenter residing at Windham, Greene Co., N. Y., b. 31 Oct., 1836, at Maryland, Otsego Co N. Y., m. 16 June, 1859, at Rensselaerville, Albany Co N Y, Almira L. Adams, b. 11

Nov., 1839, at Durham, Greene Co, N. Y., dau of Morgan Adams and wife, Lydia Earl (Methodists)

CHILDREN

1. Elmer E. (8), a farmer residing at Windham, b. 31 March, 1861, at Durham, N. Y.; m 7 Nov., 1883, at Windham, Elizabeth Case, b. 11 Dec., 1860, at Windham, dau of Henry Case and wife, Dency Andrus Has one son

    1. Harry C. (9). b 2 Feb., 1894 at Windham

2. Wilber R. (8), residing in Troy, N. Y.—occupation clerk—b 13 March, 1866, at South Westerlo, m 14 Jan 1891, at Troy, N. Y., Mary E Brockway, b 11 Feb., 1869 at Troy, dau of Wm. H Brockway and wife, Catherine Robinson, of Troy. The families are Protestant Episcopal Children

    1 Wilber C (9), b. Feb., 1892

    2 Mary Irene (9), b 19 Aug., 1894

    3. Almira (9) b 4 Jan, 1897

CHILDREN AND DESCENDANTS OF DANIEL (6) LOD-BELL AND (1) WIFE, MARY YOUNGS.

1 Melissa. 2. Alonzo 3. Sidney. 4 Gideon. 5 Mary Elizabeth

I Melissa, b. 1 Feb., 1832, at Westerlo, N Y., m Lysander Jucket.

II. Alonzo, b 1 Dec. 1834, at Westerlo; m. Jan., 1864, Augusta Comstock, dau of Cyrus Comstock of Chenango Co, N Y. The family reside at Racine Wis Is in the hardware business Has two daus., Jennie (8) and Mary Josephine (8).

III. Sidney, a farmer, b 6 May, 1836, at Westerlo; m 16 Sept., 1856, at Unadilla, Otsego Co, N Y., Mary McComber, b. 19 July, 1837, at Hoosick, Rensselaer Co, N. Y Resides at Harford, Cortland Co, N. Y

CHILDREN.

1. Jennie Elizabeth (8), b 21 Feb., 1858; m. Frank E. Ylezen.

2 Geo. Edwin (8), b. 16 June, 1862.

3 Irving Scott (8), b 28 Aug, 1876; d. 11 Oct., 1884.

IV.   Gideon, b. 19 March, 1838; m. Olive Cooley; d. at Bing-hampton, N. Y., 31 Jan., 1892.

V.   Mary Elizabeth, b 18 March, 1841, at Oneanto, N Y.; was only ten days old when her mother died and she was adopted by an aunt who cared for her until on the 26 Dec, 1865, she m. at Bain-bridge, Chenango Co., N. Y., Wm Geo. Lobdell (8), son of Smith Lobdell (7) and Eliza Bailey.

For children see Wm. Geo. (Smith).

CHILDREN OF DANIEL (6) LOBDELL BY (2) WIFE, ELIZA MARTINDALE.

Children of Daniel (6) Lobdell by (2) wife Eliza Martindale
I.   Celestia (7), b. 30 May, 1842; m. Henry Johnston
II.   Orson (7), b. 12 May, 1844.
III.   Sarah Jane (7), b. 12 Dec., 1846; d. in infancy.

CHILDREN AND DESCENDANTS OF JOSHUA (6) AND CORNELIA (FINCH) LOBDELL.

1. Zimri. 2 Rosander 3. James Elon. 4. Lucy. 5 Juliette. 6. Harriet. 7 Rovilla 8. Maria.

I.   Zimri, b. 25 Feb., 1825, d. 30 March, 1905, at Kirkwood, Broome Co., N. Y.; m. 6 July, 1853, at Kirkwood, Emeline L. Swift, b 6 May, 1833, at Lisle, Broome Co ; d. 17 April, 1892, at Kirkwood, dau. of Solomon B. and Eliza (Parks) Swift of Lisle. Zimri, with his two brothers, Rosander and James Elon, served in the War of the Rebellion, also a brother of their mother (Geo. M. Swift).

CHILDREN.

1.   Frank D. (8), b. 14 Oct., 1854, at Great Bend, Pa.; m. 28 June, 1896, at Milwaukee, Wis., Mrs. Margaret E. Dun-ning, b. 6 July, 1861, at Pittsburg, Pa., dau. of Robert L. and Jane (Buchanan) Johnson.

Mr. Lobdell resides at 288 Gregory street, Blue Island, Ill., is a passenger conductor on the C. R. I. and P. Ry. Has one step-son:

Charles F. Dunning, b 14 Dec, 1882; m. Anna M. Christensen.

2.   Anna Augusta (8), b. Jan., 1857; d. Nov., 1863.

61

3   Edwin Emerson (8), b Dec , 1860, d Oct , 1861.

4   Carrie Eliza (8), b 11 Feb , 1862.

5. Fred'k Swift (8), b. 11 May, 1866

II.   Rosander F , b 4 March, 1833, at Maryland, Otsego Co ,
N. Y.; m. 13 Dec . 1855, at Centre Lisle, Broome Co., N. Y , Nancy
A. Woodworth, b 10 Sept , 1832, at Centre Lisle, dau. of Abel
Woodworth; residence, McGrawville, Cortland Co , N Y. Rosan-
der F. Lobdell served in the "War of the Rebellion," in the 27th
Reg. N. Y Volunteers, also in the 50th N Y Engineers.

III   James Elon, b 10 Oct., 1835, at Maryland, N Y., is a mechanic, in the gun business, at Ithaca, Tompkins Co , N. Y ; m. 30
Aug., 1859, at La Porte, Sullivan Co , Pa , to Rhuma N Baldwin,
b. 30 Aug., 1842, at Montrose, Susquehanna Co., Pa , dau. of Chapman Baldwin and Lucy Nichols. She d. and left one dau , Carrie
A (8), b 22 Feb , 1862. Is unmarried.

Mr Lobdell m. 23 Aug., 1871, at Williamsport, Pa., Lucilla
Baldwin (a sister of his first wife, b 23 Aug , 1852, at La Porte,
Pa).

James Elon Lobdell enlisted in the U. S service at Wolfe Town-
ship, Pa., on 15 Aug., 1863, as a private in Co. G, 143 Regiment, Pa.
Volunteer Infantry, under Capt. Daniel J. Morton and Col. Edmund
L. Dana, to serve three years, or during the war   He was wounded
below the left knee by a minie ball at Wilderness, Va., and was in
West Building Hospital, Baltimore, Md , from which place he was
honorably discharged on surgeon's certificate of disability, on 18
May, 1865

IV.   Lucy, d. unmarried

V   Juliette, m Peter Carradine. No children

VI   Harriet, b 1828, died unmarried.   .

VII   Rovilla, b 1830; died unmarried.

VIII.   Maria, m Britton, son of Joel Lobdell and Hannah Udell,
his wife   They reside at Afton, Chenango Co , N Y

CHILDREN AND DESCENDANTS OF ROSANDER (7) AND
NANCY A. WOODWORTH LOBDELL.

I.   Willie T. (8), b 5 Dec , 1857; d 20 Aug., 1862

II.   Ralph F. (8), residing at 40 East Maine St , Ilion, N Y., is
in the gun business He was b. 20 Oct., 1860, at Center Lisle,
Broome Co , N Y ; m. 8 Dec., 1883, at Syracuse, N. Y , Czarina

Louise Ayers, b. 6 July, 1862, at Romulus, Seneca Co, N. Y, dau. of Wm. Hamilton Ayers and his wife, Czarina (Young) Barton. Mr. L is a Presbyterian in faith, a Republican in politics Has two children:

        1. Czarina Louise (9), b. 16 March, 1885
        2 Evalyn Ayers (9), b. 28 March, 1887.

III. Wallace W (8), b. 27 July, 1866; d 26 March, 1869.
IV. Mary C. (8), b 24 March, 1870
V Ernest W (8), b. 27 Nov, 1876

CHILDREN OF JAMES ELON (7) AND (2) WIFE, LUCILLA BALDWIN LOBDELL.

I. Charles E. (8), b 24 July, 1872; died —— (?).
II. Rosa May (8), b 17 May, 1874; m Charles Tyrrell.
III. Martha R. (8), b 22 Sept., 1875, at Whitney's Point, Broome Co, N Y; m. 13 March, 1895, at Troy, N. Y., Frank C. Hatch, b. 4 March, 1872, at Aurora, Cayuga Co., N. Y, son of Wm. F. Hatch and Maranda A. Reed. They reside at Sherrill, N. Y, and have three children (9)

        1. Lydia Reed Hatch (9), b 11 July, 1897
        2 Paul Elon Hatch (9), b 24 May, 1899.
        3 Benj. Thompson Hatch (9), b. 19 Dec., 1901.

IV. Myrtle L (8), b. 10 May, 1878; not living.
V. Edith C. (8), b. 20 June, 1881; not living.
VI. Herbert F. (8), b 25 April, 1886; unmarried.
VII James R. (8), b. 19 Feb, 1889; unmarried.
VIII. Ermina J. (8), b. 7 May, 1892; unmarried.
IX. Tracy B (8), b. 25 June, 1894; unmarried

SIXTH GENERATION.

CHILDREN AND DESCENDANTS OF ISAAC (5) LOBDELL, SR.

(1) Wife, Mirriam Pomeroy.
(2) Wife, Jerusha Lodbell

1. Mirıam 2 Lois. 3. Anna. 4 Isaac, Jr. 5. Joshua Pome-roy. 6. Olive. 7. Princess. 8 Jerusha. 9. Lovisa. 10 James Hervey, Sr.

By first wife, Mirriam (Pomeroy) Lobdell.

I   Mirriam, b. at Lanesboro, Mass ; m. James Jacox and resided at Westerlo. Having no children, they adopted a son and dau of Nelson Lobdell (Isaac, Jr.)

II. Lois, b. 5 Jan, 1784, at Lanesboro, d. at Chesterville, Albany Co., N Y, 25 Nov, 1828; m. at same place, 11 July, 1802, Joshua Tompkins, a farmer of Reedsville, b. 22 May, 1776, at Chesterville; d 1866 at Fulton, Schoeharie Co , N. Y. He was a Quaker, son of Elisha Tompkins

III   Anna, m Knight Bennett (no record).

IV   Isaac, Jr, a miller and farmer, b. 27 Jan., 1788, at Lanesboro; came when three years old, with his parents to Westerlo, Albany Co., N. Y., where he d. 31 Aug., 1857. He was a deacon in the Baptist church, and in politics a Whig, m for his first wife. 28 Jan, 1813, Nancy Udell, b 25 Jan, 1794, at Westerlo, where she d 14 Sept, 1837, dau of Wm and Margaret (Hogan) Udell

Isaac, Jr., m for his second wife, Lorinda (Chapin) Babcock, b 27 March, 1806, dau of Wm Chapin and widow of Josiah Hubbell Babcock of Broadalbin, N Y She d 20 Feb, 1872, at Albany, N Y. Is buried at Westerlo

V. Joshua Pomeroy. Have been unable to gain any information regarding him

VI. Olive, m. John Myers, had dau. Mirriam, b. 1825, m. Nelson Lobdell (Isaac, Jr)

VII   Princess, b 15 March, 1800, d 15 April, 1874, at Westerlo, N. Y, where she was b and m., in March, 1818, to Asa Keyes

Jackson, b 1 June, 1795, at Westerlo, where he d , son of Jeremiah Jackson and Martha Keyes, his wife.

BY SECOND WIFE, HIS COUSIN, JERUSHA LOBDELL (JOHN), CHILDREN ALL BORN IN WESTERLO.

I. Jerusha, b 5 March, 1806, d 11 Nov, 1874, at Clarksville, N Y., m at Westerlo, Frederick P Slater, b. 18 Dec. 1811, at Greenville, Greene Co, N Y.

II. Lovisa, b. 3 Nov, 1812, d. 2 April, 1861; m. first in Jan, 1835, to Francis Atkins, b. 3 March, 1812, d. 16 June, 1842, son of Elisha and Mary (Wilsey) Atkins Lovisa was b, d and m. at Westerlo

She m. second, on 4 Oct, 1843, Silas B Martin, b. 22 Nov., 1815, at W . d. 5 Jan, 1895, at Troy, N. Y, son of Joseph.

III. James Hervey, Sr., b 14 July, 1810, at Westerlo; d of Bright's disease, 19 Feb, 1868, at Fairport, Monroe Co, N. Y.; m 31 March, 1835, to Harriet Crawford, b 8 July, 1814, in Rensselaerville, N. Y., dau of John Crawford and first wife, Susanna Wilkins. Harriet d. 26 Jan, 1902, at the residence of her son-in-law, Olof Oberg, Rochester, N Y Mr. L., when first m., was a miller and farmer at Westerlo, then moved to Gallupville, Schocharie Co, N. Y., where he kept a general store In 1854 moved to Rochester, N Y., afterward locating on a farm in Fairport, N Y., where he d.

SEVENTH GENERATION.

CHILDREN AND DESCENDANTS OF LOIS (6) LOBDELL AND JOSHUA TOMPKINS, ALL BORN AT REEDSVILLE, ALBANY CO., N. Y.

I. Miriam Tompkins, b 12 July, 1803, m. Daniel Udell.

II. Wm C Tompkins, b. 12 July, 1804.

III. Isaac Lobdell Tompkins, b. 22 Sept, 1806.

IV. Joshua Tompkins, b. 13 May, 1808.

V. Anna Tompkins, b. 19 Jan., 1810; m Sidney Smith

VI Miranda Tompkins, b. 22 Aug, 1812; m Rev. Wm H Tifferny.

VII. Princess Tompkins, b. 11 Jan, 1814, m. Israel Baker, a farmer, 19 Jan, 1834, at Chesterville, N. Y, b 20 July, 1810, at

Chesterville; d 20 Aug., 1882, at Schoharie, Schoharie Co., N Y., son of Aaron and Cynthia Baker, who with their family were Quakers Princess was taken ill on Monday, 18 March, 1902, and passed away on the following Friday evening, March 21, in her 90th year The body was placed in the receiving vault at Gloversville and taken on 10 May to Esperance, Schoharie Co, and interred in the family plat.

    VIII James Jaycox Tompkins, b 13 Aug , 1816

    IX. Penolope Tompkins, b. 11 July, 1818, m Cyrus Wright

    X Elijah Tompkins, b. 23 Aug., 1820

    XI Barbary Tompkins, b. 9 Dec., 1822, m Seneca Wing

CHILDREN OF ISAAC (6) LOBDELL, JR, AND FIRST WIFE, NANCY UDELL, ALL BORN AT WESTERLO, N Y

---

    1 Luman 2. Justus. 3 Jane 4. Nelson 5 Hervey 6 Loretta 7 Margaret 8 Joshua Tompkins 9 Harriet 10 Mirriam

---

    I. Luman, a miller and farmer, b 14 June, 1814; d —— (?) at Berne, N. Y., m. 14 March, 1838, at Westerlo, Sally S Winston, b 13 May, 1817, at Westerlo, d. 29 Aug , 1869, at Berne, dau. of David and Eliza (Martin) Winston. Luman was a Baptist and a Republican.

    II Justus, a farmer of Westerlo, b 22 June, 1816, was struck by lightning and killed, 17 May, 1875, at Coxsackie, Greene Co , N Y ; m. first, 19 Oct., 1842, Mary Blackmer, b 10 Sept., 1820, m second, on 21 Nov, 1854, Ann E Stewart, b. 1 Jan., 1834, dau. of Wm. and Sally A. (Norris) Stewart

    III Jane d young.

    IV. Nelson, a miller at Westerlo. N Y , b June, 1820, d. March, 1864; m for his first wife, Mirriam Myers, b. 1825, at Westerlo, where she d 10 April, 1848, at the birth of her twin boys, Charles and James C. Mirriam was dau of John Myers and Olive Lobdell (Isaac, Sr , and Mirriam Pomeroy), and with her brother (not knowing his name) were adopted, in youth, by James Jacox and his wife, Mirriam Lobdell (Isaac, Sr., and Mirriam Pomeroy). At the death of these foster parents, their property reverted to these children

    Nelson m second. Lois O Bennett; third, Helen Anderson.

JAMES HERVEY LOBDELL, SR. (6)
(Isaac [5])   (1816-1868)
of Westerlo, Gallupville, Rochester,
and Fairport, N. Y.
(Page 65)

LUMAN LOBDELL (7)
(Isaac [6] Jr.)   (1839-1894)
of Berne, N. Y.
(Page 64)

ISAAC D. M. LOBDELL (7)
(Isaac [6] Jr.)   (1839-1894)
of Albany and Chicago.
(Page 67)

HARRY CHAPIN LOBDELL (8)
(Isaac D. M. [7])
of Albany, Chicago, and St. Xavier,
Montana.
(Page 76)

V and VI   Hervey and Loretta d young

VII.   Margaret, b. 16 Aug., 1826, m. at Westerlo, 18 Nov., 1851, Lay Ruland, b. 10 Oct., 1824, at Westerlo, where he d. 23 Oct., 1893. Lay was son of Alban Ruland and Mirriam Lobdell (Simon 5).

Miss Emily (8) Ruland, dau. of Margaret, writes me: "My grandmother Ruland's father was Simon Lobdell, a brother of Isaac (5) Lobdell, Sr., and both sons of Joshua Lobdell and Sarah Scott, so you see that my father and mother were cousins—not first cousins, but they were double cousins—as the two brothers m two sisters. Simon m. Grace Pomeroy, and Isaac m. Mirriam Pomeroy. These names have been handed down to the present generation."

On the 5th day of Feb., 1891, Margaret Lobdell Ruland was thrown from a cutter and fractured her hip, never again being able to walk without crutches, and most of the time suffering pain as the result of her fall.

On 26 Feb., 1902, at her home in Lansingburg, N. Y., she passed to the land where suffering is unknown.   Is buried at Westerlo by the side of her husband.

VIII.   Joshua Tompkins d. unmarried

IX.   Harriet m. for her first husband, Mr Jamison; m. second, Silas C. Mix   After a long illness she passed away in the spring of 1906, at her home (for over forty years) at 5 West Sunnyside, Troy, N. Y.   She had no children.   She was a member of Grace Methodist Church.   Is buried at Westerlo, N. Y.

X.   Mirriam m. John Lobdell (Simon) of Sullivan Co   They adopted Sidney, a son of Mirriam's brother Nelson.   No children.

CHILDREN OF ISAAC (6) LOBDELL, JR., AND SECOND WIFE, LORINDA CHAPIN BABCOCK.

1. Isaac D. M.   2   Mary Jane.   3. Emily M.   4. Francis W. 5   Victor B.   All born at Westerlo

I   Isaac D. M., b. 7 June, 1839, was a man of noble qualities, a man whom to know was to respect.   No better tribute to his unfailing integrity, honesty and business relations can be given than by copying from "The Haberdashers' Journal."   His residence was at Buena Park, one of the loveliest northwestern suburbs of Chicago He built his home, fashioned after his own ideas, and there hoped to spend years of happiness surrounded by his family; but Bright's disease, whose very name means death, had marked him for its victim and after an illness of five years he passed away at his home on 20 June, 1894. He m. 30 Aug., 1861, at N. Y. City, Catherine Jane McDonald, who proved herself a worthy helpmeet for the deceased. She was b. in Valatia, Columbia Co., N. Y., 18 June, 1839, and has brought up the young children left by her husband in a way that reflects honor to herself.

THE DEATH OF I. D. M. LOBDELL.

"In the death of I. D. M Lobdell, which occurred June 20 last there is a loss not easily appreciated except by those to whom his life and work are fully known Each of us in time must pass onward to complete the evolution of God's eternal purposes, and for all of us there is a peculiarly impressive lesson in the life and character of Mr. Lobdell, which leads us to make mention here of some of the more important features of his life work, in order that his hosts of friends may recall with profit the strength of that moral purpose which, undergirding his every motive, made Mr Lobdell's a stalwart figure in the moving affairs in which he participated.

Many of the haberdashers of our country are old army men, and not a few of them can recall the active work of army life in which they and he of whom we write joined hearts and hands to battle for that which must ever be the best heritage of men, Law, Liberty and Unity. Mr. Lobdell was best known in the business world in the West, and it is no exaggeration to say of him that the West collectively, as represented in the furnishing business, knew and honored him without exception.

Mr. Lobdell began to travel for Geo. B. Cluett, Bro. & Co., on February 1, 1881, and almost immediately won for himself a position of large importance in the affairs of his firm, and his value was fully recognized when his firm and the firm of Coon & Co. consolidated in November, 1889, the title then changing to the present one of Cluett, Coon & Co. Some five years since, failing health compelled Mr. Lobdell to assume a less active part in the business, but his was not a nature that could brook idleness. His physicians ordered a period of complete cessation from business cares, in the hope that thereby might come fresh vigor with which to combat the steady march of that insidious disease which finally triumphed in his decease During this period of enforced repose of body, his mind continued to employ itself in writing, and his ready pen made many an editorial for some of the leading Western papers, which successfully moulded the political opinions of many Mr Lobdell

JAMES HERVEY LOBDELL (7), JR
(J. H. L. [6] Sr.)
of Chicago
(Page 72)

was a felicitous writer on topics coming within the range of his interest and experience; as an instance we recall his lines written of a brother soldier who had died, and of whom he wrote: "His moral manliness, his modesty, his very meekness symbolized the truth that it is the shock of wheat that is heaviest which bows lowest. I never can forget how I marveled during war times at his unswerving stability of character, and the courage with which he faced every foe of either his country or his character, and how well fortified he was at every point, at that early day of his manly development, against every temptation of army life." No man could write thus without himself possessing some share of the qualities he was extolling, and those who knew Mr. Lobdell can recognize something of his own moral strength and purpose in his words.

It was about a year after the new firm of Cluett, Coon & Co. was formed, when Mr. Lobdell was obliged to stop active work; the prescribed period of rest was readily granted him by his employers whose generous kindness did not stop with mere words of hopeful encouragement, but took on that wider meaning of Christian sympathy which is practical in its expression. Mr. Lobdell's nature was strong and sympathetic, and to him his employers' action ever remained a tender evidence of their thoughtfulness for him and his, which he never alluded to without the deepest emotion and gratitude Returning from his enforced idleness, which was spent in the mountains of Montana, he again occupied his beautiful home in Buena Park, near Chicago.

When the exposition opened Mr. Lobdell felt himself sufficiently strong to manage the important duties to be imposed on someone of known ability, in the exhibit made by Cluett, Coon & Co., and his wishes were readily complied with by his firm. That he was eminently fitted for the work, those who had the pleasure of a call on him during the fair have reason to well remember, and it is a matter of no small moment to know that, though often taxed in his physical powers, Mr. Lobdell's perseverance and purpose to represent his employers' interests to the end of the exposition was in a spirit of grateful remembrance on his part, and a recognition on theirs of his sterling and heroic character to do and not die, while he had a fighting chance.

But the character of his illness was such that human skill knew and recognized its limitations, and Mr. Lobdell himself was well aware that the end would not long be delayed. It came, and found

69

him cheerful and ready, with but one regret, and that his wife and children—to leave them was to his kindly nature the one awful strain, but even in this, when the time of dissolution finally came, and his loved ones gathered at his bedside, each for a last farewell, his love seemed rested in that Higher Power which protects its own, and which in believing gave him hope for their well-being here, and reunion beyond. Mr. Lobdell died in the fifty-fifth year of his age, and in his death has given to his friends a lasting memory of all that is truest and best in manhood.

II. Mary Jane, b —— (?), d. 14 Aug., 1868.

III. Emily M., b —— (?), d. 12 Oct., 1847.

IV. Francis W., b 11 June, 1847, was like his brother a traveling salesman, he being employed by the shirt and collar firm of Miller, Hall and Hartwell of Troy, N. Y.; d unmarried. Amassed a competency and was generosity itself to those whom he wished to benefit, especially desiring his young female relatives to have the benefit of a good education. At the Lake Shore Railroad disaster at Ashtabula, O., 29 Dec., 1878, he was among the injured and suffered from the results for many years. He d. of Bright's disease at Brunswick, N. J., on 11 March, 1897.

V. Victor B., b. 7 April, 1849; d. 5 Feb., 1872

CHILDREN OF PRINCESS LOBDELL AND ASA KEYES JACKSON, ALL BORN IN WESTERLO, JACKSON BY NAME.

1. James Joseph. 2 Calvin Luther 3 Cortlandt Columbus 4 Andrew. 5. Princess Palmyra 6. Josephine. 7. Elizabeth 8. Helen Maria. 9 Mirriam Ann.

I. James Joseph Jackson, b. 6 Sept., 1819; m. Mary Elizabeth Stebbins

II. Calvin Luther Jackson, b 21 June, 1824, d young

III Cortlandt Columbus Jackson, a farmer, also a teacher in S S mission work, b. 28 July, 1825, at Marquis, Ga., m. 12 Feb., 1861, at Pleasant Grove Presbyterian church, two miles from Bluff City, Sullivan Co., Tenn., to Sallie Preston Rhea, b. 12 Feb., 1840, near Bluff City, dau. of Robert Preston Rhea and Nancy Davidson, his wife.

IV Andrew Jackson, b 20 July. 1827, d young.

70

Yours sincerely,
Julia Harrison Lobdell.
(Mrs. James H. Lobdell.)

(Page 72)

V   Princess Palmyra Jackson, b 10 March, 1829; m Baltıs Sigsbee.

VI. Josephıne Jackson, b. 27 April, 1830

VII. Elizabeth Jackson, b. 27 March, 1832, lıvıng (1902) ın Westerlo, N Y , m Aug., 1876, at Brooklyn, N. Y., Arthur Noble Sherman, b. 22 Oct. 1815, at Albany, N. Y., d. 1882 at Brooklyn, N. Y , son of Dr Abel Sherman and Martha or Cynthia Hammond of Albany. No children

VIII. Helen Maria Jackson, b. 28 Sept., 1834, is (1902) a resident of Brooklyn; unmarried

IX. Mırriam Ann Jackson, b 20 Feb., 1837, m. Geo Carl Guyer.

CHILD AND DESCENDANT OF JERUSHA(6) LOBDELL AND FREDERICK P. SLATER.

I. Edgar Slater, b. 30 June. 1851, at Westerlo, N. Y.; m. 5 Sept , 1872, at Clarksvılle, Albany Co., N. Y., Emily Le Boeuf, b 20 Jan , 1850, at Clarksville

They reside at Ravena, N. Y., have one dau., Elmyra (8) Slater, b 24 Sept., 1875; m. 25 Oct , 1899, at Clarksville, Elmer L. Bishop, b 21 Aug., 1874, at Olive, Ulster Co., N Y

CHILDREN AND DESCENDANTS OF LOVISA (6) LOB-DELL AND FRANCIS ATKINS

I   Edmund S. Atkins of Troy, N Y , b. 3 June, 1837, at Chesterville, N Y ; m (1) 1858, Emily Powell, b 20 July, 1839, at Cairo, Greene Co., N. Y, d. 1 March, 1876, at Troy. N. Y., dau. Edward and Martha Searl Powell.

CHILDREN.

1. Emma F. (8) Atkins, b. 12 Aug., 1858, d. 6 June, 1884; m. Romain Vıncent.

2   Edward F (8) Atkins, b 10 Sept., 1859; m. Sarah Cunningham.

3. Frank A. (8) Atkins, b 18 Feb , 1864; m. (1) Mary Rough, (2) Lillian Grady.

4. Fred'k (8) Atkins, b 18 Aug , 1872; m Eva Green; d. 11 July, 1898.

5. Theodore Atkins, b 18 Jan., 1875; d. 23 Jan., 1875

71

Edmund S. (7) Atkins m. for his second wife, Ida F. Pratt, dau. of Walter and Sarah Faxon Pratt of Troy. Have—

Elroy P. Atkins, b. 12 April, 1883.

II. Cordelia M (7) Atkins, b. 16 Nov., 1840, at Westerlo, where she m 4 July, 1867, Stephen Vincent, b. 19 Nov., 1843, at Coeymans, Albany Co., N. Y., son of David & Maria Marritt Vincent Cordelia d. in Troy. 1903-4 Had—

1. Hamilton Ford (8) Vincent, b. 1870, d. 1877.

2. Mary L. (8) Vincent, b. 5 June, 1874; m 1894, Fred W Curtis, a druggist of Troy, N Y

Lovisa m. for her second husband, 4 Oct., 1843, Silas B. Martin, b. 22 Nov., 1815, d at Troy, 5 Jan., 1895, son of Joseph. Had—

1. James H (7) Martin, b. 1 Feb., 1846; d 2 Dec., 1847

2. Harriet J (7) Martin, b. 23 Oct. 1848; d. 1849.

3. Joseph Henry (7) Martin, b. 5 Oct, 1852; m. Hattie McMillan.

4. Lydia (7) Martin, b. 1854, d 1857.

5 Charles F (7) Martin, b 25 Aug., 1857; m. Alida Smodell.

The children of Lovisa were all b at Westerlo

CHILDREN OF JAMES HERVEY (6) LOBDELL, SR., AND WIFE, HARRIET CRAWFORD.

I Sarah Jane, b. 28 March, 1836, d. 1838.

II. Lois, b. 28 Dec., 1837, unmarried, resides with her sister, Mrs Olaf Oberg at Rochester, N. Y.

III. James Hervey, Jr., b 22 Aug., 1840, at Westerlo, N. Y.; received a public school education, entered a wholesale shoe house in Rochester, N. Y. In this business he made himself proficient; came to Chicago in 1880 and followed the same line; later, joining with the Harry H Lobdell Wholesale Shoe Co. He m. at Rochester, N. Y., 28 Sept., 1865, Julia Ardelia Harrison, b at Rochester, 11 June, 1839, dau. of Henry and Mary (Wilson) Harrison, residents of 30 Jay street, Rochester, N. Y., for over 60 years.

They have one son—

Henry Harrison Lobdell (8), b 10 Aug., 1866, at Rochester; m. 24 Sept., 1890, at Chicago, Nellie Frost Lamson, b. 24 Sept, 1869, at State Center, Iowa, dau. of S Warren Lamson and wife, Martha Houston.

HENRY HARRISON LOBDELL (8)
(James Hervey [7] Jr.)
of Chicago
(Page 72)

of Chicago
(Page 73)

WARREN LAMSON LOBDELL

He received his education in Rochester and Chicago schools, followed the business of his father, and in 1891 opened at Chicago the wholesale shoe house of Harry H. Lobdell Co. He is a member of the Chicago Athletic Association, the Midlothian, South Shore and Exmoor Country Clubs of Chicago, and of the Athletic Association of Boston Mass. The family are Unitarians: Harry, like his father, a Republican

CHILDREN.

1. Warren Lamson (9), b 28 July, 1891, a student in Armour Institute, Chicago.

2 Ruth (9), b 3 June, 1895.

3 Harrison (9), b 22 March, 1897.

IV. Harriet. b 3 Jan., 1843, at Gallopville, Schoharie Co, N. Y ; m. at Rochester N Y, on 23 July, 1868, to Olaf Oberg, b. 29 Aug, 1836, at Hessleholm, Christiansted Co. Sweden, son of Aake Larson and Elna Olson

Mr Oberg has a beautiful residence, 543 Mt Hope Ave, Rochester, N Y, where, having retired from business, he can thoroughly enjoy his home and its environments Mrs Oberg has for the past two years been an invalid, confined to her room. They have three living children, b in Rochester

Charles Olof Oberg, the 2d child, b 6 Oct., 1870, resides at 210 Linden St, Rochester, is a custom cutter, m 22 Aug, 1896, in New York City, May Agnes Maxwell. b 12 June, 1873, at Montreal, Canada, dau. of Louis and Marie (Savard) Maxwell. No children

Albert Theadore Oberg, 4th child, b 18 Nov., 1879, for the past four years has resided in Paris, France—preparing himself for a musical career.

Mabel Lobdell Oberg, the youngest child, b 4 Jan, 1881; m. 2 July, 1906, Clarence Dale Silvernail, a graduate of the class of 1902 of the University of Rochester, and is engaged in business in New York Is son of Professor and Mrs J P Silvernail of Rochester.

Edward Sidney and Alexander Oberg, 1st and 3d children, d while young.

V. Edward Sidney, b 8 Sept, 1846, at Gallopville, N. Y., d. in Chicago of pheunomia 13 Dec., 1905, m. 28 June, 1876, at Rochester, Sarah G Spencer, b 27 Feb., 1853, at E Henrietta, Monroe Co, N. Y.,

73

dau. of Joseph Yetter and Henrietta Boucher. Had one child, Edward Albert, b. 7 Oct., 1891, d. 7 Nov., 1891.

EIGHTH GENERATION.

CHILDREN OF PRINCESS (7) TOMPKINS AND ISRAEL BAKER.

I. Dunois Baker, b. 2 Nov., 1836; m. Mary Conover.

II. Gertrude Baker, residing at Gloversville, N. Y., b. 18 May, 1839, at Dunham, Greene Co., N. Y.; m. 24 Dec., 1856, at Esperance. N. Y., Benjamin E. Bassler, b 5 Dec, 1836, at Schoharie, d. 25 March, 1900, at Gloversville, Fulton Co., N Y, son of Josiah and Jane (Van Wee) Bassler.

CHILDREN.

1. Ella P (9) Bassler, b 9 Sept, 1858; d 24 Aug., 1860

2. Nellie M. (9) Bassler, b. 5 Jan, 1861; m. H. L. Smith

3. Jennie A. (9) Bassler, b. 13 Nov., 1863; d. 28 April, 1870.

4. Menzo I. (9) Bassler, b. 17 Nov., 1865; m. Elizabeth Corneveaux.

5. Eva G. (9) Bassler, b. 24 Dec., 1867, m. Wm. A. Starr.

6. Minnie Princess (9) Bassler, b 2 Jan., 1869; m. Wm Sternberg.

7. Benjamin F. (9) Bassler, b 7 Jan, 1871.

8 Wm. D. (9) Bassler, b. 13 Aug., 1873

9. Cyrus W. (9) Bassler, b. 25 June, 1875; m. Carrie Langford.

10 Peter J (9) Bassler, b. 18 July, 1877; d. 22 Feb., 1893

11. Lottie L. (9) Bassler, b 3 March, 1882; m. Edison Platts.

III. Princess Ann (8) Baker, b. 9 April, 1847, m. John Hunter

CHILDREN AND DESCENDANTS OF LUMAN (7) AND SALLY S. WINSTON LOBDELL.

1. Adonirum. 2. Orville 3. Sidney.

I. Adonirum J., a farmer of East Berne, b. at Westerlo, 11 Dec. 1838; m. 13 Dec., 1863, at Berne, Albany Co., N. Y., Eleanor M.

ADONIRAM LOBDELL (8)
(Luman [7])
of East Berne, N. Y.
(Page 74)

REV. ISAAC V. LOBDELL (9)
(Adoniram [8])
(Page 78)

ORVILLE LOBDELL (8)
(Luman [7])
of Westerlo, N. Y.
(Page 75)

FRANK LOBDELL (9)
(Orville [8])
of Westerlo, N. Y.
(Page 78)

Vedder, b 12 Sept., 1842, at Troy, N. Y., dau. of Henry A. and Eliza (Clute) Vedder Adonirum is a Baptist, a Republican

II Orville, a practical miller at Westerlo, b. 23 Aug. 1840 His great grandfather built the first grist mills in that part of the country more than 100 years ago. It was rebuilt in 1835 by his grandfather (Isaac Lobdell) and brother, James H Lobdell The old mill still looms up proudly under the guidance of Orville, as a monument to the honesty and integrity of the Lobdell family down to its present owner Orville m 22 July, 1865, Harriet Osterhout, b 11 June, 1840, at East Berne, dau of Nicholas and Catherine (Jones) Osterhout.

III. Sidney J., b 16 Sept., 1869, d 1 April, 1871

CHILDREN OF JUSTUS LOBDELL AND FIRST WIFE, MARY BLACKMAR.

---

1. Maryetta 2 Augusta.

I. Maryetta, b. 27 Nov., 1843; m John J. Walron.
II. Augusta, b. 17 May, 1846; m. Melvin B. Calkins

By second wife, Ann E. Stewart.

1. Charlotta 2. Wm J 3 Ella 4. Georgiana. 5 Susie.

I Charlotta, b 24 March, 1856; m Geo. E. Jones
II. Wm. J., a carpenter of Troy, N. Y, b. 30 April, 1859; m. Nettie E Bull at Albany, N Y., 2 Aug. 1884, b. 18 June, 1862, at Troy, N. Y, dau of Wm H and Harriet (Nichols) Bull
III. Ella, b. 7 Sept., 1863.
IV. Georgiana, b 24 Feb., 1867, m Geo E. Lester.
V Susie, b. 28 Dec, 1872

CHILDREN AND DESCENDANTS OF NELSON (7) LOBDELL.

Wives (1) Mirriam Myers. (2) Lois O. Bennett (3) Helen Anderson.

By (1) wife

I James, no record

75

II.   Charles (8) (twin of James), a farmer residing at Westerlo, b. 10 April, 1848; m. Samantha Pitcher, 1 April, 1871, at East Berne, b. 9 Dec., 1848, at Berne.   They have two children.

      1   James W (9), b. 1 Jan., 1872, m. Belle Webster.
      2   Nellie G. (9), b. 7 Jan., 1877.

               By (2) wife

I   Montville, b. 29 Nov., 1852, m. Elizabeth Seabolt
II. Emalissa, b. 23 Nov., 1853.

               By (3) wife

I. Ann Augusta, b. 17 March, 1855
II Sidney, b. 10 Dec., 1856, was adopted by John and Mirriam Lobdell of Sullivan Co., N. Y.   He m. Belle Lewis.
III George, b. ——; m. Ella Hart.

CHILDREN AND DESCENDANTS OF MARGARET (7) LOBDELL AND LAY RULAND.

---

1. Grace L.   2   Victor Lay   3   Emily M   4   Margaret M

I Grace L. Ruland, b 10 Nov., 1854, m. Lorenzo D. Stewart, d. 1882, leaving a baby girl, who d. six weeks later.
II Victor Lay Ruland, b. 9 July, 1858, m. Althea Sanford and d when he was 32 years old, leaving four children, viz:

      1. Anna B. (9) Ruland.   2   Frank Lobdell (9) Ruland.
      3. Sanford (9) Ruland.   4   Victor Raymond (9) Ruland.

III. Emily M. Ruland, b. 2 June, 1861, and
IV. Margaret M. Ruland, b 17 Dec., 1868, reside at the homestead in Lansingburg. N. Y.

CHILDREN AND DESCENDANTS OF ISAAC D. M. (7) AND CATHERINE JANE (McDONALD) LOBDELL.

---

1   Harry Chapin   2   Byron Wellington   3   Inez Rogers.
4   Hamilton Ford (8)

I Harry Chapin, b 14 Dec., 1868, at Albany, N. Y., was educated in and graduated from Chicago schools.   His father, before his death, wishing to know that Harry was settled in business, selected Montana and established him with a hardware firm in Billings   They pushed their business further west, and himself

DR. ALBAN JUDSON LOBDELL (9)   (Adoniram [8])
of Winchester. N. H.
(Page 77)

CHILDREN OF DR. ALBAN JUDSON LOBDELL
(Page 77)

ALBAN JUDSON LOBDELL, JR. (10)   WINSTON BALL LOBDELL (10)

and partner control the only general store on the Indian Reservation (Crow), which has (1906) opened thousands of extra acres to the public Harry resides at St Xavier, where on 28 Feb., 1906, he married Ellen Reed, a teacher in the Mission school at that place

II Byron Wellington, b. at Albany 25 Nov., 1870, d 16 Aug, 1880, at Chicago.

III. Inez Rogers, b 25 Oct., 1878, at Chicago, m 22 June, 1904, Mr Frank Burns, a member of the John E Burns Lumber Co., Chicago They reside in Buena Park, have one little dau, Katherine Jane Burns (9), b 21 Sept, 1905

IV Hamilton Ford, b 18 June, 1882, at Chicago, resides at St. Xavier, Montana, where he is in the employ of his brother.

CHILDREN OF CORTLANDT C. (7) JACKSON AND SALLIE PRESTON RHEA, HIS WIFE.

1 Princess Palmyra Jackson, b 19 Dec, 1861; d 25 March, 1884

2 Rhea Jackson, b 28 March, 1864; m. Clarence Moormand Mrs Moormand is (1902) postmistress at Marquis, Ga.

3. Robert Matthew Jackson, b 24 Jan., 1867; m Mary Maude Little.

4. Nannie Virginia Jackson, b 18 Dec, 1869; m. Josiah Edward Rhea Resides Bluff City—Route 3—Sullivan Co, Tenn.

5 Cortlandt V S. Jackson, b 24 Jan, 1870

6. Augusta Lee Jackson, b 2 July, 1872; m John Jacob Stutz

7 Mary Marquis Jackson, b 19 Sept, 1876: a teacher for 6 years in suburb of Chattanooga, Tenn

8 Reverdy Preston Jackson, b 8 March, 1880; wholesale grocer, Chattanooga, Tenn

9. Paul Jackson, b 15 April, 1884

NINTH GENERATION.

CHILDREN OF ADONIRAM (8) AND ELEANOR M. VEDDER LOBDELL.

1. Alban Judson. 2. Isaac V.

I. Dr Alban Judson was born 2 April, 1868, in East Berne, N. Y. He attended the common schools of that place. At the age of 18 he began teaching, and at the same time preparing himself for the study of medicine. In 1893 he graduated from the New York Homeopathic Medical College and Hospital, receiving at the same time the diploma of its Hahnemanian Society. In 1903 he received the diploma of the New York School of Physical Therapeutics. He is a member of the Homeopathic Medical Society of Western Massachusetts, the Homeopathic State Medical Society of New Hampshire and the American Institute of Homeopathy. He has practiced since graduation in Winchester, N. H., and for several years has been a member of the Board of Health, at present is its president. He was married to Mary Grace Ball of Winchester, N. H., 25 Nov., 1896, b. 23 Nov., 1866 (dau of William Wallace Ball and Lutheda G. Willard), and two children, Alban Judson Lobdell, Jr, and Winston Ball Lobdell, have been born to them

II. Isaac V., b. 8 Oct.. 1880, at East Berne. He attended the common schools of that place At the age of 18 he entered the high school of Winchester, N H., graduating from that institution in 1901, having done its three years' work in two, and with the first honors of his class He returned to his home in East Berne and began teaching. In 1904 he entered the theological department of St Lawrence University and will graduate from that school in June, 1907, having done its four years' work in three. He then will take up his chosen work in the ministry of Jesus Christ and in the denomination of the Universalist church

CHILDREN OF ORVILLE (8) AND HARRIET OSTERHOUT LOBDELL.

1. Fred J. 2. Frank

I. Fred J, b. 10 May, 1866, d 15 Aug, 1868

II Frank W, b 6 June, 1867; m Minnie C Miller, 21 Sept. 1890, b 15 May, 1870, at Gallupville, N Y., dau. of Peter A. and Ruth (Gaige) Miller Mr. L. follows the business of his father—a miller, is a Republican and Protestant Their children are:

    1. Eleanor Miller (10), b. 17 July, 1891.
    2 Harold C (10), b. 4 June, 1893
    3. Victor (10), b 6 Sept., 1894.
    4. Paul (10), b 4 Jan, 1896.
    5. H Van Allen (10), b 24 Oct, 1897

SIXTH GENERATION.

CHILDREN AND DESCENDANTS OF JAMES (5) AND MARY (VENABLE) LOBDELL.

1. Elizabeth 2 Gilbert 3 John. 4 Sarah. 5 Mary. 6. James.

I. Elizabeth, bapt. by Rev Bostwick at Lanesboro, Mass, in 1779, married (probably) Mr. Stotts of Texas

II. Gilbert. No record.

III John, b 16 May, 1782; m. Mary Conger on 15 Sept., 1808, b 3 March, 1792, d. 6 Jan, 1835, near Vicksburg, Miss.

Mr. Lobdell was a planter residing near Vicksburg, where he d 10 Sept, 1827 In religion, a Baptist; in politics, a Whig.

As widow Lobdell, Mary m. for her (2) husband, 28 Aug., 1828, Wm Estes, by whom she had two children, viz., Sarah Chesning Lucinda Estes, b. 12 Dec, 1829, and Oscar Wm Estes, b. 21 Aug, 1831.

IV. Sarah m. Seth Rundle (her cousin). I am told that her descendants are to be found in Warren Co, Miss

V Mary m (1) John Walker, (2) John Gorman

VI. James I have been unable to secure the maiden name of his wife, or record of the birth or death of either, but am positive that they both d. young in life, leaving a family of little children. Resided near or at Vicksburg

CHILDREN.

1 Eliza m John A. Vanzile of Vicksburg, who d. in Jan., 1905. Eliza d. about one year after her marriage, at the birth of her infant, who also died. Husband. wife and child are buried in the Vanzile vault; also her brother John, who d. 11 Oct, 1850.

2 Mary m. Mr Harper of New Orleans and d. in about a year

3. James K. d. in Franklin Co, Mo, about 1889.

4 Sarah was adopted by Mrs Springer (a sister of Mr. Vanzile's). She d. in her 19th year

5 John d. 11 Oct., 1850

79

6. Elizabeth, b. 15 May, 1820, was adopted by Mrs Gordon (a sister of Mrs Springer, who adopted Sarah Lobdell). She m 27 Dec. 1842, Thomas Baldwin, a native of Missouri Elizabeth d 4 July, 1859 Left one dau., Mrs S. W. Jeannin (7) of Arcadia, Florida (who has a dau., Mrs H B. Jenkins (8), residing at Texarkana, Ark.). One of Elizabeth's sons, Judge Thomas E. (7) Baldwin of Kennett, Mo., b. 23 Oct, 1849, at Cape Girardeau, Mo, d. 27 May, 1904, at Kennett, Mo., m 18 Aug, 1872, at Clarkton, Mo, May Jones Pankey, b 27 April, 1856, at Lynchburg, Virginia, dau. of David Young Pankey and wife, Sallie B. Jones Children

CHILDREN—EIGHTH GENERATION.

1. Sallie M Baldwin, b. 25 May, 1873, m. Luther Tatum.

2. Edward Young Baldwin, b. 11 March, 1875

3 Ernest Albert Baldwin, b 19 Feb, 1878, m Carra Maye

4. Paul Baldwin, b 23 Feb, 1888

5. Lillian Ballard-Baldwin, b. 18 Nov. 1890

6 Josephine Baldwin, b 19 Nov, 1896

SEVENTH GENERATION.

CHILDREN OF JOHN (6) AND MARY (CONGER) LOBDELL.

1 Thomas Llewellyn. 2 Jonathan Conger 3 Joshua 4 Isaac Elum 5 Martha Margaret 6 Eliza Mary 7 John Venable

I Thomas Llewellyn, b 3 Dec 1810, probably in Warren Co, Miss; m Eliza Ann Grafton Left one son—Livingston Llewellyn (8) Lobdell, who m Tennessee Estelle Watson of Boliver Co, Miss., and moved to Houston, Texas They had one son, Robert Livingston (9) Lobdell.

After the death of Livingston Llewellyn Lobdell, his widow m. 22 Oct, 1895, Albert Gallatin Lobdell (James Alexander), who d. at Covington, La, 29 June, 1902, at which place the widow now resides with her son, Robert Livingston Lobdell

JOHN VENABLE LOBDELL (7), SR.
(John [6])   (1824-1859)
Near Prentiss, Miss.
(Page 81)

II. Jonathan Conger, b. 16 April, 1813, in or near Vicksburg, Miss.; m. Emily Jane Stowers Their children were all b and raised near Port Gibson, Miss , and all are buried there and names are inscribed on a monument on the square at Port Gibson. Jonathan was a prosperous cotton planter of his day, also a large slaveholder.

CHILDREN.

1. Juliet C. (8), b. 9 Nov., 1844, d. 1 Jan., 1904; m. Lewis E. Stowers; had dau , Margaret M. (9) Stowers. Sons: Benj. F. (9) and Lewis E. (9) Stowers, Jr., all single; residing at Swanlake, Miss.

2. Caleb G. (8), never m

3 Volney S. m. Amanda Hale from Albany, N. Y. Both are dead, leaving one dau. (9), who m. Lawrence Bass of Greenville, Miss. They have two sons: 1. Lawrence (10), Jr. 2 Volney (10) of Benoit, Miss.

III. Joshua, b. 3 July, 1815; d. 15 Dec., 1816.

IV. Isaac Elum, b. 8 April, 1817 d. 23 May, 1831

V. Martha Margaret, b. 8 Oct., 1820; d. 30 Oct., 1836.

VI. Eliza Mary, b. 20 March, 1822; d. 2 Sept., 1822

VII. John Venable Lobdell, b. 12 Jan , 1824, was the youngest of three brothers, the two elder being Llewllyn and Jonathan C. Lobdell.

They grew up to young manhood in Warren County, Mississippi, their father owning property on the Big Black river.

In the early 40's the three brothers came to Bolivar County, Mississippi, which was at that time sparsely settled, but gave rich promise of reward to the cotton planter.

The younger brothers, Jonathan C and John V. Lobdell, purchased in Bolivar County several sections of virgin land extending along an elevated ridge, and the first year the high cane being cut and the land planted in corn an abundant harvest followed. The following year, their barns being filled, they sold corn to many planters coming to Bolivar County, and from this incident they called their plantation "Egypt" The name applies today to one of the most prosperous portions of Bolivar County.

About 1849, John V. Lobdell, finding his health impaired, sold his interest in the Egypt plantation, and moved with his family and slaves to Brazoria County, Texas, where his father-in-law. Col Thomas J. Coffee, had preceded him to engage in sugar planting.

Purchasing a plantation on the Brazos river, he made three cotton crops there, but being entirely cured of his malady (asthma) by his sojourn in Texas, he returned to Bolivar County, Mississippi, in January, 1853, purchasing and opening a plantation on Lake Vermilion, where he again engaged in cotton planting, and there he lived until his death in 1859

He was a man of high ideals, devoted to his wife and children, loved by his slaves, and esteemed by all who knew him

John Venable Lobdell m. 5 Sept, 1848, at Louisville, Ky., Minerva Lee Coffee, b 2 April, 1830, near Canton, Madison Co, Miss, dau. of Thomas Jefferson Coffee and his wife, Malinda Graves Williams Haley Mr Lobdell was a planter, resided near Prentiss, Bolivar Co., Miss., where he d 13 Aug, 1859 The family were Methodists, Mr. L. a Whig in politics

---

Mrs Lobdell remarried to Judge Geo T Lightfoot, by whom she had one son ·

Geo. T Lightfoot, b. 12 Jan, 1871, d. 6 Nov, 1876

I was deeply grieved to hear of the death of this estimable woman, who passed away in Jan., 1907 Our correspondence I had greatly enjoyed, as she was interested in the work and took great pains to give me assistance The following tribute to her memory was written by two old friends who are themselves over eighty years old :

IN MEMORIAM.

Died at the residence of her son, Jno. V Lobdell, Mrs M L Lightfoot, a highly esteemed and beloved citizen, in her 77th year She was one of the first pioneers of Bolivar county She with her husband, John Lobdell, moved to Bolivar in 1847. She was left a widow in early life and subsequently married Judge Lightfoot, and after his death she moved to Rosedale with her son, Jno V Lobdell She has been an honored and Christian citizen She was for many years a member of the Methodist Church (which she loved), until called to be at rest with her God, whom it was her delight to serve   M B S

At a meeting of the Ladies' Aid Society of the Methodist Church of Rosedale, Mississippi, the following resolutions were adopted

It is with heartfelt feeling of sorrow and loss we tender this tribute to the memory of our departed friend and fellow member, Mrs L M. Lightfoot Gifted with a brilliant and cultivated intel-

82

CHILDREN OF JOHN VENABLE LOBDELL, JR.
of Rosedale, Miss.

lect, as she was, and devoting these gifts to God to work in service here, we felt strong to work with her to the Celestial City of God. In her careful and efficient work as secretary and treasurer of our society for years she displayed rare qualities of energy and of devotion to the work. In her life as a Christian, in her close consistent walk with God, in her faith in a prayer hearing and answering God, it was sweet for us to be in union of spirit with her. We miss her in our work, we miss her in the social circles which she graced for many years, and those of us near to her in age especially mourn the breaking of sweet ties that blossom and ripen for years. We offer loving sympathy to her son, Jno. V Lobdell, his noble wife, and the dear grandchildren, and as for ourselves, it will be our prayer that as she lived and as she died we may attain to that holy peace and resignation which was hers in the closing days of her life

I. E. R.

CHILDREN OF JOHN VENABLE LOBDELL (FIRST) AND MINERVA LEE COFFEE, HIS WIFE.

I. Henry Lee (8), b 5 Sept., 1850. d 23 Aug., 1852.

II. Elizabeth (8), b 4 Oct., 1853; m. Holland Thomas Coffee

III Florence Coffee (8), b 27 July, 1857, m. Thomas Norfleet McLemon.

IV. John Venable (8) (second), b 25 Oct., 1859, near Prentice, Miss ; m. 1 June, 1887, near Bolivar, Miss, Marie Coralie Guibert Nugent. b. 21 Jan., 1867, in New Orleans, dau. of Richard James Nugent and Marie Coralie Smith. The family are Methodists, residing at Rosedale, Miss, where Mr. L is treasurer of Bolivar county, also engaged in insurance; is a Democrat in politics.

Children of John Venable (8) (second) and Marie Coralie Guibert Nugent, his wife.

I. Richard Nugent (9), b 27 May, 1888

II. Coralie Guibert (9), b 19 Dec., 1889

III. John Venable (9) (third), b, 8 Jan., 1892.

IV. Florence Elizabeth (9), b 4 Sept., 1894; d 12 Oct, 1894.

V Lilian Hardeman (9), b. 7 Sept, 1895.

VI. Mildred Lee (9), b. 18 March, 1898.

SIXTH GENERATION.

CHILDREN AND DESCENDANTS OF SIMON (5) AND GRACE (POMEROY) LOBDELL.

1. Rebecca. 2. Simon, Jr. 3. Jacob. 4. Gideon. 5. James. 6. Daniel. 7. Enos. 8. Lydia. 9. James. 10. Grace. 11. Mirriam

A copy of the original family record of Simon Lobdell (1762) is kindly given by Mrs Rodman Dodge of Freehold, N. Y., through Mr. C S Lobdell of Windham, N Y

I Rebecca, b 4 June, 1784, at Westerlo, Albany Co., N. Y., where she d 21 July, 1854, aged 70 years, 1 month, 17 days. She is buried in Westerlo burial ground. She m Sylvester Ruland and had issue

    1. Eliza (7), b at Westerlo 30 March, 1821; m Theodorus Hart

    2 Julia (7), m Israel Lawton and lived to be nearly 85 years old. The last forty years of her life was with her family at Westfield, Wis

    3. Abraham grew to manhood, but I can find no record of him

From O'Harts' Irish Gentry I copy the following:

"Jeremiah Hart when a young man lived in Dutchess Co., N. Y. Removed to Saratoga Co., N Y. His son. Philip Hart, b about 1775, m Anna, dau of Joseph Seely and —— Millard.

Their second son, Theodorus, Sr., b 5 Aug, 1809, m Eliza (7), dau of Sylvester Ruland and Rebecca (6) Lobdell, 30 March, 1821, and had four children:

Alonzo (8) Hart

Theodorus (8) Hart, Jr

Adelia (8) Hart

Marion Ellen (8) Hart

Theodorus Jr., their second son, of Pittstown, Pa., b 10 Sept. 1847, m Rebecca, dau of Wm Dymond and Malvina (Slocum) Eyst. Children are:

   Mary (9) Hart

Lawson (9) Hart.

Dymond (9) Hart

This Mr Hart is interested in tracing his line of descent in the Lobdell family and has given me data secured by him. He is editor of the Pittston (Pa.) Gazette.

II. Simon, Jr., a farmer, b 18 Feb., 1786, at Westerlo, N. Y., where he d 11 April, 1867; m. at Greenville, N Y. (first wife), Harriet Blaisdell, b. 20 March, 1792, at Greenville, d. 11 Sept , 1827, at Westerlo, dau of Joseph and Elizabeth (Brown) Blaisdell. The family are Methodists

Simon, Jr , married as his second wife, 4 March, 1828, Phoebe Hulbert, b 23 Aug , 1788, d. 4 July, 1867

III Ot Jacob, I could find no record; b. 31 March, 1788.

IV Gideon, b. 29 Nov., 1789, d 6 Jan , 1859. He married at Freehold, N. Y., Jane Dodge, who died 8 March, 1879. They had no children

V. James, b 5 Dec., 1792; d Nov., 1797

VI. Daniel, b 25 Sept , 1794, d Nov., 1797.

VII Enos, b 8 Jan., 1796 Family record says "These three children all d Nov., 1797."

VIII Lydia, b. 15 Dec , 1797; m Mr. Ingalls. I am told they had three children Mr. Ingalls removed to Alexandria, Va , after the death of his wife

IX James, b 5 March, 1800, m Sally Cowell, living in Schoharie Co , N. Y The family afterward removed to Rock Valley, N Y, where James purchased a large section of wild woodland and constructed a sawmill I have only found record of one child, a daughter, Lucy Ann, who m in 1858 John Slater, who was killed in the Civil War.

X Grace, b 11 Jan., 1802; m Stewart Austin, and I am told was living with her son-in-law at Greenbush, N Y , when she had passed her 90th birthday Whether she had more than the one dau. I do not know I am told living at East Albany or Greenbush, N Y

XI. Mirriam, b. 26 May, 1803; m. 1821 at Westerlo. Alben Ruland, a cooper, b 5 June, 1802, at Westerlo, d 8 Sept , 1881, at Cobleskill, Schoharie Co , N Y , son of Benj. Ruland (who served seven years in Colonial war, is buried in South Westerlo cemetery) and Olive Fuller

CHILDREN.

1. Zina Ruland, b. 13 Nov., 1822; m. Annetta Waldron.

2. Lay Ruland, b 10 Oct., 1824; m. Margaret, dau of Isaac, Jr., and Nancy Udell Lobdell.

3. Eunice Ruland, b 22 July, 1827, d. 14 April, 1829.

4. Anna Ruland, b. 16 Feb., 1831; d. 19 April, 1899.

5. Enos Ruland, b 30 Nov., 1832; m. Lorena Miller.

6 Saloma Ruland b 10 April, 1837, m Hudson Jones, residence, S. Westerlo: had four daus.:

   1. Edith Jones (8), b. 10 Nov., 1866; m. Frank Stanton.

   2 Anna Jones (8), b. 18 Nov., 1871; d 19 June, 1890.

   3. Mary Jones (8), b. 1 Feb., 1874.

   4. Jennie Jones (8), b. 16 Feb., 1878.

7. Emaline Ruland, b 28 Dec, 1838; m Charles Collins.

8. William Ruland, b 18 Nov, 1841; m. Georgianna Abeal. Residence, N. Y. City

---

SEVENTH GENERATION.

CHILDREN AND DESCENDANTS OF SIMON (6) LOBDELL, JR.

1. Luther. 2 Calvin 3. Joseph 4 Elizabeth. 5 Mary. 6. Abraham 7. Wesley 8. Simon H. All b. in Westerlo.

By (1) wife, Harriet Blaisdell.

I. Luther, b. 5 Oct., 1814, was by trade a tinsmith at Westerlo, afterward moving to Brooklyn, N. Y., where both himself and wife d., he 25 Nov., 1891, she 15 Nov., 1880. He m. 16 Nov., 1835, Ellen Lampaugh at Westerlo, where she was b. 29 Sept., 1816. The family were Methodists.

II Calvin, b 22 March, 1816, d. 24 June, 1900, at Windmere, Lake Co., Ill.; m. 4 April, 1843, at Greenville, Greene Co, N. Y., Eliza Ann Williams—in 1902 living at Windmere, Ill.—b. 4 May, 1821, at Greenville, dau. of Dederick and Sarah Gavett Williams Mr. L. was a farmer of Windmere; a Republican and Methodist.

III. Joseph B Lobdell, b. 25 Feb., 1818, at Westerlo, N. Y.; m. Catherine Campbell. No children. They moved to California in the early 40's, where he d 1901.

86

IV.   Elizabeth, b. 14 March, 1820; m. 7 April, 1845, at Westerlo, where she was born, to M. J. Brown, a lumber merchant, b. 22 May, 1807, at Coeymans, Albany Co.   Afterward they removed to Waukegan, Lake Co., Ill., where Mr. B. still engaged in the lumber business.   Here he d. 4 Dec., 1878, and in Jan., 1900, it was our pleasure to meet his widow at the home of her dau. at Waukegan. The family are Methodists.   Their children:

 1. Lottie Brown (8), b. 18 June, 1849; m. James G. Smith, a real estate dealer; has an only son, who resides with his parents at Waukegan.

 2. Olin L. Brown (8), b. 16 March, 1854, m. Belle Trumbell.

 3. Emma E. Brown (8), b. 17 June, 1858; d. May, 1896.

V.   Mary, b. 5 May, 1822; m Daniel Ware.   Both dead.

I am told that two daus., Anna and Ella, reside at South Haven, Mich.   Letter of inquiry was returned by postmaster of South Haven.

VI.   Abraham, I am told, d. during the war.   Single.

CHILDREN OF SIMON, JR., BY SECOND WIFE, PHEBE HULBERT.

---

1. Wesley.   2. Simon H.

I.   Wesley, a farmer, b. 25 Dec., 1828, at Westerlo; d. 10 Sept., 1897, at Coxsackie, Greene Co., N. Y.; m. 9 April, 1857, at Westerlo, Mary Martin, b. at Westerlo 21 March, 1827, dau. of Stephen and Lydia (Boardman) Martin.

In 1902 I had a very interesting letter from the widow of Simon Lobdell, then in her 76th year.   She says: "It is nearly 50 years since we left Westerlo for Coxsackie, and the Lobdells have scattered to the four corners of the earth.   I can hardly keep track of my own children, as the oldest is here, the youngest in New York City, nearly 200 miles apart; and Simon's family, with one in California, one in New York, one in Nebraska and others I don't know where, is more than an old lady 75 years old can keep track of.   I spend my time with my children.   Am now with my dau. at Stillwater, N. Y., and expect to stay here through the winter."

VIII.   Simon H., third, a school teacher, b. 4 June, 1835, d. 11 Oct., 1889, at Ewing, Holt Co., Neb ; m 3 Aug., 1856, at Newark,

Essex Co , N. J., Susan S. Bowman, b. 30 Dec., 1832, at Philadelphia, Pa., d. 7 July, 1898, at Elgin, Neb., dau. of Charles and Susan (Shultz) Bowman. Mr. L. was a Republican, had resided in Franklin, N. Y., South Westerlo, N Y , and in Ewing, Neb.

EIGHTH GENERATION.

CHILDREN OF LUTHER (7) AND ELLEN (LAMPAUGH) LOBDELL

1. William. 2. Henry. 3 Alexander 4. Albert. 5. Ellen.

I, William, b. 2 Jan., 1837, m. at Brooklyn, N Y., 26 Sept., 1860, Louisa Tubbs, b. 15 March, 1842, in N Y City, dau. of James and Sarah (Beers) Tubbs. Wm. d at Brooklyn, 15 April, 1893.

CHILDREN.

1 Wm. A. (9), b. 14 Nov., 1862, at Brooklyn; m. at same place, 23 Oct. 1887. Mary A Pease, b 17 Dec., 1865, at Dillsboro, Dearborn Co., Ind., dau. of Wm. Pease and Susanna Mathers his wife. Mr. L. is engaged in the paper box making business, is a Republican and resides in Brooklyn, N. Y. Has four children:

    1. Arthur P. (10), b 5 Sept., 1888
    2. Agnes L. (10), b 1 April, 1890.
    3. Mary W. (10), b. 24 Dec., 1891.
    4. Victor T. (10). b. 10 Dec., 1897.

II. Henry, b 21 Dec., 1839, d. 15 Nov., 1842.

III. Alexander, b. 10 Sept , 1841; d 15 March, 1864, at Portsmouth, Va He was a sailor on board the monitor Roanoke, and served in the U. S. Navy in "War of the Rebellion " Contracted disease while on duty. Died in Naval Hospital at Portsmouth, Va. Unmarried.

IV. Albert W , Asst Supt Metropolitan Life Insurance, b. 25 Jan., 1849, d at N. Y. City 12 Nov , 1901 , m. 18 Dec , 1873, at Coxsackie, N. Y., Ellen D Burroughs, b. 27 Oct., 1851, at Coxsackie, dau. of Nathan and Ellen (Powell) Burroughs. Resided in Brooklyn, N. Y. Their children are:

    1. Bessie (9), b 27 July, 1875; d. 16 Sept , 1875.
    2. Mary E. (9), b. 24 March, 1877
    3. Harry A. (9), b 4 Jan., 1879.

V. Ellen, b. 4 Feb., 1855; unmarried 1899.

CHILDREN OF CALVIN (7) AND ELIZA A. (WILLIAMS) LOBDELL.

1 Sidney J. 2 Celestia. 3 Franklin. 4 Charles R. 5 Lewis J. 6 Mary Alice

I. Sidney J., b. 2 May, 1844, d. 21 Oct., 1845.

II Celestia. b 18 Nov., 1846, m. John F. Lewin She d. leaving two children. Adelbert and Nettie Lewin.

III. Franklin. b. 11 June, 1849, at Waukegan, Lake Co., Ill.; m. at same place, 27 Oct., 1873, Cora E. Davis, b. 1 May, 1851, at Hamsville, Lake Co., Ill., dau. of S. C. Davis and Sarah Grant, his wife. Business, an architect, religion, liberal; in politics, Republican Residence San Jose, Cal His children are.

    1. Anna R. (9), b. 4 March, 1875.
    2. Clark D. (9), b 14 Nov., 1876.
    3. Fred F. (9) b 17 April, 1878
    4. Alice M. (9), b 19 March, 1882
    5 Jessie W. (9), b. 20 Jan., 1887.
    6. Cora L. (9), b 8 Feb., 1891

IV. Charles R., b. 28 March, 1856; unmarried. Am told resides in Chicago My letter was unanswered

V Lewis, b. 28 April, 1859, in Grant township, Lake Co., N. Y, is a farmer at Windmere, Ill., m 22 Feb., 1887, at Volo, Lake Co, Ill, Eliza Tweed, b 27 Dec., 1859, at Fox Lake, Ill, dau of John L. Tweed and Barbara Strong, his wife The family are Methodists. Mr. L a Republican Have one dau

I Cora Bertha (9), b 8 Oct., 1890.

VI Mary Alice, b 10 Jan., 1863; m. John Dunn.

CHILDREN OF WESLEY AND MARY (MARTIN) LOBDELL.

1 Isadore 2 Julia Stephania 3. Francelia 4 Wilbur S. 5 Martin E.

I. Isadora, b. 13 Jan, 1853, at Westerlo; m Willman R Palmer, b. 2 March, 1849, at Livingstonville, Schoharie Co., N. Y., son of Jonathan and Mary (White) Palmer Mr. and Mrs. W. R Palmer reside at Stillwater, N Y. No children are mentioned

II. Julia Stephania, b. 10 Sept., 1855; m. D. Elliot Davis. Has one son. Fred E (9) Davis, b 1881 The family reside at Midway, N. Y.

III. Francelia, b. 15 July, 1857, m Richard E. Coon, has one son, Richard E Coon (9), b 1893; and a dau., Eleanor I. (9), b 1897. The family reside at New Hamburg, N. Y., Dutchess Co

IV. Wilbur S., b 18 March, 1865; m 10 July, 1892, at Germantown, Columbia Co., N Y., Antoinette Peary, dau. of James and Arleville (Green) Peary. Mr. L., wife and dau., Mary Arleville (9), reside at Catskill, Greene Co, N. Y

V. Martin E., b. 18 Aug., 1868. unmarried Resides in New York City.

2, 3, 4, 5 born in Coxsackie

CHILDREN OF SIMON H. (7) AND SUSAN S. (BOWMAN) LOBDELL.

---

1. Frank H 2. Edward E 3 Charles W 4 Minnie E

I Frank H., b. 10 Aug, 1857, at Franklin, Essex Co, N. Y.; m. 5 July, 1890, at Albion, Boone Co, Neb., to Linnie Lulu Lytle, b. 12 May, 1869, at Royalton, Waupaca Co., Neb., dau. of Sylvester B. and Mary M. (Sheldon) Lytle. Mr. Lobdell is a conductor on Chicago South Side Electric Railway, a Republican in politics, a Protestant. Has resided in New York state, in Nebraska, and in 1902 is at 7030 Emerald Ave., Chicago Has no children.

II Edward E., b. 20 Feb., 1859, d unmarried, 18 May, 1886.

III. Charles W., b. 23 Sept., 1860; m. Mrs. Nellie Daly, in Sept, 1890 Have three children:

1. Ollie. 2. Reuben. 3. Dudley. Their residence, Elgin. Nebraska.

IV. Minnie E., b 20 April, 1869. m Adam N. Bohn 19 Feb, 1887. They reside at Ilwaco, Washington, and have two children:

1. Hazel (9) Bohn. 2. Charles L (9) Bohn.

SIXTH GENERATION.

CHILDREN AND DESCENDANTS OF ABRAHAM (5) AND SARAH (KENNARD) LOBDELL.

1. Mary S. 2. Abraham, Jr 3. Sarah P 4. Alfred. 5. James Alexander 6 Wm Carter 7 Lydia O.

I Mary S , b 21 Dec , 1799; m Asa Conners. No children

II Abraham, Jr , b 17 April, 1801, at East Baton Rouge, La.; m 12 May, 1829, at West Baton Rouge, Caroline Broussard, dau of P. and Sophies (Molaison) Broussard (both natives of France). Mr Lobdell was a sugar planter at West Baton Rouge, where he d 1 Nov , 1867 His wife d. at Iberville, La , 7 April, 1852 They had a family of eleven children, viz (I have only the names of six, and these not in the order of their birth)

James Louis (7) (the only one who married) , he m Angelina Bird , his widow is living at Baton Rouge Abraham (7), Caroline (7), Lydia (7), Charles A. (7), b 1843, and his sister, Louisa S (7), b. 1830. These last two are the only surviving ones of this large family They reside together near Bayou Goula, La (St Gabriel).

III. Sarah P , b 1 Aug , 1804, m Mr Watson, had a son, Torrence (7) Watson (perhaps others). Their home was in New Orleans

IV Alfred, b 1 Feb , 1807. No record

V James Alexander, a cotton broker of New Orleans, b 16 Jan , 1809, d. 4 April, 1861; m 20 Dec , 1836, at Baton Rouge, Marie Rosette Celeste Allain, b 17 Oct , 1813, at Baton Rouge, d. 1 Aug , 1886, at New Orleans, dau of Franciois Allain and his wife —— (?) Blanchard.

VI Wm. Carter, b 22 Nov , 1813; m and resided in New Orleans No children

VII Lydia O , b. 7 Dec , 1816, d. unmarried

The children of Abraham, Sr., were all b. at West Baton Rouge.

SEVENTH GENERATION.

CHILDREN OF JAMES ALEXANDER (6) AND CELESTE (ALLAIN) LOBDELL

I.   Albert Gallatin. b 29 Sept. 1844, at New Orleans, La. d. 29 June, 1902, in Covington, La ; m. first, on 12 April, 1866, to Mary Hazen Pattison, b 7 Nov.. 1845, at New Orleans, d. 24 Nov., 1891 ; m. second, on 22 Oct , 1895, to (widow) Tennessee Estelle Lobdell (nee Watson), widow of Livingston Llewellyn Lobdell of Bolivar Co., Miss , and laterly of Houston, Texas   No children by second marriage   His widow survives and is living with her son, Robert Livingston Lobdell, at Covington La.

II. James Alexander. b 13 Jan., 1847 , unmarried.

EIGHTH GENERATION.

CHILDREN OF ALBERT GALLATIN (7) AND MARY (PATTISON) LOBDELL.

1   Alma Gay, b 16 March, 1867 ; m H D. Higinbotham   Resides at Arlington, N. J.

2.   Maud Holliday, b. 22 Oct., 1869, m C S Fay of New Orleans, La.

3   Celina Wright, b. 2 March, 1872; m. R. H Carter of New Orleans, La.

4.   Mary Bertha b 27 Aug , 1874; m. J H. Duggan of New Orleans, La

5.   Albert Gallatin, Jr , b 9 Nov., 1877 , m in New Orleans, 12 Feb , 1900, to Miss Ashton Pillow.   Is general freight and passenger agent of the Franklin and Abbeville Railway Co., and resides at Franklin, La   Children:

Rosemary (9), Lois Fay (9), Albert Gallatin III (9)

6 and 7   Edith and Ida, b. 9 June, 1881; Edith unmarried; Ida m. W B. Donavan of New Orleans, La.

8.   Walter Reginald, b. 18 Feb., 1885; d. 5 Dec., 1887.

9.   Marion Regina, b. 22 Sept , 1888 , unmarried.

92

THEODORUS HART, JR.
of Pittston, Pa.
(Page 84)

ALBERT GALLATIN LOBDELL (7)
(James Alexander [6]) (1844-1902)
of New Orleans, later of Covington,
La.
(Page 92)

JULIET C. (LOBDELL) STOWERS (8)
(Jonathan Conger Lobdell)
(1844-1904)
of Swan Lake, Miss.
(Page 84)

CHILDREN OF JAMES LOUIS (7) AND ANGELINE (BIRD) LOBDELL.

I. John Bird, d from disease contracted in Cuba during the Spanish-American war. His widow, Mrs. Elizabeth (Randolph) Lobdell, is at the State Normal, Natchitoches, La.

II. Belle, Mrs. Edward Phillips, is dead. She left three children. Her husband m. again and is living near Baton Rouge.

III. James Louis, killed by lightning (I am told, while horseback riding). He left a widow and two sons, near Baton Rouge.

IV. Carrie Louise, m. John Lobdell (John Little Lobdell). Reside at Thibodaux, La.

V. Lena—Mrs. Matta—lives at Baton Rouge.

VI. Pearl—Mrs. Charles McVea—Baton Rouge.

VII. Eva—Mrs. Bradford—Dallas, Tex.

VIII. Bena—Mrs. Marcus Exline—Dallas, Tex.

IX. William resides at Thibodaux, La.

X. Jennie, at State Normal, Natchitoches, La.

93

SIXTH GENERATION.

CHILDREN AND DESCENDANTS OF ABIJAH I (5) AND MARY (LITTLE) LOBDELL.

1 Abijah II 2 John Little 3 Sarah 4 James Alexander 5. Wm Scott 6. Henry Milton 7 Charles Sidney.

I   Abijah II, b 10 June, 1789, at Johnstown, N. Y As a young man he settled in Oxford, Chenango Co., N. Y., and opened a general store, marrying Sally Burghardt 22 Nov., 1810

CHILDREN—SEVENTH GENERATION.

1   Mary Ann, b 12 April, 1812; d. 22 Dec., 1872

2   Jane Eliza, b. 17 May, 1814, d 22 Feb., 1895; m John F. Hopkins, whose death preceded hers. No children

3.   Sarah Maria, b 26 Jan., 1817, at Oxford, where she d after a long illness, on 12 Dec., 1898; m 24 April, 1844, at Oxford, Geo W Godfrey, b. 26 July, 1813, at Middletown, Orange Co., N. Y., d. 12 Aug., 1857, at Oxford, leaving one dau., Augusta C Godfrey (8), b. 19 March, 1845, at Batavia, Genessee Co, N Y.

4   James Henry, b. 10 June, 1819; d 3 Sept., 1891.

5.   Helen Matilda, b 30 Aug., 1836, now (1907) living in Oxford, having the companionship of Miss Augusta C. Godfrey

In military appointments in New York state, I find, "Abijah Lobdell, Jr., was appointed ensign of 133rd Reg., infantry, Chenango Co., in 1812 Promoted to lieutenant in 1815, appointed captain in 1816 Moved" (probably to Utica) "in 1817, and Capt. Otis J. Tracy was appointed to fill his position."

Abijah moved to Utica and with Mr. Hollister as partner, was proprietor of a large drug store The location was at the old "checkered store" (now Warnicks and Brown's tobacco warehouse. In 1836 Abijah returned to Oxford with failing health, dying 9 April, that same year, leaving his widow with five children who now are all sleeping in Riverview cemetery excepting the youngest daughter. Miss Helen Lobdell, who (1907) with Abijah's one granddaughter. Miss Augusta Godfrey, are the last of this line.

94

His wife was one of Oxford's first settlers, coming here in 1794, at the age of two years, dying in Oxford 20 Jan., 1861. She was the dau. of Peter Burkhardt and Mary Church of Great Barrington, Mass. Her paternal grandfather Conrad Burghardt, is well known in history as the "founder of the Massachusetts Colony." He being a wealthy fur dealer at Kinderhook, N. Y., and understanding all the various Indian dialects, by request of the authorities removed to Great Barrington to treat with the Indians there. Later he and his sons gave liberally for the building and support of a Presbyterian church there, but being refused the privilege of Dutch preaching in the edifice once a month at their own expense, they absented themselves from the services, but were churched and obliged to still help support it. Finally Peter and two of his brothers were condemned to sit all day in the stocks, which they did with a crowd of lawyers and sympathizers around to see fair play. Then they built old St. James Episcopal church, giving the land opposite the family mansion, and also much of the expense of erection. In 1790 Peter, desiring to become a larger land owner, removed with his family westward to Oxford, a wilderness with only two or three settlers. Years later Oxford Academy was incorporated, and we find his name among the first trustees. Not many years elapsed after their coming before the first Episcopal church service was held at the house of Abijah Lobdell II, on 23 May, 1814. The Prayer Book used on that occasion, with its f's for s's, is still in perfect condition, only lacking year of publication on its title page; is sacredly held in possession by Miss Augusta C. Godfrey of Oxford, a grand dau. of Abijah Lobdell II, he having brought it from Albany, N. Y., about 1808.

When St. Paul's Episcopal church was organized, Peter Burghardt and his son-in-law, Abijah Lobdell II, are recorded as vestrymen.

The Godfreys were English. They once held a grant of land in Nova Scotia, where the city of Halifax now stands, but abandoned it and in 1769 came to the states and helped fight King George. My father's mother was Scotch, but she d. when he was a child, in Bloomingburg. His father m. a New Yorker and moved to the Genesee Valley in 1825 or 30.

Miss Godfrey has made extensive genealogical search and is proud of her ancestry. She has kindly given for the work the above interesting sketch. Her Burghardt line is:

95

1   Henrich Borghghordt.   2   Conraed Borgghordt.   3.   Peter Burghardt.   4.   Sally (Burghardt) Lobdell.   5.   Sarah M. Lobdell. 6.   Augusta C. Godfrey.

II.   John Little, b. 7 May, 1791, at Johnstown, N. Y., d. 5 Sept., 1867, at Baton Rouge, La , m 18 Dec , 1828, at Bayou Sara, La., Ann Matilda Stirling, where she also was b 2 Jan., 1811, and where she d. 8 Aug , 1890, dau. of Lewis Stirling and Sarah Turnbull.   Mr. L. was a lawyer and owner of a sugar plantation   I have given an exact copy of a letter written by him in the year 1859 to Mr. John Lobdell of Wabash Co.. Indiana, in reply to said John Lobdell's letter of inquiry concerning the whereabouts of his missing brother Nathan (page —)   Surely our works live after we have passed through the gate and joined those waiting on the other side   How little Mr. Lobdell thought of the value of that letter to Lobdell descendants years after he had laid aside the problems of earth.   The copy was kindly sent for the work. also a letter by his dau , Mrs. Sarah T. Allain of Wakefield, La   They have both been of great help to me. I found that Newtown. where he supposed was the home of the early Lobdell's, was the home of Rev John Beach. who. like most clergymen of that time, was an itinerant missionary, covering many towns in his circuit, and if the records of the church at New-town had not been destroyed, they might have revealed much of importance.   I then desired to correspond with the family of John Lobdell of Indiana, and found a kindly help in the gentleman occupying the position of Wabash Co. clerk, who gave me Lobdell names from his county records, and by writing to the different descendants I at last not only traced my John, but the "original letter," prized as an heirloom by its possessor, Mrs. Ellen J Bruner. La Fontaine. Ind.

Wakefield, La , April 11. 1899.

Dear Mrs Lobdell:

In December. 1862. my father with his family and slaves re-moved from his home in West Baton Rouge on account of its proximity to Port Hudson. then under seige; went to the parish of Natchitoches, where he bought property and remained for a year , then, just before General Banks' raid through the northern part of the state, went on to Texas, settling in Smith Co   In December. 1865, he came back to his old home, bringing the slaves with him, his health completely broken and fortune ruined.   He died in less than two years after our return.   My mother, after trying for

96

SARAH LOBDELL JOHNSON (6)
(Abijah, Sr.)   (1793-1867)
of Johnstown, N. Y.
(Page 97)

MARY CHAPMAN JOHNSON (7)
(Dr. Oran Johnson)   (1817-1865)
of Johnstown, N. Y.
(Page 101)

JAMES ORAN JOHNSON (7)
(Dr. Oran Johnson)
of Johnstown, N. Y.
(Page 101)

ANNA FRANCES LOBDELL JOHNSON
BERTRAND
(Dr. Oran Johnson)   (1832-1902)
(Page 101)

a while to re-establish the old business, gave it up and came here to live with and take care of her old mother At her mother's death, she inherited this house, with her portion of land, and died here, where she was born, leaving the house and grounds to me, after my uncle's death—he having a life interest in it. There are no children in the family except my brother John's two little girls and my own family (six children).

We have our grandfather Little's commission as a major in the militia—New York state—given in 1780 by Gov. Geo Clinton; also our father's commission as first ensign, then captain of militia in New York state, dated 1819 and 1820, given by DeWitt Clinton Dr. Wm. Scott Lobdell lost his property by the war, was made parish judge, and gradually putting away a little money, was preparing to resume his sugar planting, when he was killed by a fall in the sugar house he was having built about 1877 or '78

Charles Sidney took the oath of allegiance to the United States. By speculations he made a comfortable fortune and went back to Johnstown, N. Y., at the close of the war From there to Wisconsin, and finally to Parkersburg, Iowa, where he died last year, aged 91. I send you a copy of a paper of my father's written forty years ago The paper is partly family tradition, partly surmise and a good deal of authentic family history. I send it just as my father wrote it My father took great interest in tracing his family, and was always glad to meet or correspond with any of them.

Yours truly,

Sarah T. Allain.

III. Sarah, b at Johnstown, 21 Sept., 1793; d. at same place 2 May, 1867. She m 22 Sept., 1811, Dr. Oran Johnson (2) (Elihu), b. at Tolland, Conn., 29 March, 1783 Was a graduate of Dartmouth Medical College. Settled at Johnstown, N. Y., where he practiced his profession until his death, 12 May, 1835

IV James Alexander, b. 18 Sept., 1798, at Johnstown, where he also d ; unmarried.

V Wm. Scott, b 3 March, 1801; d unmarried

VI. Henry Milton, b. 26 Sept, 1803; d unmarried

VII. Charles Sidney It is a pleasant remembrance to both my husband and myself to have met Mr. Lobdell in 1885 Truly he was a very bright, well educated man, an easy, able conversationalist, and quick to see a joke and to give one His losses by

97

the confiscation of his cotton and belongings during the War of the Rebellion have never been adjusted—are still hanging fire at Washington, D. C. I copy from his local paper what will interest all.

OBITUARY.

Charles Sidney Lobdell was born in Johnston, New York, in 1806, and died at his home in Parkersburg, May 15, 1898, aged about 92 years

In his native state of New York he inhaled its balmy air and grew and developed into sturdy manhood. The foundation of a thorough education was laid in the meantime. July 23, 1832, he was united in marriage to Miss Susan Coffin, also of Johnston, New York. Five years later the young couple turned their backs upon their native state and emigrated to the southland, settling in Louisiana

In these early days, 61 years ago, this was a gigantic undertaking. No railroads and but few, if any, steamships. Here Mr. and Mrs. Lobdell resided for thirty years, or until nearly the close of the Civil War. Mr. Lobdell unquestionably suffered severe losses during the progress of the war and a change was deemed expedient, so from the sunny southland home to the north, settling in Wisconsin, where for a number of years Mr. Lobdell was extensively engaged in the raising of hops. In 1869 Mr Lobdell moved to Parkersburg, which place from that time was his home. He was mayor of the city for fifteen years, which attested the confidence and respect of the community. May 30, 1866, he was bereft of his wife after a married life extending over 54 years. In 1888 he was again united in marriage to Miss Elmor Perry, who now survives him. Two years ago Mr. Lobdell was stricken with paralysis which had rendered him an invalid ever since. He was not confined to his bed absolutely till just a short time previous to his death. To the last he retained his mental faculties unimpaired. He was a strong believer in spiritualism and was as firm as the granite hills of his native state in his convictions of that doctrine. What marvelous things have taken place in the world's history since Mr. Lobdell's eyes first opened to the light of day. The funeral services were conducted at the home on Tuesday, May 17, and the remains buried in Oak Hill cemetery. Thus ends in peace a long and useful life.

SEVENTH GENERATION.

CHILDREN AND DESCENDANTS OF JOHN LITTLE LOB-DELL, SR., AND WIFE, ANN MATILDA STERLING LOBDELL.

1. Lewis Sterling. 2 Mary 3 Catherine H. 4 Catharine Hereford 5 Sarah Turnbull 6 John Little, Jr 7 Anna Alston

I. Lewis Sterling, b. 26 Dec., 1829, m Lucy Susan Burton No children by this marriage. They were m 3 Jan., 1867, at Mississippi City, Miss. Lewis Sterling was corporal in Delta Rifles, Fourth La. Regt., 1861, disabled at Ship Island; detailed to home service for the remainder of the Civil War He d 25 Sept., 1897 at Lucknow, Richland Parish, La His wife d Jan., 1891, at New Orleans, La.

II. Mary d. 1855 of yellow fever.

III. Catherine H d. when eight months old.

IV Catherine Hereford, b. 12 Sept., 1839; m Dr. Irvin Edward Lewis on 22 Dec 1864, at Canton—now Troupe—Smith Co, Texas Dr. Lewis d. in March, 1877. Mrs Lewis is now at her home in Richland Pas, Lucknow, La

V Sarah Turnbull, b 22 Aug., 1845, at Bayou Sara, West Feliciana Parish, La., m 16 Jan., 1868, at Baton Rouge Villeneuve Francois Allain, b. 14 Oct., 1838, at Baton Rouge, d. 9 Nov., 1880, at Bayou Goula, son of Theophite Pierre Allain and Asparia Helene Le Blanc.

Mrs Allain lives at Wakefield, La., with her children, in the house in which her mother was born To Mrs. Allain we are all greatly indebted for her never-failing kindness in giving assistance.

VI John Little, Jr, b 11 May, 1848, at Baton Rouge, m. 16 Feb., 1887, Carrie Louise Lobdell, b 20 Dec., 1864, at New Orleans, dau of James L. Lobdell (7) and Angie Adelia Bird, and great granddaughter of Abraham Lobdell, who settled in Louisiana Mr. J L. Lobdell is a merchant in Thirbodaux, La.; of the Episcopal faith and a Democrat in politics Has two daughters, Anna Stirling, b. 4 Sept., 1888 (8); Belle Stirling, b. 30 Dec., 1891 (8).

VII. Anna Alston, b Sept., 1851; m. James A. Mhoon in Oct., 1877 Residence Lucknow, La.

EIGHTH GENERATION.

CHILDREN AND DESCENDANTS OF SARAH T. LOBDELL (7) AND VILLENEUVE F. ALLAIN.

1 Lilie Marie 2. Villeneuve Frank 3 Annie 4 Aspasie Helene. 5. Mary Aline 6 Sara Lewis

I. Lilie Marie Allain, b 15 Oct , 1868, at Baton Rouge, La ; m 9 Dec., 1896, at St Francisville, West Feliciana, La , to Robert Hereford Stirling, a traveling hardware salesman , a Democrat; a churchman; b. 24 Nov, 1865, at St Francisville. La son of Dr Ruffin Gray and Kate (Leake) Stirling They reside at Wakefield Plantation, with the mother of Mrs. Stirling Have three children
  1. Helene Allain Stirling (9), b. 23 Sept., 1897.
  2 Anna Matilda Lobdell Stirling (9), b. 13 Feb , 1900.
  3. Roberta Hereford Stirling (9), b. 9 Oct., 1902.
II Villeneuve Frank Allain. b 13 Sept., 1870 ; is a druggist in Bayou Sara, La.
  III Annie Lobdell Allain, b 29 March, 1872 , unmarried
  IV Aspasie Helene Allain, b 1 Nov , 1874 ; unmarried
  V. May Aline Allain, b 12 Nov., 1876, at Bayou Goula, Iberville parish, La ; m 14 Oct , 1902, at St. Francisville, La , to Dr Sidney Conroy Barrow. b in Nov., 1876, at Jackson, East Feliciana parish, La.; a Democrat; a Presbyterian. P O address, Torras La. Son of Hilliard B Barrow and wife, Mary Charlotte (Smith) Barrow
  VI. Sara Lewis Allain, b. 8 Dec , 1879; unmarried

Dr. Wm. Henry Johnson
(Sarah Lobdell [6] and Dr. Oran Johnson)   (1814-1868)
of Johnstown N. Y
(Page 101)

SEVENTH GENERATION.

CHILDREN AND DESCENDANTS OF SARAH LOBDELL (6) AND DR. ORAN JOHNSON.

(Johnson) by name

1. Dr. Wm. Henry 2 Charles Webb 3 Mary Chapman. 4 and 5. Elizabeth and Sarah (twins) 6 John Converse 7. James Oran 8. Anna Frances.

(Assistance on the following Johnson record is kindly given for the work by Mr Chas. W Johnson of St Paul, Minn.)

I. Dr Wm Henry Johnson (7), b 6 March, 1814, in Johnstown, N. Y , d. 6 May, 1868 A graduate of Jefferson Medical College of Philadelphia Practiced his profession in Johnstown until his death. Married 15 Jan , 1843, Harriet Livermore McCarthy, b in Johnstown 16 May, 1817 Living (1904) in Amsterdam, N Y., dau. of John and Elizabeth (Ker) McCarthy

II Charles Webb Johnson, b. 10 Aug., 1815, d. 19 July, 1854, unmarried

III. Mary Chapman Johnson, b. 16 June, 1817, d. unmarried 12 March, 1865.

IV. Elizabeth Little Johnson, b. 8 Oct , 1824, d. 31 Oct., 1832.

V Sarah Johnson, b. 8 Oct., 1824, d 11 July, 1866; m. John J. Young of Johnstown, N Y , 12 Feb., 1846

VI John Converse Johnson, b 7 March, 1821, d. 12 Jan., 1823.

VII. James Oran Johnson, b. 24 Sept., 1829, at Johnstown; m 29 March, 1853, Evaline Gardineer of Fultonville, N. Y Residence, Johnstown, N. Y.

VIII Anna Frances, b 26 Jan , 1832, d 10 Dec . 1902; m. 10 May, 1855, Lucian Bertrand, a manufacturer and importer of gloves, b at Millan, France, d at Johnstown, 28 March, 1888, son of Andra and Suzette (Treadon) Bertrand No children.

EIGHTH GENERATION.

CHILDREN OF DR. WM. HENRY AND HARRIET LIVERMORE (McCARTHY) JOHNSON.

1. Dr. Wm. Lobdell Johnson, b 17 Nov., 1843, at Johnstown; attended Trinity College A graduate of Albany Medical Col-

101

lege 1865 Began the practice of medicine in Johnstown immediately after receiving his degree of M. D. in 1865, and has continued in active practice there to the present time (1904) Married 10 June, 1868, Mary A. Clarke of Johnstown, b at Union Mills, Fulton Co., N Y, 3 Jan, 1847, dau of Richardson P. and Electa E (Ingraham) Clarke

They have one dau, Louise Clarke Johnson (9), b 23 July, 1870, in Johnstown; m (1) J. Franklin Dean, 7 Nov, 1889 He d. Dec, 1893, leaving one son Wm Franklin Dean (10), b. 7 Jan, 1894

Louise (Johnson) Dean remarried on 16 May, 1897, Joseph S Mead Children

       1 Alice Mead (10) b. 22 April, 1901
       2. Mary Clarke Mead (10), b. 29 Nov, 1904

2 Charles Williamson Johnson, b 20 Jan, 1845, at Johnstown. A graduate of Union College 1866, degree of C E Civil engineer by profession In Jan, 1867, he entered the office of the chief engineer of the Lake Shore & Michigan Southern at Chicago, and from that time has been continuously engaged in the practice of his profession with the above named railway; the Chicago and Southwestern Ry. (Rock Island), the Wisconsin Central Ry, and since March 1, 1879, as chief engineer of the Chicago, St Paul, Minneapolis and Omaha Railway, which position he now (1907) holds

Married 14 June, 1875, at Manasha, Wis, to Maria C Bronson of that place, where she was b 18 Feb 1856 Has resided at St Paul, Minn, since Oct, 1880.

3 Margaret Louder Johnson, b. 31 March, 1847, d 12 April, 1888, m 11 Aug, 1872, Dr. John Dorn of Johnstown, N Y. who d in London, England, while on a pleasure trip, 14 June, 1904 No children

4 Henry Converse Johnson, b 21 June, 1850; d. 4 April, 1854

5 Lewis Sterling Johnson, b 23 July, 1852, d 10 April, 1904

6 Harriet Johnson, b at Johnstown 12 Feb, 1855; m 8 July, 1886, Thomas Billington Had two sons, viz

       1. Louis Billington (9), b. 1 May, 1887

       2 Thomas Billington (9), b 1 May, 1887; d 3 weeks old

7 Dr Samuel Maxwell Johnson, b in Johnstown 9 July, 1856 Graduate of College Physicians and Surgeons, New York City; m 25 June, 1883, Elizabeth B Gasslin of New York Has prac-

102

ticed medicine in New York City since graduation Has held the position of police surgeon for many years. Children·

 1 Margaret Dorn Johnson (9), b in New York City 8 April, 1884

 2. Charles W Johnson (9), b in New York City 21 Jan., 1889

 3 Florence A Johnson (9), b in New York City 16 Jan., 1891; d 1 Feb., 1893

CHILDREN OF SARAH JOHNSTON (7) AND JOHN J. YOUNG (8).

1 Anna Sterling Young, b 16 Aug., 1847; m 3 Jan., 1878, Benj Ricketts. No children

2 James Oran Young. b 2 Feb., 1850; m 8 Dec., 1876, Alice M. Gross, d 23 Feb, 1884 No children.

3 Wm Henry Young, b 26 June, 1852, d 14 June, 1861.

4 Charles Johnson Young, b 27 Oct, 1853, d. 5 Dec., 1897.

5 Helen Mary Young. b 14 Nov., 1855; m. 29 Sept., 1880, Wm. J Young No children.

6. Lucian Bertrand Young. b. 15 Aug., 1857; m. 5 Dec., 1883, Dorothy Moore Children· 1 James O. Young (9). 2. Maud M Young (9)

7 Sarah Elizabeth Young, b. 27 March, 1860, d. 26 July, 1888; m 13 Oct., 1881, James D Miller, Jr No children

8 Clara Estelle Young, b 25 March, 1863; m 4 Dec., 1895, Albert Argensinger No children

CHILDREN OF JAMES ORAN JOHNSON (7) AND HIS WIFE, EVALINE GARDINEER.

1. James Oran Johnson m. (1) Martha A. France; she d. leaving two children, viz

 1 Harry F Johnson (9)

 2 Charles Oran Johnson (9)

James O m (2) Mary Griere. Had—

 3 Nellie May Johnson (9).

 4 Evaline Beatrice Johnson (9).

2. Rachel Johnson, unmarried

3 Sarah Johnson, unmarried.

4. Wm. Henry Johnson, b. 5 Aug., 1864; m. Inez Edwards. Children:

    1   Archie Oran Johnson (9).

    2. Doris Adelia Johnson (9).

5. Albert Rector Johnson m. Grace Sweet; has one child—

    1. James Oran Johnson (9).

CHILDREN OF CHARLES W. (8) AND MARIA (BRONSON) JOHNSON, OF ST. PAUL, MINN.

1. Harriet Livermore Johnson, b. 18 Dec., 1876, at Manasha, Wis.; m. 24 May, 1899, to Frederick E Mahler of St. Paul, Minn., b. 13 Nov., 1876. Children:

    1. Margaret Johnson Mahler, b. at St. Paul 26 June, 1900.

    2 Charles Frederick Mahler, b. at St. Paul 13 Nov., 1902.

2. Wm. Lobdell Johnson, b. 26 July, 1878, at Menasha, Wis., attended University of Minnesota; m. 14 June, 1905, Mrs. Cora (Hubbell) McDougal of Duluth, Minn. Has one child—

    1. Louise Cotton Johnson, b. 23 May, 1906.

3. Marie Louise Johnson, b. 26 Oct., 1882, at St. Paul, Minn.; m. Arthur E. Gilbert 9 Jan., 1901.

4. Elizabeth Ker Johnson, b. 6 June, 1891, in St. Paul.

104

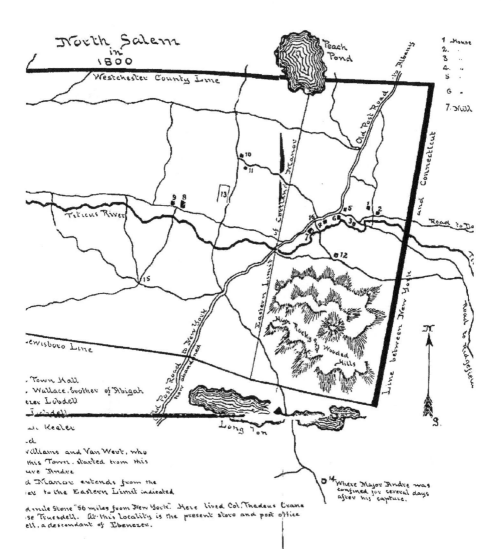

North Salem
in
1800

Westchester County Line

Peach Pond

1 House
2. "
3. "
4. "
5. "
6 "
7. Mill

Old Post Road
to Albany

Road to Connecticut

Titicus River

10
11

9 8

13

5
4 2
16 68
7 8 63

12

15

Eastern Limit of Cortlandt Manor

Line between New York and Connecticut

Road to D

Rocky & Wooded Hills

N

Road to Ridgefield

Lewisboro Line

Post Road to New York
New Orleans road

S

. Town Hall
. Wallace. brother of Abigah
ezer Lobdell
Lobdell)
.. Keeler
.d
villiams and Van Wart, who
this Town. started from this
uve Andre
d Manor extends from the
er to the Eastern Limit indicated

Long Ton

14 Where Major Andre was
confined for several days
after his capture.

d mile Stone "56 miles from New York. Here lived Col. Thadeus Crane
se Truesdell. At this Locality is the present store and post office
ell, a descendant of Ebenezer.

) represents North Salem very much as it was 75 or 100 years ago, or about as it was when it was divided
is below the "Lewisboro line" on the map and is not marked out except the Northern boundary (that i
post road is now discontinued as such, but the mile stones many of them are still standing, and one a litt
New York." No. 4, No. 6 and No. 3 are on the south side of the road with no other houses between. On
beside a little farther east, just as they have been for the last 70 years. From No. 5 westward is a sort of
ly a mile with from twenty-five to thirty dwelling houses, with two churches, two country stores, a post-off
en No. 4 and No. 7 is the store and post-office of B. R. Lobdell, a descendant of Ebenezer. No. 9 is now owne
. Lobdell). He is Town Clerk and Postmaster of what is called "Salem Center Post Office." The Academ
ch and is now the Town Hall. There are no houses at No. 10 and No. 11 now. Col. Thad Crane and Capt.
and No. 7. The village of Ridgefield is at some distance from the line but the Town adjoins. Ridgebury hil

From records of St. James Church of Salem, N Y., is copied the following, which I know will interest descendants of those whose names are mentioned The church was organized before the Revolutionary War The parsonage before 1767 was on land bounded on south by highway leading from Ridgefield to Somers; on east by land of Epenetus Howe, on north by land of Benj. Gray; on west by land of G. Howe and Charles Cable. Six acres was a donation of John Wallace and Benjamin Close.

Rev Mr. Townsend was here till about 1775. John Wallace and Ebenezer Lobdell were wardens.

The war scattered the people and the church fell into decay. The old church was taken down and sold in lots, May 25, 1797. Robert Brush. Thaddeus Husted, Uriah Wallace, Benj Close, Stephen Lobdell, John Lobdell and Jacob Lobdell bought the shingles, boards and laths.

'A meeting of the society was held at the house of John Lobdell 16 April, 1800 "

"Jacob Lobdell was collector and treasurer 1802 and 1803."

"The annual meeting of the society of St. James Church was held at the house of John Lobdell, 13 April, 1803 and 1804. Meeting of wardens and vestry at house of Jacob Lobdell, 14 Aug., 1804."

Sept., 1813, Jacob Lobdell and Zabud June were chosen delegates to represent St. James at convention in New York on first Tuesday of October next."

＋ "In 1814 Daniel Lobdell's name is mentioned."

"In 1823 Joshua Lobdell was collector."

In later years we find the name of Perry Lobdell, 1840; Jacob P. Lobdell, 1844; Benjamin R. Lobdell, as delegate, in 1865; Henry Lobdell, as secretary, 1867; Henry Lobdell, as delegate, in 1868; Darius Lobdell, 1871.

Among the communicants:

"30 June, 1839, Elizabeth Lobdell, an adult, was bapt. by me (Rev. Benj. Evans) at North Salem."

"Elizabeth Lobdell was confirmed 1839 by Bishop Onderdonk."

105

"28 July, 1838. Miss Joanna Lobdell was confirmed by Bishop Onderdonk."

1837 Wm. T. Briggs of Ulster Co. m. Mary Jane Lobdell of North Salem.

8 March, 1840, Abigail Lobdell was buried at North Salem.

Of the vestry, 1797 and 8, John and Jacob Lobdell; 1816, Anson Lobdell; 1821, Nathan Lobdell; 1835, Clark Lobdell; 1843, J. P. Lobdell; 1846, Nathan Lobdell, Clark Lobdell and Jackson P. Lobdell; 1854 and 5, Wm. Lobdell was junior warden.

CHILDREN OF EBENEZER (4) AND DEBORAH (PALMER) LOBDELL.

1 Jacob 2 Ebenezer 3. Deborah 4 Chloe 5 Anna
6 Mary De Lancey
All born at Cortlandt Manor   (Salem. N. Y)

I   Jacob Lobdell, a farmer, b about 1756. d at North Salem, N. Y., 27 Feb, 1834   He m for his first wife, at Ridgefield, Conn., 11 Dec, 1783, Betty Whitney, b 16 July, 1757, at Ridgefield, d. at North Salem, 8 May, 1795, dau of Richard and Esther (Clark) Whitney.

Mr. Lobdell resided on the farm left him by his father and was closely identified with St. James Church, of which we find him vestryman at different times.

Jacob m. for his second wife, Rebecca b 4 April, 1773, second dau and eighth child of John and Deborah (Brush) Morehouse of New Milford (the part which is now Brookfield), Conn   Her parents were probably of Ridgefield before settling in New Milford, 1769 or 70

The name of Jacob Lobdell is recorded as a private in Nov, 1781, in Capt Ephraim Lockwood's company, belonging to Fourth Westchester County Regiment of the State Militia, commanded by Col Thaddeus Crane, also that said regiment was employed in active service in the Revolutionary War

Two other children of Ebenezer Lobdell, late of Ridgefield, were baptized by Dr Deblee—Nathan, b 1758, and Robert, b. 1766—perhaps d, for I find no record or data of them.

II   Ebenezer, bapt. by Rev Dr Deblee, 30 Sept, 1764, m. Chloe Keeler, b 21 March, 1761, at Ridgefield, dau of Isaac Keeler and his second wife, Hannah (Stebbins) Keeler   Her brother, Phineas Keeler, b at Ridgefield 1 July, 1763, m. Elizabeth Lobdell (John of Salem)

Ebenezer evidently migrated with his wife and family to Goshen, Orange Co. N. Y   I find no record of the death of Chloe, but he m a second wife as his will mentions wife Sarah. He d Aug.,

1820, and is buried in the burial lot of Samuel Banker (I assume the father of his second wife)

Ebenezer was a Revolutionary soldier The musket, bayonet and knapsack worn by him are held and highly prized by his grandson, Jacob Lobdell, of East Lansing, N Y

Mrs. M C Lobdell, widow of Ebenezer, Jr., tells me that he was a member of the Masonic fraternity at Salem, N. Y. A silver badge handed down from father to eldest son gives this information

Last Will and Testament of Ebenezer Lobdell of the Town of Goshen

Dated 25 Aug , 1820, recorded in Surrogate's office, Book F, p. 347 31 Aug , 1820

"Gives to sons, Jonathan, Isaac and Nathan, $200.00 each

Gives to son Henry, $325.00

Gives to son Ebenezer, $200.00 and a two-year-old colt

Gives to daughters, Mary Williams, Annie Williams, Deborah and Minerva Lobdell, $175.00 each.

Gives to daughter Chloe Lobdell, $250.00 and one set of curtains

Gives to his wife, Sarah Lobdell, all the bedding and household goods that is remaining that she brought with her when we were married "

Appoints Henry Lobdell and Stephen Ingersol, executors

Among deeds recorded at Goshen

Deed dated 1 April, 1826, Book DD, p 480, 5 Jan , 1827   Lands in the Town of Goshen, and containing 164 acres, one-quarter and eight rods of land.

"Stephen Ingersol and Henry Lobdell, executors of the last will and testament of Ebenezer Lobdell (deceased), to Ira Hawkins."

Same parties to Samuel Banker

Deed dated 4 March, 1833, recorded Book 47, p 29 15 April, 1833 Lands in the Town of Goshen whereon the said Ebenezer Lobdell lived at the time of his death, and containing 17 acres and two-fourths of an acre, more or less

Ebenezer Lobdell and Sarah his wife, to John Yelverton, lands in the Town of Goshen and containing 182 and three-fourths acres.

Mortgage dated 24 May, 1817 To secure $1,579.08 Rec. N. p. 329 Book N

Ebenezer Lobdell and wife Sarah, to Wm. Lawrence, lands in the Town of Goshen and containing 182¾ acres

Mortgage dated 5 Aug , 1820 To secure $2,000.00. Rec. Book 2 Q, p 211, 28 Aug , 1820.

108

III   Deborah Lobdell   I have no record of her birth or death, but the latter probably occurred at South East, Putnam Co., N Y., and before the death of her husband, who as a widower lived in the family of his son, Nathan Field.

Deborah m. Isaac Field, b 1759, at Dingle. Westchester Co., N. Y, d at South East, N Y, 17 Jan., 1837, son of Solomon and Elizabeth (called Betty) (Vail) Field of Dingle

IV.   Chloe m. Nathan Brown, b. 20 Feb., 1767, son of Samuel and Susanna —— (?) Brown   Chloe's first child, Thomas Brown (6), m. Sarah Wilkinson, whose first child, Susan Ann Brown (7), m Clark Lobdell of North Salem, son of Anson and Eliza (Purdy) Lobdell.

The second child of Thomas Brown, Mary Caroline Brown, m. Hiram Reynolds of Purdy's Station N Y, whose grandson, Theodore Reynolds, m Grace, dau. of John and Sarah Eleanor (Keeler) Lobdell of Ridgebury, Conn

V.   Anna m. Benjamin Reynolds (Titus)   Their first child, Mary Reynolds (6), m. Jackson Perry Lobdell, son of Anson and Eliza (Purdy) Lobdell

VI   Mary DeLancey, bapt 27 March, 1768, by Dr Deblee at Salem, m 23 Nov, 1785, Thomas Bailey, and had Thomas Bailey (6) and Mary Polly Bailey (6)   Her grand-dau., Deborah Bailey (7), m. David Haight and d 3 Dec., 1835, aged 45.   According to the records of St Mathew's Church of Bedford, Westchester Co., N. Y. (of which church Deborah was a communicant), they had the following named children, bapt 1 Dec, 1830, by Rev Samuel Nichols:

"1. Hester Jane Haight. 2 David Lobden Haight. 3 Thomas Bailey Haight   4 Mary Lavina Haight. 5 Augusta Ann Haight "

"Married 5 Dec., 1856, at the home of David Haight, Joseph P. Johnson of New York and Hester Jane Haight from Katonah, near Bedford, by Rev. Edward B. Boggs."

In the cemetery at Bedford were found the graves of Augusta Ann, dau of David and Deborah Haight. d 30 March, 1871, aged 43 years

Thomas B., son of David and Deborah Haight, d. 20 March, 1844, aged 24

Mary Lavina, dau. of David and Deborah Haight, d 17 Nov., 1864, aged 39

109

SIXTH GENERATION.

CHILDREN OF JACOB (5) LOBDELL BY (1) WIFE, BETTY WHITNEY.

1. Anson. 2. Nathan. 3 Abigail. 4 Betsey.

Anson, b. 16 Dec., 1784, d at N. Salem, 21 Jan., 1861, m. 6 Aug, 1807, at N. Salem, Eliza Purdy, dau. of ———— Purdy and Hannah Hawley, b 4 April, 1787, at North Salem, where she also d. 24 June, 1823. Anson m for second wife, 3 Sept., 1824, at North Salem, Sarah Townsend, b at North Salem 28 July, 1793, dau of Wm Townsend and Susannah Washburn of North Salem, where she d. 9 Oct., 1867

Nathan, a mason and farmer residing at North Salem, N. Y., was b. 19 Sept., 1786, d at North Salem 27 Sept., 1810; m. 10 Aug., 1813, at North Salem, Eliza Ann Lyon, b 24 Dec., 1793, at North Salem, where she d 8 Feb., 1870, dau of Abrahan Lyon and Sarah Underhill.

Abigail, b 29 Sept., 1789, d unmarried at North Salem, 7 March, 1840, aged 50 years, 5 months, 7 days.

Betsey, b 21 April, 1793; was married by Rev. A H Partridge to Lewis Palmer, a farmer of Bedford, N. Y. (as his second wife), at North Salem, 14 June, 1841 He d at Bedford 10 Aug., 1858 She d without children at Bedford, 1 March, 1870, was buried in North Salem cemetery 4 March, 1870. Funeral services by Rev. Lea Luquer. She brought up her neice, Elizabeth Lobdell, who m Augustus Keeler, and left a legacy to St James Church, Salem, N. Y. ($500).

BY (2) WIFE, REBECCA MOREHOUSE.

1. Joshua. 2 Samuel 3 Mary

I. Joshua, a mason, b 19 April, 1798, d at North Salem 10 Dec., 1850; m. Eliza Miller for his first wife, b. 7 June, 1797, at

North Salem, where she also d. 5 May, 1833, dau. of Benj. Miller and Betsey James.

Joshua m. for his second wife, at South Salem, N Y, Sally (Braden) Stevens, in Dec., 1833, b. in South Salem 13 Sept, 1793; she d. Jan., 1871, at Ridgefield, Conn.

II. Samuel, b. 12 June, 1800, d 30 Aug., 1817.

III. Mary, b. 14 July, 1802. d. 7 Aug., 1846; m. Harvey Smith Had—

    1. Niles Smith, m. Clara Fluellen Resided at White Plains.

    2. Elbert Smith, m. Louisa Remington. Both d. about 1863.

    3. Samuel H. Smith, unmarried; resides at Purdy's Station, N. Y.

The children of Jacob were all b. in North Salem, N. Y.

CHILDREN OF EBENEZER (5) AND CHLOE (KEELER) LOBDELL.

1. Henry. 2. Ebenezer. 3 Jonathan 4. Nathan 5. Isaac. 6. Mary. 7 Deborah 8. Annice. 9. Minerva 10. Chloe.

I have made every possible search to be able to give an accurate account of this family, but the place of birth given by different descendants contradicts itself I am of the opinion that the elder children were b. in Dutchess Co

Mr. Ransom Dodge of Freedom, Dutchess Co, N. Y., sends the following as the result of his kindly, gratuitous search ·

"In examining the old school records I find, under date of 19 June, 1812, the names of Jonathan and Ebenezer Lobdell in District No. 6 of the old precinct. District No. 6 was near the old school house and the old Quaker church at Arthursburgh, now a part and parcel of La Grange."

I. Henry, b 26 Nov, 1795 at Goshen, Orange Co., N. Y., d 6 Sept, 1878, at North Lansing, N. Y.; m. 1824 at Goshen, N Y, Dorothy Denton, b 22 March, 1800, at Goshen, N. Y. d 12 March, 1860, at East Lansing. N. Y, dau of Nehemiah and Lois (Carpenter) Denton.*

Mr Lobdell was farmer, Democrat, and a Baptist.

†Denton—Rev Richard Denton was the first ancestor and came to Boston in 1630. He left five sons, Richard, Samuel, Daniel, Nathaniel and John John Denton went to Orange Co and had James James Denton had four sons—Amos, Thomas, William and John John settled in Goshen had three wives and thirteen children

II Ebenezer, b 1800 at Freedom, Dutchess Co, N Y., d 1890 at Lansing, Tompkins Co, N. Y., m Phebe Royce of Sempronius, N Y Mr Lobdell was a farmer and had the following children :

    1 Lewis lives at Ludlowville, Tompkins Co

---

* The family of Dentons were early identified with the County of Orange, N Y, Denton, from the Town of Wawayanda.

† "Ancestors from Orange Co, N Y The great battle of Minisink has made this section very interesting and most of the men living there during the Revolutionary period had a part in the history of the time."

112

2. Annice lives near Ludlowville, Tompkins Co

3. Jonathan, b 1841, lives near Ludlowville, Tompkins Co

4. Jacob lives at East Lansing, Tompkins Co.

5. Denton M lives at East Lansing, Tompkins Co.

6. Ebenezer, at Peruville, N. Y

7. Hiram. b. and d in Lansing; m. Mary Hargin, who also was b and d. in Lansing. Their children are: William, Smith and Anna

III Jonathan, of whom I have no record further than revealed by records at Surrogate's office at Goshen, Orange Co., N Y "In 1821 Daniel Denton sells to Jonathan Lobdell 13 acres of land in Goshen, and in June, 1824, Jonathan and wife Deborah sell lands" I am told that Jonathan was insane most of his later life I have no record of wife or children.

IV Nathan m Phoebe —— (?), resided in N. Y. City. Among other children, had a son named Wm Canfield (7) Lobdell, who m. 21 Jan 1864, Kate A Watkins, and also lived in N Y City. He d in 1867, leaving one son only eleven months old, named Frederick Watkins (8) Lobdell, who grew to manhood, m. Jessie Belle —— (?) and has two children, viz: Jessie Kate (9) and Edward Dunn (9) The family reside in Boonton, N. J, Mr. L. doing business in N Y City After the death of Wm. Canfield Lobdell, his widow remarried to Mr. Edward Dunn.

V Isaac m. Betsey Weaver. I have written many letters, hoping to secure the family record of Isaac, but the only answer received is from a granddaughter, Mrs. Ella Clement (8) of Freeville, N. Y., who kindly gives the only information I am able to publish She says "I will cheerfully give you all the information I possess, which is very limited I have always heard that in my grandfather's family were thirteen children Two sons served in the War of the Rebellion My father, Mr. McKinney, m two daughters of Isaac Melissa (7) was his first wife, she left one son, Wm H. McKinney (8), now living at Freeville, Tompkins Co. N Y Then my father m Esther (7); she was my mother and d when I was a child of eight years, leaving four children: my brother, George McKinney (8), lives at McLean, and Alex. (8) lives at Groton, both in Tompkins Co., N Y."

Isaac lived at Elmira, N. Y, at which place, I am told, an aged dau. lives, Mrs Sarah Roberts; but my letters of inquiry have been unanswered

113

Esther E (7), dau of Isaac (6) Lobdell, d 23 June, 1860, m. Alexander McKinney, b. 21 April, 1833, at Stewartstown, Ireland, a farmer of Freeville, Tompkins Co., N. Y., where he died 15 Sept. 1900.

CHILDREN.

1 Ella McKinney (8), b 31 Oct., 1860, at Dryden, Tompkins Co., N. Y.; m. 31 Dec., 1891, to Edwin Clement, b. 8 Dec., 1859, at Lansing, Tompkins Co, N. Y., son of Truman Clement and Amand Sellen, his wife Have one son—
  1 Harold M. Clement (9), b 18 July, 1894.

2 Ida McKinney (8), b 25 Nov., 1862, d. 29 Aug., 1871.

3 Geo. B. McKinney (8), b 29 Feb., 1864, m Susie B. Fox.

4 Alex. McKinney (8), b. 8 June, 1869, m. Maud Lobdell.

VI Mary m. Geo Williams and had seven children After her death he m. her sister Annice, she being a widow by the name of Williams.

VII Deborah, b. 1808 at Freedom (?), Dutchess Co., N. Y., d 6 Jan., 1883, m James Maloney, b Rhinebeck, N. Y., 1796, d 17 Jan., 1870

VIII Annice m. first, — — Williams; second, Geo. Williams, the former husband of her sister Mary I am told that a son, Geo Henry Williams, is an attorney and lives in Poughkeepsie, N Y (No answer to my letter of inquiry.)

IX Minerva m. Stephen Ingersol for her first husband, and one Mr. Townsend for second I am told that she left one son, but do not know further

X Chloe m Andrew Teeter, dying soon after marriage, left no children.

CHILDREN OF DEBORAH (5) LOBDELL AND ISAAC FIELD.

I. Phebe Field m Abram Kniffen.
II. Betsey Field m Daniel Baldwin
III. Athalanah.
IV. Chloe Field m 1810, Ebenezer Knox.
V. Deborah.
VI. Sally Field m Charles Terry.

114

VII. Nathan Field m. Susan Knox.

The descendants mostly reside in Putnam Co , N Y. It is told me that Joseph Field, grandfather of Isaac Field, who m Deborah Lobdell, gave the land for the Quaker cemetery near Peach Lake. Westchester Co., N Y.

CHILDREN OF CHLOE (5) LOBDELL AND NATHAN BROWN.

I Thomas Brown, b. 11 July, 1792, m Feb., 1817, Sarah Williamson. He d 24 June, 1857, she, 31 Oct , 1891

II Mary Brown m Nathan Paddock, moved to Michigan

III. Abigail Brown m Raymond Williamson, brother of Sarah (Williamson) Brown.

IV Ann Brown m Samuel Palmer. He d in N. Y. City

CHILDREN OF ANNA (5) LOBDELL AND BENJ. REYNOLDS.

I Matilda Reynolds m. Isaac Smith

II Laura Reynolds m Underhill M. Smith Had—
    1 Daniel D. Smith (7) 2 Phebe Ann Smith (7). 3 Mary E Smith (7) 4 Harrison Smith (7). 5. Willis Smith (7). 6 Alice Smith (7) 7. Samuel Smith (7).

III. Alice Reynolds m. Purdy Baker

IV. Mary Reynolds m. Jackson Perry Lobdell

V. Harrison Reynolds m. Betsey Delevan. Had—
    1 Floyd Reynolds of North Salem.
    2. Hack Reynolds of North Salem

These all were b. and lived in North Salem.

From Keeler genealogy

SEVENTH GENERATION.

CHILDREN OF ANSON (6) LOBDELL.

1. Anson. 2. Clark. 3. Maria. 4. Jackson Perry. 5. Charles Decatur. 6 Anson Whitney. 7 Almira Jeanette. 8 Betsey Maria. 9. Susan Jane. 10. Sarah Ann 11. Wm. Townsend. 12 Julia Eliza 13 Alexander Frazier 14 Almira Jeanette

CHILDREN BY FIRST WIFE, ELIZA (PURDY) LOBDELL

I   Anson, Jr., b. 30 Aug., 1808, d 17 April, 1809

II   Clark, b. 28 Dec, 1809, m 20 Dec., 1836 at North Salem, Susan Ann Brown, b. 9 Dec., 1817, at North Salem where she d. 27 Feb., 1889, dau of Thomas and Sarah (Williamson) Brown Mr Lobdell is a farmer, living at Purdy's Station, N. Y., a Democrat and a member of the Episcopal Church.

III.   Maria, b 25 April, 1812, d 12 March, 1823.

IV.   Jackson Perry was a farmer and mason of North Salem, and lived just south of his grandfather's homestead, of which he owned that part on which the buildings stood; he was b. at North Salem, 20 Dec., 1814, d. 17 July, 1889, at same place, and also m 10 Dec., 1841, Mary Reynolds, b 27 Sept, 1812, at North Salem, where she d 30 Nov., 1896, dau of Benj. Reynolds and Anna Lobdell, who was dau. of Ebenezer and Deborah (Palmer) Lobdell

V.   Charles Decatur, a farmer and mason, b in North Salem. 12 Sept, 1817, m in fall of 1856, Jane Ann Knapp of Stamford. Conn. They settled in North Salem, where he d. 20 Nov., 1861, was buried in North Salem cemetery   His only son, Charles Decatur (8) Lobdell, Jr, b 1857, resides at Peoria, Ill

Mary (8), b. 1860, d at Peekskill, N. Y., in 1893.

Sarah A. (8), b 1862; m. Geo Edwards of Yonkers, N. Y.

VI   Anson Whitney, a merchant, resided at Salem Center, where he d 1 Nov, 1872, was b at North Salem, 14 May, 1820; m. at Lewisboro, N Y, 14 Oct, 1850, Mary Abigail Jenkins, b 28 April, 1829, at Freehold, N. Y., dau. of John Flavel Jenkins and Mary Jane Thayer (Pike).

VII.   Almira Jeanette, b 26 July, 1822, d 10 Nov 1832

116

CHILDREN BY SECOND WIFE, SARAH (TOWNSEND) LOBDELL.

I. Betsey Maria, b in North Salem, N Y., 10 July, 1825, a teacher; m 29 Oct, 1849, in St James Episcopal Church at North Salem, by Rev. Erasmus H. Smith, rector, to Everett Lent, a grocer and farmer, son of James Lent and Anna Kronkhite of Cortland, N Y, where he was b. 18 Sept, 1818. They dwelt in Peekskill till 1 April, 1867, and then settled on a farm in Cortland, near Peekskill. Have no children. (Whitney genealogy.)

II. Susan Jane, b in North Salem, N Y, 29 March, 1827, m. 3 Sept., 1861, at North Salem, Abram Lockwood, a farmer, son of Richard Henry Lockwood and Sarah Wallace, his wife, of North Salem, where he was b 5 April, 1822, and where he d. 27 April, 1872. Had no children.

Susan Jane d. 9 Nov., 1902. The following from her home paper testifies to her noble life

OBITUARY.

Mrs. Susan Lobdell Lockwood.

The illness of Mrs. Lockwood ended on Sunday at 4:30 p m. She had been ill at the residence of her brother, Mr A F Lobdell, much of the time for the past two months. A severe cold and a general lack of vitality was followed by apparent weakness of the lungs and kidneys. The failing, although marked, was at first slow, and then so rapid that extreme helplessness prevailed. That condition continued during the last ten days of her illness. She was in the 76th year of her age

Mrs Lockwood, since the death of her husband, Abram Lockwood, in April, 1872, has lived in Brewster, coming here from North Salem, the home of a long line of Lobdell ancestry and kinship, always her pride and inspiration. Keeping house and providing a boarding place for teachers in the public school occupied her time as long as she cared to follow in that line, and then, giving up household exactions, she enjoyed life within the wide-open doors of a brother's home—making it her own. And thus, for thirty years, she had been well known in the village and in the Presbyterian church—the latter always commanding her most solicitous interest.

117

And beyond all that she was an active worker Ailments came, as they always come to those of advancing years, but she was largely her own doctor and never admitted physical disqualification for any service at home or in the church In fact, she rather enjoyed meeting and discharging in the most complete way duties ordinarily devolving upon others Indeed it is not often that a life of more than three score and ten draws so near to its close without requiring more often the help of others The kindly offices of those around her, during a short illness, supplemented by the close presence of a nurse for only a few of the last days, was the sum total of dependence

She was of Puritan mould, doubtful about admitting into full favor innovations of any kind The old custom, the old creed and the old Bible were good enough for her.

Very beautiful—Rev. Cornelius S Stowitts in invocation, in scripture and address, Rev A. R. Macoubrey in prayer and Miss Tuttle in song—made the funeral occasion To all the relatives and friends who assembled at Mr Lobdell's residence Tuesday afternoon the services will ever abide a precious memory.

The interment was in the family plot at the June cemetery, North Salem.

IV Sarah Ann, b. 27 Aug, 1829, d 3 Nov., 1860.

V "Wm Townsend, b in North Salem, 16 Dec, 1831, a mason, builder and contractor; m 31 Dec, 1861, at White Plains, N. Y., to Emma Jenkins, dau of John Flavel Jenkins and Mary Ann Thayer (Pike) of White Plains, formerly of Middletown, N. J., where she was b, 4 Feb, 1832 They dwelt at Salem Center, N Y, from April, 1863, till March, 1866; at Scranton, Pa., till Dec, 1866. Settled in Port Chester, N Y, 1867, and were living there in April, 1875, without children." (From Whitney genealogy.)

VI Julia Eliza, b in North Salem, N. Y., 24 Dec., 1833; m at same place, 26 Nov., 1861, Elijah Lee, a farmer, of Yorktown, N Y., son of Robert and Elizabeth Lee of Yorktown, N Y. Mr. Lee was a member of the Assembly of the State of New York from the First District of Westchester Co, 1854 Their children are (all residing at Yorktown) ·

1. Elizabeth Lobdell Lee. 2. Sarah Townsend Lee 3 John Randolph Lee. 4 Robert Perine Lee. 5. Mary Louise Lee

118

ALEXANDER FRAZIER LOBDELL (7)
(Anson [6])   (1835-1907)
of Brewster, N. Y.
(Page 119)

ALEX. FRAZIER LOBDELL II (8)
(Alex. F. [7])
of Brewster, N. Y.
(Page 128)

VINCENT PADDOCK LOBDELL (8)
(Alex. F. [7])
of Brewster, N. Y.

ALEX. FRAZIER LOBDELL III (9)
(Alex. F. II' [8]

VII. Alex. Frazier, a merchant, residing at Brewster, Putnam Co, N. Y., b. 5 Dec., 1835, at North Salem; m. 6 Sept., 1865, at South East, Putnam Co., N. Y., Julia Paddock,* b. 10 Aug., 1843, at Yonkers, N Y, dau. of Isaac Vincent Paddock and his wife, Amelia Waring

VIII. Almira Jeanette, b. in North Salem, 5 Dec., 1837 Spent one year at Yorktown, N. Y., and three years at Peekskill, N. Y, teaching in the public schools, m. at Peekskill, 25 Oct, 1869, Francis Henderson Greene of U S civil service, son of Peter and Sarah (Vought) Greene of Peekskill, N. Y, where he was b. 19 April, 1842 Their children are:

Everett Lent Greene, Jeanette Greene, Joseph Alfred Green, a lawyer at Cold Spring, N. Y., b. 29 Sept, 1874, at Brewster, Putnam Co., N Y ; m. 7 Oct., 1903, at Peekskill, N. Y., Carolyn May Wygant, a graduate of Cornell University, A B, 1896 b. 21 May, 1874 at Peekskill, N. Y, dau. of Henry B. Wygant, D D S, and Sarah Matilda Manterstock.

Joseph Alfred Greene graduated from Cornell University College of Law with the degree LL. B in 1896 and took the degree LL. M. in 1897 Is corporation counsel of the Village of Cold Spring and prominent in the Order of Odd Fellows, being a member of the Grand Lodge.

A letter of inquiry sent to the address given me for other son and dau. was returned by postmaster.

From the Brewster Standard and Putnam Co History:

"In Brewster, at his residence, Sunday morning, Feb. 10, 1907, at 2 o'clock, Alexander F. Lobdell departed this life in his 72nd year. On the Sunday preceding he was in his usual health, not in the full strength of the vigorous manhood he enjoyed until nearly three-score years and ten, but very comfortable On the last day of January he was present at the regular monthly meeting of the Putnam Co. Savings Bank, and on Feb. 2 he was at the bank and store throughout the day and evening The cause of his death was pneumonia, and the duration of the disease was less than a week, beginning on the night of Feb. 3 with a pleurisy in the right lung.

---

* Paddock genealogist tells me that Mrs. A. F Lobdell is descended from Zachariah, eldest brother of Bethia Paddock who m Philip (4) Lobdell

The attack was attended with very severe pain, and at 1 o'clock a. m. Dr. L G Newman was called and a trained nurse from New York summoned, and on the afternoon of the 4th the disease seemed to be under control. Returning pains and greater weakness on the day following required such constant treatment that a second nurse was engaged. Thereafter the condition was variable, the patient sometimes speaking naturally and inspiring hope for a few hours, and then suddenly becoming incoherent in speech and requiring heart stimulants and oxygen to keep up respiration. It was not until the evening of the 9th that hope faded; then labored breathing began, accompanied by coma and death. The funeral was held at the Presbyterian church on Tuesday, Rev A. R. Macoubrey, who had been his friend and pastor since 1867 Text, "The Lord gave and the Lord hath taken away: blessed be the name of the Lord." The interment was at the Milltown Rural cemetery. Mr. Lobdell was raised on a farm and educated at the North Salem Academy, graduating in 1853 From 1855 to 1858 he was in business in New York City, and in 1860 he became engaged in the mercantile business at Brewster, N. Y , which had since been his occupation. From 1863 to 1887 he held the position of postmaster, and since 1887 he has been treasurer of the Putnam County Savings Bank; was also a director and stockholder in the First National Bank at Brewster. But he was not all business. There was a strong religious current in his career He was not only a helper in every religious cause of public concern, but he gave when only those who received knew of the giving. Of dignified bearing, perfect as a figure, likewise in character, in dealing and in the discharge of every duty, always the Christian gentleman, are the true expressions of those who knew him—and the priceless legacy he leaves to his family.

SEVENTH GENERATION.

CHILDREN OF NATHAN AND ANN ELIZA (LYON) LOBDELL. ALL BORN AT NORTH SALEM, N. Y.

1 Mary Jane 2 Jacob Lyon 3 Abigail Frances 4 Samuel Harvey. 5 Caroline Elizabeth 6 Hiram 7 Henry.

I Mary Jane, b. 17 Sept, 1814, m 1 Jan., 1837, Wm. Townsend Briggs, b. 8 May, 1813, at North Salem; he d 7 April, 1864, at Ellensville, son of Daniel and Susannah (Townsend) Briggs

CHILDREN.

1 Susan Elizabeth Briggs, b. 9 Nov, 1840; m Wm T. Holmes.

2 Geo H Briggs, b. 23 Oct., 1842, d. 20 Feb, 1893.

The following was received—28 June, 1902—paying tribute to a noble woman:

MARY JANE BRIGGS.

Another name was dropped from the roll of our old residents Monday, when Mrs. Mary Jane Briggs passed quietly to her reward, having reached the ripe age of 87 years and nearly 9 months. For six months Mrs Briggs had been gradually failing, through weakness incidental to her age and the fact that she sustained a severe injury by the breaking of her hip a few years ago

The deceased woman was born in North Salem, Westchester county, N. Y, and was the daughter of Nathan Lobdell and his wife Eliza On New Years day, 1837, she was married to William Townsend Briggs of Briggs street, and came to that then rugged hill country to make her home. Intelligent, industrious and prudent, Mrs. Briggs became a notable housewife as she was a most excellent woman and exemplary Christian, a worthy helpmeet to her husband, a man very highly esteemed and useful, whose death nearly forty years ago was a felt loss to our best citizenship Mrs Briggs resided on the home farm until about twenty years ago she came to make her home with her son, the late George H. Briggs, in this village. The last named died in February, 1893 In recent years the deceased resided with her daughter, Mrs Susan E

Holmes, proprietor of the Walnut Mountain House, her only surviving child.

The funeral service was at the Holmes residence Thursday at 10 a. m., conducted by her pastor, Rev. Dr Travis; interment in Fantinckill.

II Jacob Lyon, b 13 April, 1817, m. 26 Sept., 1843, Mary Perry Burr. b in Ridgebury, Conn., 7 Dec., 1823, dau of Dr David Burr and Ann Maria Hickock. She d in Ridgebury, 23 March, 1844, aged 20 years Is buried in Ridgebury cemetery Her funeral sermon was preached 25 March, 1844, by Rev Zalmon B Burr (who had officiated at her marriage so short a time before) from Matthew, 25th chapter, 6th verse

Mr Lobdell m 24 Dec., 1848, as his second wife, at the home of the bride's mother in North Salem. Deborah Jane Stevens. b 17 Aug., 1827, dau of James and Sarah (Bradon) Stevens Mr L was by occupation a plasterer, a Republican in politics He lived in Westchester Co., N Y, until 1867, then moved to Ellensville, Ulster Co., N Y, where he d 12 March, 1895

III Abigail Frances, b 5 Jan., 1820, d. 20 Sept., 1887, at Norwalk, Conn.; m 20 Nov., 1841, at North Salem, Clark Hickock Osborn, b 8 March, 1819, in New York City, d 2 Jan., 1895, at Norwalk; was son of Abram Purdy Osborn and Electa Hickock, his wife. The family were all Episcopalians.

CHILDREN.

1 Ellen Amelia Osborn (8), b. 9 April, 1846; m 9 April, 1867, at Norwalk, Conn. (where she now resides at 222 East Ave, East Norwalk), to Winfield Scott Hanford, b 6 Sept., 1843, at Norwalk, son of Daniel Platt Hanford and Caroline Smith They have two children, both living with their parents.

1 Winnetta Hanford (9), b. 1 Dec., 1868; m Harrie Morehouse

2. Fred'k Osborn Hanford (9), b. 6 April, 1870.

2 Emma Caroline Osborn (8), b. 20 Feb., 1840; m 11 Feb., 1868, at Norwalk, Rufus Raymond Osborn, b 7 Dec., 1846, at Norwalk, son of Solomon Enos Osborn and Harriet Raymond They reside at Norwalk Have no children

3. Walter Doty Osborn, b 24 Aug., 1851, d. 10 Jan., 1879.

Clark Hickock Osborn served in the Civil War, was sergeant Co E, 12th Re, Conn. Vol, was wounded and taken prisoner at

ANSON WHITNEY LOBDELL (7)
(Anson [6])   (1820-1872)
of Salem Center, N. Y.
(Page 116)

HENRY LOBDELL (7)
(Nathan)
of Salem Center, N. Y.
(Page 123)

JOHN LOBDELL (7)
(Joshua [6])   (1830-1907)
of Ridgebury, Conn.
(Page 125)

WILLIAM LOBDELL (7)
(Joshua [6])   (1828-1907)
of Greenfield Hill, Conn.
(Page 124)

Cedar Creek, 19 Oct., 1864; paroled in Richmond, Va., and delivered at Harrison's Landing 5 Feb., 1865, being four months in Libby prison, the horrors of which it is hard to realize.

IV   Samuel Harvey, b. 4 Aug., 1823, a blacksmith; m. at Haverstraw, N. Y., 9 Aug., 1844, Nancy Ann Dykens, b. 2 July, 1824, at Haverstraw, d. 5 Sept., 1883, at Danbury, Conn., aged 59 years, 2 months, 3 days, dau of Thomas Dykens and Mary Babcock of North Haverstraw   Mr Lobdell d. of consumption at Patterson, N. Y., 23 Jan., 1861, aged 37 years, 5 months, 18 days

Both husband and wife, with children, Caroline Elizabeth and Ida, are buried in North Salem cemetery.

V   Caroline Elizabeth, b. 29 Jan., 1826, m. at North Salem, 12 Aug., 1857, Allen Rundle—as his second wife—a farmer, son of Ezra Rundle and Sally Downs of South East, N. Y., where he was b. 8 May, 1819. They settled near Ridgefield, Conn., where he d. 25 June, 1887, aged 68 years, leaving an only child—Arthur L. (8), b. 27 May, 1860; unmarried.

VI.   Hiram Lobdell, b. 21 Oct., 1828, a mason; d. in St. Paul, Minn., 5 Dec., 1870; unmarried   He was buried at St. Paul. He enlisted, 5 July, 1861, as a private in Co D, 2nd Reg., Minn. Volunteers, and was honorably discharged after three years' service, having been successively promoted to the grades of sergeant, second lieutenant (27 Oct., 1862) and first lieutenant

VII.   Henry Lobdell, youngest son, was b. 8 June, 1832. He is still living (1907) where he was born, on a part of the farm owned by his great grandfather, Ebenezer Lobdell. He was educated at the North Salem Academy, and at the age of seventeen began teaching   He gave up teaching in 1885 and settled on his farm. He has been a member of the vestry of St. James Protestant Episcopal Church since 1866, and senior warden since 1880   3 June, 1857, he married at Liberty, Sullivan Co., N. Y., Sarah Bethia Nichols, b. 3 Feb., 1835, at Liberty, N. Y., dau of William M. Nichols and Sally Briggs   Mr. Lobdell is a Democrat. Has three daughters, the two eldest residing with their parents:

Ella Augusta (8), b. 23 July, 1860

Alice Irene (8), b. 2 June, 1864

Sarah Edna (8), b 31 Dec, 1872, a New York State Normal School graduate, now a successful teacher in Los Angeles, Cal.

123

CHILDREN OF JOSHUA (6) AND (1) WIFE, ELIZA (MILLER) LOBDELL.

1. Samuel 2 Joanna 3 Mary 4 Elizabeth 5 William. 6. John. 7 James 8 George 9 Sarah Eliza
All born at North Salem.

1. Samuel, b. 4 Oct., 1820, d. 25 Sept., 1865, at Newark, N. J.; m. 1 Nov., 1840, at Ridgefield, Conn., Harriet Nash, b 26 Dec., 1819, at Ridgefield, d 2 May, 1887, at Newark, N. J., dau. of Charles Nash and Roxanna Nickerson Mr Lobdell was a tailor, belonged to the Republican party, and was of the Presbyterian faith.

II Joanna, b. 3 July, 1822, unmarried As the result of a fall on 3 Aug., 1904 at the residence of her brother John at Ridgebury, Conn, she d 5 Sept., 1904. Funeral at Ridgebury Wednesday, 1 p m Burial at Salem, N Y.

III Mary, b 12 June, 1824, d unmarried, 28 April, 1849.

IV. Elizabeth, b 19 Jan., 1826; m Wm. Augustus Keeler at St James Church, North Salem, by Rev. A H Partridge, on 28 Nov., 1849, moved to Bedford, N. Y., where their only remaining child, Mary Keeler, b 15 Dec., 1850, now resides in the old home Mr Keeler d. at Bedford 19 April, 1889. Mrs. Elizabeth Lobdell Keeler d. at same place 4 Feb., 1885. A dau., Anna Elizabeth. b. 30 May, 1857, d. at Bedford 20 March, 1892.

Wm Augustus Keeler was b in Bedford, N Y., 22 Oct., 1814. His father was Dr Walter Keeler (son of Timothy Keeler and Esther Kellogg). b in Ridgefield, Conn, 31 Dec., 1777, d in Bedford 15 Sept., 1871, m to Hannah Waring 31 Dec., 1801, who was b 16 March, 1783, in Long Ridge, town of Stamford, Conn, d in Bedford, N. Y, 14 Feb., 1843 Hannah was dau of Deacon Joseph Waring (a Revolutionary soldier) and Prudence Smith, his second wife

V William, b 18 Jan., 1828, at North Salem, m 27 Nov., 1849, at Weston, Fairfield Co, Conn, Galetta Angeline Wood, b 25 Jan, 1830, at Weston, dau. of Curtis and Sally (Lockwood) Wood of Weston Learned the edge tool making trade at G W. Bradley's axe factory, Weston, Conn, but poor health prevented him from working

124

at his trade. Worked the farm of his aunt, Clara Grummons, in North Salem, five years, and in the spring of 1858 bought the Eliphalet Meeker farm of sixty acres in Fairfield, Conn (Greenfield Hill), where he continued in general farming until he died. Brought up a family of five sons and three daughters, who survive him Member of Emanuel Church, Weston Served as Junior Warden of parish a number of years. Mr Lobdell passed away at Greenfield Hill, town of Fairfield, Conn , 4 Feb., 1907, having lived in the old homestead over fifty years.

VI.   John was b. at North Salem, N. Y., 15 March, 1830. When a little child the home was broken up on account of the death of his mother, and like the boys of that time he was encouraged to learn a trade, that of tailor, with his brother Samuel in Ridgefield, Conn.

When still a youth he went to California, engaged in mining and later in the clothing business in San Francisco when that city was destroyed by fire 3 May, 1851. He lost everything, seeking refuge on the now famous "Nob Hill," where he awoke next morning with but twenty-five cents in his pocket.

On returning in 1856 he m. Sarah Eleanor Keeler, b 11 June, 1832, at Ridgefield, Conn., dau. of Adonirum and Charlotte (Brush) Keeler, and for more than a quarter of a century he labored together with Brokaw Brothers, Astor place, New York City, for the best interests of the clothing business.

Mr. Lobdell's quiet attention to his business affairs, his interest in church and Sunday-school work, his complete devotion to his family, his generous hospitality and his attractive personality won for him much love and reverence from all

Although for more than a dozen years removed to the country near the old homeland of his forefathers, he kept in touch with the city of his adoption (New York) by the newspapers, which, as he had a keen appreciation of intellectual attainments, were his daily delight, and which served to kindle afresh the fires of his ardent patriotism.

Here in Ridgebury, after a long illness, he died Monday morning, 25 Feb., 1907, leaving his wife and two daughters

VII.   James, b 18 Jan., 1833, d 27 Sept., 1857, at Nichols Farms, Conn ; m at South Salem, 14 Dec., 1854, Laura Jane Keeler. Has a dau., Caravelle Estelle (8), b. 2 Oct., 1856, at Nichols Farm, Conn.; m. 12 April, 1882, Charles Elbert Brinkerhoff, at Norwalk,

125

Conn., b 24 March, 1857, at New Canaan, Conn., where they now reside. Children:

    1. James Elbert Brinkerhoff (9), b. at New Canaan, 16 March, 1883.

    2 Samuel Segbert (9), b. at New Canaan, 14 June, 1887.

CHILDREN OF JOSHUA (6) BY (2) WIFE, SALLY BRADEN (STEVENS) LOBDELL.

VIII   George, b at South Salem, 6 Jan. 1837, d. at same place, 29 Jan., 1841.

IX   Sarah Eliza, b at South Salem, 1 April, 1839, m. at North Salem, 31 Aug., 1862, Benj F Brinkerhoff and resides at 172 East 88th St., New York City. Has one dau., Georgianna Brinkerhoff (8), b 3 July, 1867 (?).

EIGHTH GENERATION.

CHILDREN OF CLARK (7) AND SUSAN ANN (BROWN) LOBDELL.

I. Sarah, b 9 Dec., 1839; d 9 Oct., 1856

II. Helen, b 28 May, 1841, unmarried; resides with her brother Darius.

III. Darius, b 19 May, 1848, unmarried, resides at Purdy's Station.

IV Almira, b. 14 April, 1853, unmarried; resides at Purdy's Station.

CHILDREN AND DESCENDANTS OF JACKSON PERRY (7) AND MARY (REYNOLDS) LOBDELL.

1. Benjamin R 2. Anna E 3 Floyd P. 4 Anson Whitney. 5 Emma E All b in North Salem

I   Benjamin R, a merchant of North Salem, b. 29 March, 1843; m. 3 June, 1873, at North Salem, Emeline Rundle, dau of Nathan and Martha Jane (Ryder) Rundle of South East, N. Y, where she was b 22 March, 1850 Mr. Lobdell with just pride says, "I am a farmer's son, educated in the common schools and the North Salem Academy." Was a teacher for seven years Has

BENJAMIN R. LOBDELL (8)
(Jackson Perry [7])
of North Salem, N. Y.
(Page 127)

ALBERT JENKINS LOBDELL (8)
(Anson Whitney [7])
of Salem Center, N. Y.
(Page 128)

GEO. W. LOBDELL (9)
(Benj. R. [8])
of North Salem, N. Y.
(Page 127)

CLAYTON R. LOBDELL (9)
(Benj. R. [8])
of North Salem, N. Y.
(Page 127)

been a merchant in North Salem, N Y., in the same location as at the present time, for thirty-five years. Is a Republican in politics and holds the position of postmaster. In the records of St James Episcopal Church we find his name as delegate in 1865. His children are:

1. Clayton R, b 11 March, 1874, d. 7 Feb., 1892.

2. Emory G., b 17 Dec., 1879; resides at North Salem with his parents. Is a dealer in antiques, possessing many old and quaint pieces

3. Geo. W., b. 22 Nov., 1881.

4. Grace H., b 19 March, 1885.

II. Anna E, b at North Salem, N Y., 1 July, 1845, m at same place, 25 Jan, 1865. Charles Hubert Vail, a farmer, son of David and Betsey Ann (Bailey) Vail of North Salem. Children:

1. David Perry Vail (9). b. 28 July, 1866, at North Salem, where he also m. Julia Quick, b. at same place 22 Oct., 1867, dau. of Gerard C Quick and Ruth A. Patrick of North Salem. Has one son, Harold Q Vail (10), b. 31 Oct., 1895.

2. Sarah E Vail (9). b. 28 July, 1866; unmarried.

3. Arthur H. Vail (9), b 14 Feb., 1876; unmarried.

III. Floyd Perry, b. 25 Nov., 1847, at North Salem; m 8 Oct, 1873, at North Salem, Julia E. Meade, b. 4 Jan., 1853, at North Salem, dau of Gilbert T. and Caroline (Bailey) Meade of North Salem.

Children, b. at North Salem, N. Y.:

1. Gilbert Meade (9), b. 27 July, 1879; m 6 March, 1901, Anna Elliott White, b. 6 Sept, 1878, at Summit, Schoharie Co., N. Y., dau. of Robert F and Lola J. (Smith) White.

Mr. Gilbert Meade Lobdell spent his early boyhood on the farm with his parents at Salem Center attending the district school. At the age of fifteen entered the Chappaqua Mountain Institute at Chappaqua, where he took a three years' course. In the fall of 1898 entered the New York Business College, from which he graduated in March, 1899. Then took up farming, in which he is still engaged, occupying the old homestead erected by his great grandfather, Jacob Lobdell, in 1782.

2. Howard Perry (9), b. 7 July, 1881; d. in infancy.

3. Florine May (9), b. 8 June, 1886.

127

4 Anson Whitney (9), b. 1 Nov., 1889.
5 Helen Amelia (9), b. 23 May, 1891.
IV. Anson Whitney, b. 8 Aug., 1851; d. 7 Jan., 1886.
V. Emma E, b 8 Feb, 1855, unmarried.

CHILDREN OF ANSON (7) WHITNEY AND MARY ABIGAIL (JENKINS) LOBDELL.

I. Albert Jenkins, a merchant living at Salem Center, N. Y., b. 7 Feb., 1854, at North Salem, N Y., m. at North Salem 5 Oct., 1881, Mary Louise Braden, dau of John Augustus and Jane Eliza (Baxter) Braden of North Salem, where she was b 25 Nov., 1862.
Children born at Salem Center:
1 Augustus Whitney (9), b. 14 Aug., 1882.
2 Cornelia Braden (9), b 11 Sept., 1884.
3 Louise Emerson (9), b 23 Dec., 1889.
4 Albert Jenkins (9), b. 6 Feb, 1893.
5. Paul Baxter (9), b 5 April, 1894.
6. Jennie (9), b. 3 July, 1895.
II. Frederick A, b. 24 Nov., 1861; d 22 Sept., 1901.

CHILDREN OF ALEXANDER FRAZIER (7) AND JULIA (PADDOCK) LOBDELL.

1. Esther 2 Alexander Frazier, Jr. 3. Vincent Paddock. 4 Susie.

1 Esther (8), b. 29 July, 1867, at South East, Putnam Co., N. Y.; m 25 Sept, 1889, Emerson Wesley Addis, b 13 Oct., 1853, at Litchfield, Conn., son of Chester and Harriet (Waters) Addis. The family reside at Brewster, N. Y. Mr. Addis is an editor and publisher, was formerly Republican postmaster, also member of Assembly of Putnam County.

CHILDREN.
1. Marjorie Addis (9), b 11 Sept, 1890
2. Barbara West Addis (9), b. 14 Dec., 1892
3 Emerson Wesley Addis (9), b 20 Oct., 1896.
4. Alex Lobdell Addis (9), b. 22 Nov., 1899.
2. Alexander Frazier, Jr., b 22 June, 1869, at South East, N. Y., for the past sixteen years has been associated with his father

in his business, and in 1904 became a partner, and during the illness of his father was empowered to act as treasurer of the Putnam Co Savings Bank in the absence of his father. He is a Republican, and in religion a Presbyterian, m. 17 Jan, 1893, at South East, N Y, Jennie Maude Lewis, b 19 Dec, 1870, dau of Wm. and Rachel (Bailey) Lewis. Has one son (9), Alexander Frazier Lobdell III.

3. Vincent Paddock, b 7 March, 1876, a graduate of Yale College (Class of 1905), having been graduated in 1896 from Phillip's Academy, Andover, Mass.

4. Susie, b 18 June, 1881.

CHILDREN OF JACOB LYON (7) AND DEBORAH JANE (STEVENS) LOBDELL. ALL B. AT NORTH SALEM, N. Y.

I. Herbert, a plasterer and bricklayer. b 10 March, 1850; unmarried

II. Amanda Jane. b 7 Aug., 1851; unmarried.

III. Isabel Carolyn, b. 9 March, 1853; unmarried

IV. William, a farmer, b 28 Feb, 1855; m 26 March, 1876, Mary Jane Blumenauer, b 2 July, 1855, at Ellenville, Ulster Co., N Y, dau of Paul Blumenauer and Caroline Ritenauer. Have four sons.

    1. Harry Jacob (9), b. 8 Nov., 1876.

    2. Frank (9), b 26 Nov., 1878.

    3. Fred'k (9), b 21 June, 1882.

    4. Willie Alvin (9), b 27 Oct., 1889.

    All residing at Ellenville, N Y.

V. Edwin Jacob, b. 13 July, 1858; unmarried

Mr Herbert Lobdell writes me: "Our family—as far as my memory goes—have all lived uneventful lives of mechanics or farmers, with one or two exceptions. My brothers have always lived on farms. I have worked at various kinds of work and rambled about some, but never met only one of the name of Lobdell. He was in Nebraska and came to see if he and I were at all related, but as he did not know the name of his grandfather we neither could gain much. My brother Will's wife met a Geo Lobdell of Kingston, Ulster Co., at the Ulster Co fair. (Mrs J. H. L. has been unable to find him.)

129

CHILDREN OF SAMUEL HARVEY (7) AND NANCY ANN (DYKENS) LOBDELL

1 Caroline Elizabeth 2 Mary Jane. 3 Geo. Henry 4 Nathan Thomas 5 Ida 6 Alida 7 Eugene Harvey 8 Hattie Cornelia

I. Caroline Elizabeth. d. 16 Feb , 1856, aged 9 years, 9 months, 7 days.

II Mary Jane, b at North Salem, 20 Oct., 1847, m 28 Oct., 1866, at Patterson, Putnam Co , N Y , Andrew J Birdsall, b 30 June, 1844, at Chappaqua, Westchester Co , N Y , son of Jacob Birdsall and Amy J. Dodge of Chappaqua

Mr and Mrs A J Birdsall reside at 300 West 144th street, New York City Have no children.

III Geo Henry, b. in North Salem 31 July, 1850, d. of Brights disease, in Danbury 20 Feb , 1904 ; m 31 July, 1873, Harriet E. Northrup, dau of Wm Northrup and Harriet Lake of Danbury, Conn Mrs Lobdell d. in Danbury 9 Aug., 1879, aged 26 years, 4 months, 12 days. leaving a son, Wm Harvey, b 4 July, 1874 Both husband and wife are buried in Kenosha cemetery, two miles west of Danbury.

IV Nathan Thomas, b 25 Jan., 1853, was a resident of Danbury when he m. Mary F Dean of Ridgefield, 3 May, 1876, who was b. 3 July, 1855, and d 25 March, 1891 Mr. Lobdell d 6 June, 1895, at Vergennes, Vt Two children were born to them:

    1 Grace May, b 9 Jan , 1878; m. Howard Reynolds (9) Manley at Croton Falls, 13 Oct , 1895

    2 Howard C , b 6 Jan , 1885

V. Ida, d 25 April, 1857, aged 2 years, 2 days.

VI. Alida, b 27 Nov , 1856-7, m Hubble Butler and had three children She d 23 Oct , 1883

    1. Cora Butler (9).

    2 Ferdinand Butler (9)

    3 Guy Butler (9), and

    Frank Butler, an adopted son.

VII. Eugene Harvey, a carpenter and living at Danbury, Conn , was b 2 March, 1859, at Patterson, Putnam Co , N Y.; m. 18 June, 1882, at Purdy's Station, Westchester Co , N Y , Hattie

C Reed, b. 13 Oct., 1859, at South East, Putnam Co., N. Y., dau of John E. Reed and Annie Merritt of Brewster, N. Y.

CHILDREN.

Ernest E, b 5 Oct., 1883, d —— (?)

Twins. Fred'k G., b. 13 Sept., 1885; died. Emma I.; died.

Minnie Essie, b. 2 July, 1887

Geneva A., b. 15 Dec., 1888

Harry R, b. at Waterbury, Conn., 29 Feb., 1892.

John Earl, b. at Long Meadow Pond, Town of Middlebury, Conn., 26 June, 1894.

I am told that a dau of Eugene Harvey Lobdell m. Geo. D Knox and d. 1902-3.

VIII. Harriet Cornelia, b 30 Jan., 1861, at Patterson, N. Y.; m. 23 Oct., 1878, at Danbury, Conn., Orrin B Gage, b. 29 Aug, 1851, son of Wm Gage and Sarah Sirrene of Danbury. Children.

Lena May Gage, b. 27 April, 1881

Carrie Louise Gage, b. 29 March, 1885.

Clarence C. Gage, b. 18 Oct., 1887.

Edith Grace Gage, b 24 July, 1889.

EIGHTH GENERATION.

CHILDREN OF SAMUEL (7) AND HARRIET (NASH) LOBDELL.

---

1. Charles Nash 2. Joshua Hudson 3. Harriet Eliza 4. Leonora Louise. 5. Aurilla Esther.

I Charles Nash, b at Ridgefield. Conn., 23 Aug., 1841. When a young man he left his home to seek his fortune in "the west." I have been unable to trace him, or get further record

II Joshua Hudson, b. at Ridgefield, Conn., 5 March, 1843; is unmarried; resides in Newark, N J A Democrat; occupies a clerical position Served in the War of the Rebellion for six months, then enlisted for three years; was promoted to commissary sergeant and served until close of the war

III. Harriet Eliza, b at Ridgefield, Conn., 19 May, 1845; m. 13 Sept, 1876, at Newark, N J, Wm Wesley Wood, b at Newark, d 30 May, 1896, at Troy, N Y, at which place he was cashier of New York Life Insurance Co No children

IV. Leonora Louise, b at Ridgefield, has resided at Newark, N. J., the greater part of her life, but in 1898 she disposed of her property in that city and since has spent most of her time in West Orange, N. J, and Mt. Vernon, N. Y., is unmarried

V. Aurilla Esther, b. at Ridgefield 27 May, 1850; m. 7 March 1867, Samuel John Gaffey, a clothier, b. at Newark, N J. Children.

       1. Lillie Belle Gaffey (9), b. 23 Jan., 1868, unmarried

       2. Leonora Runyon Gaffey (9), b 16 Oct, 1871; m. 17 Aug., 1898, Walter J. Aschenbach.

       3. James Rumsey Gaffey (9), b. 21 Aug., 1874; d in his 9th year.

       4. Samuel John Gaffey (9), b 16 Jan., 1881

       5. Ruth Hyle Gaffey (9), b. 20 March, 1886

       6 Ralph Lobdell Gaffey (9), b 15 July, 1890.

       7. Mildred Harriet Gaffey (9), b 5 Dec, 1894.

EIGHTH GENERATION.

CHILDREN OF WILLIAM (7) AND GALETTA ANGELINE (WOOD) LOBDELL.

I. John Curtis, a farmer, b. at Weston, Conn., 21 Sept, 1852; m. Lizzie Banks, at Weston, 19 April, 1876, b 10 May, 1852, at Norwalk, Conn, d. at Fairfield 22 Nov, 1905, dau of Gould Nichols Banks and Elizabeth Gregory. Children

       1. Jessie Elizabeth, b 22 Sept., 1878; m. Fred'k Clayton Banks.

       2. Wm Nichols, b. 15 Sept., 1880, d 18 April, 1902.

       3. Lura Angeline, b 12 Aug, 1885; m. Geo. Wilson.

       4. Frank Curtis, b 20 March, 1888

       5. Joanna Isabel, b 22 Sept., 1893.

II. Wm. Irving, b at Weston 5 Aug, 1854, m Harriet Bennett.

III Mary Elizabeth Proal, b at North Salem, N Y, 1857: m. 25 Sept, 1876, at Greenfield Hill, Fairfield Co, Conn, Joseph Burr Bradley, b 5 Nov. 1845, at Greenfield Hill, son of Joseph Burr Bradley and Sara Bradley. Mr Bradley is a land owner;

JOHN CURTIS LOBDELL (8)
(Wm. [7])
of Fairfield Township, Conn.
(Page 132)

WM. IRVING LOBDELL (8)
(Wm. [7])
of Fairfield Township, Conn.
(Page 132)

JAMES OLIVER LOBDELL (8)
(Wm. [7])
of Greenfield Hill, Conn.
(Page 133)

CHARLES LEROY LOBDELL (8)
(Wm. [7])
of Fairfield Township, Conn.
(Page 133)

Republican; an Episcopalian. Resides at Greenfield Hill. Have children:

1. Mary Galetta Bradley (9), b. 23 Aug., 1877.
2. Sara Eleanor Bradley (9), b 4 Jan., 1883
3. Joseph Burr Bradley (9), b 15 May, 1889; d. 16 May, 1889.
4. Frances Bradley (9), b. 13 Jan., 1894, d. 13 Jan., 1894.

IV. James Oliver, b. 29 June, 1859, at Fairfield, Conn.; m. 30 June, 1898, at Easton, Conn., Annie C Staples, b. 25 Oct., 1870, at Easton, dau. of Francis Le Roy Staples and Mary Taylor Bradley. Mr. Lobdell is a farmer, Republican, Episcopalian, and with his wife and young son, James Francis 'Staples Lobdell, b 27 May, 1899, resides at Greenfield Hill, Conn.

V. Charles Le Roy, b 8 Nov, 1861, at Fairfield, Conn., m 28 Aug, 1889, Cora B Bradley, b. 6 June, 1865, at ——— (?), Seneca Co., N. Y., 1 Jan, 1894, dau. of David Bradley and Hattie Bradley. Mr. Lobdell is a farmer, an Episcopalian Has three young sons—

1. Geo. Herbert (9), b. 21 Sept., 1890.
2. Arthur Bradley (9), b 23 June, 1892.
3. Ernest (9), b. 1 Jan, 1894.

VI. Hattie Angelina, b. 27 Aug., 1864, at Fairfield, Conn.; m. 27 Oct., 1890, at San Barnadino, Cal, Wm. Creswell Mushet. b. 22 Dec., 1860, at Glossop, Derbyshire Co., England, son of 'Geo. Mushet and Mary Cresswell. The family are Episcopalian and reside at Los Angeles, Cal. Have three children:

1. Mary Galetta Cresswell Mushet (9), b. 22 Nov., 1891.
2. Mildred Angelina Lobdell Mushet (9), b 2 April, 1896; d. 14 Jan, 1898.
3. Wm Lobdell Mushet (9), b. 22 June, 1898.

VII. Joanna, b. 8 Jan., 1866: d when 9 years old

VIII. Sarah Isabel, b. 7 Aug., 1869, at Greenfield Hill, Conn; m. 24 Dec., 1890, at Lyons Plains, Fairfield Co., Conn., George F. Sherwood, b. 3 Dec., 1864, at Westport, Conn., son of Wm. Sherwood and Esther N. Merwin. Mr. and Mrs. Sherwood reside on their farm in Westport, Conn Have no children Are Episcopalians, and Mr. S. is a Republican

IX. Samuel Everett, b 26 June, 1873, at Greenfield Hill, Conn.; m. 22 Feb., 1898, at Greenfield Hill, Mary Josephine Merwin, where she was also b. 9 Feb., 1876, dau. of Burr Merwin and

Sarah Josephine Gould Mr Lobdell has always lived at Greenfield Hill Is a farmer, Republican, Episcopalian. Has one son:
1. Burr Merwin (9), b. 14 Jan., 1899.

CHILDREN OF JOHN (7) AND SARAH ELEANOR (KEELER) LOBDELL.

I. Eleanor Justina, b. 24 Jan., 1857, d. 19 April, 1880, in New
York City.

II. Joanna Francis, b. 18 Oct., 1859; d 16 March, 1882, at
Savannah, Ga

III Jessie Clothilde, b 17 March, 1861, living with her parents at Ridgebury, Conn., unmarried. Has given me valuable
assistance in my research.

IV Grace, b. 29 Nov., 1870, at New York City; m. 12 Sept.,
1894, at Ridgebury. Conn., Theodore Reynolds, b. 26 Jan., 1870, at
Ridgefield, Conn., son of James Reynolds and Electa A. Wright.

The family reside at Danbury, Conn. Children.

1. Francis Lobdell Reynolds (9), b. 22 July, 1896.
2. Theodore Reynolds (9), b at Danbury, Conn., 25 Dec., 1900.
3 Sara Electa (9), b. 30 May. 1906, at Ridgebury
V. John, Jr., b 4 March, 1878, d 31 Aug., 1878.

SEVENTH GENERATION.

CHILDREN OF THOMAS BROWN (6) AND SARAH WILLIAMSON.

1 Susan Ann Brown, b 9 Dec., 1817, d. 2 May, 1883, at North
Salem; m. 29 Dec., 1836, Clark Lobdell, son of Anson and Eliza
Purdy Lobdell of North Salem

2 Mary Caroline Brown, b 7 Dec., 1819; m 4 Jan., 1843,
Hiram Reynolds, b. 31 Oct. 1815, d 28 Feb., 1898, at Purdy's.

3 Darius Brown, b 12 July, 1823, d Oct., 1899, m. first, Almira Frost, second, Jane Landron.

4. Chloe Elizabeth Brown, b 7 May, 1826; m. Charles M.
Bloomer 1 Feb., 1843.

5 Clarissa Margaret Brown, b 17 Oct., 1828; m. Martin Todd.
In 1904 both are living at Purdy's, N. Y.

EIGHTH GENERATION.

CHILDREN OF MARY CAROLINE BROWN (7) AND HIRAM REYNOLDS.

1. James Thomas Reynolds, b. 22 Dec., 1845, at Ridgebury; m. 2 Sept., 1868, Electa A. Wright.

2. Franklin Samuel Reynolds, b. 17 Aug., 1852, at Ridgebury, Conn., resides at Purdy's, N. Y.

NINTH GENERATION.

CHILDREN OF JAMES T. REYNOLDS (8) AND ELECTA A. WRIGHT.

1. Theodore Reynolds, b. 26 Jan., 1870, at Ridgebury, Conn.; m. Grace Lobdell, dau. of John and Eleanor Keeler Lobdell of Ridgebury, Conn.

2-3. William and Walter (twins), d. infants

4. Mary Brown Reynolds, b. 28 Oct., 1874, at Ridgebury, Conn.; m. 1 June, 1893, Charles H. Dunscomb. Reside at Sing Sing, N. Y.

5. Rufus Reynolds, b. 28 Jan., 1877, d. 24 Oct., 1877.

6. James Clifford Reynolds, b. 22 May, 1886.

SEVENTH GENERATION.

CHILDREN OF HENRY (6) AND DOROTHY (DENTON) LOBDELL.

1. Caroline 2. Amelia 3. Ebenezer 4. Stephen 5. Jacob. 6. Michael Denton

I. Caroline, b. 20 Nov, 1826, at Goshen, Orange Co., N. Y. When only six weeks old her parents moved to East Lansing, Tompkins Co., N. Y., where, on 13 Dec., 1846, she m. Daniel Bower, b. 18 Nov., 1825, at North Lansing, and d. 28 Sept., 1850, at Canandaigua, N. Y., son of Adam and Sarah (Conrad) Bower. One dau. was born to them at North Lansing:

> 1. Mary Amelia Bower (8), b. 17 Nov., 1847, and m. at Ithaca, N. Y., 1 Feb., 1865, Peter Wolverton, b. 9 Jan., 1842, at Canandaigua, N. Y., son of Joel and Mary (Sinclair) Wolverton.
>
> One dau. was b. to Peter and Mary Bower Wolverton at Canandaigua, N. Y., viz., Emma Louise Wolverton (9), b. 21 March, 1867; m. 15 Sept., 1898, at same place, Augustine Sackett, b. at Canandaigua 13 Jan., 1867, son of Henry and Delia (Parks) Sackett

II. Amelia, b. 12 Sept, 1828, at East Lansing, N. Y., d. 12 Feb, 1885, m. Anson B. Rogers, who d. 30 Sept, 1852; had two children, viz:

> 1. Carrie A. Rogers (8), b. 13 Jan, 1859; m. Irving L. Stevens. She is a widow; no children. Her husband d. 8 Oct., 1900. Her home is in West Groton, N. Y.
>
> 2. Denton A. Rogers (8), b. 11 Sept, 1860; m. Ella M. Cobb. Denton d. 20 Aug, 1888. Children are:
>
>> 1. Emmett J. Rogers (9), b. 13 May, 1886, d. 29 Sept., 1886.
>>
>> 2. Percy D. Rogers (9), b. 22 July, 1888.

III. Ebenezer, b. 12 Oct., 1830, at East Lansing, N. Y., d. 17 March, 1900, at Lansing, N. Y.; m. 25 Jan, 1853, at East Lansing, N. Y., to Mary C. Rhodes, b. 25 March, 1830, at Lansing, N. Y., dau. of Henry Rhodes and Marilda Ludlow. Had two daughters, both dead:

136

1. Ella Amelia (8), b 8 Jan., 1855; m. Michael Kennedy.
2   Etta (8), b 12 Aug., 1862; d. in infancy

IV   Stephen, b. 8 March, 1833, at East Lansing; m 9 Dec., 1857, at Locke, Cayuga Co , N Y.. Helen M. Lane, b. 8 Dec., 1838, at Locke, dau of Freeman Lane and Margaret Learn   Mr. Lobdell is living at North Lansing; is a carpenter, a Democrat, and a Methodist

CHILDREN.

1   Delmer H. (8), b. 15 July, 1861 , d 25 Aug , 1863.
2   Le Roy J (8), b. 30 May, 1864, m. Priscilla Bower.
3. Delta A (8), b. 7 June, 1872; d 17 Feb., 1873.

V   Jacob, b. 7 July. 1835, at East Lansing, m. 7 April, 1860, Calista Holden, b. 15 Nov , 1841, at East Lansing, where she was b dau of John Holden and Elizabeth Brown   Mr Lobdell resides at East Lansing , a farmer, a Democrat, a Methodist.   Has one son:
William (8), b 1 Jan , 1862, m. Minnie Norton.

VI. Michael Denton, b 31 July, 1838, at Lansing , m. Melissa Morgan, dau of Edwin Morgan and Delia Talmadge. Melissa d. 31 March. 1880, leaving five children : Charles (8), Dorothy (8), Arthur (8), Ruth (8) and Bertha (8).

Mr Lobdell m. for his second wife Catherine De Camp.

CHILDREN OF MARY (6) LOBDELL AND GEO. WILLIAMS.

1. Chloe Williams m Norton Stout, to whom were b. Geo. H. Stout in 1901, living in Streater, Ill

2   Ebenezer Williams, in 1901 living at Atlanta, Steuben Co., N Y. No children

3   Jane Williams m. Joseph Edsall ; one living offspring, Geo. Edsall (8), Ithaca, N. Y.

4   Deborah Williams. No children.

5. Betsey Ann Williams m. Wesley DeCamp; one dau , Helen Teter DeCamp (8).

6. Wm. Williams; never married

7. Geo Williams m Jane L. Munson; has dau , Mary E. Williams (8), in 1901 living at Cortland, N. Y.

This branch of the Williams name dies out with Ebenezer and Mary E. Williams

137

CHILDREN OF DEBORAH (6) LOBDELL AND JAMES MALONEY.

I. Wm. Henry Maloney, b. —— (?), d. —— (?)

II. Minerva Maloney, d —— (?); m. Nyrum Linderman

III. Geo. Maloney, a physician of Sun Prairie, Wis., b. 1833, at Lansing, Tompkins Co., N. Y.; m. Belle Woodward, b. 4 Dec. 1844, at Litchfield, Conn., d. 11 March, 1900, dau of Dr. E. H. Woodward and Mary Newton. Has two children.

    1. Florence Maloney (8), b. 29 Nov., 1869, unmarried.

    2. Ray W. Maloney (8), b. 16 May, 1874; unmarried

IV. Nathan Maloney, b. —— (?), d. —— (?), m. Mattie Peck.

V. John Maloney, b —— (?); m. Amanda Ferris, who d. leaving no children. In April, 1898, he m. for second wife, Widow Mary Douglas.

VI. Harriet Ann Maloney, b. —— (?), d. —— (?); m. Myron Miller

VII. Chloe Maloney, b. 1 July, 1889, at Lansing, Tompkins Co., N. Y.; m. 1858 at Locke, Cayuga Co., N. Y., Moses C. Lowe, b. 8 April, 1834, d. 28 Feb., 1891, son of James and Maria Van Wagoner Lowe of Locke, Cayuga Co., N. Y. Mrs Chloe Lowe resides at Lansing, N. Y., has no children. To her we—one and all—owe a debt of gratitude for giving to the work the maiden name of her grandmother. For nearly four years I have made search for the maiden name of the wife of Ebenezer Lobdell, wife Chloe. Not one of the many appealed to could give me any clew to the search. Mrs. Lowe is certain that her name was Chloe Keeler

Since my correspondence with Mrs. Lowe her husband d. and she remarried in Jan., 1906, to Rev. Wm. E. Rippey, member of the Central New York Conference (1907), stationed near Penn Yan.

VIII. Deborah Maloney m. Warren Teeter—as his second wife; his first wife was her sister, Phebe Jane. Deborah had one son, who d. of consumption Sept., 1900, aged 22.

IX. Phebe Jane m. Warren Teeter, d. two and one-half years after marriage, leaving one child 15 months old

X. Mary Elizabeth Maloney d. No record

I am told that George, John, Chloe and Deborah are living (1901).

JAMES MALONEY AND DEBORAH
LOBDELL (6) MALONEY
(Ebenezer [5])
(Page 113)

REV. WM. E. RIPPEY AND WIFE,
CHLOE MALONEY (7)
(Deborah [6])
(Page 138)

*GRANDCHILDREN OF DEBORAH (5) (LOBDELL) FIELD

BETSEY'S CHILDREN. "BALDWIN"

Phebe, b. ——, m Alason Rogers
Henry, b. ——, m Jane Dikeman
Laura, b ——; m Isaac Haviland

NATHAN'S CHILDREN. (Carmel, N. Y)

Clarissa, b. 1804; m (1) Joseph Ganning, (2) Ephraim Bedell.
Anson, b 1806; m 1838, Huldah Ambler
Sarah, b 1809, m 1838, Joseph Hobby.
Maria and Marinda (twins), b 1811 Marie m 1834, Abram Kniffen; Marinda m 1834, Alotson Dean.
Thomas, b. 1814. m 1868, Mary Travis
Isaac, b 1817; d. 24 Nov, 1818
Betsey Ann and Nancy Jane (twins), b 1819 Betsey Ann m. 1837, Nathan Lane Austin; Nancy Jane m. 1839, Cyrus Ryder of Danbury, Conn
Lyman, b 1822, m 1850, Kesia Ann Ellis.
Isaac, b 1825; m (1) Henrietta Kent, (2) Martha Knapp

CHLOE'S CHILDREN. "KNOX."

Leonard, b 15 April, 1811; d 22 Oct, 1889, m 1835, Pamelia Banks

SALLY'S CHILDREN. "TERRY."

Chloe Maria. b 1827, m ——
John, b. 1828, d 12 Aug 1833
Betsey, b 1834, m 1858, Wm. Boggs Herdman

SEVENTH GENERATION.

CHILDREN OF ANNA (5) LOBDELL AND BENJAMIN REYNOLDS.

I Matilda Reynolds (6) m. Isaac Smith.
II. Laura Reynolds (6) m Underhill M. Smith Had: **1.** Daniel D Smith (7). 2. Phebe Ann Smith (7). 3 Mary E. Smith (7) 4 Harrison Smith (7) 5 Willis Smith (7). 6 Alice Smith (7). 7. Samuel Smith (7)

---

* This list of grandchildren is kindly furnished the work by Mr **Ryder** of near Danbury. Conn.

III. Alice Reynolds (6) m. Purdy Baker.

IV. Mary Reynolds (6) m. Jackson Perry Lobdell, son of Anson Lobdell (6).

V. Harrison Reynolds (6) m. Betsey Delevan. Had:
1. Floyd Reynolds of North Salem
2. Hack Reynolds of North Salem.

These all were b. and lived in North Salem.

From Keeler genealogy.

FIFTH GENERATION.

CHILDREN AND DESCENDANTS OF JACOB LOBDELL (4), SR., AND HIS WIFE, RUTH BOUGHTON.

CHILDREN.

1 Ruth. 2 Sylvanus 3 Levi 4. Elizabeth. 5 Jacob, Jr. 6. Boughton 7 John

I. Ruth, bapt at Cortlandt Manor (Salem), N Y., Westchester Co., 22 Feb , 1761; m. Levi Lamb   One or more of her descendants, I am told, reside at Long Lake, Hamilton Co , N Y., but no answer came to me from letters of inquiry.

II. Sylvanus, bapt. at Salem, N Y , 30 Sept . 1764, d in Westport, Essex Co., N. Y., in 1836; m. Eliza Anna Knapp, who d. in 1845.

After the death of the father, Sylvanus with his mother and her children (excepting Jacob. Jr (5), who went with his uncle, Hezekiah Boughton (a brother of his mother), and with his cousins, Enos and Jared Boughton. to Ontario Co., N. Y., in 1789) to the then unbroken wilderness of the Boquet Valley of Essex Co., N. Y., settling at Elizabethtown, where Sylvanus took up the south 100 acres of lot No 9 This was probably as early as 1792 They suffered much hardship from their destitute circumstances, having to bring all their provisions from Panton, and most of them on their backs, and after the ice on the lake became sound they brought in by sleighing the house furniture they had left in Panton.   I understand that they paid $1.25 an acre for the land.

III Levi or Levy, bapt. at Salem, N Y., 31 Aug , 1766, d. at Stephentown, N. Y., about 1805 ; m Rachel Toucy and had five children, viz :

    1. Polly (6), d. in Elizabethtown. N. Y., aged 16.
    2. Eliza (6), m. Thomas Lewis.
    3. Harriet (6), m. Robert Odell.
    4. Julia (6), m. Theron Slaughter
    5. John (6), d. in Elizabethtown, aged 21.

IV. Elizabeth, m John Ayers   No answer from descendants.

141

V   Jacob, Jr., b 24 March, 1771, at Salem, Westchester Co,
N Y, d at Victor, Ontario Co, N Y, 12 Nov., 1847: m about
1793, Hannah (Waterbury) Boughton, a dau. of Levi Boughton
(brother of Ruth Boughton, who m Jacob Lobdell, Sr.), and Hannah Waterbury

Jacob Lobdell went from West Stockbridge, Mass., Berkshire
Co., in June, 1789, with his Uncle Hezekiah Boughton to the
Phelps and Gorham purchase in Ontario Co., N Y, taking with
them cattle and sheep He remained during the following winter
on Boughton Hill, Victor, to care for the stock, while his companions returned to Stockbridge He was an enterprising and prominent citizen, the first supervisor of the town of Victor, 1813, and
the first master of the Masonic Lodge there, was well known as an
early contractor on the Erie canal; at one time quite wealthy, but
became reduced financially by the betrayal of those to whom he
lent the use of his good name. He d 12 Nov., 1847, aged 76 years,
7 months, loved and mourned by all his neighbors, especially by the
poor, to whom he often rendered material aid and counsel He is
buried in Boughton Hill cemetery, near the place where he spent his
first winter in Victor among the Indians and wild beasts

(The above account is kindly given by his grandson, Mr Charles
W Lobdell, of Chicago.)

VI Boughton, b at Stephentown, N. Y, 1773, was sheriff of
Essex Co., N. Y, 1815, d 30 April, 1859, aged 86 years, m Sophronia Newell, b 1787, d at Granville, Ill., 3 Oct., 1858, aged 71 years.

CHILDREN

1   Anna (6), b. 1807, m Mr Pearson of Glen's Falls,
N Y. She d 30 April, 1881, aged 74 years.

2   Almira N (6), b. 1820 (?), lived at Warrensburg, N.
Y , d in Aug , 1902 I am told left an estate of $14,000. Be-
queathed $5,000 to the rector, wardens and vestrymen of the
Church of the Holy Cross of Warrensburg

3   Selleck Boughton (6), b 1823 (?), m —— (?), had
one child (7), who d in infancy Selleck d at Chatsworth,
Ill , 17 Sept 1868, and is buried with his family at Peru, Ill.

VII. John, b 28 March, 1776, at Stephentown, Rensselaer Co.,
N. Y, was a farmer of Elizabethtown, Essex Co., N Y, d 27 April,
1859, m for his first wife Nancy Hoisington, b 17 Oct., 1779, at
Southington, Conn., d at Elizabethtown 14 Oct., 1813, by whom
he had no children John m for his second wife, at Westport, N.

142

Y , 13 May, 1815, Emma Hoisington, b. 8 Aug , 1791, at Panton, Vt ,
d 8 May, 1855 or 58   Husband and wives are buried in the family
lot at Westport, N. Y. Nancy and Emma were daughters of James
Hoisington and his wife, Elizabeth Richards   The Lobdell family
were Universalists   John took a prominent part in the formation
of the county and dividing it into towns   Held offices from supervisor down to collector, etc   In the war of 1812 and 14 he belonged
to a company of cavalry , was in the battle of Plattsburgh, 11 Sept ,
1814   From first commission of ensign he was promoted by regular
grade to the captaincy, which rank he held in the battle of Plattsburgh, N Y   He mustered his company at 2 o'clock, p. m. of Sept
10, and was at Plattsburgh on the morning of the 11th ready for
battle—marching or riding fifty miles.

The old commissions, highly prized, are the property of his son,
Jerome T Lobdell, who has kindly given me the war record of his
father.

SIXTH GENERATION.

CHILDREN AND DESCENDANTS OF SYLVANUS (5) AND ELIZA ANN KNAPP LOBDELL.

1. Lucius. 2 Jacob 3. Seymour Boughton. 4. Polly. 5. Betsey. 6. Ruth.

I. Lucius, b. at Westport, N Y., went to Pierrepont, N. Y., soon after his marriage to Abigail Fish of Saratoga Co, N. Y., where he d. Nov , 1858

II. Jacob also went to Pierrepont, but I have found it impossible to gain any information of him He raised two children, Welthia (7) and Sylvanus (7).

III. Seymour Boughton, b. 8 Aug., 1797, at Lewis, Essex Co , N. Y., d. 1877, at Marquette, Mich. He m. Melissa Finney, b. 28 Aug., 1801, and d. 1863, at Detroit, or Jackson, Mich. (dau of Joel Finney).

IV. Polly m John Kingsley.

V. Betsey m. John Chamberlain.

VI. Ruth m. Phineas Heath, d at Westport, N. Y., where a great grandson, Harry Moyning (9) resides. All that is left of her family.

SEVENTH GENERATION.

CHILDREN AND DESCENDANTS OF LUCIUS (6) AND ABIGAIL (FISH) LOBDELL.

1 Welthia 2. Charles. 3. Jane. 4 Ezra B. 5. Emily. 6. George W. 7 Orrin. 8 Jacob Potter 9 Letitia 10. Austin.

I. Welthia m. Wm Hutchinson.

II. Charles, living unmarried at Weaverville, Trinity Co , Cal

III. Jane m L. W. Daniels

IV. Ezra B. m. Ann E Matthews

V. Emily m. L. H. Matthews

VI. Geo W., b. 3 Dec., 1827, at Pierrepont, St. Lawrence Co , N. Y., d. at same place 23 Aug., 1899; m Nancy Daniels, b. 17 March, 1884, at Pierrepont, dau of Lewis and Mary (Chase) Daniels of Pierrepont

144

Children of George (7) and Nancy (Daniels) Lobdell.

1. Mary Jane, b 25 May, 1858, m Edgar A. Hewitt. Residence, Pierrepont, N Y.

2. Ella Alberta, b. 6 July. 1861 ; m. Fred'k Sexton. Residence, Los Angeles, Cal.

3. Charles W. of Pierrepont, b. 30 July, 1863; m. Edith Bancroft.

4 Adelbert G. of Canton, N. Y , b. 19 Oct., 1865; m. Susie Leonard

5. Ezra, b 16 Jan., 1867, at Pierrepont; m. 28 April, 1891, at Pierrepont, Gertrude L. Crandall, b. 18 Oct, 1871, at Pierrepont, dau. of Enoch P and Cornelia (Pollock) Crandall Have Etta (9), b 31 Oct, 1897.

6. Myrta, b 9 March, 1869; m. Henry Crandall of Brownsville, Vt.

7 Minnie, b 29 July, 1871; m. Duane Small of Windsor, Vt.

8 Helen A , b. 16 Dec., 1874.

VII. Orrin lives at Weaverville, Cal.

VIII. Jacob Potter, a storekeeper and farmer, was b 10 June, 1830, at Westport, Essex Co, N. Y., and when about two years of age was brought by his parents to St Lawrence Co., N. Y., where they located at Highflats, where Mr. Jacob P Lobdell now resides Like all the early settlers in a new country, his life has been a very checkered one. From choice, has never been active in politics, never held any office higher than Justice of the Peace, but has done to others as he wished them to return, and is universally respected for sound judgment and excellence of character.

Mr Lobdell m 6 July, 1859, at Parishville, St. Lawrence Co., N. Y., for his (1) wife, Jane Maria Perkins, b. 15 July, 1835, at Parishville, d. 30 Dec , 1864, at Pierrepont, N. Y., leaving an infant dau., Ella Jane (8), only a few hours old Mrs. L. was dau of John Leanord and Clarissa Harlow (Brown) Perkins.

He m. for (2) wife, at Parishville, Susannah Swain, b at Briar Hill, N. Y., who d in Nov., 1897, at Potsdam, N. Y, dau. of Nathan F. and Eliza (Hutchinson) Swain By (2) wife had—

1. Clara Maude (8) (deceased), m. Dr. C. A. Barnett

2 John Nathan (8), b 25 May, 1877, at Madrid Springs, N Y Is unmarried and is (1901) occupying the position of secretary of Y. M C. A., Hartford, Conn.

Ella Jane Lobdell (8), dau by (1) wife, b 30 Dec., 1864, at Pierrepont; m 5 May, 1886, at Parishville Delmar Henry Christy, b 9 March, 1855 at Parishville, son of Charles and Betsey (Bannister) Christy Mr C is a farmer, also postmaster at Highflats, N Y., where the family reside. Their children are.

       1   Charles Harlow Christy (9), b 17 Jan 1889
       2   Clarence Cyrus Christy (9), b 28 May, 1895.
       3   John Alfred Christy (9), d in infancy (1898)

IX. Letitia, b 30 Oct., 1834, m Judge Aikins Foster, b 24 Jan, 1827 Soon after m they removed to Colton, St Lawrence Co., N Y. No children but adopted a niece of Mrs. Foster's (Alberta), m Fred L. Sexton of Cal.

X Austin No record

CHILDREN AND DESCENDANTS OF SEYMOUR BOUGHTON (6) AND MELISSA (FINNEY) LOBDELL. ALL BORN IN ESSEX CO., N. Y.

1 Luther 2 Joseph Finney 3 Elvira 4 Nancy Hoisington 5 Ann Eliza 6 Minerva Rachel 7 Sarah Polly 8 Adoniram Judson

I   Luther d young

II   Joseph Finney, b 10 Dec 1822, d 15 Aug, 1883, at Jackson or Detroit, Mich, m 2 Sept, 1857, at Detroit, Margaret Matilda Beardslee, b, 7 Aug, 1833, at Pontiac, Mich dau of Chas J. and Emily (Bonker) Beardslee Had no children, but adopted a dau, Miss Olga Lobdell, a music teacher of Detroit, Mich.

III   Elvira b 4 March, 1822, m her cousin, Wm. Wallace Lobdell, son of Jacob and Hannah (Boughton) Lobdell of Victor N Y I am told divorced her husband and is living (1902) at Osseo, Minn, with her niece, Mrs Geo. Chapman

IV   Nancy Hoisington, b 20 Sept, 1823, m Chas S Brown of Marquette Mich where she d 21 April, 1879 Her children.

       1   Ambrose Seymour Brown (8), living at Sault Ste Marie, Mich

       2   Wm. Chas. Brown (8), a broker of Marquette, Mich, b 23 Sept., 1855 at Fenton, Genesee Co., Mich ; m 15 Dec 1885, Lillie M Brown, b 9 Oct, 1861, at Detroit, Mich, dau of Jacob and Mary (Kline) Brown They have a young son, Oran Kline Brown (9), b 5 Aug, 1900.

146

3. Joseph Judson Brown (8), of Marquette (?)

4. Minnie Melissa Brown (8), of Marquette.

V. Ann Eliza, b. 10 May, 1825, d. April, 1850, at Jackson, Mich., m. at Westport in fall of 1849, Henry Abel, b. 8 May, 1824, at Elizabethtown, d. 25 Dec., 1887 at Anoka, Anoka Co., Minn., son of Charles and Mary (Ames) Abel of Elizabethtown. Had—

1. Ranson Manfred Abel (8), a wholesale produce dealer of Ironwood, Gogebic Co., Mich., was b. 9 Nov., 1850, at Jackson, Mich. When seven months old his mother died, leaving him to her sister, Minerva Rachel, who died while he was still a lad, and was taken by her sister Elvira. He made a place for himself among the business and intellectual men of his state and m. 29 ——, 1879, at Ypsilanti, Mich., to Sara Maria Curtis, b. 16 Aug., 1852, at Perrysburg, Ohio, dau. of Mark and Emeline (Palmer) Curtis of Ypsilanta, Mich. Has son, Alger Arthur Abel (9), b. 3 June, 1884, and daughter, Gretta Belle Abel (9), b. 10 Nov., 1885.

VI. Minerva Rachel, b. 30 Dec., 1828 d. at Royal Oak, Mich., 1857; unmarried.

VII. Sarah Polly, b. 3 Feb., 1831, d. Feb., 1891, at Maple Grove, Minn., m. first, Charles A. Jennison and had a dau., Lettie Dell (8), who m. Geo. Chapman and resides at Maple Grove township, Minn.

Sarah Polly m. at Maple Grove, for her second husband, Wm. M. Brooks who had a dau., who m. Chas. Prible.

VIII. Adoniram Judson, b. 18 May, 1833; m. 13 Aug., 1854, at Jackson, Mich., Rosetta E. Slade, b. 18 Nov., 1833, at Ludlow, Vt., dau. of Horace T. Slade and wife, Achsah Wiley. Mr. Lobdell is a Republican, and of the Baptist faith. From Essex and Ontario counties, N. Y., he came west to Detroit, Jackson, Grand Rapids, and finally to Marquette, Mich., where he now resides. He has one son, and I think several daughters. The son, Horace Judson (8), b. 4 Sept., 1862, at Marquette, Mich., m. 9 May, 1888, at Marquette, Sara Hughes Randolph, b. Dec. 20, 1865, at Stagner, Ontario, dau. of George and Elizabeth (Osman) Randolph. Mr. Lobdell is a bookkeeper residing at Marquette, a Baptist and a Republican. Children are.

1. Horace Randolph (9), b. 21 April, 1890.

2. Elizabeth Lucille (9), b. 20 Dec., 1893.

3 and 4. Marie Rosette (9) and Frances (9) (twins, b. 7 Feb., 1896, and I am told "the finest on earth").

147

SIXTH GENERATION.

CHILDREN AND DESCENDANTS OF JACOB, JR., AND HANNAH (BOUGHTON) LOBDELL. ALL BORN IN VICTOR, N. Y.

CHILDREN.

1 George Anson. 2. Chester. 3 Anna Palmyra. 4 Chester (2). 5. Nancy. 6. Sophronia 7 Caroline 8. Levi Boughton. 9. Hannah 10 Jacob Lyman 11 Ruth. 12 Wm Wallace

I George Anson, b 8 Nov , 1794, d 5 Jan , 1870, at Moline. Rock Island Co., Ill , m 21 April, 1824, at Victor, Almira Austin Preston, b. 24 Nov , 1803, at Victor, d. 4 Nov., 1887, at Granville. Putnam Co., Ill Mr. Lobdell was a farmer In politics a Democrat, until 1856, when he joined the Republican ranks. In religion, a Methodist.

II Chester, b 2 Oct , 1796, d in infancy.

III. Anna Palmyra, b. 5 Aug., 1798, d at South Norwalk, Conn , 12 Aug., 1872; m. at Victor 19 May, 1831, Abraham Humphrey, b 4 May, 1799, at Goshen, Litchfield Co , Conn , d 1 Nov , 1881, at South Norwalk. Conn , son of Abraham and Huldah (Baldwin) Humphrey

CHILDREN.

1. Ellen M Humphrey (7), b. 2 March, 1836; m 18 Jan , 1860, at Victor, N. Y., Seymour C. Palmer, b. 17 June, 1833. at Frankfort, Herkimer Co , N. Y , son of Adam and Mary (Fuller) Palmer. Mr. and Mrs. Palmer in 1902, resided at 25 Elmwood Ave , South Norwalk. Conn Children

1. Wm. Humphrey Palmer (8), b 30 May, 1864, at Brooklyn, N. Y ; m. 6 June, 1892, at South Norwalk. Conn , Laura G Brady, dau of Stephen and Louisa (Hyatt) Brady. They have one dau , Adelle Hyatt Palmer (9), b 15 Jan , 1894.

2 Mary Fuller Palmer (8).

2 Mary C Humphrey (7), b. 26 March, 1838, d at Victor 11 Nov , 1840

3. Jacob L. Humphrey (7), b. 27 July, 1839, d. in Victor 14 Nov., 1840.

IV. Chester (second), b. 4 June, 1801; d. unmarried 12 Aug., 1842.

V. Nancy, b. 30 Nov., 1803; d. unmarried 15 Nov., 1838.

VI. Sophronia, b. 20 Nov., 1804, d. at Flint, Steuben Co., Ind., 20 Jan., 1852; m. 25 Feb., 1835, at Victor, Amasa Maro Cleveland, b. 27 Nov., 1812, at Skeneatlas, N. Y., d. 7 Oct., 1863, at Flint, Ind., son of Asalh and Polly (Hawks) Cleveland.

CHILDREN.

1. Louise Cleveland (7), b. at Flint, Steuben Co., Ind., 8 Sept., 1839. In religion, a Spiritualist. Unmarried. Residence, San Diego, Cal.

2. Adelpha Cleveland (7), residing at Flint, Ind., b. 21 April, 1842, at Flint, Ind.; m. 8 July, 1860, George Golden, b. 8 Oct., 1835, in Genesee Co., N. Y., d. 20 May, 1892, son of Nathaniel and Elizabeth Arrah Golden. Children:

    1. Frank Golden (8), b. 12 Nov., 1862; m. 3 July, 1882, Jennie Brown.

    2. Edward Golden (8), b. 13 Sept., 1865; m. 25 Nov., 1885, Evaline Barr.

    3. Judd Golden (8), b. 10 Aug., 1871.

3. Mary Hannah Cleveland (7), b. 20 April, 1846, m. 13 July, 1867, to Dr. John Blue of Flint, Ind., b. 18 July, 1839, in Allen Co., Ind., d. 5 July, 1884, son of John and Sarah (Mercer) Blue. Children:

    1. Nellie Cleveland Blue (8), b. 13 May, 1868; m. 11 Nov., 1891, to Dr. Curtis Wolford of Grand Rapids, Mich.

    2. John Blue (8), b. 16 Nov., 1871.

    3. Ludell Blue (8), b. 27 Oct., 1876; d. 19 Feb., 1877.

VII. Caroline, b. 15 March, 1806, m. as second wife to Rufus Humphrey of Victor, where she d. Had no children.

VIII. Levi Boughton, b. 11 Sept., 1810, d. in Victor 25 Dec., 1882; m. 21 July, 1841. Frances M. Jenks, b. 12 May. 1813, d. 1 July, 1871.

CHILDREN.

1. Mary Caroline (7), b. 21 June, 1852; m. Frank E. Sale, 21 Feb., 1876, d. 27 Oct., 1887.

2. Wm. Jacob (7), b. 3 April, 1854, d. 17 April, 1854.

IX   Hannah, b 4 Feb., 1814, d unmarried 23 July, 1840

X   Jacob Lyman, b 23 Jan., 1816, d 27 July, 1855, at Victor; m 2 Feb., 1843, at Victor, Joanna Farr, b 1819, at East Bloomfield, Ontario Co., N Y., d June, 1885, at Victor, N. Y., dau. of Daniel and Lucia (Wright) Farr.

SEVENTH GENERATION.

CHILDREN.

1 Frances M. 2 Burton H 3 Byron Jacob 4 Oliver

---

1   Frances M., b 25 June, 1844, d in Victor, 27 March, 1897, m in Victor 30 June. 1874, Bolivar Ellis, b 25 Feb., 1833, at Victor, son of Henry and Isabel (Bennett) Ellis of Victor. Have one dau living at Victor, Isabell Ellis (8), b 16 June, 1875, at same place.

2   Burton II, a farmer living in Victor, b 18 March, 1846; m 19 March, 1873, at Victor, Amelia S. Ketchum, b 1848 at East Bloomfield, Ontario Co, N Y, dau of Nelson and Nancy S. (Blaney) Ketchum of Victor. In politics, a Democrat, a Universalist in religion Has two children.

Nelson L. (8), b 31 Jan., 1876, unmarried.

Marion F. (8), b 30 Sept., 1879; unmarried. Both son and dau are successful teachers.

3.   Byron Jacob, b 28 Dec., 1848, is now living at Los Angeles, Cal., m. 4 June, 1884, at Vinton, Benton Co., Iowa Mary A George Has one son—

Jacob Karl Lobdell (8), b at Los Angeles 13 April, 1887.

4   Oliver, a farmer living at Victor, was b 3 March, 1851, m. 19 Oct., 1881, at Victor, Lilla Armstrong, b 8 Dec., 1850, at Pittsford, Monroe Co., N Y., dau of Wm. Henry and Mercy Ann Olney Armstrong of Pittsford Mr Lobdell is a Universalist in religion; a Democrat in politics Children·

1   Ellery Byron (8), b 5 Feb., 1883; d 10 May, 1891.

2   Lulu May (8), b 1 Feb 1885, d 14 April, 1892

3.   Ina Frances (8), b 10 Feb., 1887.

XI.   Ruth, b. 8 Dec., 1817; d. unmarried 31 March, 1841.

XII   Wm. Wallace. b. 16 March, 1820, m first, Elvira, dau. of Seymour Boughton Lobdell (his cousin), m. second, 3 Dec., 1849, Eunice F. Hale, b. 13 Oct., 1823, at Richmond, Genesee Co., N. Y., d. 31 Oct., 1892, dau. of Solan and Eunice (Furbush) Hale. Had one child, Florence (7), b. 3 June, 1859, d. in infancy.

Child by first wife. Ruth (7), b. 9 Sept., 1843, at Victor, N. Y.; m. 2 Jan., 1876, S. Edward Fisher, b. 25 May, 1829, in New Hampshire, son of Samuel and Caroline (Cragin) Fisher. Had two children: Grace N. Fisher (8), b. 7 July, 1881, and Guy C. Fisher (8), b. 27 May, 1885, d. in infancy.

Mrs. Fisher says, "My grandfather and grandmother were cousins, my father and mother were cousins, and I am third cousin to myself—that is as far as my genealogy reaches."

I am told that Wm. Wallace Lobdell d. not long since in an asylum for the blind in California.

CHILDREN AND DESCENDANTS OF GEORGE ANSON (6) AND ALMIRA AUSTIN (PRESTON) LOBDELL. ALL BORN IN VICTOR, N. Y.

1. Maria Louise 2. DeWitt Clinton   3. Emeline Minerva.
4. Hannah Almira   5 Charles Wesley.

I. Maria Louise, b. 14 Feb, 1825, d 5 Sept., 1895, at Sioux City, Woodbury Co., Iowa, m. for first husband, Wm. Hinman. No children. M. for second husband, on 12 June, 1861, at Granville, Putnam Co., Ill., Claudius B. French, b. 15 Oct., 1817, at Hanover, Dauphin Co., Pa, son of John and Mary —— (?) French. Had one child, Claudius B French, Jr (8), b 17 Oct, 1862; m. Flora Minerva Skeel and resides at 1407 Summit Ave, Sioux City, Iowa.

II DeWitt Clinton, b 11 Aug, 1826; d. in infancy

III. Emeline Minerva, b. 22 June, 1829; d 14 April, 1847.

IV Hannah Almira, b 6 Nov., 1831, d 11 July, 1879, at Oberlin, Ohio; m 28 Nov, 1849, at Granville, Ill, to David P Jenkins, b 25 Aug., 1823, at Mt. Pleasant, Jefferson Co., Ohio, son of Israel and Elizabeth (Horsman) Jenkins

CHILDREN.

1 Annie M. Jenkins (8). b. 6 Jan.. 1851; d 28 Sept., 1858.

2 George M Jenkins (8), b. 22 Jan, 1853; m Mary A. McCarthy Resides at 1830 St. Lawrence Ave, Chicago, Ill.

3 Emma Frances Jenkins (8), residing at 1206 Broadway, Spokane, Wash, was b. 26 June, 1857, at La Salle, Ill.; m. 16 May, 1883, at Spokane, Wash., Wm Howard Rue, b. 13 Aug., 1854, at Englishtown, Monmouth Co, N. J., son of Lewis and —— (?) Baker Rue Children:

1. Annie Jenkins Rue (9). b 9 May, 1884.

2. Mabel Rue (9), b. 19 Aug., 1886.

V. Charles Wesley, b. 27 Feb, 1834; m 19 March, 1854, at Granville, Putnam Co, Ill., Eliza J Gere, b 2 Dec., 1834, at Northampton, Mass., d. 30 June, 1862, at Moline, Ill., leaving a young

CHARLES WESLEY LOBDELL [7]
(George Anson [6])   (1834-1906)
of Chicago, Ill.

son, Edwin Lyman (8). Mrs. L. was dau. of Frederick and Ruth S. (Warner) Gere.

Mr. Lobdell m. for his second wife, at Moline, Ill., on 22 Oct., 1864, Henrietta M Shaw, b. 12 Dec., 1840, at Canandaigua, Ontario Co., N. Y., dau. of Jacob and Marcia (Brown) Shaw.

I copy from one of his "old home papers" the following, which will be of interest to all who know or have heard of the courteous gentleman:

"Charles Wesley Lobdell, for years a prominent merchant in Moline, Ill., was cashier of the Moline National and Moline Savings Banks for seven years. Was secretary and director of the Moline Plow Company several years. Was president of the Moline Gas Light Company for ten years. Born in Victor, Ontario Co, New York, Feb., 27, 1834.

His father, George A. Lobdell, a farmer, was a native of the same town, his grandfather, Jacob Lobdell (second), having settled there in 1788. His mother, before marriage, was Almira Austin Preston, a native of Farmington, N. Y.

In 1848 the family migrated to Granville, Putnam Co, Ill, where the subject of this sketch received an academical education at Granville Academy and where he was fitted to enter college. Instead, however, of continuing his classical studies, he took up legal, reading law at Cleveland, Ohio. He was admitted to practice in Ohio and Illinois in 1858, and went to Mankato, Minn, and opened a law office, and in 1860 returned to Illinois and settled in Moline, where he started a dry goods store and was a successful trader until 1875, when he closed out the business. He was alderman for two terms, and connected at one time as a member of the Board of Education.

During a residence of twenty-nine years in Moline he was a public-spirited, thorough-going business man, taking pride with other local capitalists in pushing forward and developing the interests of the city. His politics are Republican, and his religious connections with the Reformed Episcopal Church.

He was first married March 19, 1854, to Eliza J Gere of Granville. She died June 30, 1862, leaving a son and an infant daughter, the latter soon following her; and the second marriage, Oct. 22, 1864, to Henrietta M. Shaw, daughter of the late Jacob Shaw of Moline, having by her two daughters, Mrs. Frances Lobdell Brown and Mrs. Marion Lobdell Bradford, both of Chicago."

153

Mr. Lobdell became a resident of Chicago in 1882. Retired from business and resided with his wife at 3861 Lake Ave.

On the morning of 1 Sept., 1906, at 5 o'clock, this good man passed away.

For over a year he had failed in health, and, hoping for added strength and vitality, he rented for the summer a cottage at Mackatawa Park, on the shore of Lake Michigan. Here he seemed to rally, and often expressed himself as happy to be surrounded by his wife, his daughters and their children, all so thoroughly enjoying themselves. On Saturday 26 Aug., Mr. L. was taken suddenly ill (his stomach refused to accept any nourishment), and his physician was at once telegraphed for, who advised immediate removal home, where he lingered until released from suffering

> "And his lifeless body, lay
> A worn-out fetter, that the soul
> Had broken and thrown away."

He is buried at Moline, Ill. beside his loved ones gone before, "and with the sanctified love of his ever-generous and thoughtful spirit, he yearns to bring the loved ones left, to the world and life where partings are unknown."

Let us all cherish the memory of Charles Wesley Lobdell, for no person was ever more loyal to his family name. It is to me a cause of deep regret that this genealogy could not have been enjoyed by him, for the work was near to his heart and eagerly waited for.

CHILDREN AND GRANDCHILDREN OF CHARLES WESLEY LOBDELL (7).
CHILDREN.

---

1. Edwin Lyman 2. Lillie. 3. Frances Eliza. 4. Marion Emma

By (1) Wife, Eliza J. (Gere) Lobdell.

I. Edwin L. (8) Lobdell was b. in Granville, Putnam Co., Ill., 14 July, 1857. His boyhood was spent at Moline, Ill., where his family settled prior to 1860. He was educated in the public schools of Moline

In 1874, at the age of seventeen years, he commenced his business career in Chicago as clerk in the First National Bank of that

EDWIN LYMAN LORDELL (8)

city, Lyman J Gage, then cashier of that bank, and more recently secretary of the treasury of the United States, under President Mc-Kinley, being his first employer

His progress in the bank was rapid and he served successively as receiving and paying teller until 1881, when he started the firm of Edwin L Lobdell & Company, Bankers and Brokers

His firm, with some changes in its personnel from time to time, has been in active business in Chicago continuously since that date.

He was married in 1883 to Miss Annie Philpot, daughter of Brian Philpot, a leading citizen of Chicago for many years.

His children are Charles W (9), a graduate of Yale College, class of 1905, S ; Adeline (9), a graduate of Mount Vernon Seminary, Washington, D C, class of 1906; and Edith (9), now a pupil in the Northampton School for Girls, Northampton, Mass.

He is a member of the Union League Club, Chicago Athletic Association, Exmoor Country Club, Midlothian Country Club, Twentieth Century Club, Coleman Lake (fishing) Club.

His energy and perseverance are the two characteristics which have contributed most largely to his successful business career.

II Lillie, d in infancy.

Children by (2) Wife, Henrietta (Shaw) Lobdell.

I Frances Eliza (8), b 3 July, 1866, at Moline, Rock Island Co, Ill, m 16 Oct, 1888, at Moline, Robert Patterson Brown, b 6 Nov., 1859, at Chicago, Ill, son of Andrew Jesse and Abby Louise (McCagg) Brown Children.

    1. Robert McCagg Brown (9), b 4 Feb, 1891 Is (1907) a high school graduate of Chicago

    2. Arline Henrietta Brown, a student (1907) of Chicago University (preparatory)

II. Marion Emma, b 26 July, 1869, at Moline, m 12 Feb, 1895, at Chicago, Josiah Bradford, b 29 Nov, 1858, at Romulus, N. Y. (son of Theron and Mary Elizabeth (Draper) Bradford of Syracuse, N. Y.) They have two sons (both b at Chicago), viz: Wm. Josiah Bradford (9), b 26 Oct., 1899, and Charles Lobdell Bradford (9), b 21 April, 1907 (the youngest representative in the Lobdell Genealogy) These sons are lineal descendants of Gov. Wm. Bradford of Massachusetts, who was one of the 'Mayflower" passengers, 1620

SIXTH GENERATION.

CHILDREN AND DESCENDANTS OF JOHN (5) AND EMMA HOYSINGTON LOBDELL. ALL BORN AT WESTPORT, ESSEX CO., N. Y.

CHILDREN.

1. Erastus. 2 Levi 3 James 4. Jacob 5 Nancy 6 Caroline. 7 Rosamond 8. Jerome Theron.

I. Erastus, now living at Elizabethtown, Essex Co., N. Y., b 12 Sept, 1816; m 12 June, 1853, at Essex Co, N. Y, Mary A Nichols, dau of Roland and Betsey (Durand) Nichols Children

      1 Wm H (7), b at Elizabethtown m Viola Hodgkins
      2 Jenny (7), b at Elizabethtown, m. Moses Smith.
      3. Edward J. (7), b at Elizabethtown; m Belle Hodgkins
      4 Ella (7), b at Elizabethtown, m. Albert Emnott

II. Levi, a carpenter and millwright. b 6 June, 1818, d 12 May. 1896, at Delhi, Iowa ; m 11 Nov., 1845, at Addison, Vt , Jane Goodale, b 21 Oct , 1818, at Addison, Vt., d Sept., 1893, at Dubuque, Iowa, dau of Jared and Patience (Sumner) Goodale of Vermont.

CHILDREN.

1. Amelia J. 2 Rosatha A 3 Levi Jerome 4 John C 5. Jared Charles 6 John William 7. living

      1 Amelia J (7), living at Delhi, Delaware Co., Iowa, was b 9 Dec., 1846, at Westport, Essex Co, N Y ; m. 19 Oct, 1887, at Dubuque, Iowa, Edwin H King, b 30 Aug, 1845, at Clayton, Iowa, son of James and Maryetta Bartlett King of Canada Has one dau (8) m and living in Buchanan Co., Iowa

      2 Rosatha A (7), residing at Minneapolis Minn , b 22 Nov., 1848 at Elizabethtown, N Y., m. in Dubuque, Iowa, 12 Sept , 1876, Henry C Ehrlick, b at Youngstown, Ohio, son of Fredrick and Katherine (Fair) Ehrlick of Elkader, Iowa Has two daughters:

156

FATHER AND GRANDSONS OF CHARLES WESLEY LOBDELL (DECEASED) OF CHICAGO

Geo. Anson Lobdell (6)
(Jacob, Jr. [5])   (1794-1870)
of Victor, N. Y., and Moline, Ill.
(Page 148)

Charles W. Lobdell (9)
(Edwin L. [8])
of Chicago, Ill.
(Page 155)

Robert McCagg Brown (9)
(Frances E. [8])
of Chicago, Ill.

Wm. Josiah Bradford (9)
(Marion E. [8])
of Chicago, Ill.

1. Florence A. Ehrlick (8), b. at Minnesota City, 25 Sept., 1879

2. Josephine Mae Ehrlick (8), b at Elkader, Iowa, 8 Nov, 1883

3. Levi Jerome (7), living at Dubuque, Iowa, b 9 June, 1852, at Canton, St Lawrence Co, N. Y ; m at Dubuque, Iowa, 31 Aug, 1876, Lilian C Hickock, b 8 May, 1858, at Dubuque, Iowa, dau. of Sylvester and Frances (Terry) Hickock of Dubuque. Mr Lobdell is a machine woodworker, a Republican, and a member of the Congregational Church.

Children of Levi Jerome (7) and Lilian (Hickock) Lobdell, all born in Dubuque.

1. Charles Elmer (8), b. 13 July, 1877; d. 22 Sept., 1898, at Jacksonville, Fla

2 Willard LeRoy (8), b. 9 July, 1879

3. Harry Allen (8), b. 4 July, 1881.

4. James Edward (8), b 3 Feb., 1884.

5 Jerome Orville (8), b. 18 Feb, 1887; d. 1 Sept, 1891.

6 Leonard Irving (8), b. 11 May, 1889

7. Francis (8). b. 18 Jan, 1892; d. 11 Feb, 1892.

8. Jerome Leslie (8), b 7 April, 1895

9 Lillian Frances Jane (8), b 3 March, 1899

4. John C. (7), b. 7 Nov., 1853, d. in childhood.

5. Jared Charles (7), a brass worker, living at Minneapolis, Minn, b. 22 June, 1856, at McGregor, Clayton Co., Iowa; m. at Dubuque 31 Oct., 1878, Elvira A. Hodge, b 9 Nov., 1860, at Eau Clair, Wis., dau of Fredric O. and Sarah (Werner) Hodge Mr. Lobdell is a Baptist in Religion. In politics, a Republican. Children:

1. Henry James (8), b. 30 March, 1880.

2 John Fred'k (8), b. 18 Oct., 1882; d 3 July, 1883.

3 Judson Charles (8), b 5 May, 1891, d. in infancy.

6 John W (7), b 12 Jan, 1860; m Matilda Kaufmann.

7 Irving (7), a clerk, living at Dubuque, Iowa, was b. 26 Oct., 1863, at McGregor, Clayton Co, Iowa; m. at Dubuque 28 Aug., 1889, Mae Nuss, b 24 Feb, 1869, at Sauk City, Wis., dau of Henry and Marie (Helm) Nuss of Sauk

City. Mr. Lobdell is a Republican in politics. Has one son, Earl Leslie (8), b 6 Oct., 1892, at Dubuque.

III. James, b. 27 Oct., 1820, d 19 April, 1896, at Pleasant Valley, Scott Co., Iowa; m. Jane Knapp, who d May, 1874, at Saranac Lake, N. Y. Mr. Lobdell was in religion a Methodist, in politics, a Republican, and by occupation, a blacksmith

Children of James (6) and Jane (Knapp) Lobdell.

1 Nellie E (7), deceased; m Dr H Roberts.

2. Myria A. (7), m John Little of Port Henry, N. Y.

3. John Ambrose (7), the only one of the children of James (6) and Jane Knapp Lobdell of whom I have obtained record, was b. 17 June, 1848, at Elizabethtown, N Y, d. 21 July, 1894, at Westport, N. Y., m. 20 Jan., 1875, at Elizabethtown. Alma A Bull, b 8 July, 1847, at Westport, N. Y., dau. of Ephraim J. Bull and Mary N. Green Children:

1. Pearl A (8), b. 30 April, 1876

2 Nellie R (8), b 26 Aug., 1879

3 Mary E (8), b 4 March, 1882, at Westport, is a successful teacher at Wadham's Mills, Essex Co, N. Y.

4 Harley A (8), b 20 Nov., 1885.

5 Charles A (8), b. 22 March, 1888

4 Charles W. (7), m. Mary Clemons

5. Herbert (7) of Saranac Lake, m. Mary Peck

6 Emma (7), deceased

7 Ernest (7) of South Dakota, m. Myria Sawyer

8. Elmer (7) of Saranac Lake, m. Carrie Wood

IV Jacob, b 18 Feb., 1823, d 18 Jan., 1894

V. Nancy, b 8 Aug., 1826; m Julius Vaughan. Had one son. John Lobdell Vaughn; not knowing his residence.

VI Caroline, b 12 Sept., 1828; m Calvin Pratt, one dau., Mrs Emma Simonds, not knowing residence.

VII Rosamond, b 6 Feb. 1833: unmarried, resides at Elizabethtown, N Y

VIII Jerome Theron, b 19 Feb., 1835, at Westport, N Y; m 19 Jan. 1861, at Lewis, Essex Co, N Y, Helen Deyoe, b 5 Dec., 1838, at Elizabethtown, dau of Jacob and Mary (Woodruff) Deyoe. Mr. Lobdell is a Universalist in religion, a Republican in politics Is now (1902) living at Elizabethtown, N Y on the same farm on which he has lived since 1 April, 1848, and where, he says, he will stay until called to his home beyond. He has never held public office, from choice preferring to lead a more quiet life, but in the community no man is more respected for genuine, sterling worth than Mr. Lobdell

SEVENTH GENERATION.

CHILDREN OF JEROME (6) THERON AND HELEN (DEYOE) LOBDELL

1. Mary Emma 2 Lewis Levi 3 John Erastus 4 Edith A. 5. Clifford 6 Harry

I Mary Emma, b. 25 March, 1862; d. 17 April, 1862.

II Louis Levi, living at Saranac Lake, Franklin Co., N. Y., b. 19 Nov., 1863, m 6 Sept. 1896, at Plattsburg, Clinton Co, N. Y. Catherine Mihills, b at Wilmington, Essex Co., N Y. (dau. of Sylvester and Sarah (Hazelton) Mihills of Saranac Lake). No children

III John Erastus, living at Elizabethtown, Essex Co, N Y., was b 24 April, 1866; m 18 Dec, 1889, at Elizabethtown, Lena A. Lewis, b 25 Oct., 1866, at Elizabethtown, dau. of Alva M and Anna (Southmaid) Lewis of Jay, Essex Co, N Y.

CHILDREN.

1. Walter R (8) 2. Anna H (8) 3 Mabel E (8)

4. Rosamond (8). 5. Kittie (8)

IV. Edith A, b 6 Feb., 1870, m. 10 July. 1901, at Elizabethtown, Frank Vaughn

V. Clifford, b 15 Jan. 1874; m 4 Nov., 1896, at Elizabethtown, Rose Mary Lewis, dau. of Alva M and Mary (McKay) Lewis of Elizabethtown. No children

VI Harry, b 20 March, 1881.

The family of Daniel (4) and Elizabeth (Lockwood) Lobdell lived at Cortland Manor, Salem, Westchester Co., N Y., on a farm adjoining his brother Ebenezer's and west of his brother John's. We have no record if his departure from his Salem home, but it was after 1766—31 Aug.—at which date his son Joseph was baptized. Daniel with his family migrated to what was called "The Royal Grant"—New York state.

Sims' History Schoharie Co. and border wars of New York tells us:

"The Royal Grant contained nearly 100,000 acres of choice land, mostly situated in the County of Herkimer, was formerly the property of Sir Wm. Johnson, granted 1761, the title to this land being confirmed by the British government, hence called "The Royal Grant."

Daniel Lobdell settled in a place called Salisbury, which was peopled before the Revolution by persons friendly to the Crown. That they suffered privations in the new country, such privations as we of the present day cannot even realize, is beyond doubt.

From Revolutionary records, Vol. 16 of manuscript, entitled "Assembly papers." I find the following:

"Montgomery County, N. Y.

This may certifie that Daniel Lobdell of Palentine Town in the County aforesaid did belong to Capt. John Cuizer's Company of Militia in my Ridgment in the year of our Lord one thousand Seven Hundred and Eighty, and was so fare in actual service as to be held ready for service at a minute's warning, and being at home at his own house in the Royal grant on the third day of April in the year aforesaid was taken prisoner by a party of Indians, himself and three sons, one of abought sixteen years of age, the other two younger, and carried prisoners to Canady and theire cept three years and a half, stript of his property sutch as they could carry away, and left his wife with the remaining part of his children in distressed surcomstances

February 12th, 1793   Jacob Klock,
John Keyser.   Led Corl."

As Herkimer Co. was not organized till 1791, when it was taken from Montgomery Co., so that Daniel served in a militia organization of the later county.

Daniel must have returned to Salem after the war, as on 23 Feb., 1799, he was one of the witnesses of his brother Ebenezer's will

FIFTH GENERATION.

CHILDREN OF DANIEL (4) AND ELIZABETH (LOCK-WOOD) LOBDELL.

1 Daniel 2 Joseph. 3. Zadock 4. Isaac. 5 A dau 6 A dau. 7 Samuel.

I. Daniel, bapt. at Salem, N Y., by Rev. Dr. Diblee, 25 Aug., 1765. All that I have been able to find of Daniel after moving to Herkimer Co is kindly given me by Judge Geo. W. Smith of Herkimer, who found the following memoranda among his father's papers:

"April 3rd, 1826

Daniel Lobdell began work with me, Samuel Smith (2nd), for the term of two years, for the sum of two hundred and fifty dollars, together with the privilege of mending his own family's shoes and for the purpose of learning the tanning and currying and shoemaking business."

Also—

Margaret Lobdell, Cr., by 8 lb., 1 oz calfskin, 0.81 Dr. to balance our account, 0.12½; to 1 pr morocco shoes, 1 50

Also—

From an old account book, April 3rd, 1827. Cr by his labor: one hundred dollars to balance in full of all over work account up to this date.

April 19th.   Samuel Smith, 2nd.
                                         Daniel Lobdell."

II Joseph L. was bapt. at Salem, N. Y., 31 Aug, 1766, by Dr. Deblee. With his father's family he moved to Herkimer Co N. Y. Revolutionary records at Washington, D. C, give

"Joseph Lobdell, a soldier in the Revolutionary war, a private m Capt John Keyser's Co., Col Klock's Reg't, enlisted at Little Falls, Herkimer Co., N. Y.; says he was taken prisoner in March or April, 1777, by Tories and Indians, at a place called Yankee Bush, seven miles north of Little Falls, was taken to Canada and kept until the war closed."

He probably returned to Westchester and Albany counties where many of his relations lived, and I think entered the army where many of his relations lived. He m. Dorcas Holcomb, b. in Simsbury, Conn., 25 May, 1766, dau. of Josiah and Dorcas (Smith) Holcomb. Her parents moved to Nassua, Rensselaer Co., N. Y., and while here Joseph was drowned—the sad accident occurring five months before the birth of his only child Joseph Lobdell Jr.

His widow re-married at Nassua to Mr. Clark, by whom she had two children—Cynthia and Lewis Clark. Mr. Clark d. and Dorcas m. for her third husband. Jesse Stuart, living at Scipio. Cayuga Co., N. Y., a native of Vermont, by whom she had three children—Orsemus Stuart, Polly Stuart and Francillo Stuart, who m. Lucinda Davis, a sister of the wife of Joseph Lobdell Jr.

Dorcas d. 1848, aged 82, at the home of Francillo Stuart, Springwater, Livingston Co., N. Y.

III. Zadock. Revolutionary records say that he was about eleven years old when captured by Indians with his father and brothers, in 1777; say that he was sold by Indians to a British officer and kept by him for seven years. His name is found in the account book of Samuel Smith, second, of Herkimer—as a farmer—and exchanging his farm products with Mr. Smith. This was in the year 1827. He m. Miss Castler and had children; moved to Theresa, Jefferson Co., N. Y., where he d. at the home of his son-in-law, John Boyer, and is buried in the village grave yard.

IV. Isaac of whom I can find no trace.

V and VI are daughters of whom I could gather no information only as given in the letter of Mr. John Little Lobdell, page 341, that one m. Mr. Lounsberry, the other Mr. Rundell

VII Samuel, the youngest, was with his sisters left with the mother when his father and brothers were taken captives by the Indians, he being too young to walk. He was probably born at Salisbury, Herkimer Co., where he m. Lois Greenfield. There were their children born and there they lived until about 1834, when they went to live with their oldest son, Lockwood Lobdell, who had made for himself a comfortable home in Cherry Valley, Ashta-

162

bula Co, Ohio Samuel had been an invalid for years, having suffered from what was called "a stroke of palsy," and one day in the summer of 1836 he was found in the cornfield, where he had feebly gone to try to work, prostrated by another shock, from which he soon after died His widow survived until 1868

SIXTH GENERATION.

CHILD OF JOSEPH, SR., AND DORCAS (HOLCOMB) LOBDELL

I Joseph, Jr, b 1788, probably in Nassua, Rensselaer Co N Y, m Sarah Cordelia Davis, and resided in Ontario Co, N Y, until five of their children were born, then removed to Lower Sandusky, Ohio, where both died, he in 1843, she in 1844 Was a farmer

The parents of Sarah Cordelia Davis were David Davis and his wife, Renewa ——— (?) (Can any one send to me her maiden name?)

Sarah Cordelia's sister, Lucinda Davis, b 1810, m. Francello Stuart, a half-brother of Joseph Lobdell, Jr

SEVENTH GENERATION.

CHILDREN OF JOSEPH, JR., AND SARAH CORDELIA (DAVIS) LOBDELL.

1, 2, 3, 4, 5, b near Richmond, Ontario Co, N Y

1 Sarah Cordelia 2 Orren Seth 3 Eretus Davis 4 Philetus 5 Joseph Judson 6 David 7 Elizabeth Ann

I Sarah Cordelia m James Battles, by whom she had one dau, Emma, now living (1905), but I greatly regret having mislaid the record sent me by Mr Battles, who resides at North Fields Farm, Mass

Sarah Cordelia d in 1856, is buried in Michigan City, Ind

II Orren Seth, b in Ontario Co, N Y., 23 Oct, 1818, d. near Barcley, Sangamon Co, Ill, 20 March, 1865, m at Groton, Erie Co, Ohio, 1 July, 1842, Elizabeth M Crippen, b. 3 Dec, 1820, at

163

Oxford, Huron Co , Ohio, d. at Calumet, Ind , 1854, dau. of Stephen Crippen—his second wife was Nancy Caryl.

Mr. Lobdell was a blacksmith; Republican, Methodist. Had resided in Ohio, Indiana, Minnesota and Illinois.

Orren Seth Lobdell enlisted in 1st Ill. Cavalry, Sangamon Co , 1861; served one year, when the regiment disbanded. In 1862 he served as cook six months at Bird's Point. In fall of 1862 he enlisted in Company C, Vaughn's Battery, Springfield Light Artillery, served until 20 Feb . 1865, returned home and d. 20 March, 1865. just one month after reaching home.

III. Eretus Davis, b 1821, near Richmond, Ontario Co , N. Y., d. in 1855, at St. Charles, Minn., m. 1843. at Sandusky, Ohio, Emily Crippen, b. 18 Feb . 1823, at Pipe Creek, Ohio, d. 6 March, 1881, at Spring Valley. Minn., dau of Stephen Crippen and wife, Laura Harrington. Mr Lobdell was a Democrat; in religion, Universalist.

IV Philetus, b 20 June, 1825, d. 30 Jan., 1863. at Monroeville, Huron Co . Ohio . m for his first wife. Mary Ann Olmstead, by whom he had one dau. He m. for second wife, on 28 Oct., 1852, Margaret Duncan, b 2 Aug., 1830, d. 5 Feb., 1899 Mr. Lobdell enlisted in the U S. service in War of the Rebellion and was killed while on his way to be mustered into the service.

V. Joseph Judson, b. 22 Feb., 1830; m. 28 Oct., 1853, at Chicago, Ill., Elizabeth Maria Napier, b 5 Dec., 1833. at Blissfield, Monroe Co.. Mich., dau. of Wm. and Ruth Hoag Napier, d. at Chicago at the home of her dau , Dr. Effie Lobdell, 10 Dec , 1904 Interment at Green Bay, Wis , at which place Joseph Judson Lobdell also d 5 May, 1886 He was a lake pilot and captain; a Whig Universalist in religion

Has three daughters. viz

1. Addie Cordelia (8), b. 21 April, 1857, m. Wm. H. Marvin

2. Jennie Belle (8), b 24 Aug, 1865; m. Roscoe Elroy McCann

3 Effie Leola (8), b 1 Jan., 1867, at Washington Island, Wis , educated at Green Bay, Wis, until 1886 Graduated from Ft Wayne (Indiana) College of Medicine (now the Medical Dept of Purdue University) in 1891 Immediately came to Chicago and began practice of medicine

ERETUS DAVIS LOBDEL] (7) AND WIFE
(Joseph Jr. [6])   (1821-1855)
of Spring Valley, Minn.
(Page 164)

ORREN SETH LOBDELL (7)
(Joseph [6])   (1818-1865)
of Sangamon County, Ill.
(Page 163)

PHILETUS LOBDELL (7)
(Joseph [6])   (1825-1863)
of Fremont, Ohio
(Page 164)

CAPT. JOS. JUDSON LOBDELL (7)
(Joseph [6])   (1830-1886)
of Green Bay, Wis.
(Page 163)

In 1893 was appointed by Gov. John P. Altgeld to medical staff of Eastern Illinois Hospital for Insane at Kankakee, Ill, being first woman physician so appointed. In 1895 was appointed Obstetrician to the staff of Mary Thompson Hospital for Women and Children in Chicago, which position she held until 1902 In 1901 was appointed as attending physician on staff of Cook County Hospital by Board of Cook County Commissioners and re-appointed to the same position 1903 This was the first appointment of a woman to this position Was surgeon to Frances Willard Hospital, Florence Crittenton Anchorage, and Supt of Harvey Hospital for several years. With Dr. Frances Dickinson established Harvey Medical College, the first night school of medicine in Chicago At present devotes herself to private practice of surgery in Chicago Office, Marshall Field Building

From the Wisconsin State Gazette

"The death of Capt. Lobdell made a break in the ranks of the older lake navigators, and was a passage to the other shores of one whose presence will be missed by many old comrades Joseph Judson Lobdell was born Feb 22, 1830, in Ontario Co, N Y. His family moved into Ohio when he was seven years of age and resided in and near Sandusky At the age of fourteen he was bereft of both parents, his father and mother dying within a year of each other. As a boy he engaged in sailing and sailed for some four or five years out of Sandusky, on Lake Erie. In the spring of 1850 he went to the straits of Mackinac and was one of the first settlers of Pine River, Michigan, now called Charlevoix In the summer of 1853 he went to Detroit Harbor. In the same fall he was married to Elizabeth M Napier Subsequent to this he went with his brother, David Lobdell, to Beaver Island, and at the time of the Mormon excitement there, when the prophet Strang was killed, in 1856, he was keeping the lighthouse at the head of the Beavers. It became unpleasant for him, as for all gentiles there, in the unsettled period there that succeeded the tragedy, and he left the island. He afterward took part in the raid of the gentiles there, when the Mormons were driven from the island He then settled on Washington Island, where he remained eighteen years, being engaged in the fishing business with Wm. Craw for fourteen years, and with Wm. P. Ranney four years. He then removed to Green Bay, where he continued to reside until his death. Capt. Lobdell ran a schooner on Lake Superior one season. He was with Capt. Gaylord one season on the old propeller Rocket, and later one season on the Canisteo. After coming to Green Bay he followed sailing most of the time, being with Hagen & English several years as master of the steam barge Minnie. He was a good sailor and was well acquainted along the entire chain of lakes, having pilot's papers accordingly.

Captain Lobdell's widow and three daughters survive, namely Mrs. W. H. Marvin of Green Bay, Miss Jennie Lobdell of Michigan and Effie L. Lobdell of Green Bay.

The deceased was a man of friendly and social qualities, one who bore the reputation of being honest and who had many staunch friends. Like all men who follow the water and are compelled to exercise and cultivate judgment—to act quickly in responsible situations, and who have the quality of observation sharpened, he was a man of good practical ideas and one to be trusted with great responsibility. A fondness for reading kept him posted on all current events. The sickness that preceded his death was a long and painful one, but through it all he preserved hope and exhibited great tenacity of purpose that almost seemed to keep death remote. During his sickness he was held in kindly remembrance by many friends. The family have much sympathy in the bereavement that takes away its head."

VI. David Davis, a farmer. b. 4 Nov., 1830, d. 30 Nov., 1897, at Alexandria, La., m. 15 Oct., 1862, Eliza A. Holcomb. b. at Fremont Sandusky Co., Ohio, dau of Thomas Holcomb (b. in Granby, Conn.) and Agnes Leforce, his wife. b. in Normandy, France.

Mrs. Lobdell for the past three years has been with her sister, Mrs. Gillette, at Lansing, Mich. I have greatly valued her correspondence. She is really a mine of reliable, valuable information. She tells me that the sons of Joseph were all tall, Eretus looked like his father.

They had five children. Two boys and two girls died in infancy. A dau., Harriet (8), grew to womanhood, a woman of character and education. I am told by several descendants that she was a

166

MR. AND MRS. MICHAEL OBERST
of Fremont, Ohio
SARAH LUCINDA (8)
(Philetus [7])
(Page 169)

STEPHEN C. LOBDELL (8)
(Eretus D. [7])
of Spring Valley, Minn.
(Page 168)

DR. EFFIE LOBDELL (8)
(Capt. Joseph Judson [7])
of Chicago, Ill.
(Page 164)

WILFORD NORRIS LOB-
DELL (8)
(Orren Seth [7])
of Rochester, Ill.
(Page 166)

ORREN R. LOBDELL (8)
(Orrin S. [6])
of Belle Plain, Kansas
(Page 167)

particularly charming person She was b in Green Bay, Wis , d
of malarial fever at Alexandria, La., 22 June, 1897 Was educated
at Chicago, Ill , and Nashville, Tenn ; then sent to St Louis, where
she finished her musical education

VII Elizabeth Ann, b 15 July, 1839, at Groton, Huron Co ,
Ohio, m at Valparaiso, Ind , 25 Sept., 1856, by Rev. J. C Brown,
James Anderson Walton, a farmer, b 17 Jan , 1834, in Ohio, d at
Benton Harbor, Mich., son of John and Nancy Blake Walton.
James and Elizabeth after marriage moved to Lake Station, Ind ,
afterward coming to Benton Harbor, Berrion Co , Mich , where
Mr. Walton died in 1890 Mrs. W is, with all her children, living
at Benton Harbor

EIGHTH GENERATION.

CHILDREN OF ORREN SETH (7) AND ELIZABETH MINERVA (CRIPPEN) LOBDELL.

1 Huldah   2. Charles   3 Orren R

I   Huldah R , b 5 March, 1843
II   Charles S , b 16 March, 1845

III. Orren R , a blacksmith, residing at Belle Plaine, Kansas,
b 2 May, 1848, m 3 July, 1871, for his first wife—at Springfield,
Ill.—Ida Freeman; m second and third time, but I am unable to
give maiden name of wives Mr. Lobdell is a Grand Army man,
having served in same Co. as his father during the "War of the
Rebellion " Is a Republican, and Protestant Formerly resided
in Barcley, Ill.

O R. Lobdell left Ohio with his parents in 1853, went to Indiana, where they stayed until 1855, went to Minnesota, and in
1858 moved to Illinois. He started out for himself in 1882, choos-
ing Kansas as his destination, at that time on the boom. Was
successful, but in 1890 lost his wife and met with severe pecuniary
losses, but stayed by Kansas with its hot winds and cyclones and
other ups and downs until he recovered all he had lost in property;
then traveled over Missouri, Arkansas, Nebraska and Indian Territory, but liked Kansas the best, and returned and will probably
end his days there.

IV. Stephen C , b. 8 Nov , 1851

167

V. Wilford Norris, a farmer, b. 2 May, 1853, at Monroeville, Huron Co., Ohio, resides at Rochester, Sangamon Co., Ill., since 1858; m. 4 Dec., 1878, Mary Minerva Garretson, b. 9 Sept., 1860, at Rochester, Ill., dau. of Samuel and Amelia Jane (Dickerson) Garretson. In religion, Protestant. Prohibition in politics.

VI Mary A., b 8 Nov., 1858.

VII. Ida M., b. 18 May, 1860.

VIII. Anna M., b 16 Oct., 1861.

CHILDREN OF ERETUS D. (?) AND EMILY (CRIPPEN) LOBDELL.

I Stephen C., b 6 June, 1844, at Sandusky City, Ohio, m. 8 Sept., 1865, at Wabasha, Wabasha Co., Minn., Josephine E. Farman, b. 23 Sept., 1844, in England. Mr. Lobdell was a resident of Monroeville, Ohio, 16 years; St. Charles, Minn., three years; Wabasha, Minn., three years, was in U S service, Civil War, two and a half years, and has been a resident of Spring Valley, Minn., nearly 40 years. Is a hardware merchant; belongs to the Republican party, and is a Liberalist in religion.

Stephen C Lobdell enlisted 18 April, 1861, for three months in 24th Ohio Volunteer Infantry, re-enlisted for three years, or during the war, in same company, mustered at Camp Chose, Ohio. Went to the front with 23rd, 24th, 25th and 26th O. V. I regiments, Aug., 1861. Was a comrade and friend of the late Wm. McKinley, 23rd O. V. I. Regiment followed line of march into Western Virginia, to Clarksburg, thence to Cheat Mountain, where they had several engagements. Left at Clarksburg on account of sickness; followed regiment in the fall of 1861 and was in the engagement at Gaully river against rebel General Floyd. Marched through Kentucky and was in the battle of Shiloh, where, on the third and last day of the fight, was wounded in right leg; was sent back to Cincinnati, O., and from there "home, to die." Arrived in Monroeville, Huron Co., Ohio, unconscious; rallied and went to Columbus, Ohio, and enlisted in the 88th O. V. I., to drive John Morgan out of Kentucky. Returned to Columbus and was mustered out after 27 months' service.

II. Laura Crippen, b —— (?); m John Henry Davis. Resides at Dover, Minn.

III Xachary Taylor Lobdell d in childhood.

EIGHTH GENERATION.

CHILDREN OF PHILETUS (7) LOBDELL AND FIRST AND SECOND WIVES.

1. Mary. 2 Francello Stuart 3 Sarah Lucinda 4 Eliza Jane. 5. Orren. 6. Hannah Furgeson 7 Harriet Anstress.

By First Wife, Mary Ann Olmstead.

I Mary, b —— (?); m (1) John Allen, (2) John Rowlins. No answer to my letter of inquiry

By Second Wife, Margaret Duncan.

II Francello Stuart, b. 28 June, 1853; unmarried, a farmer, residing near Fremont, Ohio

III Sarah Lucinda, b 18 July, 1854, at Fremont, Sandusky County, Ohio, at which place she was m , her children were born, and where (I am told) they have a lovely country home, m on 27 Nov., 1873, to Michael Oberst, a prosperous farmer, also b same place. 8 Dec., 1848, son of Michael and Anna Mohler Oberst.

I am greatly indebted to Mrs. Oberst for assistance in making clear the line of Joseph Lobdell

IV. Eliza Jane, b 16 April, 1856, at Fremont, Ohio, m 8 Sept, 1874, Silas George, a carpenter b 18 Nov., 1843, at Clyde, Sandusky Co Ohio, son of Silas and Eliza Grover George The residence of Silas George, Jr, is at Millbury Wood Co., Ohio. Is a Democrat. They have no children In religion, a Methodist.

V. Orren S, b 18 May, 1858, d. 2 April, 1860.

VI Hannah Furgeson, b 30 Sept, 1860, at Fremont, Ohio, where she m. 14 March, 1882, Stillman George, b 2 Dec., 1846, at Fremont, son of Silas and Eliza (Grover) George. Reside at Rothbury, Mich.

CHILDREN.

1 Carl George (9), b. 17 Oct, 1883.
2 Elmer M George (9), b 6 Sept., 1887.
3. Howard George (9), b. 22 May, 1894

VII. Harriet Anstress, b 2 Dec., 1862, at Fremont, Ohio, m. 4 Nov., 1883, at Fremont, Walter Whited, a farmer, b. 11 Feb, 1887, at Deer Park, Orange Co, N. Y., son of Charac and Sarah (Carr) Whited. Mr W is a Democrat. The family, Presbyterians

Residence, Green Spring, Seneca Co, Ohio. Have two daughters, viz:

    1. Bessie Myrtle Whited (9), b 11 June, 1880; m. Elbert Emery

    2 Nessel May Whited (9), b. 2 Dec., 1888

CHILDREN OF ELIZABETH ANN (7) LOBDELL AND HER HUSBAND, JAMES ANDERSON WALTON.

1 Emma Arvilla 2 Marcellus Adelbert 3 Florence Mary. 4 Alma Vidette

    I Emma Arvilla Walton, b. 3 July, 1858, m. 1879, Wm Wing. Emma d. 11 Aug., 1882 No children.

    II. Marcellus Adelbert Walton, b. 20 July, 1860, d 30 Sept., 1865

    III Florence Mary Walton, b 4 Dec., 1863, m. Wm Crowell Hovey, 15 Sept, 1883, at Benton Harbor, where Mr. Hovey is engaged in the manufacturing of carriages and wagons. They have one son, Don Jacob Hovey (9), b 23 April, 1887

    IV. Alma Vidette Walton, b. 4 May, 1866; m. Adelbert J Covelle of Benton Harbor They have one son, Carlton James Covelle (9), b 5 Sept, 1891

NINTH GENERATION.

CHILDREN OF ORREN R. (8) LOBDELL OF BELLE PLAIN, KAN.

I. Eugene, b 12 Oct., 1871.

II. Gertie, b. 5 June, 1873.

III. Bertha E, b 17 March, 1876

IV Bert O, b 17 Nov, 1883

V Clyde F, b 12 Jan, 1885

VI Millie E., b. 23 April, 1887, a teacher.

VII Ben H, b. 16 Sept, 1888

The sons are all "railroad" men

CHILDREN OF WILFORD NORRIS (8) LOBDELL AND WIFE, MARY MINERVA GARRETSON.

I. Cora Etta, b 7 Feb , 1882.
II. Leslie Crippen. b 25 Sept., 1885.
III. Bruce Earl, b. 10 Feb , 1891
IV. Orren Samuel, b 13 Nov., 1892.

CHILDREN OF STEPHEN C. (8) AND JOSEPHINE (FARMAN) LOBDELL.

1. Laura Renewa 2. Lodwie Tabor 3. Lovina Celina. 4. Emily Louise. 5 Emma Josephine. 6 Stephen Crippen, Jr 7. John Henry

I. Laura Renewa, b 3 June, 1866, at Wabasha. Minn ; m 1 June, 1887, at Spring Valley, Minn Henry Ernest Kalb, a druggist, of Spring Valley, b 12 May, 1859, at Rochester, Minn., d. 9 June, 1890, at Spring Valley, Minn., son of Henry and Fredrika Roediger. Christian Scientist in religion

II. Lodwie Tabor, a merchant of Spring Valley, Minn., b. 20 Feb , 1868, at St. Charles, Minn , m 20 June, 1893, at Winona, Minn., Clara Man, b. 21 March, 1869, at Westville, N. Y., dau. of Buel A. Man and wife, Abigail Towne Westcott. Liberal in religion ; Republican in politics

III Lovina Celina, b 20 Feb., 1868, at St Charles, Minn.; m. 8 Sept , 1897, at Spring Valley, Minn , Albert Marvin Smith, b 8 Sept , 1868, at Austin, Minn , son of Hiram Sofford Smith and wife, Evaline Allen Stuart Republican; liberal in religion.

IV Emily Louise, b 25 Jan 1870, at Spring Valley, Minn ; m. 2 Sept., 1895, Elmer Milliard Lloyd, b 10 July, 1870, at Spring Valley, Minn., son of LeRoy and Evaline Smith Lloyd. Residence, Spring Valley Republican Liberal in religion

V Emma Josephine, b 25 Jan , 1870, at Spring Valley; m. 2 Sept., —— (?), Roy Viall, b. 27 June, 1871, at Preston, Fillmore Co , Minn., son of Burke and Florence Butler Viall Mr. Viall is a Republican, and liberal in religion

Capt. Roy Viall enlisted 28 April, 1898, at Spring Valley, Minn., mustered in as captain, commanding Co. F, 12th Minn. Vol. Inf., 6 May, 1898; Camp Ramsey, Minn ; at Camp Geo. H. Thomas,

Ga., 19 May- 22 Aug., 1898; at Camp Hamilton, Ky., 23 Aug.-15 Sept., 1898, at Camp Mueller, Minn., 17 Sept.-22, 1898, furloughed with reg't 22 Sept.-21 Oct., 1898 Mustered out 5 Nov at Camp Mueller, New Ulm, Minn

VI Stephen Crippen, Jr. a merchant of Spring Valley, b. 20 Aug., 1874, at Spring Valley, Minn., m. 7 June, 1899, at Chicago, Ill., Amy Wightman Johnson, b 6 Aug., 1869, at Australia, dau of John and Rebecca (De Warren) Wightman—Republican and Liberal.

VII John Henry, b. 27 Jan. 1879, d 7 May, 1879.

CHILDREN OF SARAH LUCINDA (8) LOBDELL AND MICHAEL OBERST.

1. Olive Elenora 2 Chas Wm. 3 Lucy Webb 4 Franklin Philetus 5 Anna Leon 6 Earl Monroe. 7 Clair Rutherford 8 Wilber Lobdell

I. Olive Elenora Oberst, b 17 July, 1874, m 11 Feb., 1902, at Fremont, Charles Henry Zeigler, a farmer, b 18 Sept., 1871, at Fremont, son of John and Mary Ann (Jacobs) Zeigler Mr. Z. is a Democrat, religion Lutheran Have one little dau., Corinne Helen Zeigler (10), b. 23 Jan., 1903.

II. Charles Wm. Oberst, b 17 Dec., 1875.

III Lucy Webb Oberst, b 22 July, 1877, m 10 June 1903, at Fremont, Clarence Edward Wolf, an architect and carpenter, b 4 July, 1877 at Fremont, son of George and Isabel (Reed) Wolfe Has Dallas Edward and Doris Evaline Wolfe (twins).

IV Franklin Philetus Oberst a farmer, b. 23 July, 1879; m 28 April 1904 at Breckenridge, Gratiot Co., Mich., Mary Ellen Crowell Mr. Oberst is a Republican, in religion, Methodist

V. Anna Leona Oberst, b 5 Oct., 1881; m A Leedy Cocanour. Has a baby boy (1907), Clair Everett Cocanour

VI Earl Monroe Oberst, b. 29 Sept., 1887.

VII. Clair Rutherford Oberst, b 9 Jan., 1892.

VIII Wilber Lobdell Oberst, b 8 May, 1900

172

SIXTH GENERATION.

CHILDREN OF ZADOCK (5) AND MARGARET (CASTLER) LOBDELL.

1. Daniel. 2 Zadock 3. Susan. 4. Nancy. 5 Margaret. 6 Betsey 7 Morillus

I Daniel, b. 1792 at Manheim, a town adjoining Salisbury, Herkimer Co, N Y., m for his first wife. Nancy Barnes, dau. of Elijah Barnes (a Revolutionary soldier) and Lucy Hunter, Nancy, b 18 June, 1897, at Salisbury, and d. 5 April, 1832, at Theresa, Jefferson Co, N Y. To them were born four sons.

Daniel m for second wife, Emiline Broughton of Theresa About the year 1840, with his wife and their five little children they moved to Swan, and afterward to Avilla, Noble Co, Ind.

On the 25th of March, 1850. Daniel started with his son Zadock, a boy of 14 years, and others in the company, for the gold fields of California, going the overland route. In the month of June they came to an alkali spring or lake. They were all very thirsty, but knew the danger of a draught. Daniel would drink, and there he died. Zadock went on with the company to California, and nothing has been heard of him since 1857, when he was at Oro City, Cal Five sons were in the War of the Rebellion, some from start to finish and of the five, four returned home

II Zadock No record only as above.

III Susan m Asa Duran, a farmer, living in Lewis Co., N Y.

IV Nancy m John Lamberson, a farmer, living at Rushford, Allegany Co N. Y. Mr. A. J Lamberson a grandson living at Rushford, writes "John Lamberson has been dead for 25 years, and his family are all gone except one who is 76 years old (1903) She can tel you nothing "

V Margaret m Samuel West, a farmer, living at Salisbury, Herkimer Co, N Y

VI. Betsy m John Boyer of Theresa, N. Y.

VII. Morillus m. Samuel Platt of Herkimer Co, N Y. Two of their sons were killed in the War of the Rebellion.

173

SEVENTH GENERATION.

CHILDREN OF DANIEL LOBDELL (6) AND FIRST WIFE, NANCY BARNES, ALL BORN AT SALISBURY, N. Y.

1 William 2 George. 3 Elijah 4. Charles

I   William, b 29 April, 1820, d. 5 Feb, 1856, in De Kalb, St Lawrence Co, N Y ; m 4 Jan., 1843, Electa J Potter, b. 3 March, 1827. dau of Erastus and Jane (Dickey) Potter of Salisbury, N Y.

Mrs Lobdell remarried to Mr. E J Wright and is now living at Waterloo, Iowa

II   George. b. 10 June, 1824; m 15 Oct., 1843, at Fairfield, Herkimer Co, N. Y., Nancy Potter, b. 27 May, 1825, at Fairfield. N Y., d 12 Oct., 1889, at De Kalb, St. Lawrence Co, N Y, dau of Erastus and Jane (Dickey) Potter.

Mr Lobdell is a farmer, residing at De Kalb Junction, N Y I am told is a man of influence, highly respected by his fellow citizens in and around his town.

III   Elijah Caryl, b 6 Sept, 1827; m. Sept, 1862, at Newport, Herkimer Co, N. Y., Cynthia E Farmer, b. March, 1838, in Wisconsin. dau of Geo Farmer

In 1865 Mr. Lobdell moved to New Jersey, located half way between the City of Philadelphia and Atlantic City, on the line of two railroads, about half an hour's ride to each city. Has retired from business and at his home in Hammonton, N. J, enjoys a comfortable old age

IV   Charles, b 2 Aug, 1830. When about eight years old he went to live in the family of Lawrence Timmerman of Theresa, Jefferson Co. N Y, and there remained until he was twenty-one. He was always looked upon as one of the family by both Mr. and Mrs Timmerman, and as a brother by the six daughters and one son He m. Abi Jones of Jefferson Co and had one son, Clarence (8). b 18 Sept, 1852. who m his cousin, Nellie Lobdell. b. 1863. dau of Elijah Caryl Lobdell a brother of Charles Clarence has one son, who makes his home with his grandfather at Evans Mills, Jefferson Co., N. Y

174

LUMAN LOBDELL (7) AND WIFE
(Daniel [6])
of Avilla, Ind.
(Page 175)

SAMUEL EVERETT LOBDELL (8)
(Wm. [7])
of Greenfield Hill, Conn.
(Page 133)

ROY P. LOBDELL (8)
(Frank P. [7])
of Plattsburgh, N. Y.
(Page 313)

CHILDREN OF DANIEL (6) AND EMELINE (BROUGH-
TON) LOBDELL, HIS SECOND WIFE.

1. Luman. 2 Luman 3 Asbury 4 John W. 5. Mary Ann 6. Nancy. 7. Taylor. 8 Millard.

V. A son, d aged 12 years

VI. Luman A , b. 28 May, 1834, at Salisbury, N Y, resides at Avilla, Noble Co , Indiana, where he has held different town offices Has been town marshal several times, justice of the peace, and is now (1901) councilman of his ward

Was in the War of the Rebellion for one year. On 25 March, 1855, he m at Swan, Noble Co , Ind., Elizabeth Bricker, who d 8 Nov., 1863, leaving two sons and two daughters

On 4 May, 1864, he m. widow Sarah S Eddy, who d 6 May, 1880, leaving three sons He m for his third wife, on 20 Jan , 1881, widow Cornelia Isabel.

VII Asbury was in the Civil War, gave his life for his country, dying in the hospital at Beaufort, S. C , April, 1865, of small-pox contracted in the army.

VIII. John W., b. 15 May, 1840, at Swan, Ind , is a farmer, residing at Swan, was in the war of 1862 until its finish, m 28 Dec , 1865, Damie Porter, b 10 Feb , 1849, dau. of Noah W. and Henrietta (Allen) Porter of Swan.

CHILDREN.

1. Francis A. (8), b. 9 July, 1871, m. Carrie F. Cramer.
2. Willis E (8), b. 1 Aug , 1874.
3 Albertie W (8), b 28 March, 1876, m Della M. Long.

John W Lobdell (7) of Swan. Ind , at the age of 21 enlisted as private in Co. F, 30th Reg. Ind. Vol , 1st Div., 2nd Brig , 4th A. C First enlistment was 24 Aug , 1861. from this was discharged 19 Jan , 1864, at Whiteside Station, Tenn. Next day enlisted in Co D, same regiment; was furloughed for 30 days, rejoining company at Buzzard's Roost 27 April, 1864 He participated in all the noted battles of the Army of Tennessee

IX. Mary Ann, b 13 July, 1838, in Herkimer Co., N. Y.; m. 25 April, 1863, James Fisk, b 14 Sept., 1842, at Genesee Co , N. Y , son of Fred'k and Eliza (Beswick) Fisk They reside at Swan, Ind Have five children, viz.

1. Clyde W. Fisk (8), b. 20 Jan , 1865.

2 Frank M. Fisk (8) b. 13 May, 1868, m. Alma Clemens.

3. Emma E. Fisk (8), b. 7 Oct., 1871

4 Clara M. Fisk (8), b. 5 Oct., 1873

5 Harry D. Fisk (8), b. 5 Oct., 1875; m. Estelle Weaver.

X. Nancy m. a Mr Fisk and resides at Fort Wayne, Ind. No answer to my letter of inquiry.

XI. Taylor is living in Mulhall, Okla.

XII Millard, b 16 July, 1850, is living at Kansas City Mo (?) He was b. four months after his father started for California, so he never saw his father.

EIGHTH GENERATION.

CHILDREN OF WILLIAM (7) AND ELECTA J. (POTTER) LOBDELL.

---

1. Rosetta 2 Helen M. 3 Herman Willis 4. Frank 5. Brayton 6 Merriam 7 William

---

I. Rosetta J., b 25 Dec. 1843, at Manheim, near Little Falls, Herkimer Co, N Y; m 20 Jan, 1864, to Wm Moody and resides at Tripoli, Bremer Co, Iowa Has no children

II. Helen M, b 26 July, 1845, at Fairfield, Herkimer Co, N. Y.; m 5 Jan, 1867, at Canton, St. Lawrence Co, N. Y., A C Hine, b 31 March, 1842, at Hammond, St. Lawrence Co., N. Y, son of A. A and Evaline (Case) Hine. From De Kalb Junction, St. Lawrence Co, N. Y., they removed to their present home at Waverly, Iowa, where also their children reside, viz..

1. Minnie M Hine (9), b. 16 Oct., 1869, m Geo. Leytze

2. Walter C Hine (9), b 20 March, 1872, m. Bertha S Scobey

3. Blanche E Hine (9), b 9 March, 1877.

4. Murray N. Hine (9) b 23 April, 1882

III Herman Willis, b. 7 Aug, 1847, in Salisbury, Herkimer Co, N. Y; m 2 July, 1870, Mary J Martin, b 20 Oct. 1847, at Adams, McHenry Co, Ill, dau. of Asa T and Harriet A (Branch) Martin. Mr and Mrs L reside at Beloit, Kan No children.

IV. Frank, residing at Beloit, Kan, b. 8 Oct, 1849, at Salisbury, N. Y, m Florence E Mason, 26 Sept, 1873, d 4 Feb, 1898, dau of Wyman and Roxey (Smith) Mason

176

CHILDREN.

1. Mason F. (9), b. 20 Aug., 1880.
2. Benj. W (9), b. 2 Feb., 1885
3 Helen E. (9), b. 1 Sept, 1891
4. Ray R. (9), b 5 June, 1893.

V. Brayton, b. 1851, m. Mary —— (?)

VI. Merrian E., b. 1853; m. Addie Pitts Resides at De Kalb Junction, N Y

VII. William, b. 1856, was adopted by a family named Rundle. Resides in Dakota, but I have been unable to find him. He m Mary —— (?)

CHILDREN OF GEORGE (7) AND NANCY (POTTER) LOBDELL.

1 Seymour, b. 1 Nov., 1844, d. 16 Nov., 1864, from wounds received while serving his country in "War of the Rebellion"

2. John A, b 26 March, 1846; m Martha Bennett.

3 Nancy DeEtte, b. 18 April, 1848; m. Seymour T Walker

4. Amelia J., b 22 Dec, 1850; m. Charles W. Austin

5. Malina, b. 15 June, 1853; m James Baxter.

6 Ida Ann, b. 30 July, 1856, d. 25 Aug, 1859

7 Minnie Adella, b. 8 Nov, 1860, d 22 March, 1862

CHILDREN OF ELIJAH CARYLE (7) LOBDELL AND WIFE, CYNTHIA E. FARMER.

1 Mellie. 2 Ida E. 3 Martha 4. Fanny 5. Frank Caryl

I. Melly, b. 1863; m Clarence Lobdell (her cousin, son of Charles) Reside at Evans Mills, N Y

II Ida E, b 7 June, 1864, at Rushford, Allegany Co., N. Y.; m 26 Nov., 1886, at Atlantic City, N. J, Arthur Knaner, a native of Pennsylvania Residence, Atlantic City, N. J. Mr. Knaner is proprietor of a jobbing printing house. A Republican, Protestant.

CHILDREN.

1. Edna M. Kraner (9, b. 18 March, 1887. at Atlantic City, N. J

177

2   Carroll H Kraner (9), b 17 April, 1890, at Atlantic City. N J.

III. Martha, b. 12 Jan , 1867, at Hammonton, N. J.; m Jan., 1888, Charles W. Austin, a machinist. Democrat; Protestant. Resides at Hammonton, N. J.

IV. Fanny. b 2 Feb , 1872, at Hammonton, N. J ; m 5 March, 1893, at Hammonton (where they now reside), John Measley, son of Frederick and Marie Measley. Mr Measley is a farmer; Democrat, Protestant.

CHILDREN.

1   Horace J Measley (9). b 12 July. 1895
2   Mabel Measley (9) b 18 April, 1898
3   Cora Measley (9). b 30 Nov . 1901

V Frank Caryl. b 1 June. 1874. at Hammonton. N. J., m. Ella Dunkle, b. at Waterford, N J Mr. Lobdell is a farmer at Hammonton A Republican; a Protestant

CHILDREN, ALL BORN IN HAMMONTON (9).

1   Florence E.
2   Helen
3   Mildred.
4. Stella M

CHILDREN OF LUMAN LOBDELL (7) AND FIRST WIFE, ELIZABETH BRICKER.

---

1   Orlan W.   2 Charles E   3. Emma L   4. Ora A.

I Orlan W , b in Avilla. Noble Co , Ind., 3 Jan., 1856, is in the transfer business at Mulhall. Okla., m. 11 Sept., 1875, at Avilla. Ind , Eliza J Williams. b 3 Oct. 1857, at Noble, Ind A Republican, and in religion, A. F. and A. M. Came direct from Indiana to Oklahoma in 1889, arriving 2 March

CHILDREN.

1   Edna M. (9), b 14 Oct., 1876.
2   Velma M (9), b 26 Nov , 1878
3   Arthur G. (9). b 3 Feb . 1881
4   Walter A. (9). b 16 Aug , 1891.

178

II   Charles E., b. 27 April, 1857, m 9 Sept., 1880, at Hicksville, Defiance Co., Ohio, Nancy E. Fredricks b. 18 Feb., 1858, at Ankenytown, Knox Co., Ohio, dau of Peter and Catherine (Bolyard) Fredricks Mr. Lobdell is a farmer, residing at Mark Centre, Defiance Co., Ohio A Republican in politics

CHILDREN.

1 Elmer F. (9), b 25 May, 1881.
2 Ethel F. (9), b. 28 March, 1895.

III. Emma L., b 10 July, 1858, at Swan, Ind ; m 3 Feb., 1878, at Garrett, De Kalb Co., Ind., Thomas Kelham, b 5 April, 1853, at Shelby, Richland Co., Ohio, son of Edward and Sarah (Downing) Kelham. A farmer, resides at Avilla. A Democrat. Protestant

CHILDREN.

1. Annetta M Kelham (9), b 29 Dec., 1878; m Samuel Scheurich

2. Alda Z. Kelham (9), b. 10 Aug., 1880; m. LeRoy Zellers

3 Frank C Kelham (9), b. 15 Sept., 1882.

4. James W. Kelham (9), b 16 May, 1885.

5 Frederick T Kelham (9), b. 5 Oct., 1887

6. John C. Kelham (9), b 30 March, 1893.

The children of Thomas Kelham all reside at Avilla, excepting Mrs. Le Roy Zellers, whose residence is at 1420 Swinney Ave., Ft. Wayne, Ind

IV. Ora A., b 10 Jan., 1860, at Avilla, Ind., m 30 March, 1880, at Cedar, Ind., Nicholas Lung, b. 9 Sept., 1860, at Cedar, Ind., son of Philip and Margaret S (Ott) Lung The family reside at Cedar, De Kalb Co., Ind. Mr. Lung is engaged in agriculture, is a Democrat and a Protestant.

CHILDREN.

1 Alonzo C Lung (9), b 5 Jan., 1881; m Lizza Zern Resides at Garrett, Ind

2 Merrett C. Lung (9), b. 31 Aug., 1886. Resides at Cedar, Ind

3 Forest E Lung (9), b 28 April, 1889. Resides at Cedar, Ind.

CHILDREN OF LUMAN (7) LOBDELL BY SECOND WIFE, SARAH S. EDDY, ALL BORN IN AVILLA.

V Luman A., b. 19 Feb , 1865, resides in Chicago, Ill,, is employed by I C R R My letter of inquiry was returned to me by postoffice not finding the address given

VI. John D , b 30 March, 1867 , m. 4 Sept.. 1888, at Avilla, Emma Stapf, b 31 March. 1866, at Kendallville, Ind., dau of George and Amelia (Bush) Stapf Mr. Lobdell is a railroad man, living at Elkhart. Ind. A Socialist, and in religion, English Lutheran

CHILDREN.

1 Clara Cornelia (9), b. 16 Aug , 1888.
2 Emma Amelia (9), b 19 Aug , 1891
3 John Charles (9), b 13 March, 1894

VII Uri, b 17 Aug , 1869; m 1 June, 1891, at Fort Wayne, Ind., Lillie Smith, b 3 Sept., 1867, at Ft Wayne, dau. of Geo and Eliza (Klinger) Smith Mr and Mrs. Lobdell reside upon their farm, four miles north of Ft. Wayne, on the Goshen road No children Universalists in religion. A Republican.

LOCKWOOD LOBDELL (6)
(Samuel [5])   (1805-1803)
of Cherry Valley, Ohio
(Page 181)

HENRY LOCKWOOD LOBDELL (7)
(Lockwood [6])
of Madison, Ohio
(Page 184)

BETHUEL LOBDELL (6)
(Samuel [5])   (1821-1902)
of Hartford, Mich.
(Page 181)

ELIJAH CARYL LOBDELL (7)
(Daniel [6])
of Hammonton, N. J.
(Page 174)

SIXTH GENERATION.

CHILDREN OF SAMUEL (5) AND LOIS (GREENFIELD) LOBDELL.

1 Lockwood 2. Gideon 3 Seth. 4. Angeline 5 Esther 6 Bethuel

I. Lockwood b 4 Feb., 1805, at Salisbury, Herkimer Co, N Y, d 1893, at Cleveland, Ohio; m. 1829, Fanny Krum, b 24 Dec, 1808, at Chatham, Four Corners, Columbia Co., N. Y., d 1 Aug (about 1885 (?), at Cleveland, Ohio, dau. of Peter and Sarah (Trowbridge) Krum

II Gideon, b. (?), m Margaret Farley, d in Cherry Valley, Ohio. No children

III. Seth, b 24 April, 1817, at Salisbury, N Y, d May, 1872, at Andover, Ashtabula Co, Ohio, m 2 Sept., 1841, Olive, dau of Jesse Beverly.

IV. Angeline, b —— (?): m Wm Taylor; no children; d —— (?) at Andover, Ohio.

V Esther, b. —— (?), m Daniel Rand of Cherry Valley, Ohio, where he also died After his death, Esther, with her children, went west with her father-in-law's family. I have written several letters, but no notice has been taken of them.

VI. Bethuel, a farmer, resided at Hartford, Van Buren Co, Mich., b. 24 March, 1821, at Salisbury, N. Y.; m at Warren, Trumbull Co., Ohio, to Henrietta Ryan, b at Black Rock, N Y. Her father d. at Port Stanley, Canada West, of cholera in 1832

Mr. Lobdell d Monday, 21 July, 1902, at his home in Hartford, Mich. His widow d suddenly 10 Oct, 1903.

Obituary from his local paper·

Bethuel Lobdell was born at Salisbury, Herkimer Co., N. Y., March 24, 1821 In his early youth his parents moved to Cherry Valley, Ashtabula Co, Ohio, where he grew to manhood

In 1845 he was united in marriage to Miss Arretha Ryan of Gustavus, Ohio, who survives him.

181

Twelve years of his life were spent in Canada. In 1865 he brought his family to Michigan and settled in Van Buren county, where he has ever since resided, universally respected and held in high esteem

He was the father of six children, all of whom are now living: The eldest, Mrs R. M. Rowe, of Berlamont; Willis, who resides three miles southwest of town and with whom he and his wife have made their home since January last, Howard, recently supervisor of the town; Mrs. George Lammon. Ira and Levi Lobdell, all of whom reside in Van Buren county. He had eight grandchildren and six great grandchildren, so that four generations were represented in the family.

He died on Monday, July 21, and was the last survivor of a family of six children. Beside his immediate family only two relatives survive him, viz Mrs. Elvira Lobdell Bushnell of Chicago and her brother, Henry Lobdell, of Ohio

The following letter from Mr. Bethuel Lobdell (1897) I hope will be as interesting to descendants as it is to me, for I fully enjoy every word, having had the pleasure of meeting this fine old gentleman, also all of his family. He says

"I was born in Salisbury, N. Y., 24 March, 1822, and when 5 years old left my parents and with my oldest brother, Lockwood, went to the then wilderness of western Ohio. We finally settled in Cherry Valley My father's name was Samuel I have heard him tell that his father and brothers were all taken prisoners by the Indians, to Canada, during the Revolutionary war My father was left with my grandmother, as he was too young to walk so far. My mother's name was Lois Greenfield I am the youngest and only one living of our family. I have four sons and two daughters living near me I came to Michigan in 1861 John B. Lobdell then kept a hotel at Grand Rapids I do not think this family is of our line I saw recently in a Michigan paper a notice of the fiftieth anniversary of the marriage of Ammon Lobdell of Chessaning, Mich I do not know of him, but the name always attracts me My son found Lobdells in Mississippi, and in 1845, while coming from Buffalo, N. Y, I heard of two families—at Hamburg, on Lake Erie I shall always owe you a debt of gratitude for your interesting letter, as it is the only information I have of my ancestors; yes, I may say of my relatives, other than my own family. My father was an invalid before my knowledge, caused by a shock

182

of palsy. When about 14 years old I left my brother and went to Pittsburg, Pa., and found employment as a cabin boy on a steamboat This occupation I followed for about three years on the Ohio, Mississippi, Missouri and Illinois rivers, leaving the last boat hard and fast aground on the upper rapids of the Mississippi After staying at St Louis until short of money, and finding no further employment in that line, I found on the market an old farmer who took me home with him to Harrisonville township, Ill., where I worked for three years Then I decided to go to Oregon, but by the persuasion of friends I wrote to my mother in Ohio, and when the answer came that all the living members of my family were there, I concluded to visit them before going to Oregon. I married at Ohio, and learned that my wife's father had left a valuable estate, that legal proceedings had been commenced and died out. I went, and by bill of errors renewed the legal battle and kept at it seven years, receiving a judgment of $25,000 but was beaten on execution I settled in Michigan in 1861, having rambled over the rocky hills of New York and Pennsylvania, the forests of Ohio, the mountains and valleys of Virginia, Kentucky, Tennessee and Alabama, the prairies of Indiana, Illinois, Iowa, Missouri and Kansas, or gliding on the western rivers and northern lakes I have never felt lack of hospitality or friendship and can truly say that I have no reason to be afraid or ashamed to meet any person at any time or place I am now nearly 78 years old (22 Nov., 1899) and death has never broken my family circle. Hoping for you every success in your great undertaking, and that I may live to receive a copy of your genealogical history, I am very respectfully,   BETHUEL LOBDELL.

Hartford, Van Buren Co., Mich "

SEVENTH GENERATION

CHILDREN AND DESCENDANTS OF LOCKWOOD AND FANNY (KRUM) LOBDELL.

1 John Marshall 2. Elvira Jane. 3 Henry Lockwood. 4. Clarence Dudley.

I. John Marshall, b 6 Jan, 1832, at Cherry Valley, Ohio He received a fair education for the times and became a young man of great promise, universally liked and worthily popular for sterling qualities. While teaching his first school, he was stricken with a fever and died 12 Feb., 1852, when barely 20 years old.

II Elvira Jane, b 29 May, 1833, was of a social disposition and with unusual conversational powers, she was fitted to attract people and make acquaintances On 20 Nov., 1859, she m. Corydon L. Bushnell, b. 12 Oct., 1826, at Monroe, Ohio, d 29 May, 1881, at Cleveland, Ohio

CHILDREN (8).

1. Emory L. Bushnell (8), b 12 Oct, 1861, m. —— (?); d 27 Nov., 1892

2. Lee S. Bushnell (8), b. 15 June. 1865; m —— (?)

Both sons died suddenly of heart disease at Chicago

III. Henry Lockwood, b. 17 Feb., 1840, with a decided bent for music and literature, in the way of being an inordinate reader, has taught school, taught music, and beside being a farmer, has mainly sold musical instruments for a livelihood Unmarried, he resides at Madison, Lake Co, Ohio Independent in politics. In religion, a freethinker

IV. Clarence Dudley, b 8 Feb, 1846, was an unusually bright boy. He enlisted in the 105th Ohio V. I, 5 Aug., 1862, was wounded at Perryville 8 Oct, 1862, sent to hospital and was discharged for disability. In Sept, 1864, enlisted in the 40th Ohio, was detailed to serve in the Tod Barracks band In the spring of 1865 was transferred to the front, and was with his regiment in Virginia at the close of the war After pursuing various occupations he enlisted in the regular army about 1880 and d at Columbus barracks, Ohio. in 1882 He m 8 April, 1860, at Jefferson, Ohio, Julia Miner, b 2 April, 1848, at Wayne, Ohio, dau. of Jonathan T and Sarah (Krum) Miner. Had—

Sarah Miner (8), b 6 March, 1862, at Cleveland, Ohio; m 23 Jan, 1902, at Cleveland, Charles Robert Ross Resides in the state of Florida

---

The name and address of Henry Lobdell was given me and I at once wrote him at Madison, Ohio, and his immediate reply will be appreciated particularly by descendants of Daniel L He says:

"Your letter was received last evening and I was both surprised and gratified by its contents. You could not have been more pleased to learn of me than I to know of what you have told me. The name Lobdell is a strange one to most persons. Aside from

184

my father's family, I have never but three times seen any one of the name. We have always considered ourselves a kind of lost people, but you have built up a genealogic tree of which I am undoubtedly a member, and I do not feel quite such an unknown quantity. My father's brother once lived near several families by the name in Byron, Mich., but they were unable to trace any relationship. My father was b. in Salisbury, Herkimer Co., N. Y., 4 Feb., 1805. My grandfather was probably in poor health, and at best not fitted to make his way in the world. At all events the family were poor. As a boy, when old enough, he lived a good deal from home. Finally he was apprenticed to a carpenter and learned the trade, afterward worked with a millwright, so that he became proficient as a workman. He was of a very sensitive disposition and never liked to talk much about what he endured from poverty. When he was about 23 he and my mother, Fanny Krum, aged 20, were m. She was b. on a farm at Chatham, Four Corners, Columbia Co., N. Y. This farm of 100 acres was lost by her father's mismanagement, and the family of half-grown children went to face life in the wilds of Montgomery Co., N. Y., at Oppenheim, and there the two found each other. In the spring of 1829, they with my uncle, Abel Krum, moved to Ashtabula Co., Ohio. At first my parents settled in Wayne, where they bought 30 acres of land, moved into what had been a stable, and with not much but their hands began the struggle for a home and competence. Both were inured to poverty and privation. Both were industrious and economical. My father worked at his trade and tended his farming between spells, with the aid of my mother, who could plant, hoe and do all outdoor work women undertook at all. She was also a tailoress and plied her needle as well. With her it was work-work, until it became second nature. After I could remember, it was the usual thing for her to work half the night and be the first one up in the morning. What could it have been when they were beginning, it is difficult to guess. Their success was perhaps the greater part due to her. Patient, persevering, exemplary in every way—never was a woman of more worthy motives. My father, too, would teach school winters and walk home some four miles at night to work on the house he built, after he sold in Wayne and moved to Cherry Valley when only 29 years old, and on the Western Reserve lived for years, afterward built for himself the first frame house and barn in that township. Both were

honest and true and beyond reproach in all their dealings My
father was of a generous disposition, and always the home was a
haven for some one that was needy. The only thing he could be
blamed for was a moroseness that I ascribe in a great measure
to what he had endured and the lack of appreciation of his liberality
and the abuse of his generosity, which, I am sorry to say, are
common in the world I must say that I think my mother a
blameless woman, and never heard any one say otherwise Am I
not entitled to a just pride in such ancestors? My father held various township offices at Cherry Valley and was postmaster till
1877 As I said, outside of our immediate family, we knew no one
bearing the Lobdell name, and were always attracted whenever
we found or heard of the name. About 1855 a man and wife
named Lamberton, visiting friends in Trumbull Co, Ohio, came
to see us, and she was a relative of my father's About 1858 an
Elijah Lobdell, then living in Cuba, Allegany Co., N. Y., made us
a visit. He was first or second cousin of my father, in whom the
feeling of kinship was strong. My grandmother told a more or
less mythical story about a Daniel Lobdell, brother or father of my
grandfather, being captured and with his children marched into
Canada by the Indians, and they becoming dispersed was the reason no one knew anything of grandfather's relatives As a boy I
used to like to ask questions and hear my grandmother tell of her
family and of my grandfather's family. Her maiden name was
Lois Greenfield and the name of her mother, Lois Rose. One
time I took down the names of the children of Daniel Lobdell and
also of the children of her brother's family (Rose), and although
I have many, many times thought to destroy them as of no value,
I have, I am now glad to say, kept them and forward same to you,
and I (Mrs J. H. L.), hoping they may be of value to others, place
them before you Children of Charles Rose, viz.

Willard, Charles, Betsey, Rhoda, Mollie, Sally and Harriet.

Children of Wyatt Rose (one of the early settlers of Stephentown, Rensselaer Co., N. Y.), viz:

Patty, John, Lucy and Abigail.

Children of Nathaniel Rose, viz:

Mercy, Mollie, Thankful, Susanna, Thomas, Peter, Olive,
Bathsheba, Susan, Lillian and Dilly

Wishing you success   H. L. LOBDELL."

186

CHILDREN OF SETH (6) AND OLIVE BEVERLY LOBDELL, ALL BORN IN ANDOVER.

I. Dennis   2. Eliza   3 Almon A.   4. Flora.   5 Austin N. 6 Jesse J.

I.   Dennis, b 10 June, 1846

II.   Eliza, b 9 Nov., 1848; m 16 April, 1874, at Buffalo, N Y , Edward A Howard, b. 27 Sept., 1825 (?), son of Geo E and Mary Ann (Barber) Howard. Reside at Orwell, Ohio.

CHILDREN.

1   Georgie E Howard (8), b. 12 Oct., 1876, at Buffalo, N Y ; m 15 Nov 1898, Wm G McCorkle, a printer, b. 24 Sept., 1856, at Bazetta, Trumbull Co, Ohio, son of Andrew and Margaret (Hoagland) McCorkle. Reside at Cortland, O. One child—
Mildred Howard McCorkle (9), b 12 Sept., 1899.
2.   Edward A Howard (8), b. 24 April, 1879
3.   Jesse E. Howard (8), b. 8 Oct., 1880.
4.   Flora H Howard (8), b 15 June, 1887.

III.   Almon A., b. 10 July, 1851; m. in 1875, Amelia Potter. Reside at West Andover, Ohio One child—
1.   Wallace Alanson, b 25 May, 1883.

IV   Flora, b 8 Oct , 1853

V.   Austin N., a mechanic b 25 June, 1857. Resides at Ashtabula, O., unmarried A Republican; a Protestant.

VI.   Jesse J , b 31 July, 1860, m 27 March, 1880, Norma E. Platt, b. 28 July, 1860, at Richmond, Ashtabula Co, Ohio dau of Perry J and Elizabeth (Bassett) Platt Residence, 22 Vine St., Ashtabula, Ohio. Mr Lobdell is vice president of Ashtabula Camera and Supply Co.; also a letter carrier. Is a Republican, and Protestant

CHILDREN.

1   Ernest E , b. 1881
2   James S., b. 1886.
3   Jesse C, b 1890

187

CHILDREN AND DESCENDANTS OF BETHUEL AND HENRIETTA RYAN LOBDELL.

I. Emma Ann, b. 10 Feb., 1847, at Cherry Valley, Ohio, m 29 May, 1866, at Allegan, Mich., Rufus Murray Rowe, b 22 Sept., 1840, son of Dr Nelson and Lovisa (Camp) Rowe of Chautauqua, N. Y. Dr Nelson Rowe, a college graduate, was a talented and patriotic man, who gave his three sons to the service of his country in War of the Rebellion, Rufus being the only one of the three who returned alive Reside at Lawrence, Mich

CHILDREN.

1. Florence Rowe (8), b. 18 Dec., 1867, at Lawrence, Van Buren Co., Mich., at which place she m 18 June, 1890, Edwin H. Luce, b 1 May, 1861, at Breedsville, Mich., son of Charles W and Nancy Hinckley Luce. Mr. E. H. Luce and family reside at Lawrence, Mich., where he is the proprietor of a "general store" Children

    1. Zora Luce (9), b. 5 Jan., 1892.
    2. Genevieve Luce (9) b 1 May, 1893
    3 Rufus Rowe Luce (9), b. 8 Nov., 1895.
    4 Charles Willis Luce (9), b 18 Dec., 1900.

2 Mattie Rowe (8), b 20 Dec., 1872, at Lawrence; m 9 March, 1892, at Hartford, Van Buren Co., Mich., Albert C. Barnes, b. at Lawrence, son of Wm M and Fanny (Gates) Barnes. Children.

    1. Leland M. Barnes (9), b. 26 Dec., 1894.
    2. Roland Barnes (9), b 31 Aug., 1899.

II. Willis, a farmer residing near Hartford, Mich., b. 27 Jan., 1849, at Ashtabula, Ohio; m 13 Aug., 1878, at Watervalley, Zallabusha Co., Miss., Virginia Beauregard Turner, b. 7 Aug., 1861, at St. Joseph, Buchanan Co., Mo., dau of Isaac and Caroline (Menefee) Turner.

Willis Lobdell enlisted 22 Aug., 1864, at Grand Rapids, Mich., was consigned to Co H. First Mich Engineers; joined company at Mechanicsville, Ga., marched to Atlanta, helped burn the city: then marched to Savannah under General Sherman. There, in Jan., was stricken with typhoid fever and remained there until 14 April. On that date the troops embarked, sailed to Morehead City, then marched to Newburn, N. C ; there took passage on transport and after a voyage of six days arrived at Washington, D C., May 24.

188

CHILDREN AND DESCENDANTS OF BETHUEL LOBDELL (6)
(Samuel [5]) of Hartford, Mich.
(Page 188)

Was in review of the western army. Afterward was sent to Jackson, Mich., and discharged 6 June, 1864. They have one dau.—

    Bessie Menefee (9), b. 20 Aug., 1880. She is m., living near Hartford, and has one little dau., but no record has been sent to me.

III   Howard, a farmer near Hartford, Mich., b. 4 May, 1851, at Vienna, Canada West; m. 18 March, 1879, at Hartford, Eva Taylor, b. 22 Dec., —— (?), at Hartford, dau. of Howland C and Emma A. (Goodenough) Taylor. Is a Democrat. No children.

IV.   Fannie, b. 30 Jan., 1855, at Vienna, Elgin Co., Ontario; m. 28 Nov., 1875, at Hartford, Mich., Geo G Lammon, b 21 June, 1854, at Lorain, Jefferson Co., N. Y., son of Gilbert and Helen M (Avery) Lammon. Mr. Lammon is a farmer near Hartford, Mich. Is a Democrat. No children.

V.   Ira, b. 13 Nov., 1857, at Vienna, Ont ; m. 19 Oct., 1880, at Bangor, Mich., Josephine Byers, b. 7 Nov., 1857, at Koseoska, Ind., d. 4 Jan., 1899, at Hartford, Mich., dau. of A. S. and Henrietta (Lee) Byers. Is a farmer; a Democrat. Residence, Hartford, Mich. Mr. L. re-married, but I have no data.

CHILDREN.

    1. Elsie A , b 19 May, 1882, m. —— (?).
    2. Myra C., b. 2 July, 1885, m —— (?)
    3. Gale D., b 21 Feb , 1895.

VI.   Levi Ryan, b 9 Jan., 1861, at Port Stanley, Ontario; m. 12 March, 1895, Kittie O'Rourke, b. 17 Jan., 1872, at Mt. Morris, Genesee Co., Mich., dau. of A. H and Mary (Vodden) O'Rourke. Resides near Ludington, Mich.

CHILDREN.

    1. Eva M., b. 30 Dec., 1895.

    2. Meredith, b. 21 July, 1901, in Hamilton township, Van Buren Co., Mich.

    3. Howard M., b. 30 March, 1904, at Custer, Mason Co., Mich.

FIFTH GENERATION.

CHILDREN OF JOHN (4) AND ELIZABETH (SHERWOOD) LOBDELL.

1. Elizabeth. 2. John. 3. Jerusha 4 Tertullas. 5 Stephen. 6. Daniel 7. Nathaniel 8. Sarah Sherwood. 9. Ruth 10 Mary. 11. Theodosia 12 Lewis All born in Salem, N. Y.

I. Elizabeth, b. 5 April, 1765; m. Phineas, son of Isaac, and— his second wife. Hannah (Stebbins) Keeler of Ridgefield, Conn., b at Ridgefield 1 July, 1763 They lived in North Salem until after their first child was b., then moved to West Milton, Saratoga Co., N Y., where Elizabeth d Phineas m. for his second wife, Mary Ellis, and d 31 Oct, 1847 .

II John, b 22 March, 1767; m Esther Ressequie. b 23 Nov. 1771, dau. of Alex. and Eunice (Blackman) Ressequie of Ridgefield. They settled in Sherburne, Chenango Co., N. Y.

III. Jerusha, b 3 March, 1769; m. as his second wife, Isaac, son of Joshua and Sarah (Scott) Lobdell (her cousin) They resided at Westerlo, Albany Co., N Y., where she d. 2 May, 1849

IV. Tertullas, b. 25 Dec, 1770; m. Deborah, dau. of Abijah and Elizabeth (Keeler Wallace), b 11 Oct, 1774, of North Salem, N. Y. They removed to Coxsackie, Green Co., N Y, but were there only a short time when Tertullas d of typhoid fever. Deborah returned to North Salem and re-married to Elnathan Smith, 1 Nov., 1809 She d in Amsterdam, N Y, 16 Jan, 1851

The extended record of the descendants of Tertullas Lobdell is kindly given to the work by Mrs Julia Lobdell (Dean) Stark of Randolph, Wis

V. Stephen, b. 23 Jan, 1773; m Ruth, dau of Gilbert and Ruth (Wallace) Webb of Stamford, or Darien, Conn They settled in Albany, N Y, where in 1813, we find his name as constable in Fourth ward No record of his death, but his widow d in Albany 17 July, 1834, aged 60 years. 3 months They resided at 50 Church street

190

JERUSHA LOBDELL LOBDELL (5)
(John [4])   (1769-1849)
of Westerlo, N. Y.
(Pages 190, 64, 65)

HIRAM LOBDELL (6)
(Lewis [5])   (1816-1896)
of Sherburn, N. Y.
(Page 197)

LEWIS R. LOBDELL (7)
(Hiram [6])
of East Granby, Conn.
(Page 197)

JULIA LOBDELL DEAN STARK (7)
(Anna [6])
of Randolph, Wis.
(Page 205)

VI. Daniel, b. 10 May, 1775; m. Sally, dau. of Jeremiah and Lydia (Keeler) Keeler. They settled in Cazenovia, Madison Co., N. Y., where both died

VII. Nathaniel, b. 16 April, 1777; m. for his first wife, Polly Baker, dau. of Josiah Baker of Westerlo, Albany Co., N. Y. She d. in 1822, at Mentz, Cayuga Co., N. Y. He re-married, but do not know to whom

VIII. Sarah Sherwood, b. 27 May, 1779; m. Wm. Stewart and settled in Sherburne. Chenango Co. They had no children, but after the death of Polly Baker, the first wife of Nathaniel Lobdell, they adopted Albert, her little motherless son, then 18 months old. Both Mr. and Mrs. Stewart d. of consumption and are buried in the Episcopal cemetery at Sherburne.

IX. Ruth, b. 19 June, 1781; m. Elisha Ray and settled in Sherburne, where both are buried

X. Mary, b. 4 Feb., 1783; d. 23 Feb., 1783.

XI. Theadosia, b. 29 April, 1785; m. for her first husband, Edmund Perlee Smith, b. at Ridgefield 22 March, 1779, who d. 5 Dec., 1805, no children. She then m. Samuel Shaw, b. 18 Aug., 1778, at Spencertown, Columbia Co., N. Y. He d. 8 Nov., 1836, at Sherburne, where also his wife d. 21 July, 1846.

Samuel Shaw was deputy sheriff of Columbia Co., N. Y., in and around 1817.

XII. Lewis, b. 18 Feb., 1787; m. Eunice Shaw and moved to Sherburne, where he d.

SIXTH GENERATION.

CHILDREN OF ELIZABETH (5) LOBDELL AND PHINEAS KEELER.

---

1. Theadosia   2. Isaac   3. John.   4. Tertullas.   5. Ruth

I. Theadosia Keeler, b. at North Salem, N. Y., 24 Aug., 1798; m. first, 26 Aug., 1821, Edmond Millard and settled at Clarendon, N. Y. No children. She m. second, Benj. Thomas. No children. Died 1886 in Illinois.

II. Isaac Keeler, b. at West Milton, N. Y., 1 Sept., 1800; m. 12 Feb., 1828, Susan Wheeler and settled at Akron, N. Y., where he d. 1853

191

III. John Keeler, b. at West Milton, N. Y., 25 April, 1802; m. 25 May, 1824, Selinda Boss. They settled in Clarendon, N. Y. He d. in Worcester, Mass., 3 April, 1871; buried in Fredonia, N. Y.

IV. Tertullus L. Keeler, b. at West Milton 25 May, 1804; m. 26 Feb., 1828, Rebecca Hayes and settled at West Milton, where he d. 27 May, 1890.

V. Ruth Keeler, b. at West Milton 22 May, 1806; m. 27 Feb., 1828, David J. Rockwell. She d. 24 May, 1842, at Akron, N. Y.

(From Keeler Genealogy.)

CHILDREN OF JOHN (5) AND ESTHER (RESSEQUIE) LOBDELL.

1. John Sherwood   2. Sally.   3. Ann.   4. Almira.   5. Abigail.

I. John Sherwood, b. 1811 at Sherburn, N. Y., m. Zeruah, dau. of Andrew and Caroline —— (?) Robinson. They lived at or near Sand Lake, which is about 13 miles from Stephentown, N. Y., and 10 miles from Troy, N. Y. He was a weaver by trade, and d. at Sand Lake. His wife d. Feb., 1881, at Lebanon Springs, Columbia Co., N. Y.; is buried at Sand Lake.

II. Sally, of whom I have no record.

III. Ann, probably m. at Sherburne 16 Sept., 1835, James Pelton, b. at Warwick, Orange Co., N. Y., 8 Jan., 1815. Ann d. 18 April, 1853 (Pelton Genealogy.)

IV. Almira, no record

V. Abigail, no record

CHILDREN OF STEPHEN (5) AND RUTH WEBB LOBDELL.

1 John Wallace. 2 Stephen 3 Joshua 4 Ruth. 5 Tertullas.

I. John Wallace, b. about 1796 at North Salem, N. Y., when a young man settled in New York, where he followed the business of last making and where he m. Elizabeth Minard, dau. of James and Catherine (Harrison) Lyvere, b. about 1802. They had three children, but all d. young. He d. about 1822 and is buried in St. Paul's Church yard, New York City. His widow came to North Salem

192

and m. Wm Pettit Baxter of North Salem, whose dau, Mrs. F J. Rockwell of South Norwalk. Conn., has kindly given this information

II Stephen. Never married.

III Joshua, b at North Salem, July, 1800; m Lydia, dau. of John and Margaret (Morgan) Tillotson of North Salem, N. Y They settled in Sherburn, Chenango Co., N Y

IV. Ruth m. Benajah Salisbury and settled in Albany, N Y. Had two children Ruth Helen Salisbury, residing in Albany, 1901, and Henry Wallace Salisbury, who was in the army and d in Washington 18 or 20 years ago

V. Tertullas, a boy soldier. Shot in the War of 1812.

CHILDREN OF DANIEL (5) AND SALLY (KEELER) LOBDELL, ALL BORN IN NORTH SALEM, WESTCHESTER CO., N. Y.

1 Lydia. 2 Lewis. 3. Nancy. 4 Polly. 5 Jane. 6 Eliza. 7 Julia 8 Harry S. 9 George. 10 Floyd.

I Lydia, m. Philander Badeau, lived in Nelson, N. Y. Had one dau.

II. Lewis, m Phebe, dau of Jonathan Truesdall; lived in Cazanovia, N. Y.

III. Nancy, b 30 Sept., 1801 ; m. 16 June, 1822, at North Salem, N. Y., Jacob Wright Webb, b 31 Aug., 1798, at Darien, Fairfield Co, Conn Mr. Webb, with his brother-in-law, David Wing, came to Belvidere, Boone Co, Ill., in 1845, coming from Cazanovia, N. Y. Both bought farming land, and Mr. Webb successfully carried on the merchant tailor business All were members of the Methodist Church Mr and Mrs Webb d in Belvidere, he 7 Dec., 1867; she 28 Dec., 1882 He was a son of Gilbert Webb and Ruth Wallace (of North Salem), who was dau. of John and Martha (Schoefield) Wallace of Middlesex (Darien), Conn.

Jacob Wright Webb was brother of Ruth Webb, who m Stephen Lobdell, a brother of Daniel, the father of Mrs Jacob Wright Webb, both being sons of John and Elizabeth (Sherwood) Lobdell of North Salem. N Y

IV. Polly m. Hiram Jackson of North Salem and after his death went to Nelson, N. Y., where she m Seldon Andrews, moving to Belvidere, Ill, in 1846, where they both d.

V. Jane m. David Wing, came to Belvidere, Ill., in 1845, where both d.

VI Eliza m. Wm. Sherwood.

VII. Julia d. unmarried at the home of Mr. Floyd K. Lobdell, near Belvidere, April, 1900, aged 88 years.

VIII. Harry S. m Mary Ann Southerly, moved to Spring, Ill., where both d., he aged 49 years, 11 months, 12 days, she 38 years, 2 months, 5 days. Three children were b. to them at Cazanovia, Madison Co., N. Y.:

    1. Mary Jane (7), b. 20 Aug., 1844; m. Bela C Needham in 1864. Three children (8) were b. to them; two daus are now living Mrs. Needham d aged 45 years, 8 months

    2 Elizabeth M (7), b 18 Aug., 1849; m. 6 Feb, 1875, Benj F. Brooks They reside at Spring. Ill., have no children

    3 Charles H (7), b 4 Oct, 1854, m. in 1878 to Jennie Sweet Have two sons (8)

IX. George m Cordelia Stranahan d leaving a widow and three daughters.

X. Floyd, b 31 May, 1825, m 30 March, 1847, at Spring, Boone Co, Ill., Clarinda Dewolf, b. 23 Nov, 1827, at Conneaut, Ashtabula Co, Ohio, dau of Stephen and Bethe (Ellis) De Wolfe. Mr. Lobdell came to Illinois in 1846, bought a farm eight miles southeast of Belvidere, still owned and occupied by his widow and two sons, James Monroe (7) and Jesse Wing Lobdell (7) Here Mr Lobdell d 24 July, 1881 He was a Methodist, and in politics a Republican.

CHILDREN AND DESCENDANTS OF NATHANIEL (5) AND POLLY (BAKER) LOBDELL.

---

1 Mary Ann. 2 Jacob Baker 3 Albert.

---

1. Mary Ann, b in 1815, was taken, after the death of her mother, into the family of Wm. Griggs of Mentz, N Y, where she was afterward m to Joseph Russell of Nunda, N. Y.

II Jacob Baker, a boss carpenter, b 30 Aug., 1818, at Mentz, Cayuga Co, N Y; m. 2 Oct, 1842, at Warsaw, Wyoming Co, N Y., to Lucy M Mungar, b 22 Oct, 1818, dau of Harmon Mungar and Sophia Knapp, dau of a Revolutionary soldier Mr Lobdell was foreman for Brown & Upton, threshing machine company, Battle Creek, Mich., for 16 years; was, during the "War of the Rebellion," a private in 13th Mich. Infantry from Aug., 1864, to June, 1865, under Colonel Culver and Capt. Silas Yerkes. Was at the taking of Savannah, Georgia. When I last heard from him he and his wife were in Muskegon, Mich., at the home of their dau.

CHILDREN.

1. Franklin Eugene (7) d. young.
2. Lora Elmore (7) d. young.
3. Frances Ophelia (7), b. 1 Dec., 1846; m. Harry H. Range. They have—
    1 Edward W. Range (8).
    2 Charles L. Range (8)
4. Helen Amelia (7), b. 28 Nov., 1848, d. aged 32.
5. Cora Adelia (7), b 25 Dec. 1850; d. aged 30
6. Victoria Rosalie (7), b 19 Aug., 1852; m. Charles S Marr, a lawyer of Muskegon, Mich.: has one dau., Margaret Marr, m. Robert Grife.

III. Albert, b. 20 May, 1820, at Rensselaerville, N. Y., was adopted by Mrs Wm Stewart (his father's sister), m. Eliza Ann Lobdell of Sherburne, b. 28 Aug., 1825, dau of Joshua (6) Lobdell, son of Stephen (5), a brother of Nathaniel (5) They moved to the town of Aylmer, Elgin Co., Canada, where Albert d 6 Jan., 1876 Had one dau., Jerusha.

1. Jerusha (8), b 5 Dec., 1845; m W. H. Miller.

By second wife (name unknown) Nathaniel had—

IV. Jerusha V. John. and VI. Hiram, of Battle Creek, Mich., who has two daughters, one of whom has taken the vows of sisterhood. Hiram was in "War of the Rebellion." in a Michigan company of heavy artillery, at Newport News and Baton Rouge; discharged in 1865

CHILDREN OF THEADOSIA LOBDELL AND SAMUEL SHAW (HER SECOND HUSBAND).

I Marvin Shaw, b —— (I do not know whether the older children were b at Spencertown. Columbia Co., N Y., or at Sherburne, N Y.) 8 Feb., 1808; m. Jane Smith.

II Edmond Shaw, b. 12 Feb., 1809, m. Ersula Ray.

III. Wm Stewart Shaw, b 4 Feb., 1811; m. Ruth Ann Strong. I am told that he left Sherburne, Chenango Co., N. Y., when a young man, bought a load of merchandise and, making sales on his way, settled at Elgin, Ill., where he, with two or three other families, laid the foundation of Elgin. He built the first hotel in the place, which was still standing when my information was given He m. his wife at Elgin, and had a family of ten children. Willis and Eugene were sons. Eugene was killed on the railroad.

Mr. Shaw went to Elgin in 1836, was a resident for 60 years, dying there in 1896.

He owned the first omnibus and was the first constable in Elgin, and at the time of his death owned a farm deeded him by the government. He worked under James T Gifford, owner of the town site, in erecting the First Congregational Church, which now stands. He was a thoroughly progressive man and leaves to his family a precious legacy in his good name and true life.

IV. Hiram K. Shaw, b 17 April. 1813, m Maria Eaton

V. Geo. W Shaw, b 15 Nov , 1815; m Orsaville Maxon.

VI Daniel L Shaw, b 15 Feb , 1817; m Amy Harris

VII. Harriet Shaw, b 31 March, 1821; m Jerome Pratt.

VII. Elizabeth Keeler Shaw, b. in Sherburne 15 June, 1825, is the youngest and the only living child of Theadosia (Lobdell) Shaw. She m. twice (2) Almon Cook, and (1) James D Harris, b. 25 Dec , 1820, at Sherburne, d 1 Dec., 1865, at Sherburne, son of Dexter and Amy (Hall) Harris, by whom she had two children.

> 1. Theadosia Irene Harris (6), b. 14 July, 1847, d 10 May, 1854
>
> 2. Eva Cephantus Harris (6), b. 30 Sept, 1854; m. F. T. Zellers and resides with her mother in Sherburne (1903)

The religion of the Lobdells of this branch was Episcopal, and Mrs Cook has an old Episcopal prayer book given her by her aunt. Elizabeth Lobdell, dated 23 Nov , 1767.

CHILDREN AND DESCENDANTS OF LEWIS (5) AND EUNICE (SHAW) LOBDELL.

1 Eliza 2 Sally Ann 3 Hiram 4 Francis

I Eliza No record.

II Sally Ann, probably m Reuben Davis, Jr , b in Somers, Conn , lived in Sherburne, N Y , son of Reuben and Mehitable (Sexton) Davis.

III.   Hiram, b in 1816 in Sherburne, N. Y.; m. Maria, dau. of Jacob Smith. He d. 1896 at Sherburne. Had three children.

    1.   Smith S. (7), b 1846; m. Etta Crandall.

    2   Lewis R. (7), b. 19 March, 1850, at Sherburne, m. 23 Dec., 1873, Mary E., dau. of Hiram C. and Elizabeth Warren Bassett, b. 1855 at Columbus, Chenango Co. They have one dau., Fern D. (8), b. 31 Dec., 1881, m. Charles S. Clark. Mr. Lobdell moved from Sherburne to Baltic, Conn., and thence to East Granby, Conn., where he is a progressive and influential citizen. Has held the position of justice of the peace for the past four years, and is extensively engaged in raising tobacco in Conn., both Havana and shade-grown Sumatra. Previous to this he was in the creamery business for twenty years.

    3   Francis (7), b. 1855. m. Jennie Weldon.

SEVENTH GENERATION.

[4]CHILDREN OF ISAAC AND SUSAN (WHEELER) KEELER OF AKRON, ERIE CO., N. Y.

1. Cordelia.   2. Emma.   3. Mark.

    1.   Cordelia Keeler, b. at Clarendon, N. Y., 4 Oct., 1833; m. 15 Feb., 1860, Ambrose B. Comstock and resided at Sylvania, Ohio. No children.

    2.   Emma L. Keeler, d. unmarried.

    3.   Mark Keeler, b. Akron, N. Y.; m 3 Oct., 1860, Amelia Klinek, resided in Rochester, N. Y.

[4]CHILDREN OF JOHN AND SELINDA (BOSS) KEELER.

1. Truman Phineas.   2 Amelia.   3. Ann Adelia   4. Melinda 5. Wm. Henry.   6. Elizabeth Lobdell.

    1.   Truman Phineas Keeler, b Camillus, N Y., 3 Dec., 1826; m. 16 Feb., 1851, Candice Cumming of Worcester, N Y., where Phineas d 28 April, 1889.

    2   Amelia Keeler, b. at Camillus. 12 March 1829; m. 14 Feb., 1857, Wm H. Smith and settled in Fredonia, N. Y.

---

*Rockwell and Keeler Genealogy.

3. Ann Adelia Keeler, b. in Orleans Co., N. Y., 10 April, 1834; m. Ludulphy P. Osmer. He d. in New Mexico. She afterward made her home with her son at Jamestown, N. Y.

4. Melinda Keeler d. unmarried.

5. Wm. Henry Keeler, b. 1838; m. Susie A. Pedler and moved to California. Afterward in Detroit, Mich.

6. Elizabeth Lobdell Keeler, b. 1841; d. in Fredonia 1860.

*CHILDREN OF TERTULLUS L. AND REBECCA (HAYES) KEELER OF WEST MILTON, N. Y.

1. Mary Elizabeth Keeler m. Silas Walker. She d. at West Milton 7 May, 1878.

2. Henry Keeler m. Hannah Young. Home at West Milton.

3. Isaac Keeler m. Clarissa Olds and settled at Washington, D. C.

CHILDREN OF JOHN SHERWOOD (6) AND ZERUAH (ROBINSON) LOBDELL.

1. Caroline m. Abraham Slighter of Nassau, Rensselaer Co., N. Y.

II. Levi m. Mary A. Rogers.

III. Rowland never married.

IV. Lewis m. Eleanor Craver.

V. Cornelius, b. 1837 at Chatham, Columbia Co., N. Y.; m. Mary H., dau. of Stephen and Polly (Flint) Vickery, b. 24 March, 1839, at Alps, Rensselaer Co., N. Y. Mr. Lobdell resides (1901) about six miles from Stephenstown, Rensselaer Co., N. Y., on a farm purchased about 18 years ago. He suffers greatly from rheumatism, but has the assistance of his son William, who lives on the farm and is m.; has three little children. William (8), Clara (8), and Ella (8).

Mr. C. Lobdell has another son, Irving, living at Housatonic, Mass., m. and has two little ones. Lawrence (8) and Marion (8).

Irving E., b. at Chatham, N. Y., 2 Oct., 1865; m. Lena Dunham.

Wm., b. at Troy 22 Aug., 1867, m. Minnie Knapp.

VI. Eugene, unmarried.

---

*Rockwell and Keeler Genealogy.

CHILDREN AND DESCENDANTS OF JOSHUA (6) AND LYDIA (TILLOTSON) LOBDELL.

1. Eliza Ann 2 Stephen Wallace. 3 Sarah Jane

1 Eliza Ann, b. 28 Aug., 1825, at Sherburne, m (1) Albert Lobdell, son of Nathaniel, and moved to Canada, where her husband d 6 Jan., 1876 She re-married to Mr Scott, a farmer, a native of Canada, and both are living in Sherburne with their dau. and son-in-law, Mr W. H Miller

2. Stephen Wallace, b 22 Nov., 1826, at Sherburne; m 18 Nov., 1850, Permelia Purdy, b 12 April, 1832, at Sherburne, dau. of Stephen and Nancy (Crandall) Purdy. Mr Lobdell (1901) conducts a large business at Sherburne in grain and feed, and daily is at his store Has three sons; one is bookkeeper for the father, one a farmer, the other a conductor on M. C. railroad, residing in Canada. Children·

      1 William Wallace (8) m Ophelia Wicks
      2. Charles A. (8) m. Carrie Miller.
      3 Albert E (8) m. Cora Bryant

3 Sarah Jane m. Mr. Abbott; d and left four children 1. Joshua. 2 Henry 3 Ella, and 4 Frank Abbott.

CHILDREN OF NANCY LOBDELL (6) AND JACOB WRIGHT WEBB.

1. Henry. 2 Mary Jane 3 Wm Wallace. 4. Charles Wesley. 5 James Edward 6 Lucius Allard

1 Henry Webb. b. 8 March, 1823, m. Mary Abbott After his death, his widow and two little daughters went to live with her people in Columbus, Ohio, where one dau d

II. Mary Jane Webb, now living (1903) in Belvidere, Ill., was b 7 Jan , 1825, at North Salem, N. Y , m. at Belvidere 14 Oct., 1846, John Martin Glasner. b. 18 Dec., 1817, at Harmony, Warren Co, N. J., d. 11 April, 1897, at Belvidere. He was the son of Peter Glasner, b 25 July, 1775, and Elizabeth (Martin) Glasner, b 30 March, 1781; m. 13 May, 1800, of Harmony, N J. The family are Presbyterians and consist of—

      1 Mary E Glasner (Lillie) (8) m. Enos T. Gage. Has one little dau Resides at Belvidere. Ill

2. Emma Glasner (8) m. Wm. H. Pettit of Belvidere.

3. Wm. A. Glasner (8) m. Cora L. Gilman. Residence, Chicago, Ill

III. Wm. Wallace Webb, b. 13 Dec., 1827, m. Lydia A. Ray, d. 15 May, 1897. No children.

IV. Charles Wesley Webb, b. 21 April, 1830; m. Mrs. Adeline Eaton. Is now (1903) living with his son, Benj. Webb, in Elroy, Wis.

V. James Edward Webb, b. 21 July, 1832, m. Mary McMahon, d. Has one dau., Mrs. Lillie E. Wearne, Omaha, Neb.

VI. Lucius Allard Webb, b. 14 June, 1838; m. Asenath Lisdall. Resides at Portland, Ore. Has one dau., Mrs. Clara J. Harvey (8) of Woodlawn, Portland, Ore

---

SEVENTH GENERATION.

CHILDREN AND DESCENDANTS OF FLOYD KEELER (6) AND CLARINDA (DE WOLF) LOBDELL.

---

1. James Monroe 2 Wilber Fisk 3 Bartow Stewart 4. Mervin H. 5 Luceba J. 6. Luella J. 7 Albert. 8. Alice J. 9. Marett Elizabeth. 10 Gertrude 11. John Ellis. 12. Jesse Wing.

I. James Monroe, b. 26 April, 1848, in Boone Co., Ill.; unmarried

II. Wilber Fisk, b. 17 Oct., 1849; d. unmarried 30 March, 1880.

III. Bartow Stewart, a commercial traveler, residing at Janesville, Wis., was b. 28 May, 1853, at Belvidere, Ill ; m. 22 March, 1878, Mary Della Smith, b. 11 April, 1855, at Bolivar, Allegany Co., N. Y., dau. of Richard De Los Smith and Margret Lodema Andrus.

CHILDREN.

1. Bartow S, b. 9 Dec., 1887.
2. Kenneth L., b. 23 Nov., 1897.

IV. Mervin H., b. 2 Feb., 1855; m. Jean Concannon.

V. Luceba J., b. 26 April, 1856; m. Wm. M. Ray, b. 21 Jan., 1858, at Belvidere, Ill., son of Adam and Mary (Hadley) Ray. They reside at Belvidere, where the following children were b. to them:

1. Jennie I. Ray, b. 16 March, 1882.
2. Ethel C. Ray, b. 22 May, 1884; d. 25 Jan., 1892.

200

3 Walter W. Ray, b. 10 April, 1886

4 Floyd A Ray, b. 12 July, 1887.

5 and 6 Ruby L Ray and Jessie W. Ray, twins, b 14 Jan , 1892, Ruby d 25 Sept , 1892

VI. Luella J., b. 1858, d. 1861.

VII and VIII. Albert J. and Alice J , twins, b 1860, d. 1863

IX. Maret Elizabeth. b 7 Jan., 1863, at Belvidere. Ill., m. 30 Sept., 1889, at Rockford. Winnebago Co., Ill., Wilson James Grover, b. 26 Feb., 1865, at Ulysses. Potter Co., Pa., son of Wm. Wilson and Cynthia (Perkins) Grover. Mr. Grover is a Republican, and the family are Methodist They removed from Belvidere to Brookings, S. D , where they now reside Have one son, Donald Dana Grover, b. 25 May, 1895. Their little dau., Marguerite Gertrude Grover, b. 9 Oct., 1893, d. 18 Sept., 1894.

X. Gertrude M , b 15 Nov., 1864, is a teacher, residing at Belvidere, Ill.

XI. John Ellis, b 17 March, 1868, at Belvidere, m. 21 Nov., 1897, at North Redwood Falls, Minn , Carra Pearl Caverhill, b. 23 Feb., 1875, at Needah, Adams Co., Wis., dau of Palmer and Nellie (Jefferson) Caverhill Mr Lobdell has no children; is a farmer, residing at Fessenden, Wells Co , N D

XII Jesse Wing, b. 19 Jan , 1869, at Belvidere, Ill ; m. 24 Feb., 1894, Anna Wander. b 19 Oct , 1877, in New York City, dau. of Adam and Mary Ann (Kranz) Wander. Mr Lobdell is the youngest of twelve children and is living on the old homestead eight miles southeast of Belvidere. bought by his father over fifty years ago, still owned by his mother, who, with her oldest son, James Monroe, who is blind, lives with Mr Jesse Wing Lobdell, who has three children

1. Floyd Adam (8), b 9 July, 1895.

2 Gladys Maria (8), b 31 May, 1897.

3. Luceba Clarinda (8), b 13 May, 1899.

Given by Mrs Julia Lobdell (Dean) Stark of Randolph, Wis. ·

Tertullius Lobdell, b. 25 Dec., 1770, d. 7 Aug., 1803, at Coxsackie, Green Co., N. Y., of typhoid fever. He went there to make a home for his family from North Salem, N. Y. He m. at North Salem —— Deborah Wallace, dau. of Abijah and Elizabeth (Keeler of Wilton, Conn) Wallace She was b 11 Oct., 1774, d 16 Jan., 1851, at Amsterdam, N. Y., and buried there. Children :

Fanny, b. 22 Dec., 1793.

Anna, b. 1798.

Fannie Lobdell (Tertullius), b. 22 Dec., 1793, d. 1 July, 1829; m. James Hayes 30 Aug., 1812. He was b. 30 Sept., 1791, d. 5 Dec., 1885, at Ballston Spa, N. Y. He was son of Henry and Mary (Ferris, she was called Molly) Hayes. Molly was dau. of Sylvanus and Mary (Mead) Ferris. James Hayes was grandson of Freegift and Fanny (Perritt) Hayes. He was elder in the West Milton Church, N. Y., for over sixty-five years. Although a farmer, he was leader in his community and respected by all for his integrity and judgment. He was m. five times, all of his wives being excellent women. Children by first wife:

Harriet Hayes, b. 19 May, 1813, Galway, N. Y.; d. 12 April, 1814.

Henry Wallace Hayes, b. 24 Nov., 1815, Galway, N. Y.

Deborah Hayes, b. 17 Nov., 1818; d. 15 July, 1838; unmarried.

Fanny Hayes, b. 28 May, 1820, Galway, N. Y.; d. 2 Sept., 1822.

James Hayes, b. 10 July, 1823.

Fanny Hayes, b. 22 Aug., 1828.

Anna Lobdell (Tertullius), b. —— 1798; d. 9 Dec., 1840, at Amsterdam, N. Y. She was dau. of Tertullius and Deborah (Wallace) Lobdell, who lived at North Salem, N. Y. She m. 13 Feb., 1818, Jehiel Dean, son of Jehiel and Lydia (Arnold) Dean. He was b. 26 Feb., 1795, at Galway, N. Y.; d. 21 Jan., 1858, at Amsterdam, N. Y. He was a merchant and at one time owned a carpet factory. Children:

Lydia Ann Dean, b. 9 Nov., 1819, at West Galway, N. Y.

George Dean, b. 18 April, 1824, at Mannys Corners, N. Y.

Edward H. Dean, b. 1 April, 1831, at Galway, N. Y.

Francis Elizabeth Dean (called Libbie), b. 9 July, 1836.

Julia Lobdell Dean, b. 15 Nov., 1840, at Amsterdam, N. Y.

Henry Wallace Hayes, son of James and Fanny (Lobdell) Hayes, b. 24 Nov., 1815, d. at Galway, N. Y., 14 June, 1844, aged 28 years, 6 months, 24 days. "Married Mary Ann Knox at her home by Rev. Andrew Johnson May in the year of our Lord 1838." She was b. at Broadalban, N. Y., 10 Aug., 1817, was dau. of Peter and Jane (Clow) Knox. She d. in New York City 15 Dec., 1891, aged 73 years, 4 months and 8 days. She was matron at the Institute for the Blind in New York City nineteen years. From the tombstone of Henry Hayes:

"Husband, thy love is not forgot.
Affection marks the hallowed spot
Where thou art laid, and hope is given
To meet thee yet again in Heaven."

Child, Julia Hayes, b. 24 March, 1839, at Galway, N. Y.

James Hayes, son of James and Fanny (Lobdell) Hayes b. 10 July, 1823, d. 10 July, 1881, at Three Rivers, Mich.; m. 4 Sept., 1849, at West Galway, N. Y., Isbella Mead, dau. of Ralph and Isbella (Stewart) Mead. She was b. at West Galway 3 May. 1827, and d. 24 March, 1881. at Detroit, Mich. James Hayes was a merchant. Children.

Henry Wallace Hayes b. 17 Feb., 1851, at West Galway, Fulton Co., N. Y.

Elizabeth Mead Hayes, b. 1 Sept., 1853, at Hagamans Mills, Montgomery Co., N. Y.

Isabella Hayes. b. 22 July, 1855. at Wallace, Steuben Co., N. Y.

James Hayes, b. 13 April, 1857. at Wallace, Steuben Co., N. Y.

Fannie Hayes, b. 8 April, 1862, at Ballston Spa. N. Y.; d. 30 Sept., 1874. Centerville, Mich.

Ralph Alexander Hayes, b. 20 Sept., 1865, at West Galway, N. Y.

Fannie Hayes, dau. of James and Fanny (Lobdell) Hayes b. 22 Aug., 1828; d. 31 March, 1897, at Detroit, Mich. She m. 13 Dec., 1848, Richard Halloway Steele, A. M., D. D., son of Rev. John Beatty and Eliza (Holloway) Steele. He was b. 17 Sept., 1824, at Watervliet N. Y. and d. 5 April, 1900, at Detroit, Mich. He graduated from Rutgers College. New Brunswick, N. J., in 1844. Received degree of A. M. in 1847. Graduated from the Theological Seminary at New Brunswick, N. J., in 1847. Was licensed by the classes of Schenectady, N. Y. 23 July, 1847. He was engaged to supply the pulpit of Charlton Church, N. Y., for six months, commencing 12 Sept., 1847, and elected as pastor 29 Dec., 1847. He was ordained and installed 16 Feb., 1848. In 1850 he took charge of the church at Ballston Spa and remained two years. From 1852 to 1863 was pastor of the Reform Church at Nassau, N. Y., from there he went to New Brunswick N. J., where he remained seventeen years, from 1863 to 1880, in one of the oldest and largest churches of the denomination, First Reformed (Dutch) Church, founded in 1717. In 1880 he was called to the Presbyterian Church of Ann Arbor, Mich., where he remained until 1887. He retired after forty years of ministry and in 1888 he removed to Detroit, Mich. Thirteen of his sermons are published, also his history of the First Reformed Church of New Brunswick, N. J. From about 1865 he was a constant contributor to secular and religious periodical literature—his last article being published six months after his death. Children

Charles Henry Steele, A. M., M. D., b. 18 July, 1851, at Ballston Spa, N. Y.

Emma Frances Steele, b. 16 Oct., 1855, at Nassau, N. Y., m. 2 June, 1903, by Rev. David M. Cooper, to Duncan K. McNaughton, b. 22 May, 1845. Reside at Detroit, Mich.

Wallace Halloway Steele, b. 13 March, 1867, at New Brunswick, N. J., d. at Ann Arbor, Mich., 10 Sept., 1888.

Lydia Ann Dean, dau. of Jehiel and Anna (Lobdell) Dean, b. 9 Nov., 1819, d. 28 Feb., 1885, at Ripon, Wis; buried at Forest Home, Milwaukee, Wis. She m. 18 June, 1844, William Lewis Gillette (7), son of Stephen and Nancy (Lassell) Gillette. He was b. near Jamestown, N. Y., 6 Feb., 1816; d. at Ripon, Wis., 7 Feb., 1907, the morning after he was 91 years old. buried at Forest Home, Milwaukee, Wis. Children:

Wallace Clisbe Gillette, b. 1 Sept., 1845, at Amsterdam, N. Y.; d. 4 March, 1864, at Randolph, Wis. He was buried at Forest Home, Milwaukee, Wis.

Walter Stephen Gillette, b. 22 Feb., 1848, at Amsterdam, N. Y.

Anna Nancy Gillette, b. 18 March, 1850, at Amsterdam, N. Y.

Mary Alice Gillette, b. 22 April, 1852, at Amsterdam, N. Y.

Ellen Gillette, b. Dec., 1853, at Amsterdam, N. Y.; d. Feb., 1855.

George Dean, son of Jehiel and Anna (Lobdell) Dean, b. 18 April, 1824, at Mannys Corners, N. Y., m. 26 May, 1852, at Amsterdam, N. Y., Laura V. Bunn, dau. of Thomas and Elizabeth (Button) Bunn. She was b. at Tribis Hill, N. Y., 31 March, 1829, and d. at Amsterdam, N. Y., 19 April, 1900. They lived in California from 1859 to 1882, when they returned to Amsterdam. Children:

George Thomas Dean, b 14 Nov., 1856, at Amsterdam, N. Y.

Anna Elizabeth Dean, b 24 Oct., 1859, at Amsterdam, N. Y.

Mary Bunn Dean, b. 1 March, 1867, near Oakland, Cal.

Edward H. Dean, son of Jehiel and Anna (Lobdell) Dean, was b. 1 April, 1831, at Galway, Saratoga Co., N. Y., d. 28 Sept., 1906, at Albany, buried at Amsterdam; m. at Amsterdam, N Y., 2 Oct., 1854, Mary Elizabeth Stone. She was dau. of Charles and Comfort S. (Bell) Stone, was b at Fondas Bush (now, 1901, called Perth), Fulton Co., N Y., 28 March, 1835. Edward Dean went into the New York Central freight office 1 April, 1855; later spent six years in California. When he returned he went back into the same office and is still there (March 1901). Children:

Mary (called Minnie) Stone Dean, b. 21 July, 1855, at Amsterdam, N. Y.

Ella Palmer Dean, b. 14 Dec, 1856, at Amsterdam, N Y.

Charles Stone Dean, b. 23 Oct., 1858, at Albany, N. Y.

Albert Edison Dean, b 1 Jan, 1862, at Albany; d 5 Aug., 1862.

Frank Godine Dean, b. 27 May, 1863, at Amsterdam, N. Y.

Elizabeth Dean, dau. of Jehiel and Anna (Lobdell) Dean, was b. 9 July, 1836; d. at half past two o'clock Saturday morning, 15 April, 1899, at Ripon, Wis. She was m at Amsterdam, N. Y, 28 June, 1858, to Ira DeWitt Hedding of Milwaukee, Wis He was b. in Chazy, Clinton Co., N Y., 1 Jan, 1828. He was son of Simeon and Lucinda (Chamberlain) Hedding. Lucinda Chamberlain was dau. of Ira and Lydia (Dewey) Chamberlain. Simeon Hedding was son of H. James and Ruth (Ferguson) Hedding. He was the youngest, and Bishop ——— Hedding of the Methodist Episcopal Church of northern New York was the oldest of a large family of children. The older members of the family moved from Vermont to New York in an early day.

Julia Lobdell Dean, dau. of Jehiel and Anna (Lobdell) Dean, b. 15 Nov., 1840, at Amsterdam, N. Y.; m. at Randolph, Wis., 29 Oct., 1867, John Given Stark. He was b. 15 Sept., 1836, at North Lyme, Conn.; came to Dodge Co., Wisconsin, in 1853. He was son of Abial (Nathan, Nathan, Abial, Aaron, Aaron) and Jane

Alice (Ely) Stark He was postmaster at Randolph for several years; was a member of the village board several times, also clerk of the board. Children

 Stella Louise Stark, b Wednesday, 22 July, 1868, at Kenosha, Wis

 Anna Pearl Stark, b 27 June, 1871, at Randolph, Wis.

 William Henry Stark. b 7 April, 1873, at Randolph, Wis.

 James Stark, b. 1 July, 1875, at Randolph, Wis

 Frank Stark, b. 17 May, 1877, at Randolph, Wis

 Walter Stark, b. 12 Sept., 1878, at Randolph, Wis.

Julia Hayes, dau of Henry and Fannie (Lobdell) Hayes & Mary Ann (Knox) Hayes. She was b at Galway, N Y, 24 March, 1839, and m James Moor Pfleger 18 April, 1865, by the Rev. Richard Steele, D. D, at his house in New Brunswick, N. J. (his wife being Julia's father's sister) J M Pfleger was b. 26 Jan., 1832, at Strouchburg, Pa.; was son of George and Lavinia Ruth (McConnell) Pfleger He d 29 March, 1898, at New York City. Salesman for H. B. Claflin & Co., New York City, N. Y., for thirty-four years Children·

 Wallace Jeremiah Pfleger, b 6 Feb, 1866, at Brooklyn, N Y.

 Lilly Pfleger, b. 22 May, 1870, at Brooklyn, N. Y.; d 20 May, 1872.

 Spencer Day Pfleger, b 2 June, 1873, Brooklyn, N. Y.

 Merrin Lavinia Pfleger, b 6 Sept, 1875, at Brooklyn, N. Y

Henry Wallace Hayes, son of ( ) James and Isabella (Mead) Hayes, was b. 17 Feb, 1851; m. Florence Bliss Jewett 27 May, 1879. She was b 4 April, 1855, lived and m at Florence, St. Joseph Co, Mich; was dau. of Joseph and Mary Almira (Farrington) Jewett. H. W. Hayes is Michigan Central Railroad agent at Ann Arbor, Mich Children :

 Pauline Jewett Hayes, b 3 Jan, 1884, at Ann Arbor, Mich

 Wallace Farrington Hayes, b 27 Jan, 1888, at Ann Arbor, d 3 Sept, 1890, at Ann Arbor

 Inez Robinson Hayes, b 10 Aug, 1892.

Elizabeth Mead Hayes, dau of James and Isabella (Mead) Hayes, was b 1 Sept, 1853, at Hagamans Mills, N. Y. She was m at the residence of her brother, Henry W. Hayes, at Ann Arbor,

Mich., 20 March, 1887, by Rev. R. H. Steele, to Charles Knox Fletcher. He was b. at Centerville, Mich., 16 March, 1847, son of John Wilken and Sarah (Knox) Fletcher. A farmer. Children:

John Wilken Fletcher, b. 28 July, 1888, Centerville, Mich.

Katherine Isabella Fletcher, b. 19 June, 1892, Centerville, Mich.

James Hayes, son of James and Isabella (Mead) Hayes, b. 13 April, 1857, at Wallace, Steuben Co., N. Y.; m. Abigail McHenry 24 March, 1888, at Chicago, Ill. She was b. ———, and dau. of William and Abigail (Colby) McHenry of Chicago. James Hayes is a merchant. Children:

Benton Hayes, b. 5 Dec., 1888, at Chicago, Ill.

An unnamed babe d. one month old at Chicago, Ill.

James Colby Hayes, b 10 June, 1892, at Chicago, Ill.

Dorothy Hayes, b. 6 March, 1895, at Chicago, Ill.

Charles Henry Steele, A. M., M. D., son of Fanny Hayes and Richard Steele, D. D., was b. 18 July, 1851. Studying medicine in New York City and finding his health failing, he went to San Francisco, Cal., about 1874, became doctor on the ships of the Pacific mail, and for a time in the U. S. Army with a winter station on an island in the beautiful San Francisco Bay. Later practiced his profession twenty-two years in San Francisco. He m. there on 1 Nov., 1882, Hattie Bailey McKee. She was b. there 1 Nov., 1865, was dau. of William H. and Clara (French) McKee. Children:

Fannie Steele, b. 26 July, 1886, at San Francisco, Cal.

Arthur Halloway Steele, b. 4 April, 1890, at San Francisco, Cal.

Mary A. Gillette, dau. of Lydia Ann Dean and William Gillette, b. 22 April, 1852, at Amsterdam, N. Y., m. at Ripon, Wis., by Rev. Father Prescott, Thursday, 13 Aug., 1885, at St. Peter's Episcopal Church, to Charles Cowan. He was b. at Worthington, Ohio, son of Ira and Mary (Gilman) Cowan. Mary Gilman was dau. of Israel Gilman. Children:

Imogene Cowan, b. 24 June, 1886, at Ripon, Wis.

William Prescott Cowan, b. 16 Dec., 1889, at Ripon, Wis.

George Thomas Dean, son of George and Laura V (Bunn) Dean, b. 14 Nov., 1856; m. 23 July, 1888, Mary E. Bartleman. She was dau. of David and Mary (Stacy) Bartleman and was b. at Pekin, Niagara Co., N. Y., 2 July, 1864. They live at Amsterdam, N. Y.

Anna E. Dean, dau. of George and Laura V. (Dunn) Dean, was b. 24 Oct., 1859; m. at Amsterdam, N. Y., to James Addison Barkhuff, Tuesday, 17 Nov., 1885, at one o'clock p. m. He was b. 16 Nov., 1857, at Amsterdam, N. Y., and was the only child of Robert and Henrietta (Pulver) Barkhuff. Children:

Laura Etta Barkhuff, b. 2 Jan., 1887, at Amsterdam, N. Y.

Raymond Addison Barkhuff, b. 28 May, 1889, at Amsterdam, N Y.

Ella P Dean, dau. of Edward and Mary (Stone) Dean, b. at Amsterdam, N. Y., 14 Dec., 1856; m. at Albany, N. Y., Thursday, 21 Oct., 1886, to George Warren West. He was b. 11 April, 1856, at Ballston Spa, N. Y., was son of Henry L. and Mary (Scidmore) West. Children:

Mabel Minnie West, b. 28 July, 1888, at Amsterdam, N. Y.

Edison Stone West, b. 7 March, 1890, at Amsterdam, N. Y.

Charles S. Dean, son of Edward and Mary (Stone) Dean, b. 23 Oct., 1858, at Albany, N. Y.; m. Thursday, 29 Sept., 1887, at Troy, N. Y., to Marie Louise Toles, b. 24 Dec., 1865, at Troy, N. Y., dau. of Perry E. (b. at Danville, N. Y.) and Martha D. (Lindsay) Toles (b. at Hartsville, N Y.). Children:

Rena Stone Dean, b. 21 Dec., 1888, at Troy, N. Y.

Dorothy Dean, b. 26 June, 1890, at Troy, N. Y.

Frank G. Dean, son of Edward and Mary (Stone) Dean, b. 27 May, 1863, at Amsterdam, N. Y.; m. 2 June, 1884, Marguerite Audell Jackson, dau. of Benjamin Rush and Harriet E. (Wells) Jackson, and b. 22 March, 1867, at Dushore, Pa. Children:

Ethel S. Dean, b 25 Sept., 1887, at Amsterdam, N. Y.

Edward Jackson Dean, b. 11 July, 1889, at Amsterdam, N. Y.

Stella L. Stark, dau. of Julia (Dean) Stark and J G. Stark, b. at Kenosha, Wis., 22 July, 1868. She was m. by Rev. J. V. Trenery at Randolph, Wis., 22 Aug., 1894, to Charles William McGill of Grand Rapids, Mich. He was b 14 July, 1865, at West Stephentown, N. Y.; was son of Hugh and Eunice Ann (Newton) McGill. He is a lawyer and served four years as Circuit Court Commissioner of Kent County and as representative in the Michigan Legislature in 1897-1898.

Anna P. Stark, dau. of Julia (Dean) Stark and J. G. Stark, was b. 27 June, 1871, at Randolph, Wis.; m. by Rev. J V. Trenery at

Randolph, Wednesday, 11 Sept., 1895, Frederick Elmer Sexton of Grand Rapids, Mich. He was b. 15 July, 1865, at Bloomfield, Crawford Co., Pa., son of Lyman Platt (b. 16 April, 1837, McKee Co., Pa.) and Abigail Enos (Sweet) Saxton. (She was b. 15 March, 1836, at Philadelphia, Pa.) She (Abigail) was dau. of Benjamin P. (b. in New York state) and Catherine Eliza (Burroughes) Sweet (b. in New Jersey). Lyman Saxton was son of Lyman Langworthy and Dorothy (Goodwin) Saxton. Children

Julia Saxton, b 23 July, 1896, at Grand Rapids, Mich.

Dean Frederick Saxton, b 9 Aug., 1897, at Grand Rapids, Mich.

Wallace J. Pfleger, son of Julia (Hayes) Pfleger and J. M. Pfleger, b 6 Feb. 1866, at Brooklyn, N Y ; m 4 July, 1894, Mary Warner, dau of William and Anna Gates (Lewis) Warner. She was b 25 Sept, 1868 Child·

Kenneth Warner Pfleger, b 22 July, 1899, at Arlington, N. Y.

Additions by Mrs Julia Lobdell Stark (1907)

My dau., Anna Pearl Saxton, d. at Traverse City, Mich. (and buried there) 10 Dec., 1903. Her child, John R. Saxton, b. 10 Dec., 1903.

My son, Walter Dean Stark, b 12 Sept, 1878; m. by Rev. Charles Storey at Clintonville, Utah, 14 Feb., 1905, to Blanch Parker, dau of Maximilian and Annie Parker. She, b. at Beaver, Utah, 5 Nov, 1881. Children Twins, b. 26 Nov., 1905, at Bingham, Utah—John Boyd Stark and Bryce Parker Stark.

My son, Frank Stark, m at Mt. Pleasant, Mich., 30 Aug., 1905, to Helen Elizabeth Leaton, b. 29 May, 1880, dau of John J. and Stella (Gaylord) Leaton

The wife (Louise) of Charles Stone Dean (Edward), d 19 March, 1902. He m. Charlotte Janet Velsey 27 Feb, 1905, at Troy, N. Y

FOURTH GENERATION.

CHILDREN OF MARY (3) LOBDELL AND SAMUEL PLUMB.

1. Samuel. 2. Zuriel. 3 Joshua 4. Jared 5 Mary. 6. Samuel. 7. Susanna. 8. Jared

(Copied from Plumb Genealogy.)

I. Samuel Plumb, b 12 April, 1729

II Zuriel Plumb, b 8 April, 1731.

III. Joshua Plumb. b 24 June, 1734.

IV. Jared Plumb, b. 15 January, 1736, d. before 1749.

V. Mary Plumb, b 27 February, 1738; m Daristus Baldwin.

VI. Samuel Plumb, b. 18 April, 1741; m Eunice ——; d. 17 Oct , 1795, aged 54 years.

VII Susanna Plumb, b. 23 April, 1744; m Claudius Bartholemew

(From Bartholomew Genealogy.)

Claudius Barteleme was the son of a merchant and was born in Marseilles, France. At the age of 17 he engaged in the regiment "Royal Rolison" and shortly after came to America with Montcalm.

Claude Barteleme came to Derby in 1760, and soon after married Susannah, daughter of Samuel and Mary (Lobdell) Plumb.

Susannah was born 23 April, 1744; her father came from Milford and was one of the first settlers of Derby County.

He built a house on the opposite side of the street from the "Jewett house" at "Uptown". After settling in Derby he became a sea captain and eventually a large ship owner. In his religious views Claude was a devout Catholic, and his Catholic Bible containing the family record written by him is still preserved

He died in Derby 10 Oct , 1824, aged 87 Susannah died 26 Jan , 1818. Children all born in Derby.

210

VIII. Jared Plumb, b. 18 March, 1749; m 8 Aug., 1771, Ruth Fowler. He d. 1821, aged 72 years

The record of Revolutionary soldiers in Massachusetts has Jared Plumb of Westfield, Mass. He answered the call for the "Lexington Alarm." Afterward lived in Amsterdam, N. Y. and in 1820, when he applied for a pension, was nearly blind.

His name is on the muster rolls in the state house, Boston, Mass.

Children and Descendants of
Ebenezer [3] Lobdell, (Joshua [2], Simon [1])
Wife, Rebecca Benedict

FOURTH GENERATION.

CHILDREN OF EBENEZER (3) AND REBECCA (BENE-DICT) LOBDELL.

1 Elizabeth. 2. Ebenezer 3 Thomas 4 Uriah 5 Rachel. 6 Eunice. 7. Sarah. 8. Burwell 9. Rebecca. 10. Samuel 11. Sarah. 12. Susanna 13 Jared. 14 Josiah.

(All born in Ridgefield, Conn.)

I. Elizabeth, b. 21 Sept., 1733; m. at Ridgefield, 5 Dec, 1755, Henry Whitney, son of Henry and Elizabeth (Olmstead) Whitney of R., where Henry was b 29 July, 1715. They settled in R. and there d.—he, 9 or 10 July, 1794 of cholera morbus; she, 15 Aug, 1816, at the house of her dau , Rebecca (Whitney) Olmstead. Both are buried in Titicus cemetery.—(Whitney Genealogy)

II Ebenezer, Jr., 13 July, 1735; m. Eunice Bradley. He probably moved to Courtland Manor, for the record of baptism of his son Nathan by Dr Deblee, at Salem, 29 Oct , 1758, says· "Nathan, son of Ebenezer Lobdell—late of Ridgefield ' I have no record of the death of either Ebenezer or Eunice.

III. Thomas, b 2 Nov., 1737, evidently migrated with others of his family to Orange Co , N Y , as from Ridgefield records "Thomas Lobdell migrated to Warwick, Orange Co , N. Y., 1768 "

In 1782 in Ridgefield deeds he is given as Thomas Lobdell of Warwick, Orange Co , N Y. About that time there was an exodus of families from Orange Co. to Hunterdon Co , N. J., and probably Thomas was among them

From New Jersey men in the Revolutionary War I find "Thomas Lobdell, private, Hunterdon Co., N. J." "Thomas Lobdell, teamster, Capt. Scudder's team brigade "

I can find no record of his m. or death

IV. Uriah, of Ridgefield, b 11 March, 1740, m. Phoebe Chapman, dau of Phineas Chapman, of whom he bought (according to Redding, Conn , land records) 71 acres of land, 17 Jan , 1771 Ridgefield records give. "Uriah Lobdell moved to Philipstown,

N Y., but returned to Ridgefield " His name is found on the muster roll of Capt. Thomas Hobbies ' Co.

V Rachel, b 22 May, 1742, m. Wm. Hurlbutt and went to "the Butternuts", Otsego Co., N. Y.

VI Eunice, b 17 Sept., 1744. From Congregational Church records of Ridgefield "Eunice Lobdell, d. 29 Oct., 1825, aged 82 years."

VII Sarah, b. 10 Sept., 1746, d. 1751. Miss Jessie Lobdell of Ridgebury tells us that in Ridgefield cemetery, she found a small blue soap grave stone, all out of the ground. On it·

"Here lies the body of Sarah Lobdell, who died in ye fifth year of her age, April the 17, 17— ' "The last two figures were faint and I could not be sure if they were 21 or 51."

Evidently the grave of little Sarah

VIII. Burrell (or Burwell, as I understand it), probably given the family name of his paternal grandmother (Mary Burwell), was b 24 Feb., 1749. He m 9 March, 1772, at Wilton, Conn., Anna St. John, dau of Noah and Jane (Smith) St. John, and moved to Wilton, around Georgetown, where his children were born. Norwalk records say that he was a land owner at Georgetown, his property being bounded by that owned by John Morgan

He was alive in 1814, but probably d. about July, 1817, as on that date the last mention is made of Burwell, only the widow afterward, in Dr. Chichester's account book. Buzzell (Burwell) Lobdell enlisted in Conn. troops, 2 May, 1775; discharged, 8 Oct., 1775

IX. Rebecca, b. 20 Feb., 1751; m. John Chappell and went to live at "the Butternuts, Otsego Co., N Y, where her sister Rachel resided This data is given by a descendant. There was one Rebecca Lobdell, b about 1751, who m Josiah Davis, who enlisted as musician in Col Heman Swift's Co from Middletown, Conn., 1777. They had a dau Eunice Davis, m Joseph Griffen and moved from Connecticut to New York state about 1812. Judge Josiah Davis Ensign, of Duluth, Minn, is a great grandson of Rebecca, but who this Rebecca is I cannot prove

X Samuel, b 12 July, 1753 I have no proof of the identity of this Samuel, but I assume that he m and according to Dr. Chichester's account book the Dr. made a call on him 21 May, also 23 May, 1809, traveling five miles, and in 1819 traveled the same distance for professional calls on the widow (not knowing her maiden name) Norwalk land records give: "Samuel Lobdell, owner of a mill near Ridgefield and Redding line, apparently between Branchville and Sandford Station."

(From Redding Land Records.)

"Samuel Lobdell lease from Daniel Dean of Ridgefield of two inches of the depth from ye surface and five inches in length on the surface of the pond at the outlet commonly called the Great East Meadow Pond, otherwise sometimes called Burt's Pond, from the fifteenth day of March till the fifteenth day of April, inclusive, annually, in order to catch fish Rec'd of Samuel Lobdell and to his heirs and assigns, etc, for the term of ninety-nine years from the date hereof, the privilege of making a dam to stop the water on my land at or near the outlet of said Pond in such a manner as he the said Lobdell, his heirs or assigns, shall see necessary with free Liberty to pass along side the Brook and my Heirs and Assigns to repass over my Land to and from said Outlet, reserving to myself the Priviledge of Two inches in Depth and five inches in Length on the Top of said Dam at the Outlet of the Pond as aforesaid Only. In witness whereof I do hereunto set my hand and seal the 13th Day of Feb., A D, 1769

"Recorded May 25, 1774." Vol. 2 p. 45. (Copied)

XI. Sarah Lobdell (4), b. 5 Aug, 1755; m. Michael Warren of Ridgefield as his second wife.

XII. Susannam Lobdell (4), b 9 July, 1758; m. Daniel Riggs, an only child, born about 1762 at Stamford, Conn , d. 6 June, 1793; son of Joseph Riggs and Mary Keeler, his cousin. They resided at Ridgefield, where their children were born and where Susannah d. at the home of her granddaughter, Mrs Sarah Ann (Gray) Roberts, 5 Aug., 1841, aged 83 years.

(From Riggs Genealogy)

XIII. Jared Lobdell, b 1759, d 1759.

XIV. Josiah Lobdell, b 14 Aug , 1760; m. 20 Oct., 1787, Widow Miriam Hickock, b. 14 Aug , 1760, d. — June, 1837. They resided at Ridgefield, and both d there

Josiah enlisted in April, 1781, served as a private one month— on guard duty. Under Capt. Knowles Sears in Oct., 1781. Was private three months with Col. Heman Swift, April, 1782. Was private one month under Capt Doolittle in Oct., 1782. Served two months under Capt. Booth Was a pensioner, act of 1832

FIFTH GENERATION.

CHILDREN OF ELIZABETH (4) LOBDELL AND HENRY WHITNEY.

(Whitney). 1. Betty. 2. Sarah. 3. Rebecca. 4. Elizabeth.

(All born in Ridgefield.)

I. Betty Whitney, b. 30 April, 1756; m. in Ridgefield, Jeremiah Mead as his third wife.

II. Sarah Whitney, b. 23 July. 1759; m. her second cousin, Matthew Olmstead.

III. Rebecca Whitney, b. 18 Feb., 1761; m. Josiah Olmstead.

IV. Elizabeth Whitney—a twin of Rebecca; m. Daniel Jackson. They moved to Stratford, Conn.

(From Whitney Genealogy.)

FIFTH GENERATION.

CHILDREN AND DESCENDANTS OF EBENEZER, JR. (4) AND EUNICE (BRADLEY) LOBDELL.

I. Nathan. 2. Ben. 3 Abigail. 4. Thomas. 5. Robert. 6. James. 7. Samuel.

I. Nathan (5), bapt. 29 Oct., 1758 at Salem, Westchester Co., N. Y, d. in Fairfield, Franklin Co.. Vt. He m. 10 Jan., 1793, Abigail, dau of Benj. and Patience (Smith) Hoyt.

As Widow Lobdell, she died at the home of her son, Benj. Hoyt Lobdell, in Fairfield, Vt.

Nathan was a devout Christian man—a member and worker of the Episcopal Church, the following an example: He took a most arduous horseback ride of nearly 150 miles, through a wilderness, on business for the church he loved so dearly and served so faithfully. From the effects he d.

II. Benj., bapt. at Salem, 23 Aug., 1767, probably d young.

III. *Abigail, born 30 July, 1770; m. 1 Dec., 1787, Sherwood Whitney, b. in Fairfield or Stratford, Conn., 22 Sept., 1767. They

---

* Whitney Genealogy

217

lived in western part of Connecticut, but later moved to Fairfield, Vt., where he d 28 Feb 1848; she, 23 June, 1851.

CHILDREN.

1. Esther Whitney (6), b at Redding, Conn ; m 1809, Joseph Soule of Fairfield, Vt. He took part in the battle of Plattsburg, 1812

2 Silas Whitney (6), d. young.

3. Clarissa Whitney (6), d young.

4. Harriet Whitney (6), b. 22 Nov., 1795; m Salmon Soule

5. Eunice Whitney (6), b 3 May, 1800, m Anson Buck, of Fairfield, Vt

IV Thomas.—Mrs. Abigail H. Buck of Johnson, Vt., kindly gives to descendants the only record "Penelope ———— was the wife of Thomas Lobdell (a brother of grandfather Nathan Lobdell). He d. in the town of Georgia, Franklin Co, Vt. They had three children one son, Ebenezer, went to California. Sophie m. Mr Everts of Georgia She d many years ago Polly, the youngest, after the death of her father, with her mother spent the winter of 1848 at my father's (Andrew Buck). The next summer they went to Michigan, where Aunt Penelope d. Polly m and had two children "

V. Robert, bapt. at Salem, 31 Aug., 1776, probably d. young. No data can be secured regarding him.

VI James, m in Fairfield, Vt, had a dau Betsey (6) and a son James (6), by first wife Betsey was brought up by her Grandfather Lobdell as his own child She m Parker Farnsworth. They had two children, viz.

1 Susan Farnsworth (7), d. in childhood.

2 James Farnsworth (7), was a soldier in the Civil War, was taken sick at the front and d on his way home, at the hospital in New York City James m Jeanette Buck and had five children, two boys who d in childhood and three daughters

1. Susan Farnsworth (8)

2 Hattie Farnsworth (8)

3 Jennie Farnsworth (8)

All were Episcopalians.

VII Samuel, b. 31 Oct, 1783, at Ridgefield, Conn., d. 25 June, 1849 at Dickinson, Franklin Co, N. Y; m 5 Nov, 1809, Roxey

218

Colburn, b 18 Oct, 1789 at Lebanon, Madison Co., N Y, d. 21 Jan., 1853 at Dickinson, N Y.

I know the descendants will be interested in the letter I received from Mrs. Clara (Buckley) Wakeman of Allerton, Mass., in reply to inquiries as to the family of Samuel Lobdell (Ebenezer, Jr.) She says. "There were no other family of Lobdells in Fairfield, Vt. I am quite positive. I remember Mrs Whitney. She was aunt to my mother I do not think there were either Robert or Benj. There were Samuel and James, brothers of Nathan. Both had families Samuel's children were: Jason, Alex. Vietts Griswold (named for Bishop Griswold) and Orissa. I think Samuel m a second time and had one dau. Polly, who m Mr North and moved from Vermont to Wisconsin

---

CHILDREN OF NATHAN (5) AND ABIGAIL (HOYT) LOBDELL.

---

1. Esther (6). 2. Rachel (6). 3. Bradley (6). 4. Benj. Hoyt (6). 5 Amelia

---

1. Esther, b 17 Jan., 1798, at Fairfield, Vt., d. 8 Oct., 1848, at Fairfax; m. 1 March. 1827, Andrew Buck, a farmer of Fairfax, 20 Sept, 1797, at Fairfax, Franklin Co.. Vt., who d 22 Oct, 1896 at Fairfax, son of Gould and Hannah (Burritt) Buck. The family were Episcopalians

II. Rachel, b 7 April, 1800 at Fairfield. Vt, where she also d 28 Nov, 1872, m. at Fairfield 13 Feb, 1827, Horatio Wakeman, a farmer, who d 10 Sept., 1868 at Fairfield, son of Isaac and Sarah (Bradley) Wakeman. Sarah Bradley was dau. of Ezekial Bradley, who m. three times and had 12 children. Oldest was Ezekial, b. 1763; the youngest Lewis, b. 1791. One wife was Ruth ———; one, Eunice———. The last one, I do not know her name She had no children. He came from some place on the Hudson River, New York state Is buried at Fairfield, Vt.

III. Bradley, m for his first wife, Mary Bradley of Fairfield, Vt After her death he m Mahala Trowbridge of Indiana, to which state Bradley had moved. They were Episcopalians. Had no children

219

IV. Benjamin Hoyt, b 22 June, 1804 at Fairfield, Franklin Co., Vt, d 27 Feb, 1880 at Bartlett, Cook Co, Ill, m. 31 July, 1836 at Fairfield, Vt, Anna Andrus, b 15 Jan, 1810, at Shaftsbury, Vt, d 16 March, 1880 at Bartlett, Ill, dau of Benjamin Andrus and Freelove Milliman of Fairfield, Vt. Mr Seth Lobdell of Bartlett, Ill, tells us "Father left Fairfield Vt, in Sept, 1846 There were at that time three young children, the eldest 11 years. We came as far as northern Indiana and stopped a short time with Uncle Bradley Lobdell, leaving there we arrived at Dundee, Ill in Oct, 1846 My parents moved to Bartlett, Ill in 1877, where father and mother both died "

V. Amelia—of whom I have no record

Feb 27, 1880. Benj H Lobdell died at his residence, with inflammation of the lungs, aged 75 years, 7 months His funeral was attended at the Congregational Church on Sunday, Feb. 29, Rev H Munroe preaching the funeral sermon. Monday his remains were laid to rest in the family ground at Dundee Mr. Lobdell was born in Fairfield, Vt., and in 1847 removed to Illinois, and for thirty years remained upon one farm in Dundee But from increasing age and decreasing strength to meet the demands of hard labor, he sold his farm, and three years since purchased a home in Bartlett, where he remained to the time of his decease. He leaves behind him a devoted and faithful companion. Almost a half century of time attest the faithfulness of their lives. Truly a good man has gone from our midst He was honored and loved by our whole community.

His was a uniform Christian life. He exemplified in all his acts the spirit of Him whom he had professed to love for over half a century He rests from his labors, and his works do follow.

(From Local Papers)

Mrs Annie, widow of the late Benj H Lobdell, died after an illness of only four days, of inflammation of the liver, at her late residence in Bartlett, March 16, 1880, aged 70 years The funeral was held in the Congregational Church the 18th, at 10 a. m., Rev. H H. Munroe officiating.

Her remains were taken to Dundee and laid beside her late husband, who was buried there only two weeks before. She was born in Shaftsbury, Vt., in 1810

220

BENJ. HOYT LOBDELL (6)
(Nathan [5])   (1804-1880)
of Fairfield, Vt., and Bartlett, Ill.
(Page 220)

SETH LOBDELL (7)
(Benj. Hoyt [6])
of Bartlett, Ill.
(Page 224)

She early joined the Episcopal Church and remained a true and consistent member, until transmitted to the church triumphant In 1847, with her husband, she settled on a farm at Dundee, and remained there until three years ago, when they purchased the home in Bartlett. She was a most estimable lady, quiet, unassuming, rendering a helping hand in every case of need. Having been called to pass through a series of afflictions in the loss of husband, daughter and daughter-in-law—all within five weeks, she bore it all with remarkable calmness.

Having lived the life of a Christian, she died as she had lived. "Blessed are the dead who die in the Lord, for they rest from their labors and their works do follow them."

(From Local Papers)

SIXTH GENERATION.

CHILDREN OF SAMUEL BRADLEY LOBDELL AND WIFE, ROXEY COLBURN.

1. Hiram Colburn. 2. Jason Bradley. 3. Hiram R. 4. Alex. Vietts 5. Mary Bradley. 6. Orissa Parmelia.

I. Hiram Colburn, b. 10 Oct., 1810, d. young.

II Jason Bradley, b 7 Feb., 1812, at Fairfield, Vt., d 17 Jan., 1883 at Minneapolis, Minn : m. 21 April, 1838 at St. Albans, Vt., Eunice Jane Brigham, b. 9 April, 1823, at North Brookfield, Conn., d 24 Jan., 1857 at Dickinson, Franklin Co., N. Y., dau. of Dr. Lemuel Hawley and Betsey Ayers Brigham.

Mr. Lobdell in for his second wife, at Minneapolis, on 24 Jan., 1864, Maria Eliza Woodward, b. 11 Nov. 1829, at Fitchburg, Worcester Co., Mass., at which place—5 Bluff Ave—the widow resides (1903). Mr. Lobdell was a farmer; in religion, Universalist; Republican in politics. No children by second wife.

III. Hiram Restored, b 18 Jan., 1814, d. 1817.

IV. Alexander Vietts Griswold, b 1 Oct., 1817; named by Bishop Griswold; d. unmarried 10 April, 1885, at Minneapolis, Minn.

V. Mary Bradley, b. 10 Feb., 1825, d. 26 Oct., 1827.

221

VI. *Orissa Permelia, b 11 Oct., 1830, m 1861 at Richfield, Henepen Co, Minn, Adams Rogers Decrow. She d. 1863. Her husband was in the Union service at Vicksburg and was killed in a Confederate raid in 1864. No children

SEVENTH GENERATION.

CHILDREN OF ESTHER (6) LOBDELL AND ANDREW BUCK.

1. Infant son. 2 Betsey Ann Buck. 3. Nathan Lobdell Buck. 4 Cornelius Henry Buck. 5. Martha Jane Buck. 6. Mary Ann Buck. 7 Mahala Trowbridge Buck. 8. Andrew Bradley Buck

(All born at Fairfax, Vt.)

I. Infant son, died

II. Betsey Ann Buck, d in infancy.

III. Nathan Lobdell Buck, b. 16 Jan., 1831, m. Elmira S. Norton

IV. Cornelius Henry Buck, b 23 April, 1833; m. May Griffeth

V. Martha Jane Buck, b. 15 Feb., 1835, d. 15 Sept., 1884; m. Daniel J. Norton.

VI. Mary Ann Buck, a twin of Martha Jane, b. 15 Feb., 1835; m 24 Jan., 1856 at Fairfax, Abijah H Buck, b. 29 Nov., 1833 at Fairfax, son of Nathan and Sarah (Hawley) Buck of Fairfax. They reside at Johnson, Vt Are Episcopalians. 'Tis sad to record that their children have all preceded them to the other shore, where awaiting their arrival are

CHILDREN.

1 Wilmot Andrew Buck (8), b 28 Sept., 1857, d. unmarried, 24 March, 1879.

2 Sarah Buck (8), b 13 Nov., 1860, d. 16 Oct., 1861.

3 Ida Mahala Buck (8), b 8 Nov, 1863, d 1886; m. Lyman Jones

4 Nathan Abijah Buck (8), b 11 March, 1868, d 19 Nov., 1892.

VII Mahala Trowbridge Buck, b 9 July, 1837; m. Hiram Allen Soule.

VIII Andrew Bradley Buck, b 6 Dec, 1838, d unmarried

*John Rogers Genealogy

222

CHILDREN OF RACHEL (6) LOBDELL AND HORATIO WAKEMAN.

1. Seth Bradley. 2. Abigail. 3 Sarah C. 4 Sanford H. 5. Clara 6. Isaac C. 7 Walter

I. Seth Bradley Wakeman, b 30 Nov., 1827; m Cynthia B. Houghton

II. Abigail Amelia Wakeman, b 13 June, 1829; (m Van Rensaeller Skinner) entered peacefully into life eternal, at her home at Bakersfield, Vt, on the morning of 2 Dec, 1897. "Numbered with Thy saints in glory everlasting." (From the Churchman).

III. Sarah C Wakeman, b 17 Sept, 1831; m. Timothy Jarvis.

IV Sanford H Wakeman, b. 7 Jan., 1834, m Theresa V. Sampson.

V Clara Buckley Wakeman, b 16 Nov, 1837 at Fairfield, Franklin Co., Vt ; m 19 June, 1868 at Fairfield, Smith Farrand Sturgis, b 3 Oct, 1839 at Fairfield, Vt, son of Seth and Eliza (Bearse) Sturgis of Fairfield, Vt Mr. and Mrs S. F. Sturgis reside at Allerton, Mass. Are members of the Episcopal Church. Have two children·

    1 Mary Rachel Sturgis (8), b. 19 March, 1870; m. Alvin James Perham

    2. Walter Horatio Wakeman Sturgis (8), b 10 Feb, 1873; m. Anna Turner Sylvester

VI Isaac C. Wakeman, b. 30 Aug, 1839

VII Walter Wakeman, b. 25 Jan, 1843 at Fairfield, Vt, m. 1 June, 1876 at Lynd, Lyon Co, Minn., Eva J. Watson, b. 20 Feb, 1856 at Redwing Goodhue Co, Minn, dau. of W. L. and Jane A. (Howard) Watson. Mr. Wakeman and family reside at Marshall, Minn

CHILDREN.

    1. Howard Guy Wakeman (8), b. 21 Feb., 1877, d. 8 July, 1882.

    2. Minnie May Wakeman (8), b. 27 July, 1878, d. 2 Sept., 1882.

    3. Hazel June Wakeman (8), b. 26 June, 1884

    4 Walter Earl Wakeman (8), b. 24 April, 1888

CHILDREN OF BENJ. HOYT LOBDELL (6) AND WIFE, ANNA ANDRUS.

1. Seth 2. Nathan 3. Charles Henry 4. Mary Abigail.
5. Esther Ann.
(1, 2, 3 and 4 were born at Fairfield, Vt.)

I. Seth, b. 22 May, 1834. When a child 11 years old left Fairfield, Vt., and after sojourning at several places, his parents located in Bartlett, Ill in 1877 On Dec. 31, 1861, at Fond du Lac, Wis., he m. Emeline Holland,* b 15 April, 1844 at Painesville, Ohio, dau. of Peter and Julia (Walker) Holland.

He m. for his second wife, 16 Jan., 1881 at Kaukauna, Wis., Mrs G. W. Mann. The family reside at Bartlett, where Mr. Lobdell deals extensively in lumber, coal and feed.

II Nathan, a retired merchant, resides at 213 West St., Rockford, Ill. Was b. 18 Sept, 1839; m. 4 March, 1862 at Marengo, McHenry Co., Ill., Sarah Dimon, b. 15 Oct., 1842 at Weston, Fairfield Co, Conn., d 19 Jan., 1897 at Rockford, Winnebago Co, Ill., dau. of Thomas and Sallie E (Treadwell) Dimon. Mr. Lobdell remarried to Helen M Smith He is a Christian Scientist, a Republican in politics.

III Charles Henry, b 1 May, 1844, d in infancy.

IV Mary Abigail, ·b. 18 Jan, 1846; m. 1 Jan., 1873 at Elgin, Kane Co, Ill, Warner Towne, b 31 March, ——, at Hadley, Mass, son of E. Warner and Sophia (Hawks) Towne. Mr Towne and family reside at Sac City, Iowa, where he is interested in real estate He is a Republican The family are Presbyterians

CHILDREN.

1. Etta Sophia Towne (8), b at Monticello, Iowa, 29 April, 1877: m. 18 Jan, 1874 at Earlville, Delaware Co,

---

* Died at her home in Bartlett, Feb 10, 1880, aged 34 y, 10 m
Mrs Lobdell came to Bartlett about 4 years ago and during her residence here has endeared herself to all who became acquainted with her.
For several years her health has been poor, and her intimate friends could but feel that she was soon to be taken away
She suffered an exceedingly severe illness until relieved from all earthly troubles by that kind Providence who doeth all things for the best. A husband, four children and a host of friends mourn their loss
Her remains were taken to Dundee for burial —Local paper

224

Iowa, son of Geo M and Louisa P Van Derveer Parker

2 Roy Lobdell Towne (8), b 9 Dec, 1879. Is in business at Boone, Iowa

3 Benjamin Warner Towne (8), b 7 June, 1886.

V. Esther Ann, b 15 Sept., 1848 at Dundee, Kane Co., Ill., d 28 Feb. 1880 at Bartlett, Ill ; m 25 Dec, 1872 at Dundee, Ill, Bascom Bartlett, b 9 April, 1848 at Bartlett, Ill, son of Luther and Sophia Celia Bartlett One son, Ira Bartlett (8), a farmer, b 24 Feb, 1874, resides at Bartlett, Ill ; another, Walter Bartlett (8), at Elgin, Ill.

"The day after the death of her father (Benj Hoyt Lobdell), his daughter—wife of Bascom Bartlett—followed her father to the long home, never more to return She leaves three little ones and a dear companion to mourn her loss. She had endeared herself to us all The funeral was largely attended at the Congregational Church, Rev. H Munroe officiating, after which her remains were laid away in the family ground, while some who knew her well, sung over her grave. "Sister, thou wast mild and lovely," etc.

"From the first to the last the neighbors were unceasing in their attention, rendering every aid within their power These demonstrations of love and kindness are appreciated by the surviving friends of these stricken families."—(Local paper.)

EIGHTH GENERATION.

CHILDREN OF SETH AND EMELINE (HOLLAND) LOBDELL.

1 Allie Isadora (8) 2 Chloe May (8). 3. Ralph B (8)
4 Roy (8).

I Allie Isadora, b 8 Nov., 1862, at Fon du Lac. Wis , m. 18 Feb., 1885 at Bartlett, Cook Co., Ill. Jay Wylie Carr, b. 9 Dec., 1857 at Elgin, Ill, son of John Calvin and Julia M. (Smith) Carr. The family reside at Aurora, Ill., where Mr Carr is in the creamery and butter business The family are members of the Congregational Church.

225

CHILDREN.

1. Roy Leslie Carr (9), b. 29 March, 1886 at Bartlett, Ill.
2. Irene May Carr (9), b. 20 March, 1892 at Sheridan, La Salle Co., Ill

II Chloe May, b 11 April, 1882, d. at her home in Bartlett, 16 Nov., 1899, at 12.45 p m., aged 17 y. 7 m. 5 d. She had been ailing in health for several months and on 29 Oct. was taken ill of typhoid fever and gradually grew weaker until the cold hand of death took her away She had attended the public schools in the village and upon graduating became a student in the Elgin Academy, but after a short time was compelled to leave school, owing to poor health

About four years ago, she united with the Bartlett Congregational Church, and always took an active part in the Sunday School and the young people's societies

The funeral services were held at her late home on Sunday, Nov 19, at 10 o'clock.

Rev. C. F. Bauman conducted the last sad rites, assisted by Rev Stratton of Wheaton. Rev. Bauman based his remarks upon the words "She is not dead but sleepeth" The white casket was a mass of flowers. A large audience was present, showing the sincere respect felt for the bereaved family.

The remains were taken to Dundee for interment, where loving hands had almost covered the white lining of the grave with evergreens

Rev. W. R. Hench of Dundee conducted the services at the grave She leaves to mourn her untimely end, a father, mother, grandmother, two brothers and one sister, and a host of other relatives and friends. May was a beautiful, Christian girl and won the love and respect of all by her loving and kind disposition She will be sadly missed in the home circle by the young people of Bartlett, with whom she was closely associated, and in the Sunday School, of which organization she was organist

The bereaved family have the sympathy of all in this their sad hour of affliction "

"Blessed are the pure in heart for they shall see God "

III. Ralph B., b 24 May, 1874 at Burlington, Des Moines Co, Iowa; m 27 June, 1899 at Chicago, Ill, Zenetta H. Powers, b. 12 March, 1871 at Maryville, Nodaway Co., Missouri, dau. of Alfonso E. and Inez (Noe) Powers Mr Lobdell is a miller, residing at Bartlett, Ill.; Republican

226

CHILDREN.

1. Marion (9), b at Bartlett, 19 Dec, 1900
2. Letha (9), b. at Bartlett, 11 March, 1902.

IV. Roy, a farmer of Bartlett, Ill, where he was b. 28 Jan, 1877; m. 20 Oct., 1897 at Bartlett, Alverda Catherine Dice, b. 13 July, 1875 at Skippensburgh, Franklin Co, Pa, dau of Geo. Franklin and Alice Eliza (Coldsmith) Dice

Has one son

    1 Harvey Seth Lobdell (9), b. 4 Feb., 1899 at Bartlett, Ill.

EIGHTH GENERATION.

CHILDREN OF NATHAN (7) AND SARAH (DIMON) LOBDELL

---

1. Charles H (8). 2. Vincent D (8).

I Charles H., b 5 Sept., 1863 at Langworthy, Jones Co., Iowa, m Lula Heath, b 6 July, 1864 at Elgin, Ill., where she d. 25 Oct., 1897., dau. of Aaron and Mary (Fisher) Heath, leaving three children, viz ·

    1 Harold M (9), b. 9 April, 1887
    2 Ralph V (9), b. 20 Sept, 1889
    3 Ruby E (9), b. 29 Jan, 1891

Mr. Lobdell remarried 24 Dec, 1898 at Cresco, Howard Co., Iowa, to Katherine Garrett, b 11 Dec., 1872 at New Orange, Iowa, dau of Wm. S and Lucy (McMillian) Garrett, by whom he has one dau ·

    1 Lucy Olivia (9), b. 2 Nov, 1901

The family resides at Elgin, Kane Co., Ill., and are Congregationalists. Mr. L. is connected with one of the large factories.

II Vincent D., b. 23 Dec, 1866 at Cass, Jones Co, Iowa; m 23 Dec, 1891 at Cresco, Iowa, Bertha Louise Wentworth, b. 12 Dec, 1870 at Bethlehem, N. H., dau of Nelson John and Lucinda A (Blake) Wentworth. They have two children:

    1 Paul Vincent (9), b. 2 Aug., 1900.
    2 Vera Irene (9), b. 25 Sept, 1902

227

SEVENTH GENERATION.

CHILDREN OF JASON BRADLEY LOBDELL (6) AND FIRST WIFE, EUNICE JANE BRIGHAM.

I. Mary Lucretia, b 22 Oct., 1840 at St Albans, Vt., d 14 Jan., 1886 at Minneapolis, Minn ; m in Oct., 1859 at St. Paul, Minn. to Amos Foster Blanchard, a painter and decorator of Minneapolis, b 2 May, 1817 at Wilton, Hillsborough, N H , d. 14 Nov., 1895 at St Louis Park, Henepen Co., Minn , son of Isaac and Betsey (Foster) Blanchard of Wilton, N H.

CHILDREN.

1 Mattie Jane Blanchard (8), b 13 March, 1862; m. Dewaine Hall, deceased No children

2 Arthur Foster Blanchard (8), b 31 Dec., 1876 Living at Minneapolis In 1903 unmarried.

II Cassius Hawley, b 30 Jan , 1847, d May, 1867.

III Henry Jason of Minneapolis, b. 2 Dec., 1849 at Dickinson, Franklin Co., N Y ; m. 2 Oct , 1888, to Anna E MacKeever, b 24 Jan., 1859 at New Bedford, Bristol Co , Mass., dau. of Frederick H and Susan W. (Emery) McKeever

CHILDREN.

1. Annie Margarette (8), b. 23 June, 1890, d. 22 Nov , 1891.

2. Gladys Bingham (8), b 5 May, 1892

IV. Millie Jane, b 4 April, 1850 at Dickinson, N. Y.; m 3 Dec., 1879 at Auburn, Minn., Charles Fremont Nevens, b 30 Oct , 1853 at Fremont, Franklin Co , Minn , son of Frederick and Harriet (Mitchell) Nevens Mr Nevens is a manufacturer; resides at Paxton, Keith Co., Neb , a Republican; in religion, Universalist. They have no children

228

FIFTH GENERATION.

CHILDREN OF URIAH (4) AND PHOEBE (CHAPMAN) LOBDELL.

1 Benj 2 Phineas 3. Ebenezer 4 Sarah. 5 Mary. 6. Eunice 7. Huldah.

I. Benjamin, b. 1767; m. Lydia Sellick. He d 18 Jan , 1812. His widow remarried to Mr. Daniel Wood, by whom she had one son, Wm or Darius Wood, whose widow was a resident of Norwalk

In the cemetery south of Starrs Plain, just east of Sugar Hollow road near Danbury, Conn., are found the graves of the family of Benj Lobdell

"In memory of Benjamin Lobdell, who died Jan , 18, 1812, aged 46 years "

"In memory of Lydia, widow of Daniel Wood and relict of Benjamin Lobdell, who died Sept 23, 1845 in the 71 year of her age "

The stones are of marble and more or less mossy and gray with age

Benjamin evidently lived about three miles from the center of Wilton, Conn., as in Dr Chichester's old account book is found:

"In account with Benjamin Lobden.

Nov , 1798.	S.	D.
To a Par of worm Pow......................................		9
March to a visit Tral., 3 mild medicins... 3		9
6 April to a visit Trav'l, 3 mild medicins................ .3		9
7 To a visit Trav'l, 3 mild medicins....................3		9
8 To a visit Trav'l, 2 mild medicins................. 3		9
9 To a visit Trav'l 3, mild medicins... 3		9
10 To a visit Trav'l 3, mild. 2		9
11 To a visit Trav'l 3, mild 3		8

Ct. by 8 lb of Iron

(Dr. Chichester.)

II. Phineas, m Lydia Bronson, whose brother, Rev Levi Bronson, was for a long time minister at Starrs Plain.

In an old grave yard at entrance to "Sugar Hollow", on main road from Danbury to Ridgefield, near the back of the yard, no mark of other graves near, is a tall, plain, white slab. On it:

"In memory of Phineas Lobdell, who died Jan., 1, 1844, aged 75 years.

III. Ebenezer Lobdell, b. about 1771, probably at Redding, Conn. Migrated from Ridgefield, Conn. to Philipstown, Putnam Co., N. Y. in 1759 where from county records we would judge that he was an owner of considerable land. Here he m. Phebe Hustis, dau. of Wm., whose ancestors were among the first settlers of Philipstown. No record of his death.

IV. Sarah (or Sally), b. about 1773; m. David Burr, both of Ridgefield; he, the son of Abel and Sarah (Cadwell) Burr of Eaton, Conn. David d. 1856, aged 83. Sarah, in 1846, aged 73. David and Sarah are buried in Stairs Plain cemetery.

V. Mary (called Polly), b. about 1775 at Ridgefield, d. 1863 at Warren, Trumbul Co., Ohio; m. three times: (1) John White, by whom she had two children, viz.:

      1. Charles Benjamin White (6)

      2. Uriah Burr White (6).

      Charles Benjamin White I am told was a wealthy contractor (carpenter) residing on 2nd Ave., New York City, and having a summer home at Norwalk, Conn. While a lad his father d. and he was brought up in the family of his uncle and aunt (Mr. and Mrs. David Burr.)

Mary m. for her (2) husband, Wm. Weeks of Tarrytown, N. Y.

Mary m. (3) John Davenport. No issue. She d. about 1864 It is said at or near Tarrytown, N. Y.

VI. Eunice, m. James Holt, d. 1825 at Martinsburg, N. Y. No children.

VIII. Huldah Ann, b. 1779, unmarried; lived with her mother.

SIXTH GENERATION.

CHILDREN OF BENJAMIN (5) AND LYDIA (SELLECK) LOBDELL.

1. Benj., Jr. 2. Selleck. 3. Polly. 4. Betsey. 5. Ann. 6. Sally. 7. Huldah.

I. Benj., Jr. is buried in Bridgeport, Conn.; m. Hannah Curtis. No children.

II Selleck m. Lucy Wood. Selleck d. 1848 Lucy d. 1881.
They and their children, Betsey Ann, aged 6 y., 25 d., and Edward,
aged 8 m., 13 d., are buried in South Starr's Plain cemetery Selleck and his sister Sally, both m. descendants of Daniel Wood
(their stepfather).

From Redding land records: "Selleck Lobdell of Danbury
buys land of Russell White at Long Ridge, bounded south by
Uriah Griffin's lands, 4 June, 1847."

III Polly m. David Dauchy, had

    1 Edward Dauchy (7), who lived in New Castle.

    2 David Dauchy (7)

    3 Burr Dauchy (7), who went to sea and never re-
turned

IV Betsey of Ridgefield, m. Hanford Bates of Danbury, 5
March, 1817, a son of Nathan and Ruth Bates. Hanford d. 7 March,
1867, aged 71 y., 10 m. Betsey d 4 Dec., 1884, aged 82 y., 6 m., 8 d.
Both buried at Starr's Plain   .

V. Ann (a twin of Betsey) m. John L. Ambler. No children.

VI Sally m. 7 Feb., 1810, Isaac Jones (both of Ridgefield).
After his death she m. Abijah Wood (her stepfather's son). They
moved to Michigan.

VII Huldah, b. 8 March, 1807; m Judson White, 3 Nov., 1824,
son of Gideon and Esther White. He d 30 Jan., 1853 in his 50th
year She d 11 May, 1845, aged 38 y., 2 m., 3 d. Are buried in
cemetery south of Starr's Plain. Judson remarried to Marie Hor-
ton, 19 Nov., 1845

SIXTH GENERATION.

CHILDREN OF EBENEZER (5) AND PHOEBE (HUSTIS) LOBDELL.

1 Wm. 2. Harry. 3. Katy. 4. Mary 5. Phoebe. 6.
Jane. 7 Eliza

1 Wm. lived and d. about 1845 to 50 on his own farm in the
Highlands (Putnam Co., N. Y.) back of Cold Spring; m. Sarah
Davenport and had two children, viz.: Wm and Mary.

    1. Wm., Jr (7), b. 1849 at Philipstown, N. Y.; m. Char-
lotte Hultz and resides at Buchanan, N. Y.; has two children, viz :

1   Daniel (8), b. 1880
2   Emma (8), b. 1883
2   Mary E. (7), b. 1842 in the Highlands; says: "My parents d. while I was very young and from the time of their death I was among strangers, so that I heard little of my ancestors." She m. at Earlville, Ill., Mr. S. M. Warren, who was b. 7 Jan., 1842 and was also raised in the Highlands. They reside at Earlville, La Salle Co., Ill. Have one son:
1. Ellison Warren (8), b. 19 July, 1870 or 76.
II. Harry, came to Ill. in 1853, d. at Paw Paw, Ill., in 1883. Two of his children live there now, John and Armena; Benj., Ebenezer and Alfred are dead   (Letter of inquiry unanswered.)
III. Katy m. Wm. Wright and lived near Garrison on the Hudson Had a family of children, but I reached no descendant.
IV. Mary m. Ezekiel Cary and lived at Kingston, N. Y. Had children, but I have found no descendants.
V. Phoebe m Gilbert Townsend and they lived at the High-
VI. Jane m. Stephen McKeel or Markell. All d.
VII. Eliza, never m.

FROM PUTNAM CO. CLERK'S OFFICE.

List of conveyances with the name "Lobdell" either as grantor or grantee from 1812 to 1865:

"Deed 1. Ebenezer Lobdell and Phoebe, his wife, 15 April, 1818, to Peter Warren, 20 acres, $1,100, Philipstown.

Deed 2. Same, to John Davenport, 3 Aug., 1825, $400, one acre at Philipstown.

Deed 3. Same, to Elijah Knapp, 2 Aug., 1825, $2,200, 40 acres at Philipstown.

Deed 4. Same, to Gilbert Ireland, 27 Oct., 1827, $36, 10 acres at Philipstown.

Deed 5. Same, to David Knapp, 28 Oct., 1827, $75, one-quarter acre at Philipstown

Deed 6. Huldah Lobdell from Samuel Riggs, 10 Nov., 1828, $280, 6 acres at Philipstown.

Deed 7. Phoeber, Harry, Mary Jane and Phoebe J. Lobdell to Wm. Lobdell, $90, 10 acres at Philipstown, 28 July, 1845.

Deed 8. Wm. Lobdell from Luke Wood, 1 May, 1851, $950, 45 acres at Philipstown.

Deed 9. Wm. Lobdell from Jesse Lawrence, 13 March, 1844, $600, 25 acres at Philipstown.

Deed 10. Phoebe, Harry, Eliza, William and Sally Ann Lobdell to Caleb Hustis, 19 Feb., 1830. $550, 25 perches land in Philipstown.

Deed 11. Harry Lobdell from Wm. Hustis, 4 Feb., 1831, $330, 5 acres at Philipstown.

Deed 12. Samuel H. Lobdell from J. A. Taber, 31 March, 1857, $199, 5,700 feet near railroad at Patterson, N. Y.

Deed 13. Harry and Mary A. Lobdell to S. W. Davenport, 17 Sept., 1856, $800, 5 acres at Philipstown.

Deed 14. Samuel H Lobdell and Nancy, his wife, to T. W. Akin, 1 April, 1859, $575, 5,700 feet in Patterson, N. Y.

Deed 15. Nancy A. Lobdell from J. A. Taber, 29 Sept., 1859, $400, 1,000 square feet in Patterson, N. Y.

Deed 16. Nancy A. Lobdell to Alex. Hall, 23 March, 1861, $1,000, 10,000 square feet in Patterson, N. Y.

Deed 17. Wm Lobdell from Caleb Hustis, etc., 21 Aug., 1854, $400, 25 perches of land in Philipstown.

Deed 18. Wm Lobdell from David Knapp, 1 April, 1846, $50, one-half acre land in Philipstown."

New York State Gazeteer, p. 542, Putnam Co :

"The first settlement in Philipstown was made by Thos. Davenport about 1715, and during that year he built the first house in Coldspring. David Hustis settled in the town 1730."

CHILDREN OF SALLY (5) LOBDELL AND DAVID BURR.

1 David Barlow Burr. 2 Caroline Burr 3. Polly Burr.

1. David Barlow Burr, b. Jan, 1799, m. Abigail, b. about 1805, dau. of Noah and Esther (Hecock) Dibble. David d. 26 April, 1891, aged 92 years, 4 months; Abigail, 17 July, 1889, aged 84. Both are buried in Ridgefield cemetery

II. Caroline Burr never married.

III. Polly Burr m. Samuel Baxter. She and three little children, who d in infancy, are buried in the Burr plat in Starr's Plain cemetery. Polly d. 4 Aug., 1862, aged 69 years.

In the same plat with David and Sarah Burr lie their children: Caroline Burr d 29 Jan, 1833, aged 29 years; Maria Louisa Burr d 2 July, 1832, aged 13 years, Sally Burr d. 13 June, 1822, aged 21 years; Sally Burr d 1 Aug., 1790, aged 5 years. Also Charles Benjamin Burr, son of David Barlow Burr, d. 16 Aug., 1852, aged 20 years, 8 months, 22 days.

CHILDREN OF MARY (5) LOBDELL AND HER (1) HUSBAND, JOHN WHITE.

(White). Charles Benjamin—Uriah Burr.

Uriah Burr White, a bridge builder, b 11 Feb'y 1811, at Norwalk, Conn, d. 3 March, 1890, at Des Moines, Iowa, m 7 Nov, 1833, at Tarrytown, N Y Mary, b 15 March, 1812, at Tarrytown, d 8 Jany, 1881, at Mitchelville, Iowa,—dau. of Daniel Warren.

CHILDREN.

1. Uriah Height White, b 25 Nov, 1834, m three times
2. John A White, b 21 Oct 1836, m Florida Boone.
3. Warren White, b 27 Oct 1838, m Abbie Severs
4. Martha J White, b 1 March, 1841, m Samuel Curtis
5. Mary E White, b 13 March, 1843
6. Alvah C White, b 17 July, 1846, m Mary Clegg
7. Theophilus White, b 11 May, 1849
8. Hanna White, b 11 Sept, 1851, at Warren, Trumble Co., Ohio, m 11 Sept, 1888, at Marion, Linn Co, Iowa, Jesse Davis Wilson a mechanic, b 21 June, 1833, at Warren Springs, Bath Co, Virginia, son of Wm Wilson and Elizabeth Davis Residence, Colfax, Jasper Co., Iowa No children Methodist Republican.
9. Charles Henry White, b 16 April, 1854; m. Helen Cady

CHILDREN OF MARY (5) LOBDELL AND HER SECOND HUSBAND, WM. WEEKS.

(Weeks). 1 Wm Henry 2 John L 3 Mary Esther 4 Evaline

I Wm Henry Weeks, b July, 1815, at Philipstown, N Y, d. 2 April, 1878, at Cedar Rapids, Iowa, m. 11 Nov, 1838, in New York City, Frances Noble, b 17 Dec, 1821, at Nova Scotia, B C., d. 28 July, 1892 Her parents resided in New York City, where they both d of cholera, 4 July, 1832.

234

CHILDREN—SEVENTH GENERATION.

1. John Noble Weeks, b. 22 Oct., 1839, m. (1st) Emeline Kenmie. (2nd) Miss Lane.

2. Ann Elizabeth Weeks, b. 25 Jan., 1844; d. in infancy.

3. Wm. H. Weeks, b. 9 Sept., 1845, m. Helen Bates.

4. Charles Benj. Weeks, b. 24 Feb., 1848; m. Amelia Fuller Pear.

5. Julia Weeks, b. 18 Oct., 1853, at New York City; m. 5 Jan., 1874, Gold D. Pettit, b. at Flushing, Queens Co., N. Y., d. 13 Feb., 1905, at Cedar Rapids, Iowa, son of Henry and Joanna (Aaroson) Pettit. Mrs. Julia (Weeks) Pettit resides at Waterloo, Iowa, and has one son (8)—

    1. Fred G. Pettit, b. 31 July, 1875; m. Josephine Lee Buchanan.

6. Mary Weeks (a twin of Julia), b. 18 Oct., 1853; m. Joseph Stoddard.

7. Nellie Venitia Weeks, b. 15 Feb., 1859.

II. John L. Weeks.

III. Mary Esther Weeks, b. Dec., 1823, at Cold Springs, N. Y.; d. 1897 in Chicago, Ill., m. at Tarrytown, N. Y., Wm. Geo. Darley, b. 1815 in London, England, d. 25 Dec., 1893, at Marshalltown, Iowa. Children—

    1. Venetia F. Darley, b. 5 April, 1844, at Tarrytown, N. Y.; m. 30 Nov., 1865, at New Castle, Pa., T. M. Humphreys, b. 2 Dec., 1843, in Butler Co., Pa., son of Thomas A. and Ruth (Thorn) Humphreys. Children—

        1. Wm. A. Humphreys, b. in New Castle, Pa.

        2. Lea M. Humphreys, b. in St. Louis, Mo. Residence, Chicago, Ill.

    2. Edward C. Darley, b. 1846; m. Elenora Walton.

    3. Wm. B. Darley.

    4. Mary M. Darley, b. 28 July, 1855, at Warren, Trumbull Co., Ohio, m. 15 Dec., 1896, Charles Henry Anderson, b. 9 Nov., 1854, at Griggsville, Ill., son of Wm. F. and Laura E. (Gilpin) Anderson. Residence, St. Louis, Mo.

    5. Kittie Darley, d. young.

    6. Richard M. Darley, b. 1863; m. Harriet Chamberlain.

IV. Eveline Weeks, who d. in her girlhood.

SEVENTH GENERATION.

CHILDREN OF BETSEY (6) LOBDELL AND HANFORD BATES.

1. Caroline. 2. Benjamin 3 Henry 4 Nancy 5. Eliza 6 Ann

1. Caroline Bates m. Chas. B Weed Reside in Bridgeport, Conn
2 Benjamin Bates m. 13 March, 1855, Frances L. Burr. Resides at Starrs Plain, near Danbury, Conn
3. Henry Bates m. first, Emma Lee, second, Sarah Gregory
4. Nancy Bates m. Timothy Ambler.
5. Eliza Bates m Henry Ambler
6 Ann Bates m. Henry Taylor Reside in Danbury.

CHILDREN OF HULDAH (6) LOBDELL AND JUDSON WHITE.

1 Benj White m first, Rhoda Boughton, 8 Sept, 1845; second, Ellen M Boughton
2. Joel White m. Sarah Maynard 7 Sept, 1855.
3 Mary White m. F W Force, 2 Jan, 1856; living at South Norwalk, Conn (1902)
4 Martha White m. Joel W Hatt 25 Dec, 1860
5 Judson White, Jr, m Sarah Morris 11 Nov., 1863.
6 Eliza Ann White
7. John L White d 2 Oct, 1861

From tombstones found in Starr's Plain cemetery:
Gideon White d 1876, aged 99 years, 18 days Esther, his wife, d 1869, aged 83 years, 11 days
Judson White d. 30 Jan, 1853, aged 49 years, 9 months, 12 days. Huldah Lobdell, his wife, d. 11 May, 1845, aged 38 years, 2 months, 3 days An infant son d. 29 April, 1845.
Eliza Ann White d 10 Nov 1847, aged 18 years, 3 months, 12 days.

Nathan Bates d 25 June, 1855, aged 83 years, 5 months, 11 days. Ruth, his wife, d. 19 Aug., 1849, aged 73 years, 7 months. (Parents of Hanford Bates, who m. Betsey Lobdell.)

CHILDREN OF DAVID (6) BARLOW AND ABIGAIL (DIBBLE) BURR.

1. Mary Esther 2. Daniel Dibble 3. Emily. 4 Wm. Seely 5. Chas. Benjamin. 6. Caroline Louise. 7. Marie Antoinette. 8 Elbert. 9. Lucy Abigail.

I. Mary Esther Burr, b. 2 Nov., 1828, at Ridgefield; m. 1 Jan., 1850, at Ridgefield, Burr Taylor, b. 17 April, 1822, son of Noah and Pamelia (Burr) Taylor of Ridgefield They reside about two miles and a half from Starr's Plain, on the road toward Ridgefield. Have two sons—

Elbert Burr Taylor (8) m. Catherine Johnson, and Jerome Taylor (8) m. Jennie Frisbie 26 Jan., 1885.

2. Daniel Dibble Burr, b. 1826, d. 1901.

3. Emily Burr, b. 5 Jan., 1829; m. Theodore Mayhew, b. 1 April, 1822 They have no children

4. Wm. Seely Burr, living in Bridgeport, Conn., b 1831, m. Harriet Lane

5. Chas. Benj. Burr, b. 1832, d. 1852.

6. Caroline Louise Burr, b. 23 May, 1834; m. Elbert W Gilbert, 30 July, 1854; Caroline d. 30 April, 1885.

7. Marie Antoinette Burr, b. 21 Jan., 1836; m. first. Le Grand Hull, 17 July, 1862; had—

1. Cornelia M. Hull (8). b. 4 July, 1863, m. Daniel O. Depew.

2. Sarah E. Hull (8). b. 27 June, 1866; m. in 1885, Wm. S. Thompson.

Widow Hull m. 8 Oct., 1872, Elijah Morris, b. 28 June, 1832. They reside in Danbury, Conn., and have one dau. and one son:

1. Jessie Eliza Morris (8), b. 30 Sept., 1874; m. Clinton Thompson.

2. Benj. Franklin Morris (8), b. 16 Oct., 1876; m. Lena Moran, 14 Nov., 1900.

8. Elbert Burr, b. 1838, d. 1840.

9. Lucy Abigail Burr, b. 28 Sept, 1846; m. Johann Hornig, who d. 8 March. 1903

CHILDREN OF BENJAMIN AND FRANCES (BURR) BATES.

1. Della E.   2. Cora R   3. Jennie N.

1 Della Elizabeth Bates, b 20 Feb , 1856; m. 14 Sept., 1878, Charles F White.* Their only child. Carrie Frances (9) White, b. 21 Aug., 1884, m. Wm. M. Hoffman 17 June, 1902.

2. Cora R. Bates, b. 19 Dec., 1858; m Charles A Abbott

3. Jennie N Bates. b 26 Jan , 1861; m 1876, Richard Hoyt. She d. Aug., 1895

> Their son, Ernest (9) Hoyt. b Aug ,1877, m Bertha Lent, March, 1901.

CHILDREN OF BENJAMIN WHITE (7) AND RHODA BOUGHTON.

(White). 1 Geo Henry 2 Chas. Judson 3 Jane 4. Wallace A 5. Edward Allison. 6. Ward. 7. Lewis B 8. Mary E

1. Geo Henry White, b 18 Sept , 1848; d 14 Oct , 1852.

2 Chas. Judson White, b. 12 June, 1851; d 28 March, 1872

3 Jane White. b. 29 April, 1854; d 28 March, 1855.

4 Wallace A White, b 14 March, 1856; m. 2 Dec , 1877, Ida Northrup

5. Edward Allison White, b 6 March, 1858, m. 14 Jan., 1877, Laura E. Hummiston.

6. Ward White, b 9 Jan , 1864

7. Lewis B White, b. 12 June, 1866.

8. Mary E White, b. 26 Nov , 1871; m Oct , 1890-1, George A. Ferguson

FIFTH GENERATION.

CHILDREN OF BURWELL AND ANNA (ST. JOHN) LOBDELL.

1. Polly. 2 Annis 3 Betsey 4 Samuel 5 Lewis. 6 Joseph.

I Polly m. Noah St. John Had Hiram (6), John O. (6), Samuel (6) and others. A grand dau (7) is living in Norwalk

II. Annis (probably Eunice) m. Moses Jennings. Annis d. a young woman, and Moses Jennings m for his second wife, Hannah Squires. Moses d and was buried in New Jersey, where he was at work. Both wives are buried at Osborntown cemetery, Georgetown.

III Betsey, m 25 May, 1800, d. 13 Sept, 1825, at Georgetown; m Matthew Bennett, who d 7 Jan., 1851, aged 68 years. Matthew Bennett had 21 children by his two wives He with his two wives and several children are buried in Osborn cemetery, Georgetown. He m for his second wife, Polly Scribner She d 21 Sept., 1849, aged 54 years.

IV Samuel, bapt 20 May, 1784, by Dr. Debles; residence of parents given as Norwalk (which part was after 1802 called Wilton) I assume that he d. a young man, about 25. Danbury Probate Records, Vol 10. p 188, 12 Dec., 1809 "Letters of administration on the estate of Samuel Lobdell, late of Reading, in the District of Danbury, are granted by this court to Lewis Lobdell of said Reading." The estate was found insolvent. Inventory taken 26 Dec., 1809. Amount $100.53, and recorded same day Settlement and order to pay dividend, 20 July, 1810. No wife nor children mentioned

V. Lewis, b. 7 Feb., 1788, at Georgetown, Conn., m. Aug., 1820, at Wilton, Conn, Rebecca Noyes, b. 3 March, 1794, at Fairfield, Conn, dau of Joseph and Amelia (Burr) Noyes Mrs. Lobdell was a direct descendant of John Alden and his wife, Priscilla Mullins. She d. 6 Sept, 1826, at Wilton, Conn., and Lewis m as his second wife. on 4 April, 1827, Sarah Foot, b. 6 June, 1799.

Lewis d. 6 April, 1834, at Wilton, and on 22 April of the same year Noah St. John was appointed administrator of his estate, and on 27 Dec, 1834, Joseph Levy of Wilton was appointed guardian to Lewis and James Lobdell, sons of Lewis and Rebecca (Noyes) Lobdell (This from Norwalk Probate records.)

Widow Sarah Lobdell m. for her second husband, Eleazar Taylor, son of Ebenezer Taylor of Bethel, Conn. She d 30 March, 1866, aged 66 years, 10 months. This is copied from her grave stone in Zion Hill cemetery at Wilton.

In the cemetery at Osborntown, near Georgetown, are the graves of Lewis and Rebecca (spelled Lobdill)

<table>
<tr><td>In</td><td>In</td></tr>
<tr><td>memory of</td><td>memory of</td></tr>
<tr><td>Lewis Lobdill,</td><td>Rebecca, wife of</td></tr>
<tr><td>who died</td><td>Lewis Lobdill,</td></tr>
<tr><td>April 6, 1834,</td><td>daughter of Joseph</td></tr>
<tr><td>Ae. 46 years.</td><td>and Amelia Noys,</td></tr>
<tr><td>Also</td><td>who died</td></tr>
<tr><td>Levi, his son,</td><td>Sept. 6, 1826,</td></tr>
<tr><td>who died May 20, 1834,</td><td>Ae. 32 years.</td></tr>
<tr><td>Ae. 6 months.</td><td></td></tr>
</table>

(Descendants will notice the names spelled Lobdill and Noys, instead of Lobdell and Noyes, as at the present day)

From Wilton land records:
"David Coley of Weston sells land to Lewis Lobdell, who lived at Georgetown. 1812 The land was at Long Hollow"

From Wilton town records:
"The cattle ear-mark of Lewis Lobdell was a swallow fork near ear, and half-penny under side of ear"

VI Joseph No record of his birth nor of his life, only from Dr. Chichester's books During the month of May, 1794, the doctor made him three visits, traveling two miles to reach the home of Joseph. Records give:

"Joseph Lobdill of Wilton, Ct. (Georgetown), on 12 Sept, 1797, bought lot and dwelling house at Wilton, Conn, and sold the same in 1799 to Luke Keeler"

SIXTH GENERATION.

CHILDREN OF ANNIS LOBDELL (5) AND MOSES JEN-
NINGS.

1. Eunice 2. Sally 3. Angeline. 4 A son.

1 Annis (Wilton records give her name Eunice) Jennings, b. 1797, d. on Olmstead Hill, Wilton, Conn., 20 April, 1881; m. Stephen Scribner. who d several years before his wife. Both are buried in Zion's Hill cemetery, Wilton. A dau. (7), Mrs. Burr Patrick, b. 1826, resides (1902) at North Wilton, Conn.

2. Sally Jennings m Beach Whitehead. Both are buried in Tempawaug cemetery. Children:

    1. Alonzo Whitehead (7). probably lives in Roxbury, Conn.

    2. Georgianna Whitehead (7) m. Geo Dudley.

    3 Sarah Whitehead (7) m Mr Sanford.

    4 Angeline Whitehead (7) m. Morris Jennings

    5. Ambrose Beach Whitehead (7) went west.

    6 Eleanor Whitehead m. John Partrick, a brother of Burr Partrick

    7. Jane Whitehead, unmarried

3 Angeline Jennings m Geo Shute of New York, buried in Osborntown cemetery.

4. A son, enlisted in the U. S Army. Never heard from.

Moses Jennings by (2) wife had Thomas, Polly, Abby, Jane, Charles, Delia, Ann, Orrin.

CHILDREN OF BETSEY LOBDELL (5) AND A. MATTHEW
BENNETT.

1 Aaron 2. Henry 3. Noah. 4 Sherman. 5. Sarah 6. Geo. L. 7 Aaron. 8 Alvira. 9. Betsey Ann.

1 Aaron Bennett d. young

2. Henry Bennett, b. 7 Feb., 1806, at Georgetown, Fairfield Co., Conn , m 11 Sept., 1833, at Amenia, Dutchess Co., N. Y., Sarah B., dau of Moses and Amy (Hibbard) Witherall, b 25 Oct., 1814, d. 19 Feb., 1867, at Norfolk, Conn., Litchfield Co

Henry Bennett, with his brother Noah, went to Amenia when they became of age, and both m and lived there until 1848, when Henry and his family moved into the next town (Sharon, Conn.), and in 1864 came to Norfolk, Conn. His son Henry, b 1835, tells me "Since 1864 it has been our home and the burial place for our dead Here I hope to spend the remainder of my days. There are but three of our family now living "

CHILDREN.

1. Geo H. Bennett (7), b 14 Oct., 1834, d. young.

2 John Henry Bennett (7), b. 13 Nov., 1835, is unmarried and living (1902), together with his brother Charles, on the old homestead in Norfolk, Conn. The infirmities of age obliged him to give up a position held for over twenty years in the Norfolk & New Brunswick Hosiery Co., as foreman of the finishing room. Was employed by the company nearly 32 years, ten years on machine button holes and looking after the machines Rheumatism has so crippled his hands that it is almost impossible for him to use them, but he patiently waits the call of Him who will release him from suffering. He says: "The good Lord has taken care of me and I am about through with this world "

3 Geo. M. Bennett (7), b. 26 July, 1837; d 9 Oct., 1864 Was in War of the Rebellion.

4. Fred'k H Bennett (7), b 9 July, 1840; m Mary E. Bennett, a cousin He was in War of the Rebellion

5 Aaron M Bennett (7), b 23 Oct., 1842; m Sarah F Emory He was in War of the Rebellion Is now (1902) living at "The Soldiers' Home," Norton Heights, Conn.

6 Moses W Bennett, b 12 March, 1845; was in War of the Rebellion; d of yellow fever at Newborn 19 Oct, 1864.

7 Charles B. Bennett (7), b 20 June, 1858; m Julia A Myers Is living on the old homestead (1902)

Four other children d in infancy making eleven in all

3 Noah Bennett, b 10 March, 1808, m (1) Clarinda Hutchinson, (2) Minerva Hurst, d April 1894 He d 13 Aug, 1891, in Easton Center, Conn

CHILDREN

1 Sarah E. Bennett (7), b 25 Dec, 1833; m 25 Dec, 1856, Eli B. Godfrey; she d 9 July, 1891 Has one son, Wm. B. Godfrey, living in Danbury, Conn. (1902)

2 Pauline Bennett (7) d. in childhood.

3 Joel Bennett (7) d. in childhood.

4 Geo. Henry Bennett (7) killed in War of the Rebellion

5 Joseph Bennett (7) d. in childhood

6. Charley Bennett (7) d. in childhood

7. Albert H. Bennett (7), b Oct., 1847. Resides at New Haven, Conn.

8 Ezra M Bennett (7), b 25 Dec., 1849. Resides at Worcester, Mass.

4 Sherman Bennett m. Jeanette Sherwood, d in Wilton 22 Nov., 1825, aged 22 years Buried at Branchville. Two of his daughters are living in Georgetown, Conn.

Mrs Fanny St. John (7) and

Mrs Mary Bennett (7) (1902).

5. Sarah Bennett d. 1900, aged 90 years; m. Ezra Brown of Georgetown A dau., Martha A. Brown (7), m as second wife. 28 June, 1874, Nathaniel Boughton, b 30 Dec., 1830, son of Joseph and Betsey (Bixbee) Boughton of Norwalk, Conn.

Sarah was brought up by Dr and Mrs. David Willard "She had a number of children, all very smart."

6. Geo L Bennett d. at South Norwalk 31 Dec., 1897; m Mary Smith, dau. of Ebenezer and Rachel (Disbrow) Smith. She d 17 Aug., 1889 Has a dau., Mrs Esther Wheeler (7), East Norwalk.

7 Aaron Bennett, b 14 Aug., 1817; m 24 April, 1844. Caroline Phillips, b Jan., about 1827, d. 30 Nov., 1899, dau of Thomas and Caroline (Godfrey) Phillips. Residence, Westport, 1902.

8 Alvira Bennett, b. 30 July, 1819; m 4 May, 1848—as his second wife—Francis Godfrey, b 23 July 1811 (son of Stephen) He d 4 April, 1890.

9 Betsey Ann Bennett d. unmarried, 14 April, 1884, at Westport, Conn Was a very bright woman.

Matthew Bennett, by his second wife, had—

Matthew, Jr., d 18 Dec., 1854

Harriet Bennett, b. 8 Nov., 1842.

Mary Elizabeth Bennett, b 3 Aug., 1832; m. 23 Jan., 1850. Wakeman Bates, b 22 Feb., 1825, d. 26 Aug., 1897. Widow Bates resides in Georgetown, Conn., 1903.

Stephen Bennett and perhaps others

243

CHILDREN OF LEWIS (5) LOBDELL AND HIS FIRST WIFE, REBECCA NOYES.

1. Noyes 2 Lewis 3 James.

1. Noyes, b. at Georgetown 10 June, 1821; probably d. in infancy, as no record, except that of his birth, found in M. E. Church records, can be found.

2 Lewis, Jr., b 23 Jan , 1823, at Georgetown, Conn.; m. Abby Jane Lockwood, dau. of Isaac and (Sturges) Lockwood, b. at Weston, Conn The family removed to Sharon, Kalkaska Co., Mich., where Lewis d 10 Aug., 1865

3. James, b. 3 Feb., 1825, at Wilton, Conn.; m 26 Sept., 1846, at Weston, Fairfield Co, Conn, Elizabeth A. Lockwood, b 6 March, 1825, at Weston, dau of Albert and Rachel (Ogden) Lockwood. They removed to Bridgeport, Conn., where James d. 2 Nov., 1878 His widow resides in Bridgeport (1902), and from letters written by her I know that she must be a wonderfully bright and well preserved woman James served one year in the "Civil War," enlisting in the 23rd Reg't . Co E, Conn Volunteers.

CHILDREN OF LEWIS LOBDELL AND HIS (2) WIFE, SARAH FOOT.

1 Eli Lobdell, b. about 1828, as we find in the distribution of his father's estate. 8 Nov . 1834, his mother was appointed his guardian, he then being six years old. He m Clarissa Olmstead, dau. of Seth and Polly (St. John) Olmstead They had no children Eli enlisted in the War of the Rebellion, Co. C, 17th Reg't Conn. Volunteers I think he d. away and his body was returned home and buried in Zion Hill cemetery at Wilton.

" Eli Lobdell,
Member of Co C,
17th Reg't, C. V ,
Died
Feb 5. 1864,
Ae. 34 y 9 m.
and 21 days
He sleeps his last sleep,
He has fought his last battle ,
No sound can awake him
To glory again "

244

Clarissa m. for her second husband, Samuel Williams, who d. 12 Jan., 1864, aged 62 years, 3 months, 8 days; and she m. third, Edward Fryer, who survived her. Is now living (1904) She is buried in her father's lot in the cemetery near Batterson's corners at Georgetown. Found on tombstone.

"Clarissa,
Wife of Edward Fryer,
Died Jan. 19, 1837,
Ae. 57 y., 7 m."

2. Noyes Lobdell was about 4 years old when his mother was appointed his guardian, 8 Nov, 1834, m 7 Feb., 1852, Mary Elizabeth Gunn, b 8 Jan., 1835, dau of Ariel and Harriet (Flynn) Gunn. They removed to New Jersey, he enlisted on a whale ship and wrote to his wife from Carolina, since then was never heard of. His wife re-married to a Mr. Crosby of Georgetown.

3. Amelia Burr, b. 4 Jan., 1832, now (1904) living in Georgetown, Conn., on being interviewed by Miss Jessie Lobdell of Ridgebury, tells us:

"My father was Lewis Lobdell He lived and d in the old house on the hill (Georgetown) All of his children were b. there. Father and his first wife are buried right up the road in Osborntown graveyard. My two brothers, Eli and Noyes, one b. in April, the other in May, one year apart, were both older than I. I m. 12 May, 1850, Charles Osborn, b. July, 1829, d. 26 Aug., 1872, son of Isaac and Hannah (Knapp) Osborn. My husband and two children are buried in cemetery, Zion Hill, at Wilton."

CHILDREN.

1 Geo. Turney Osborn (7), b. 11 July, 1855; d. 22 Dec., 1876.

2. Charles Noyes Osborn (7), b. 26 Dec., 1857; d 19 April, 1861.

3. Clarence Lincoln Osborn (7), b. 3 March, 1867; m. 10 June, 1896, Eliza Jane Officer, b. 15 Dec., 1869, dau. of David and Jane (Holmes) Officer. Resides at Georgetown, Conn.

4. A son, Levi, who d. about one month after the death of his father, aged 6 months.

Matthew Bennett and Lewis Lobdell must have lived near to each other, as in Dr. Chichester's books the accounts are together, viz:

245

MATTHEW BENNETT AND LEWIS LOBDELL

20 Oct., 1819, to a visit travel four miles, medicine. 4.6
21, to a visit, travel four miles, medicine 4.6
23, to a visit, travel four miles, medicine..... . . . . 4 3
21 June. A D. 1822. to a visit, travel four miles, medicine...... 4.9
22, to a visit, travel. medicine.. . . . . 4 9
23. to a visit travel. medicine... . . . . 5.
24. to a visit, travel, medicine 3 6

SEVENTH GENERATION

CHILDREN OF LEWIS, JR., (6) AND ABBY JANE (LOCK-
WOOD) LOBDELL.

1. Henry. 2. Edward J 3. Rebecca

1   Henry d. young.
2   Edward J. b. 20 Jan., 1859, at Sharon. Mich., m Grace A.
Dunbar In 1899 he was a resident of Marietta. Ohio, engaged in
the manufacturing of carriage stock, also bicycle rims He now
has valuable interests in the lumber districts of northern Michigan.
being located in Onaway, Presque Isle Co.   Children
        1   Faith (8). b 30 Nov., 1893
        2   Edward J, Jr (8). b 3 Aug 1895.
3   Rebecca, b 1864; m Daniel Gage

CHILDREN OF JAMES (6) AND ELIZABETH A. LOCK-
WOOD LOBDELL.

1 Augusta Ogden 2. Rebecca Noyes. 3 James Benjamin.

1. Augusta Ogden. b 8 July 1849, m Fred'k Converse.
2   Rebecca Noyes. b. 31 Dec., 1852; m John S. Fray.
3   James Benj, b. 12 Nov, 1855, in Fairfield Co. Conn., in
what is now called Branchville, near Georgetown.   When eight
years old he moved with his parents to Bridgeport, Conn, where
he lived for over thirty years   In 1896 he went to Marietta, Ohio,
and is now located at Onaway, Mich., engaged and interested in
the lumber business On 8 April, 1886, he m. at Pittsfield, Mass.,
Berkshire Co, Addie L Lockwood, b. 25 Sept, 1856, at Weston,
Conn, dau of Joseph R and Anna E. (Reeves) Lockwood.

CHILDREN.

1. Alida Lewis (8), b. 1 March, 1887; d. 4 March, 1887.
2. Elizabeth Reeves (8), b 8 Nov, 1889; d 8 March, 1896.
3. Benjamin Noyes (8), b. 28 June, 1898.

FIFTH GENERATION.

CHILDREN OF SUSANNAH (4) LOBDELL AND DANIEL RIGGS.

I. Samuel Riggs, b. 20 May, 1785; m Elizabeth Haight of Dutchess Co, N. Y.

II Isaac Riggs, b. 5 March, 1787; m Marinda Smith.

III Polly Riggs, b 6 July, 1791; m Lockwood Gray.

IV. Daniel Riggs, b. 16 May, 1793, m. Lumeric Ryerson.

From Riggs genealogy

CHILDREN OF JOSIAH (4) AND (WIDOW) MIRRIAM (HICKOCK) LOBDELL. BORN AT RIDGEFIELD.

1 Jared. 2 Jacob 3 Sarah 4. Rebecca 5. Amy. 6. Eunice

I. Jared, b. 25 May, 1788, d in 1799

II. Jacob, b. 14 March, 1790; no record.

III Sarah. b. 4 Jan., 1793; no record

IV. Rebecca, b. 13 Feb, 1797; m 30 April. 1821, Philo Webb Jones, b. 27 May, 1802, at Stamford, Conn, son of Daniel and Elizabeth (Pardee) Jones Philo Webb Jones resided at Westport, Conn., where he d 31 July, 1876, and Rebecca 5 Jan., 1876.

V. Amy, b 26 March. 1798, resided with her sister Rebecca (during Rebecca's life). d in Wilton, Conn., 9 Oct., 1878, aged 81 years.

VI *Eunice. b 17 July. 1800; m Thaddeus Mead Benedict, b 3 Jan., 1801, m. 4 May, 1826. Eunice d. 26 Aug, 1850. Children:

    1 Mary Ann Benedict (6), b. 1827 at Norwalk, Conn.

    2 Sarah Maria Benedict (6), b 1828, d 20 Sept, 1835

    3 Wm. Edward Benedict (6), b. 24 June, 1830, m. 2 April, 1857, Antoinette, dau. of Ira and Thirza Barrett of Bedford, b. 11 Jan., 1832 Resides at Ridgefield, Conn.

In Ridgefield cemetery are two low, narrow, connected gravestones, erected by loving hands to the memory of Josiah and Miriam Lobdell:

Died

" Oct 21. ———. Miriam. wife of Josiah Lobdell, ae. 69 years.
Her face was tranquil and serene,
No sorrow in her looks was seen,
Her Saviour's smiles dispelled the gloom
And smoothed her passage to the tomb."

" In Memory of Josiah Lobdell, who died June 4, 1837, aged 77 years."

*From Benedict Genealogy.

SIXTH GENERATION.

CHILDREN OF REBECCA LOBDELL (5) AND PHILO WEBB JONES. BORN AT WESTPORT, FAIRFIELD CO., CONN.

1 Edward Jones d. in infancy

2. Sarah Maria Jones, b 24 Aug., 1826, at Titicus, Fairfield Co., Conn., d. 14 Aug., 1899, at Wilton, Conn.; m 12 May, 1847, at Westport, Conn., Sherman Platt Fitch, a merchant of Wilton, b. 21 Nov., 1822 at Wilton, where the family resided and he d 16 Feb. 1894 The family were Episcopalians

3 Charles Henry Jones m. Phoebe Raymond

4 Oscar J. Jones m. Elizabeth —— (?)

5. John Jones m. Mary Elwell

6 Mary Robinson Jones, unmarried

7 Philo Jones m Mary —— (?)

SEVENTH GENERATION.

CHILDREN OF SARAH MARIA JONES (6) AND SHERMAN PLATT FITCH.

1. Edward Sherman Fitch, b 7 Feb., 1848, at Wilton, Conn.; m 16 Nov., 1870, Ella Louisa Chauncey, b 1 June 1849, at Brooklyn, N Y., dau. of Michael and Maria Louisa Chauncey Residence, West 72nd street, New York City

Edward Sherman Fitch was in the banking and brokerage business from 1870 to 1884, when he accepted a position with the Western Union Telegraph Co, as special inspector of the gold and stock department. He was an exhibitor in space "R," Electrical building, World's Fair, Chicago, 1893, of printing telegraphs.

In Nov., 1893, was appointed general agent of the Union Telegraph and News Co, No 1 Broadway, New York, and was the first to place in actual operation in New York the Page Printing Telegraph system under the patents of S V Essick, an apparatus by means of which messages can be transmitted and recorded in plain Roman characters over a thousand miles on a single wire.

CHILDREN.

1. Maud Louisa Fitch (8), b 1 Jan , 1872
2. Ethel Chauncey Fitch (8), b. 11 July, 1876
3. Harry Sherman Fitch (8), b at Ridgewood, Bergen Co , N J, 28 Sept , 1877, is the last male issue of Sam'l Fitch, the Crown's Justice, and from him the descent is as follows:

Samuel Fitch, Jr.
    Samuel, son of Samuel, Jr.
        Joseph Platt Fitch
            Sherman Platt Fitch
                Edward Sherman Fitch
                    Harry Sherman Fitch

2 Arthur Treat Fitch, b. 6 Aug., 1849, is unmarried and resides in London, England.

3 Helen Elizabeth Fitch, b. 6 Feb , 1853; m John Burr Sturges.

4 Agnes Jones Fitch, b 10 Nov , 1854, m David B Ogden.

5. Harriet Robinson Fitch, b. 10 Jan., 1857; m Daniel B. Telford

6. Frances Fitch, b. 5 Sept., 1861; m. John M. Belden.

7. Richard Henry Fitch, b. 5 June, 1866; m. Bertha Brady. Resides at Wilton

FOURTH GENERATION.

CHILDREN OF SUSANNA (3) LOBDELL AND SEABORN BURT.

I.   Thankful Burt, b. 3 Nov., 1738.

II.   Ben. Burt, b. 29 Dec , 1741.

III.   Joshua Burt, b 21 March, 1743; m 12 Sept., 1770, Lydia Smith.

IV   Mary Burt, b 12 May, 1746

V.   Susannah Burt, b. 18 Aug., 1748

VI.   David Burt, b. 14 Feb , 1750.

VII.   Theopilus Burt, b. 14 May, 1752, d 1753.

VIII.   Theopilus Burt, b 31 March, 1756.

(From Burt Genealogy.)

CHILDREN OF SARAH LOBDELL (3) AND JABEZ NORTHRUP.

Born at Ridgefield.

I.   Eunice Northrup, b. 6 Oct., 1735.

II   Jabez Northrup, b. 14 Aug , 1737.

III.   Sarah Northrup, b. 21 June, 1741.

IV.   Lois Northrup, b. 16 Feb., 1743.

(Northrup Genealogy)

Children and Descendants of
Caleb [3] Lobdell (Joshua [2], Simon [1])

(1) Wife, Elizabeth ——— ?
(2) Wife, Bethia Paddock
(3) Wife, Ruth ——— ?

CHILDREN OF CALEB (3) LOBDELL, BY (1) WIFE, ELIZABETH ——?

1. Caleb, Jr.

I. Caleb, Jr., b 2 June, 1751; m. Susanna ——?, 1779

CHILDREN.

1. Caleb (5). b. 11 Jan., 1781; no record
2. Polly (5), b 13 Nov., 1782, d 27 Nov., 1801
3. Jeremiah (5), b. 1784; m. Sarah Elizabeth Abbott dau. of Joel Abbott). They resided at Litchfield, Conn., until 1806, when they ,removed to Washington, Ga.. where Jeremiah d. Elizabeth Abbott Lobdell d in 1850 at Denmark, Tenn. Children:

    1. Sarah (6) 2. Caroline (6). 3. Cornelia (6) 4. Jane (6).

    1. Sarah (6), b. in Litchfield, Conn., 1803; m. Joseph Moseley of South Carolina, in Washington, Ga. She d. in 1868 in Jackson, Miss Children: Mary (7). Caroline (7) Sarah (7) Frances (7) Lucretia (7); all b in Washington, Ga. Caroline m. Mr. Barrows of Jackson, Miss.; had dau. Mary and son Charles Mary (8) m. Dr. Wirt Johnson of Jackson, Miss ; lived only a few years and d. without children. Charles Barrows (8) is a physician in New York City. The two younger sisters—the only remaining of the five daughters of Sarah Lobdell Moseley—are Mrs. Peyton of Raymond, Miss, who has three grown sons (8) and two daughters (8), and Mrs T M. Nash (widow of Dr. Nash) residing at Little Rock. Ark

    2. Caroline (deceased), m. Professor Lewis of Oxford. Miss ; has one dau. living in Texas.

    3 Cornelia. d unmarried

    + "Miss Jane Lobdell, aged 79 years, an aunt of Mrs. D M Barrows. d. suddenly at the residence of Major Barrows this a m " (1895)—(N O. Paper.)

BY (2) WIFE, BETHIA (PADDOCK) LOBDELL.

1. Paddock. 2 Philip.

I. Paddock, b. 20 July, 1760; no record

II. Philip, b. 7 Oct., 1761, at Ridgefield, where he d. 19 Dec., 1793, aged 32 years; m 27-8 Sept., 1788, Sarah Smith, dau of John and Clemence (Mills) Smith, b. 26 Sept, 1763 at Ridgefield They had one child:

    1. Philip Paddock (5), b at Ridgefield 6 April, 1790, d. in Galletin, Texas, 2 Oct, 1833, aged 35 y., 5 m., 26 d., buried on his father's lot in Ridgefield cemetery; m Temperence Titus Smith, dau of Reuben and Susannah (Phillips) Smith, b. in Caravel, N Y., 10 Feb, 1793 They were m by Isaac Smith, Esq. North Salem, N Y., 22 Feb, 1812.

    Widow Temperance Titus (Smith) Lobdell remarried to Wm. Barhite, son of Andrew and Mary (Dies) Barhite, b. 30 May, 1799; m. by Rev Reuben Harris at North Salem, 6 Jan., 1825 She d. in Ridgefield 2 July, 1870, aged 71 y., 1 m., 2 d.

Sarah remarried (as his second wife) on 17 March, 1803, to Epenetus Platt of New Milford, Conn., and had one child, Marshall Platt, who m. Tryphena Merwin of Milford, on 20 March, 1825.

In Ridgefield cemetery are the graves of Philip and of his son, Philip Paddock Lobdell and of "Sarah, widow of Epenetus Platt and formerly relict of Philip Lobdell, who d 8 Aug., 1846, aged 83."

SIXTH GENERATION.

CHILDREN OF PHILIP PADDOCK (5) AND TEMPERANCE TITUS (SMITH) LOBDELL.

---

1. Cynthia 2. Susan.

1. Cynthia, b in N. Salem (Knoxtown), 16 Jan, 1813, d. in South East, N Y., 16 Nov., 1827

2. Susan, b. in N. Salem (Knoxtown), 19 Sept., 1815, d. suddenly of nephritis and old age at the home of her dau., Mrs. Frank E. Olmstead on Maple St. in Ridgefield, Conn., Saturday morning, 27 Feb., 1904, in her 89th year She was m to Sylvester Main in Ridgefield 27 May, 1838, by Rev Nathan Burton, P. E. Sylvester

Main was son of Joshua and Hannah (Gilbert) Main, b. Weston, Conn., 18 April, 1817, d. in Norwalk, Conn. (Grantville), 5 Oct., 1873, aged 56 y., 5 m., 17 d Children (born at Ridgefield):

SEVENTH GENERATION.

1. Hubert Platt Main (7), b 17 Aug., 1839; m. 18 Sept., 1865, Ophelia Louise Degraff, b. 13 Feb., 1842. Mr. Lobdell and family reside in Newark, N. J., he doing business in New York City, "The Bigelow & Main Co., Music Publishers, 135 Fifth Ave."

2. Julian Sylvester Main (7), b 28 Sept., 1841, d 19 Nov., 1865.

3 Helen Ida Main (7), b. 21 Oct., 1844, d. 22 May, 1889

4. Cynthia Isabella Main (7), b. 17 Aug., 1849; m. Frank E. Olmstead; resides at Ridgefield.

EIGHTH GENERATION.

CHILDREN OF HUBERT PLATT MAIN (7) AND OPHELIA LOUISE DE GRAFF.

---

1. Carrie Virginia. 2. Lewis Arthur 3 Lucius Clark. 4. Hubert DeGraff.

---

1. Carrie Virginia Main, b. in New York City, 18 Nov., 1866.

2. Lewis Arthur Main, b in New York City, 24 July, 1868, d. 14 Sept., 1868 in New York City.

3. Lucius Clark Main, b. in New York City, 1 March, 1874; m. at Newark, N. J., 26 July, 1899, Etta Stuart Burke, b 26 July, 1874 at Bayonne, N. J

CHILDREN.

1 Stuart De Graff Main (9), b 3 June, 1900 at Newark, N. J.

2. Donald Gage Main (9), b. 7 Sept., 1901 at Newark, N. J.

4. Hubert DeGraff Main, b 2 Dec., 1884 at Newark, N. J.

The above line of Philip Lobdell is kindly given by Mr Hubert Platt Main of Newark, N. J.

Children and Descendants of
John (3) Lobdell, (Joshua (2), Simon (1))
Wife, Ruth Sherwood

FOURTH GENERATION.

CHILDREN OF JOHN (3) AND RUTH (SHERWOOD) LOBDELL.

1. Ruth. 2. John 3 Caleb. 4. Sarah. 5. Abigail. 6. Hannah. 7. Daniel. 8 Lewis. 9. Chloe.

All born in †Brookfield, Conn

I Ruth, b. 26 March, 1745, m Mr Bradley. It has been impossible to find any descendants or reach any records that will reveal parentage or given name of Mr. Bradley I assume it to have been Nathan Bradley, as the name is repeated in every generation, to the present day, in the family of Daniel Lobdell—a brother of Ruth.

Ruth Lobdell Bradley was dead 28 June, 1782, at which time was the distribution of her father's will, in which is mentioned "To the heirs of Ruth Bradley."

II.   John, b. 21 Sept, 1746, m. Abigail Barlow. Her parentage I have not been able to trace, but she was a sister of Nehemiah Barlow, b 15 April, 1740, who m Jerusha Sherwood (dau. of Daniel Sherwood and Jerusha Whitney.) John was, with his brother Caleb, administrator of his father's estate 30 June, 1777.

III.   Caleb, b. 4 July, 1748; m. at South Salem, Westchester Co, N. Y., 4 Nov., 1773, Patience Boughton, b. 30 March, 1756 at S. Salem, dau. of Ebenezer and Abigail——? Boughton. Caleb and Patience made a home in Brookfield, but soon after the British raid in 1777, Caleb and his brother Daniel moved to New York State.

They evidently stopped in Rensselaerwyck,* where the families of their cousins Jacob and Joshua lived, rented land of Stephen Van Rensselaer, in that portion of the estate which afterward was

---

† The town of Brookfield, Conn, was incorporated in 1788, taken from the towns of New Milford. Newton and Danbury, probably the family of John Lobdell lived in that part of Danbury which was in 1788 included in the town of Brookfield

* Rensselaerwyck, or, the manor of the Van Rensselaers, included parts of the present Columbia, Rensselaer and Albany counties.

Hudson, Columbia Co. We have no record of the time they remained there but each had one or more children born while there. Both, with their families, moved to Northville (then called Old Ford), Fulton Co., N. Y. Here Caleb and Patience both d.; he, 23 Jan., 1829; she, of apoplexy, 30 Oct., 1819.

IV. Sarah, bapt. 14 April, 1749; m. Mr. Peck.

V. Abigail, b. 4 May, 1753; m. Mr. Dunning.

VI. Hannah, b. 4 June, 1755; m. Mr. Hepburn.

VII. Daniel, b. at North Brookfield, Conn., 22 Sept., 1757; m. for his first wife, Rachel Osborn, b. 13 Dec., 1757 at New Milford (now Brookfield), Conn., dau. of James and Elizabeth (Mead) Osborn. Daniel with his brother Caleb were of Northville, Fulton Co., among its earliest residents.*

Rachel d. at Northville 13 July, 1821, and Daniel remarried to Betsey Bryant of Northville, where Daniel d. 13 June, 1843. He was the owner of a large farm, also having other interests. Politically was a staunch Whig. Had three sons by first wife. None by second.

VIII. Lewis Lobdell, b. at Brookfield, 7 March, 1760; m. Elizabeth Osborn, 22 Sept., 1780, b. at Brookfield, 18 Oct., 1760 (sister of Rachel, the wife of his brother Daniel. They remained in Brookfield, where they both died; he, in 1813; she, 12 May, 1851. (Whitney Genealogy.)

IX. Chloe Lobdell, b. 1764-5; "was joined in marriage with Elijah Bauldwin on the tenth day of July, A. D., 1782" (Recorded at Newtown, Conn.) After 1790 they moved to Stamford, Delaware Co., N. Y.

FIFTH GENERATION.

CHILDREN OF JOHN (4) AND ABIGAIL (BARLOW) LOBDELL.

---

1. Orpha. 2. Dennis Barlow. 3. Huldah. 4. Phebe Ruphina.

---

* Each buying land near the other and began a settlement. Samuel Olmstead and Zadock Sherwood, relatives of the Lobdells, having located there in 1786 from Ridgefield, was the inducement for Daniel and Caleb to visit Northville, and were prevailed upon to locate there. The four families being the first settlers of Northville, N. Y. Daniel was a soldier in the Revolutionary War; in service six years.

259

1. Orpha Lobdell; m. Walter Cleever, no record.

2. Dennis Barlow Lobdell, of Brookfield, Conn., b. 8 Dec., 1777, where he d 1838; m. 1803, Clara Northrup, b. 29 July, 1782, at Ridgefield, d 1870 at Bridgeport. After the death of Dennis Barlow Lobdell, his widow remarried to Elijah Barnum, whose first wife was Phebe, a sister of Dennis Barlow Lobdell. (Elijah Barnum had a brother, John Barnum, a soldier in the Revolutionary War, who was taken prisoner in New York harbor, put in the old sugar house prison, and starved to death.) His one sister. Zeruah Barnum, m Darius Bristol of Brookfield.

3. Huldah Lobdell, b at Brookfield, 1779; m. Thaddius Gray, b at Fairfield, Conn., 27 Oct, 1730, son of Wm Gray and Elizabeth Meeker, his wife.

CHILDREN.

1. John Gray (6), b 1811; in 1843 m. Lucy Ann Lobdell, dau. of Ormond and Prudence (Bostwock) Lobdell. Lucy Ann was b. in Brookfield, 2 Jan., 1815, where she d., 17 Dec, 1888 Had son Henry Gray (7) (only child), d 15 Nov., 1900.

2. Abby Gray (6) m. Mr. May.

3. Mary E. Gray (6), d. at Danbury 15 Nov., 1899-1900; m. Mr. Dauchey.

4. Phebe Ruphina Lobdell, b in 1782 at Brookfield (I am told that the old house in which she was born is still standing, but has passed into stranger's hands), m Elijah Barnum, b. 1770 at Danbury. Phebe d. at Danbury, 21 April, 1838, aged 56 years. Elijah (son of ―― Barnum and Temperance Nichols), d. 5 Nov., 1854, aged 84 years Elijah m for his second wife, Clara Northrup Lobdell, widow of Dennis Barlow Lobdell.

SIXTH GENERATION.

CHILDREN OF DENNIS BARLOW AND CLARA (NORTH-RUP) LOBDELL.

---

1. Henry Clark 2. Anna Maria. 3 Chloe Eliza. 4 Harriet Elizabeth. 5. Jerome Bonepart 6. Susan. 7 John Carmen. 8. Walter C 9 Wm 10 Betsey Bradley.

1 Henry Clark, b. 18 May, 1804, at Brookfield, Conn, was afterward a resident of Danbury, Conn, and later of Brooklyn,

HARRIET E. LOBDELL ALVORD (6) (Dennis Barlow [5]) (1866-1904)
CLARK ALVORD (7) of Bridgeport, Conn.   MRS. EDWARD SPARGO (8)   EDWARD SPARGO (9)
(Page 261)

N. Y., where he d. 12 April, 1877 He m. Almina Meeker, b. 2 March, 1805, at Norwalk, Conn, d. 25 Aug., 1891 at Buffalo, N Y., dau of Joseph Steel and Rebecca (Youngs) Meeker, who was dau. of Richard Youngs of Stamford, Conn. The family of Henry Clark Lobdell were brought up in the Methodist faith, but as they attained manhood and womanhood became members of other denominations.

2. Anna Maria, b. 2 Feb., 1806, d. aged two weeks.

3. Chloe Eliza, b. 15 Jan, 1807; m Wm Terrill, a Southern gentleman, resident of Waterbury, Conn. Her first child, Frederick E Terrill (7), followed the sea On April 1, 1873, on the ship "Samuel G Glover" on which he was steward, bound for Havre, he was injured, from the effects of which he died shortly afterward.

2 Henry Terrill (7), d in Norwalk, Conn.

3. Augustus Terrill (7), was with "Farragut" during the war of 1861 and 1864.

4. Julia Terrill (7)

5. Frank Terrill (7), d young.

6 Wm Terrill (7), and George Washington Terrill (7), went to Michigan, taking the widowed mother with them, where she died many years ago

4. Harriet Elizabeth, b 15 Dec., 1809, at Brookfield, Conn ; m 1 Aug., 1827, Chauncey Hart Alvord, b. in East Hampton, Conn., 16 Dec, 1803, who d in 1881 at Morris, Conn Today (Aug. 1902) Mrs. Alvord is living at Morris, Conn in the old homestead into which they moved in 1872 She has always been a bright, active woman. In April, 1901, she had a sickness, which in all probability "was the beginning of the end." Previous to that time, she was always bright and cheerful; even at her age she never sat idle, always had some work in her hands. Since she was eighty years old she had pieced 19 throwdowns, all silk—and they are done nicely. The last one she pieced was entered in the Agricultural Fair held in Waterbury in Sept, 1901, and took the premium She has not worn glasses for ten years. A good Christian mother Her children rise up and call her blessed. Three years passed away and her Master called; she had long been preparing her marriage robes of righteousness and was ready for his summons

" The angel of death has brought sorrow to many hearts during the past week April 12 Mrs. Harriet E Alvord passed away

after a short illness To those to whom she bore the sacred name
of mother the death summons brings with it a sorrow deep and
lasting. Mrs. Alvord was born in Brookfield, December 15, 1809.
Her maiden name was Harriet Elizabeth Lobdell. She moved in
her childhood to Goshen and in August 1, 1827, she married Chauncey Hart Alvord of Chatham (East Hampton). In 1844 they removed to Morris, purchasing the Job Clark place, and in 1872
they removed to their present home. Their golden wedding occurred in 1877. She leaves two daughters and four sons, Mrs. N. S.
Markham of Willimantic, Mrs L. Millaux of Waterbury, Joseph H.
of Elmwood, Edwin Clark of Bridgeport and Edgar A. Alvord,
with whom she lived She also leaves 17 grandchildren and 7
great-grandchildren. She was the last of a family of 10 children
and the oldest person in the town, and feeling the weight of years
she was more than usually bright and active for one of her age.
She made a profession of faith in Christ in 1829, uniting with the
Methodist Church. The funeral took place from the Congregational Church Thursday afternoon, the Rev. Mr. Fletcher officiating, assisted by the Rev. Mr. Toles, pastor of the Methodist Church
of Bethlehem, of which Mrs. Alvord was an active member. A
quartet sang two selections, "Thy Will Be Done" and "Asleep
in Jesus." The floral tokens were many and beautiful. The interment was in the East Cemetery beside her husband. The pall
bearers were Frederick F. Wadhams, Francis F. Wadhams, Lyman
L. Whittlesey and Henry C. Goslee. (From local paper, 1904.)

5. Jerome Bonapart, b. 12 June, 1812 at Brookfield, d. 28 March,
1888 at Bridgeport, Conn.; m. Catherine Smith Raymond, b. 23
Aug., 1811 at Patchogue, Long Island, N. Y., d. 15 Dec., 1891 at
Bridgeport, Conn., dau. of Simeon Raymond of Norwalk, Conn.
He was a Democrat in politics, in religion an Episcopalian.

6. "Susan, b. 14 March, 1814, d 6 March, 1895." These records
were copied from their gravestones, in the cemtery of Danbury,
and given by Mrs. Julia E. Partrick of Danbury, whom we may all
thank for much valuable information, most cheerfully given. Susan
m Sidney Smith, b. 18 Dec., 1809, d. 30 Dec , 1884. Son of Mc-
Pherson and Sally (Benedict) Smith of Brookfield. Children all
b. in Fairfield Co., Conn.

    1 Mary Josephine Smith (7) m. Edward Fairchild,
of Danbury, Conn., a retired merchant, died at Danbury.
Both are dead Left no family.

2 Rockwell Smith (7).

3. Charles Smith (7).

4 Clarence Smith (7), m. twice.

5 Henry Smith (7).

6 Frank Smith (7).

7. John Carmen, b. 28 Apr., 1816 at Danbury, Conn., d. 25 Feb., 1878 at Washington, Litchfield Co., Conn., m. 11 Aug., 1845 at New Milford, Litchfield Co., Conn. to Laura Ann Wheeler, b. 18 Feb., 1819 at New Milford, d. 2 July, 1893 at Northville, Litchfield Co., Conn., dau. of Denmon and Ruth Ann Hawley Wheeler Mr Lobdell was a Methodist.

8 Walter C., b. 13 Feb., 1819 at Danbury, Conn.; at Norwalk, he m. Eulalia Maria Cleveland, dau. of Wm. Cleveland She d in New York City in 1870. Children all born in Norwalk·

1 Sarah Frances (7), d. in New York City

2 Mary Eliza (7) m. at Yonkers, N. Y., James Tallman, of Newburgh, N. Y

3 Eulalie (7), d young.

4. Wm Henry (7)

5 Edward Francis (7).

6. Oscar (7), on the 18 of March, 1868, was killed on the L. I. R. R., near Newtown, Conn.

7. Ida (7).

8 Walter (7).—(Cleveland Genealogy.)

9 William, b. 23 March, 1822

10 Betsey (or Elizabeth) Bradley, b. 20 April, 1827 at Brookfield, Conn., d 10 Aug., 1894 at Danbury, where she also m. on 10 Nov., 1844, Wm. Byfield, b 14 Jan., 1823 at London, England, d 28 June 1891 at Wilton, Conn., son of Richard and Sarah (Rowcliffe) Byfield.

SIXTH GENERATION.

CHILDREN OF PHEBE (5) LOBDELL AND ELIJAH BARNUM.

---

1. Polly Ann. 2. Orra. 3. Annis. 4. John 5. Starr. 6. Henry G. (All born in Danbury.)

1. Polly Ann Barnum, m Turner Barnum of Bethel. They moved soon after to Moscow, Livington Co., N. Y.; had eight children, five girls and three boys.

Herman Barnum (7), the oldest son, has spent his life as a missionary in Turkey; m there—has one daughter (8) and two sons (8) now in this country being educated.

Harriet Barnum (7), the third dau., m. ——? Smith and resided in Chicago. She left two sons (8) now in business in Chicago.

2 Orra Barnum, b. 3 April, 1809, d. at Danbury 24 May, 1887; m. same place 9 Jan., 1832, Darius H Dikeman, a farmer, b 4 Sept., 1807 at Danbury, where he d 4 Nov, 1840, son of Benj. and Mary (Crofoot) Dikeman, both b at Danbury. Mr. Dikeman was a Democrat in politics and formerly the family were Methodists; in later years Universalists

3 Annis Barnum, b. 23 April, 1811; m twice, —— Curtis was her first husband, Amas Bishop her second She had two daughters (7); one d. young The other (7) is living at Danbury

4. John Barnum married a lady from Poughkeepsie, N. Y Both are dead, as are also their two daughters, who grew to womanhood

5 Starr Barnum joined Santa Anna's army to go to Mexico The last the family ever heard of him, they had reached St Louis. Never married.

6 Henry G Barnum, b. 1820, d 24 Aug., 1876; in Eleanor Demming They lived in New York and had one son and daughter The daughter (7) d. young. The son (7), named P. T. Barnum 2d (7), d. in New York 2 Dec, 1901, aged 45 He m. Susie Travis

Henry G. Barnum promised P T. Barnum, who had no sons. many years ago, that if he ever had a son, he should be named Phineas Taylor Barnum, second.

P. T. Barnum 2d left two sons H. G. Barnum, Jr. (8), aged 23 and P. T. Barnum 3d (8), aged 18.

SEVENTH GENERATION.

CHILDREN OF HENRY CLARK (6) AND ALMINA (MEEKER) LOBDELL.

1. Harriet. 2 Hannah 3 Francis. 4. Mary Louise. 5. Henry. 6. Susan Rebecca.

1. Harriet Augusta, now residing (1902) in New York City, was born 22 Sept., 1824 at Norwalk, Conn., m for her (1) hus-

REV. FRANCIS LOBDELL (7)
(Henry Clark [6])   (1835-1900)
of Buffalo, N. Y.
(Page 265)

band, John M. White in 1842, at Bethel, Conn., who d in Danbury, Conn., 29 Sept., 1857, son of John White of Danbury. Mrs. White remarried at New York City 8 Feb., 1865 to John I. Doane, who d 1 March, 1877 at Brooklyn. By her first husband she had two sons:

    1. John Henry White (8), b. 28 Aug., 1844, d. 4 Sept., 1898; m. Margaret Pryor and had 5 children, viz:
        1 John Norton White (9)
        2. Thomas White (9)
        3. James White (9).
        4 Mary Augusta White (9)
        5 George Francis White (9), b. 26 Oct., 1879
    2. George Russell White (8), b 4 Jan., 1847, d. 11 June, 1889.

  2. Hannah, b. 23 Dec, 1829, is buried in Bethel cemetery (about 9 miles south of Brookfield, Conn The inscription on her gravestone reads: "Hannah, wife of Joseph M. Barnum, passed to her spirit home from Brookfield, 15 March, 1867, aged 38 y., 2 m., 20 d." Hers was a lovely character, and she possessed a remarkably sweet voice Children:

    1. Lucius Russell Barnum (8), lies beside his mother; d. 10 Sept., 1855, aged 4 y., 4 m., 10 d

    2 Frank Mortimer Barnum (8), b. in Aug., 1850; m. 17 June, 1873, Evie Watts, b. 12 May, 1852. They have one dau. Emily Keene Barnum (9), b. 29 March, 1874 All reside in Paris, France.

    3. Francis, b. 25 March 1835 at Danbury, Conn., d. at Buffalo. N. Y., 26 Oct., 1900; m. for his (1) wife on 6 Sept., 1859, Julia A Danforth, b. 29 Sept., 1836 at Middletown, Conn, d. 18 Aug., 1869 at Cincinnati, Ohio, dau. of Deacon Josiah Danforth and his wife Almira Camp, dau of Ezra and Anna (Coe) Camp. M. for his (2) wife on 6 Sept., 1870, Harriet Toucey, d. 22 April, 1872. M. third on 17 June, 1874, Julia Goodall Doon, b. 9 Nov., 1847, dau. of John Glasgow Doon of Savannah, Ga. The widow resides at Buffalo, N. Y.

Rev. Francis Lobdell, D. D., L. L. D., a graduate of Amherst College (1849) was fitted for college at Phillips (Andover) Academy. He studied theology at Union Seminary and was ordained 3 Nov., 1859 at Warren, Conn. Was pastor of the First Congregational Church at Warren until 1863 and of Second Congregational

Church in Bridgeport, Conn, from that date till 1865. While in this pastorate he was a member of the United States Christian commission, whose mission was the care of the sick and wounded. He was present during the final battle of Petersburg, Va, and had charge of the commission work in that city from the day of its surrender till the close of the war. On the 31st of Aug., 1865, he was ordained to the deaconate of the Episcopal Church, and advanced to the priesthood on Nov. 19 of the same year. Was rector of the Church of the Advent, Cincinnati, O., 1865-1869.; St. Paul's Church, New Haven, Conn., 1869-1879; St Andrew's Church, New York, 1879-1887, and Trinity Church, Buffalo, N Y., 1887 until his death, 26 Oct., 1899. While rector of St. Andrew's Church he was elected Secretary of the Diocese and a member of its standing committee. From 1892 he was a delegate to the general convention of the Episcopal Church, serving on many important committees. For several years he held the office of arch-deacon of Buffalo, N Y. Hobart College conferred on him the degree of S T D in 1881 and of L L D in 1894. For many years he served as chaplain of the 65th Regiment.

4. Mary Louise, b 13 Nov, 1837, d. 13 Jan., 1875, m first Charles Snedeker, by whom she had one son, Charles Snedeker (8), who is now (1902) Dean of St Paul's Protestant Cathedral, Cincinnati, O. She m second David Simonson Hillyer. Residence, Brooklyn.

CHILDREN.

1. Alice Almira Hillyer (8), b. 23 Oct., 1863, m first Howard E. Turner, no children; m second Horace P. Gould, by whom she had one son:

    1. Pierson Hillyer Gould (9), b. 21 Nov., 1900.

2 John Blake Hillyer (8), b. 15 Feb., 1868; m. Jessie A. Lipman. Children.

    1. Douglas Van Alen Hillyer (9), b 25 May, 1893.

    2. John Blake Hillyer (9), b 11 Jan., 1901

3. Ellison Hillyer (8), b. 15 July, 1870; m. Lottie Belle Taylor; one son, Kenneth Ellison Hillyer (9), b. 25 Sept., 1895

4 Francis Lobdell Hillyer (8), b. 3 July, 1872

5 Henry (Rev.), b. in Danbury; m. Lucy Cornelia Williams, b in Ridgefield, 27 Nov, 1827 He was appointed to go to the Turkish Empire, where—at Mosul—he d, greatly lamented as a

man of rare enthusiasm and of the most devoted consecration to his great work. Two children were b. to them, Mary, one of the leading soprano singers of Brooklyn, who passed away in early life, and Julius Henry, of Chicago, Ill

6. Susan Rebecca, b. 1841, d 1877; m Rev. R Henry Gidman, a Congregational minister who lived at North Madison, Conn., at time of her death She left one child:

1. Thusa Lindsay Gidman (8), a graduate of Northfield School, Wellesley College, b. 25 March, 1874.

CHILDREN AND GRAND-CHILDREN OF HARRIET ELIZABETH LOBDELL AND CHAUNCEY CLARK ALVORD.

1. Anna 2. Joseph Hart 3 Eliza Chloe. 4 Jerome Lobdell 5. Edwin 6 Edgar.

1. Anna Alvord, b. in Goshen, Conn., 23 May, 1828; m N. S. Markham of East Hampton, Conn , 19 Nov , 1846. He died in Windham Co., Conn , 2 Oct., 1882. Three children:

1 N. Augustus Markham (8), b in E Hampton, 16 Sept , 1847, d in Thomasville, Ga., 27 Dec , 1880.

2. Arthur L. Markham (8), b in E Hampton, 21 Aug , 1851, d same place 25 Oct , 1854.

3 Herbert S Markham (8), b in E Hampton, 18 April, 1855, d. 12 Aug , 1873.

2. Joseph Hart Alvord, b in Goshen, Conn , 12 Dec , 1830; m. Betsey Lathem Had two daughters, b in Glastonbury, Conn

1 Carrie Alvord (8), d young

2 Annie Alvord (8), m E M. Hewit of Detroit, Mich.

3. Eliza Chloe Alvord, b. 26 Feb., 1834 at Cornwell, Litchfield Co , Conn , m 21 Aug , 1853, Ludovic Millaux, b 22 Feb., 1832 at Paris, France, son of Louis Paul and Caroline —— Millaux. They reside at Waterbury, Conn Mr Millaux is by profession a musician, a Republican in politics Two sons were born to them, both d in childhood·

1 Geo Ludovic Millaux (8), b 28 Jan , 1854, d 13 March, 1860.

2. Edwin Ludovic Millaux (8), b 10 May, 1864, d. 8 May, 1865

267

4. Jerome Lobdell Alvord, b in Goshen, 12 Dec., 1835; m. Emily V Daniels, in E. Hampton, Conn, 31 May, 1857. He d in Glastonbury. Conn, 14 July, 1871 Had four children:

      1 Frances Alvord (8), d. young in E Hampton

      2 Minnie Alvord (8), b. 16 June, 1860, m 14 Jan., 1888, Leland M Strong of Middle Haddem, Conn

      3 Bertha Alvord, b in E Hampton, 12 Nov., 1867, m Dr. C. Art Ward of Waterbury, Conn.

      4 Emma Daniels Alvord, b in E Hampton, 18 Oct, 1869. Is clerk in Waterbury Post Office

5 Edwin Alvord, b in Goshen, Conn, 12 March, 1840; m Susan Birch of Woodbury, Conn Has six children

      1 Harriet M. Alvord (8), b in Woodbury, Conn

      2 Jerome Lobdell Alvord (8), b. in Thomastown, Conn

      3 Raymond Alvord (8), b. in Thomastown, Conn

      4 Alfred Alvord (8), b. in Thomastown, Conn.

      5 Frederick Alvord (8), b in Thomastown, Conn

      6 Frank Alvord (8), b in Bridgeport, Conn.

6 Edgar Alvord, a twin of Edwin, b in Goshen, Conn, 12 March, 1840, m. Helen Waugh of Morris, Conn They have four children

      1. Henry Chauncey Alvord (8).

      2 May Emma Alvord (8).

      3 Herbert Markham Alvord (8)

      4. Clark Leander Alvord (8), m. Georgie Parda of Thomaston, Conn., and has two children, b at Thomaston.

           1. Lilla Alvord (9), b. 14 July, 1875.

           2 Harry C. Alvord (9), b. 5 May, 1878

CHILDREN OF JEROME BONAPART (6) AND CATHARINE SMITH (RAYMOND) LOBDELL.

1 Charles, b 24 June, 1833, d 18 Dec., 1867.

2. Julia, b. 2 Oct., 1835, d unmarried, 16 Nov, 1873.

3 Ruth, b 3 June, 1838, d 13 May, 1874

4 John R, b 1 Sept., 1843 at New York City, is a resident of Bridgeport. Conn, engaged on the "Bridgeport Standard", a Democrat in politics, a Catholic in religion. Married Bridget Burns, b. 7 June, 1847 at Longford, Longford Co, Ireland, dau of James and —— Niernay Burns They have no children.

268

5   Thomas, b. 25 Nov , 1846, d. unmarried 13 June, 1871.

6   Susan, b. 21 Sept., 1848 at New York City , m. 20 Feb , 1868 at Bridgeport, Fairfield Co , Conn., Charles H. La Field, b. 21 Feb., 1843 at Bridgeport, Conn , son of Geo and Elizabeth Shelton La Field Mr. Chas La Field is a grocer, residing at 93 North Ave., Bridgeport. Is a Democrat. In religion the family are Episcopalians. They have three children

    1   Howard La Field (8), b. 6 May, 1869, unmarried (1902.)

    2. Grace La Field (8), b 23 Sept., 1872, unmarried (1902.)

    3. Clara La Field (8), b 11 Oct., 1874, m. 30 Dec , 1897, Wm. A Platt of Milford, Conn. No children.

7   Clara, b. 23 May, 1863, d. unmarried 6 Nov., 1876.

CHILDREN OF JOHN CARMEN (6) LOBDELL AND HIS WIFE, LAURA ANN WHEELER.

1   Mary E. 2   Ellen J. 3. John H.

1. Mary E , b. 13 May, 1846; m Milo C Parsons. She d. March, 1891

2. Ellen J , b. 21 July, 1847 at New Milford, Conn.; m. 11 March, 1868 at Wolcottville, Litchfield Co , Conn., John W. Bird, b. 20 Jan., 1842, son of James and ——— (Wilson) Bird. The family are Episcopalians and reside at Ringsville, Canada

CHILDREN.

    1. Clarence W. Bird (8). b. 26 April, 1872.

    2. Myra A. Bird (8), b. 2 Dec., 1874.

    3. Laura C. Bird (8). b 18 Nov., 1876.

3. John H., b. 29 June, 1849; m Kate Hagany. I have been unable to get authentic record of John H. I am told that he formerly lived at Cassville, Oneida Co , N Y., that he d. in 1900-1, and that his widow lives in Waterbury, Conn.

CHILDREN OF BETSEY (BRADLEY) (6) LOBDELL AND WM. BYFIELD.

1. Wm. Edward. 2. Charles Henry. 3. Clara L. 4. Arthur L. 5. Frederick M. 6. Sarah H.

1. Wm. Edward Byfield, b. 26 Sept., 1845, d. 17 Oct., 1898; m Mrs. Orpha Lane.

2. Charles Henry Byfield, b. 9 Dec., 1847, m. 25 Dec., 1871, Hettie N. Strong, resides at Sawpit, Colo.

3. Clara Lobdell Byfield, b. 1 Jan., 1852, at Beaver Brook, Fairfield Co., Conn.; m. 31 July, 1877 at New York City, Edwin N. Landon, b. 21 Jan., 1851 at New York City, son of John E. and Allison R. (Couthill) Landon. Edwin N. Landon served seven years in militia, 12th Regiment, Co. I, National Guards, State of New York. Reside at 1116 East Main St., Bridgeport, Conn.

CHILDREN.

1. Edwin Burdette Landon (8), b. 17 July, 1878.

2. Harold Richard Landon (8), b. 7 July, 1880. Both unmarried (1902).

Harold Richard (8) is (1902) bugler in 87th Co. Coast Artillery stationed at Fort Totten, Willets Point, N. Y.

4. Arthur Rocliffe Byfield, b. 28 March, 1854, d. 1 Sept., 1873.

5. Frederick Mortimer Byfield, 22 March, 1856; m. 23 Dec., 1883, Mary Spooner.

6. Sarah Helen Byfield, b. 19 Dec., 1864; m. 16 June, 1886, Geo. L. French, and resides at North Bridgeport, Conn.

CHILDREN OF ORRA BARNUM (6) AND DARIUS H. DIKEMAN.

---

1. Darius H. 2. Frances A. 3. Julia E.

1. Darius H. Dikeman of Danbury.

2. Frances A. Dikeman, b. 21 Oct., 1832; m. James G. Hagan.

3. Julia E. Dikeman, b. 7 July, 1840 at Danbury, m. 25 June, 1861, Edgar J. Partrick, b. 2 Feb., 1829 at Patterson, Putnam Co., N. Y., d. 14 June, 1877 at Danbury, son of Lewis Partrick, b. at Ridgefield, Conn., 2 May, 1798 and Mary Heartwell, b. at Patterson, N. Y. Mrs. Julia Partrick has one dau.

Mary H. Partrick (8), b. 22 Feb., 1865; m. Francis T. Austin. Resides in Danbury.

The sad information of the "going home" of this truly noble woman was sent to me and if they who tenderly loved her will think of her "as one of those angels into whose charge the Lord has given them, that in angelic hands, they may be borne lest plagues come nigh their dwelling or lest they dash their feet against

270

a stone, they will find occasion for sweet rejoicing in the superior relation which she now bears to them."

(From Local Paper, 1907.)

Mrs. Julia E. Partrick, a lifelong resident and descendant of one of Danbury's oldest families, died at her late home, 393 Main Street, last evening, at 6 o'clock, at the age of sixty-seven years, after an intermittent illness, dating from the early part of last January. For a few days prior to last Thursday, Mrs. Partrick had shown a marked improvement, when a sudden collapse set in, from which she was unable to rally

Born July 7, 1840, the daughter of Darius H and Orra Barnum Dikeman, she was a descendant of the Barnum family, one of the first settlers of Danbury and was of the fifth generation of this honored family to live in the present home. She was the wife of the late Edgar J. Partrick, well known as a public man of this city.

She as a woman of choice life, unostentatious and home-loving, whose quiet charities seemed to be governed by the scriptural injunction to let not the left hand know what the right hand doeth. Like her mother, she was a life-long member of the Universalist Church

She is survived by one daughter, Mrs. F. T. Austin, and two granddaughters, Misses Julia A. and Fannie C. Austin

The funeral service will be held at her late home, 393 Main Street, on Monday at 2 o'clock, followed by interment in the family plot in Wooster cemetery.

EIGHTH GENERATION.

CHILDREN OF REV. FRANCIS LOBDELL (7).

1. Eleanor. 2 Frederick Danforth, and 3 Frank, twins. 4. Harriet. 5. Marion Doon 6 Margaret Dunning. 7. Leighton.
(By First Wife.)

1 Eleanor, b. 29 May, 1861, at Warren, Litchfield Co., Conn; m. 17 June, 1880 at New York City, Rev Edward William Worthington, an Episcopal clergyman, (1902) rector of Grace Episcopal Church, Cleveland, Ohio, who was b 10 May, 1854 at Batavia, Genesce Co, N Y, d. 15 April, 1906—son of Gad B. and Anna M. (Dixon) Worthington Children:

271

1. Eleanor Worthington (9), b. 1 Sept., 1881.
2. Agnes Seabury Worthington (9), b. 14 Nov., 1884, d. 2 March, 1900.
3. Edward Lobdell Worthington (9), b 2 June, 1886
4. Donald Worthington (9), b. 13 Jan., 1893.
5. Dorothy Worthington (9), b. 10 April, 1895

2. Rev. Frederick Danforth, b 8 Oct., 1862. Is a member of the Order of the Companions of the Holy Savior, Philadelphia, Pa.

3. Frank, twin of Frederick, b 8 Oct., 1862, d in infancy.

4. Harriet, b. 1 Dec., 1863 at Bridgeport, Conn., m. 17 June, 1885 at St Andrew's Church, New York City by Rev. Francis Lobdell to Vernon Mansfield Davis, b 29 Jan., 1855 at New York City, son of Robert Vernon and Mary (Semler) Davis. Mrs. Harriet Lobdell Davis has for several years held the office of Registrar of the New York City Chapter, Daughters of the American Revolution and is descended from many interesting lines of Colonial ancestry in New England. Mr. Vernon M. Davis, residing at 194 Lenox Ave., New York City, is a Democrat in politics Was twelve years Assistant District Attorney and succeeded Col John R. Fellows as District Attorney for a short time Was elected to the Supreme Court of New York in 1902. He is a member of the Board of Education and a member of many of the leading clubs. He succeeded Elbridge T. Gerry as President of the Society for the Prevention of Cruelty to Children They have no children.

(By second wife, Julia Goodall Doon.)

5. Marian Doon, b. 4 March, 1877 at New Haven, Conn., d. at Buffalo, N. Y., 3 June, 1900; m 28 Sept., 1898 at Buffalo, N. Y., Thos. B. Lockwood, a lawyer residing 465 Niagara St., Buffalo, at which city he was b. 7 Feb., 1873, son of Daniel N and Sarah E. (Brown) Lockwood No children.

6. Margaret Dunning, b. 30 Aug., 1878; m at Trinity Church, Buffalo, N. Y. on Tuesday, 17 June, 1902, by Rev Frederick Danforth Lobdell, assisted by Rev. Cameron J. Davis, to Wm Algernon Brackenridge.

7. Leighton, b. 19 Nov., 1884.

FIFTH GENERATION.

CHILDREN OF CALEB (4) AND PATIENCE (BOUGHTON) LOBDELL.

1. Jerusha. 2. Lucy. 3. Daniel. 4. Caleb. 5. Noble. 6. John Boughton. 7. Ruth. 8. Lanie. 9. Jacob Elias 10. Melinda. 11. Samuel. 12. Abigail. 13. George Rodney. 14. Pliny.

I. Jerusha, b. 22 April, 1774 at Brookfield, Conn., d. 18 Dec., 1848 at Fonda, Montgomery Co (afterward called Fulton Co.), N. Y.; m. Samuel Olmstead, one of the first settlers of the town of Fonda. Their children were all b. at Northville, Fulton Co.

CHILDREN.
1. Ormond Bradley Olmstead (6).
2. Samuel Olmstead (6).
3. Miranda Olmstead (6)
4. Melissa Olmstead (6)
5. A dau. (6), who m Ezra Lyon.
6. A dau. (6), who m. Dr. Mitchell.

II. Lucy, b. 15 Nov., 1775 at Brookfield; m. Cornelius Van Ness, resided at Hamburg, Erie Co , N. Y., where Lucy d. in 1839.

CHILDREN.
1. Cornelius Van Ness (6)
2. Jacob Van Ness (6).
3. John Van Ness (6)
4. Rachel Van Ness (6).
5. Jerusha Van Ness (6).

III. Daniel, b. at Brookfield, 7 Sept, 1777; m. Polly Sackett of Dutchess Co, N. Y. They removed to Genesee Co., N. Y., where Daniel was drafted into the army, in the war of 1812, but was too ill at the time to serve and soon after d. of quick consumption. His widow remarried to Mr. Lewis Barnes

IV. Caleb, Jr., b. 16 June, 1779; m. Elizabeth Hammond. b at Northville 4 May, 1786, dau. of Paul Hammond Caleb and Elizabeth lived near Watertown. Their children were: Samuel,

273

John B., Jerusha, and another dau.—who probably d. young. (Hammond genealogy.)

V   Noble, b. 17 April, 1781, (?) was a resident of Northville, and in 1807 a neighbor of his brother Caleb on (now) Main St He m, 1810, for his first wife, Sarah Clark, dau. of Caleb Clark, b. in Montgomery Co, N Y., by whom he had five sons and one daughter The family moved to Hamburg, Erie Co., N. Y., where the mother d. 1825 or 6.

Noble m for his second wife, Mary Adelia Sly (called Polly) and removed to Waukesha Co, Wis., where he d 13 Oct., 1861. His wife d. 29 Dec, 1866.

VI.   John Boughton, b (?) 23 Feb., 1782; m. Flora Judd, dau. of Sherman Judd of Connecticut, where Flora was b 26 July, 1780 They moved to Hamburg, Erie Co, N Y, afterward moving to Michigan, where Flora d., 1860 John Boughton d. 1861.

VII   Ruth, b 26 Feb, 1785 (?), d. at Brandt, Erie Co., N. Y. 17 Sept., 1863; m 1 May, 1803, Benoni G. Hammond of Brandt. Hammond Genealogy says: "Two of their children with Aunt Mary went west with the Mormons."

CHILDREN.

1. John Hammond (6)
2. Laney Hammond (6)
3. Samuel Elias Hammond (6).
4 Ammon Hammond (6).
5. Wm Hammond (6).
6. Harry Hammond (6)
7. Mary Elizabeth Hammond (6).

VIII   Lanie, b. 9 Feb., 1787, d. 28 March, 1854; m. Edie Cole

CHILDREN.

1 Harriet Cole (6), never married.
2 Maria Cole (6) in Mr Phillips.
3 Clorinda Cole (6), never married.
4 George Cole (6).

IX   Jacob Elias, b 30 June, 1789 at Hudson, now Columbia Co., N Y He was probably named after a friend of his father, one Jacob Elias, of Hudson, of whose will in 1786 Caleb Lobdell, Peter Sylvester and Thomas Whitlock were executors He moved with his parents to Northville, or Northampton, Fulton Co, N. Y, where he m. 2 Sept, 1810, Rachel Van Ness, b. 15 Dec, 1791, dau

NOBLE LOBDELL (5) AND MARY ADELIA SLY—HIS SECOND WIFE
(Caleb [4])   (1781-1861)
of Waukesha County, Wis.

(Page 274)

of Garrett and Effie (Sharp) Van Ness Husband and wife d. at Northampton, he 12 Oct., 1842, she, 16 March, 1888.

X   Melinda, b. 14 April, 1791, d 1 Nov., 1859; m Reuben Vibbard.

XI   Samuel, b. 6 April, 1793 (?), was also one of the early settlers of Northville, where he d. 22 Sept., 1860; m. Lydia Randall, 24 Jan., 1814 for his first wife Having no children they adopted Samuel's niece, Matilda Lobdell, youngest dau. of his brother Daniel.

His wife Lydia d 20 Sept, 1849 at Northampton, N. Y., and Sam'l remarried 25 Sept., 1850 to Widow Harriet S Aylsworth (Cornell) One child was born to them

> Samuel Henry Lobdell (6), b. 15 Nov., 1851, d 5 Nov., 1868 at Northville.

XII. Abigail, b. 13 May, 1795, d, aged 9 years.

XIII. George Rodney, a farmer, b at Northampton, 11 Nov., 1798, d. Dec, 1849 at Hamburg, N. Y.; m. Abigail Dart, b. 21 Aug, 1805 at Danby, Vt., d 6 Sept., 1870 at Fairplains, Montcalm Co. Mich. The family were Universalists.

XIV. Pliny, a farmer, b. 2 Jan., 1800 at Hudson, N. Y., d. 7 Nov, 1863 at Hamburg, Erie Co., N. Y ; m at Hamburg in 1819, Nancy Pierce, b. 8 Aug., 1802 at Long Island, N. Y., d 16 Aug, 1888 at Chesaning. Saginaw Co., Mich, dau of Roland Pierce, who lived near Paris, Canada Mr. L was a Methodist, Republican in politics.

CHILDREN.

1. Electa (6). 2. Seymour (6). 3. George (6). 4 Amanda (6). 5 Ammon (6) 6. Patience (6). 7 Matilda (6). 8. Mary (6) 9. Martha (6).

3. George resides at Mankato, Minn. No answer to my letter of inquiry

5. With Mr. Ammon H, I had a very pleasant correspondence in 1900, but probably failing health was the cause of no reply to my last letter He is a farmer residing at Chesaning. Saginaw Co., Mich., b 3 Dec, 1830 at Hamburg, Erie Co., N Y, where he m. 7 Oct., 1849, Caroline Northum, b 27 July, 1831, also b at Hamburg, dau. of Levi and Lucy (West) Northum. Children:

275

SEVENTH GENERATION.

1. Ida Gertrude, b 15 Aug, 1850; m. Erastus Wierman.

2. Emma Lillian, b. 22 Nov., 1853, m. Geo. Mc-Cormick

3. Martha Amelia, b. 10 Jan., 1856, m. Douglas Coleman.

4 Lois, b. 22 April, 1858; m. W. W Day.

5. Florence May, b. 18 Jan., 1860; m Arthur Lewis.

6 Pliny b 15 Sept., 1863, deceased.

7. Austin K

8. Seymour.

9 Alice. b. 13 July. 1857; m Elmer Swift

10. Carrie, b 17 Sept., 1869, deceased

11. Gabriella, b 17 May, 1872, m Merton Card

12 Charles E , b 20 May, 1875.

SIXTH GENERATION.

CHILDREN OF DANIEL (5) AND POLLY (SACKETT) LOBDELL.

---

1. Smith. 2 Mary. 3. Eliza 4. Matilda

1. Smith, b. 1805, d ——?

2. Mary, b. 7 June, 1807 at Northampton, Montgomery Co. (now Fulton Co); m 26 Sept, 1821 at Norway, Herkimer Co.. N. Y, Benj. Austin, b. 2 Jan., 1802 at Salisbury, Herkimer Co, N. Y. (son of Wm., son of Benj). Wm Austin was b in Rhode Island 27 March. 1767, d 19 Jan , 1849 With his wife (I think her name was Sweet) Wm. Austin came in 1797 or 8 to the town of Fairfield, Conn , bought land, cleared quite a large tract, built a house, when to their dismay parties came and claimed the land by a previous title, proving Mr. Austin's deed not good They then moved further north. One brother, Stephen, of Connecticut, or a descendant of the same name, settled in Texas, and from him the capital of the state derives its name

Mr. Benj Austin d. 15 July, 1877 at Norway, Herkimer Co, N Y , Mary d 12 March, 1887.

3 Eliza, b. 1 April, 1811; m Stephen Judson Gage, b. 9 June, 1802 at Norway, Herkimer Co, N Y., d. in same place 27 Oct., 1882 Eliza d. also at Norway, 5 Nov., 1850

4 Matilda, b 17 June, 1813 at Penfield, Monroe Co., N. Y., was adopted after the death of her father by her uncle Samuel Lobdell, with whom she lived until 10 Jan, 1833, when at Northville, Fulton Co., N. Y. (the home of her Uncle Samuel), she m. Alexander St John Lobdell, b. 18 Nov, 1810 at Northampton, Fulton Co, N. Y, d 14 Nov, 1865 at West Troy, N. Y. Alex. St. John Lobdell was son of James and grand-son of Daniel and Rachel Osborn Lobdell.

CHILDREN OF NOBLE LOBDELL.

---

1. Abby. 2. Caleb 3 Daniel 4 David Clark. 5. Henry. 6 Miles 7. Sally. 8. Harriet 9 Gilbert 10 Noble Burlen. 11. Mary. 12. Abby. 13. Caleb. 14. Melinda. 15. Maria. 16 Pliny 17 Wm Daniel. 18 Emmet Lee 19. Lora Nash.

(By (1) Wife, Sarah (Clark) Lobdell)

---

1. Abby, b. 1800 at Northville; m. Asa Fuller She d in 1830, leaving five children

CHILDREN.

1   Esther Fuller (7)
2. Sarah Fuller (7).
3   Henry Fuller (7).
4   Charles Fuller (7)
5. And a little dau, Adelia Fuller, only four months old, who was taken by the second wife of Noble Lobdell (Abby's father), who at that time had a little dau. Harriet, four weeks old. She cared for Adelia until she was eleven months old, when her father took her

2 Caleb, b at Northville, d. unmarried in Troy, N Y.

3. Daniel, b at Northville, d. in South Bend, Ind.; m. Lucy Ann True of Indiana Had four children:

1. Harriet Ann Lobdell (7).
2   Florence Lobdell (7).
3. David Miles Lobdell (7).

277

4. Geo. Lobdell, a saddler and harness maker, residing at Racine, Wis.

4. David Clark, b 7 Jan., 1818 at Hamburg, Erie Co., N. Y., was reared to the life of a farmer. At the age of 21 he m. Martha Sly and soon after moved to Norwalk, Huron Co., Ohio There he first engaged in agricultural pursuits, and then bought an interest in a stone quarry, which he assisted in operating three or four years

In 1856 he moved with his family to Waukesha Co., Wis., and engaged in farming. In 1861 he came to Wanewoc township and bought a farm of 160 acres, which was nearly as it had been designed by nature. In Sept., 1881, he exchanged this farm for a house in Wanewoc, where he lived and died, in May, 1893. He was one of the pioneers of Jeneau Co. His wife d 3 April, 1888. They had a family of nine children, six sons and three daughters.

Mr. Lobdell was well known and worthy of the high esteem in which he was held by his fellow citizens.

(The above is copied from their local paper. Both himself and wife were members of the Campbellite Church.

5. Henry, d. when two years old.

6. Miles C., b. 30 March, 1824 at Hamburg, N. Y. Of the children born to Sarah (Clark) Lobdell, three d. in infancy and she d. leaving five; Miles was her youngest, seventeen months old His mother gave him to her brother, Henry Clark, who d. when Miles was 16 years old. Two years later his aunt remarried to Silas Wheelock and Miles remained with them until he m. (six days after he was 20 years old. He came to Wisconsin in 1848 and bought a farm in the town of Mukwonago. In 1880 he moved to North Prairie, where he has owned and cared for a large farm, but declining years and inability to do farm work caused him to sell it in the fall of 1903 and buy a smaller one of 13 acres on which he now lives (1904). 81 and 80 years, the ages of himself and wife, represent struggles, sickness and sorrow, all borne with Christian patience and fortitude. All who know them prize the acquaintance of such true Christians, who so faithfully have served their Master, both in the church, in the home circle and among friends and neighbors. In Mr L.'s last letter he says: "We wait and watch for the call of our Master." On 24 April, 1844, Miles m. at Hamburg, Sarah M. Littlefield, b. 25 Dec., 1823 at Hamburg, dau of Wray S. and Nancy (Green) Littlefield. Mrs. Lobdell's

DAVID CLARK LOBDELL (6)
(Noble [5])   (1818-1893)
of Wanewoc, Wis.
(Page 278)

MILES CLARK LOBDELL (6)
(Noble [5])   (1824-1904)
of North Prairie, Wis.
(Page 278)

HARRIET LOBDELL MOODY (6)
(Noble [5])
of Plainfield, Wis.
(Page 279)

CHARLES WEBB JOHNSON
(Dr. Oran Johnson)   (1815-1854)
of Johnstown, N. Y.
(Page 101)

father was in the "War of 1812"; an epaulette worn by him is held by a descendant. He was sheriff of Erie Co., N. Y., in 1822, the "Thars" being hung during his term of office.

CHILDREN OF NOBLE AND HIS (2) WIFE, MARY ADELIA SLY.

1 Sally, b 8 Nov., 1828; m. 1848 John Sugden, d. about 1873 Sally had 13 living children; ten of them are now living (7). She lives with her second son in Hubb City, Richland, Wis.

2. Harriet, b. 1 April, 1830; m. Lewis Moody, b. 23 April, 1824. They reside at Plainfield, Wis.

3. Gilbert, b. 1831, d. at the age of 2 y., 7 m.

4. Noble Burlen, b 1833, was named after his father and a friend of his father. He never married.   •

5. Mary, b. 24 Feb., 1834; m. Russell Richardson. She had fifteen children; eleven (7) are living in Minnesota.

6. Abby. b. 16 Dec , 1636. d 1893; m. Fred Oorh. She had eight children. He d. leaving five children living.

7. Caleb. b. 7 July, 1838. Enlisted in the Civil War, 1861; served three years. Lives in Bellewood, Nebraska (unmarried.)

8. Melinda, b. 10 Feb., 1840; m. Wm. Fairbrothers. He enlisted 1861, in the Civil War and served till its close; came home and died, leaving a widow and four children (7) living in Woodstock, Richland Co, Wis

9 Maria, b. 1841; m. in 1873, Thomas Erickson, who d. leaving her with three children (7), who all live in New Lisbon, Jeneau Co., Wis.

10. Pliny, b. 1842. d 1856. Buried in Wisconsin.

11. Wm. Daniel, b 1844. He enlisted 1861 in the Civil War, when only seventeen years old; remained three years and three months. He m. Sarah Coarts on Coats. Have two daughters (7), Annie and Alice. Reside in Bellewood, Neb.

12. Emmet Lee, b 1846. Enlisted in Civil War in fall of 1864. The following April he d. of apoplexy.

13. Lora Nash, b. 1848; m. Ellen ——?. They have five children (7).

To Mrs. Moody, I feel indebted for much valuable information regarding this family. She also tells us:

"My father lived close by Uncle John (he moved to Michigan), Uncle Rodney, Uncle Pliney, Aunt Ruth and Aunt Lucy. All lived in New York State, town of Hamburg, Erie Co I knew them well. Uncle Rodney lived and died close by us. Uncle Pliney lived four miles from us on shore of Lake Erie, eight miles from Buffalo."

CHILDREN OF JOHN BOUGHTON LOBDELL AND FLORA (JUDD) LOBDELL.

1. Sherman. 2. Eliza Ann 3 Polly 4. Sherman Judd. 5. Caroline 6. Andrew P 7 Solon D

1. Sherman, b 14 May, 1810, on Monday, d. at 2 years of age.

2. Eliza Ann, b. 11 July, 1812, on Saturday, m Lewis Clark, d. 70 years old Had one dau. named Jane Clark (7). All dead Lewis Clark hanged himself shortly after the death of his wife.

3 Polly, b 18 Sept., 1814, on Tuesday; m. Wm. Birdsall, a Methodist minister She d aged 77 years.

CHILDREN.

1. George Birdsall (7).
2 Jacob Birdsall (7).
3. John Birdsall (7).
4 Andrew Birdsall (7).
5 and 6. Emily and Alice Birdsall (7).

4 Sherman Judd, b. 19 Aug., 1816, d. 5 Nov., 1880 at Mt. Morris, Genesee Co., Mich., m. 1 Oct, 1835 at White's Corners, Erie Co., N Y., Irene Wheelock Lines, b 19 Aug., 1827 in Vermont, d. 28 March, 1896 at Caro, Tuscola Co, Mich, dau. of Elijah and Olive (Wheelock) Lines. Mr. Lobdell was probably born in Buffalo, N. Y. By occupation, a wheelwright. In politics, a Whig.

CHILDREN.

1. Franklin Eugene, b 3 July, 1845, m. Effie Holmes.

2. Francis Marion (7), a farmer of Clio, Mich, b 29 April, 1848 at Waterford, Oakland Co, Mich.; m 3 July, 1878 at Mt. Morris, Genesee Co, Mich, Nettie M Shelley, b. 13 Nov., 1857 at Delhi, Delaware Co. Iowa., dau of Aaron J. and Mary (Curtiss) Shelley. Has two children:

1 Lee Augustas (8), b 29 Aug., 1879.
2. Sherman Judson (8), b 4 Sept., 1882.

3. Eliza (7), b. 23 Jan., 1852, m. Brooks Serven

5. Caroline Ann, b. 13 Sept., on Tuesday; lived the life of a true Christian woman. Passed to eternal peace at the home of her nephew, Porter Lobdell at Flint, Mich., 3 July, 1902, aged 82 y., 3 m.

6. Andrew P., a farmer of Tarrant, Wis., was b. 25 June, 1824, on Saturday, at Buffalo, Erie Co., N. Y.; m. 20 Aug., 1846, Angelina Ward, b. 13 Jan., 1828 at Buffalo, N. Y., d. 18 May, 1896, dau. of Elanson and Jerusha (Van Ness) Ward. The family are Methodists.

CHILDREN.

1. Julius (7), a carpenter, residing at Chetek, Barron Co., Wis., b. 6 Sept., 1848, at Clark, Mich.; m. Evelyn Sabin on 1 May, 1870, b. 4 April 1853, at Broadhead, Wis., dau. of Nelson and Abigail (Bruster) Sabin Children—

    1. Abigail D., b. 5 June, 1871; m. Arthur B. Holman

    2. John Boughton, b. 18 Feb., 1873; m. Emma Hockenback

    3. Maria A., b. 27 Jan., 1879, m. William A. Nickel

2. John B. (7), b. 30 June, 1853.

3. Ward E. (7) b. 16 July, 1864; m. Maggie Chase.

7. Solon Demothsenes, b. 20 July, 1830, on Tuesday, d. 23 April, 1899 of heart trouble at Flint, Mich., m. 20 April, 1854 in Michigan, Caroline M. Shepard, b. 25 Nov., 1836, d. 22 Sept., 1866 at Flint, Mich., dau. of Phineas Shepard of Sparta, Mich.

Mr. Lobdell was a contractor and builder, coming from New York state to Michigan, residing in Fenton, Saginaw, Flint and Coronna, Mich. Died aged 69 years

CHILDREN.

1. DeWitt Ernst, b. 29 March, 1856, d. in infancy.

2. Julian A., b. 22 Aug., 1858, m. Julia Crocker, has a son, Leslie Lobdell (8), living in Detroit, Mich.

3. Andrew Porter, b. 14 Aug., 1861; m. Catherine Smith. Has: Ethel (8), Earl (8) and Sadie (8). Resides at Flint, Mich

4. Elmer E., b. 16 July, 1863, d. 25 Sept., 1864

5. Flora B., b. 2 March, 1866; m. Edward Conner No children. Resides at Detroit, Mich

CHILDREN OF JACOB ELIAS (5) AND RACHEL (VAN NESS) LOBDELL.

1. Simon Van Ness. 2. Lydia. 3. Garrett. 4. Effie. 5. Mary. 6. Clorinda. 7. Lany. 8. Sarah. 9. John. 10. Laura. 11. Samuel. 12. Matilda.

(All born at Northampton, Fulton Co., N. Y.)

1. Simon Van Ness, b. 29 Jan., 1812, d. 30 March, 1900 at Taberg, Oneida Co., N. Y.; m. (1) Mary Jane Gilbert, b. 27 Jan., 1814, d. 25 Dec., 1852. They were m. 22 Oct., 1834, Hon. N. B. Lobdell, Esq., performing the ceremony Children·
Aseneth (7). Helen (7) Sidney A. (7).

1. Acenath Caroline, b. 24 Sept., 1835, d. 29 Aug., 1872; m. 28 Sept., 1855, to Andrew J. Bacon, a farmer and blacksmith, (both of Trenton Falls, N. Y.) son of David and Julia Bacon.
One son was b. to Acenath, viz.: John C. Fremont Bacon, b. 5 May, 1857. Residence, Orange, Mass.

2. Helen Mary, b. 15 Oct., 1837, d. 8 May, 1864; m. 25 March, 1858, Timothy D. Powers, a master mechanic. They lived in Chicago, Ills., where Helen d.

3. Sidney Alexander, a merchant and farmer residing at Bowie, Texas; b 30 Sept., 1839, at Northville, Fulton Co., N. Y.; m. 13 Oct., 1864, at Princeton, Bureau Co., Ill Eliza J. Minnerly, b. 11 Dec., 1841, at Crestline, Ohio, dau of Albert B. and Eliza J. (Cox) Minnerly Sidney A., moved with his father from Taberg, Oneida Co., N. Y., to Illinois in the year 1857, to a small town situated on the Illinois Central R. R., in Iroquois Co. He enlisted for the Civil war in a Board of Trade Reg't of Chicago, known as the 113th Reg't. Ills. Vol. Infantry, on 26 Aug., 1862. Was wounded in the left elbow at the battle of Chickasawby in Feb'y., 1863, and sent up the Mississippi river to Jefferson barracks, Mo., was then transferred to the V. R. C. and attached to the Hospital service and had charge of "Ward F" until the close of the war, when he was mustered out of the service. Is a Republican in politics. In religion, a Methodist. Is proud of the name of Lobdell and has often heard his father say that he never knew one of the' name that was ever arrested for a crime Mr. and Mrs. Lobdell have been m. nearly 43 years—have resided in N. Y., Ill., Oklahoma and Texas; have four sons.

EIGHTH GENERATION.

CHILDREN OF SIDNEY ALEXANDER AND ELIZA J. (MINNERLY) LOBDELL.

1. Wm. Albert 2. Herbert Edwin. 3. Van Ness Joseph. 4. Francis James

1 Wm. Albert, a furniture dealer of Bowie, Texas; b. 3 Dec., 1866, m. 5 Oct., 1888, to Sallie Nichols, dau. of Widow Endora W. Nichols

CHILDREN.

1. Lottie M., (9) b. 29 July, 1889; d. 23 Oct., 1889.
2. Laura, (9) b. 3 May, 1892
3. Roy, (9) b. 22 Dec, 1894
4. Endora W., (9) b 6 Feb'y, 1896.
5 Lyde J., (9) b. 17 April, 1897.
6. Wm. Albert, (9) b 10 April, 1901.
7. Sidney Alexander (9) b. 6 Dec., 1902. d 15 Jan'y, 1903.
8. Bertha Mary (9) a twin of Sidney Alex.

2. Herbert Edwin, a lawyer of Denton, Texas; b. 24 Nov, 1872, at Watseka, Iroquois Co, Ills; m 19 Feb'y, 1896, at Gainesville, Texas, Maggie M Beck, dau. of La Fayette and Marie Theresa Beck Mr. L. is attorney for G. C and Santa Fe R. R. Co, with headquarters at Gainesville. Is a Democrat No children.

3 Van Ness Joseph, b in Denton, Texas, 13 Sept., 1880; m 27 Sept, 1903, to Etalia Adalaide Hughs, dau of Rev. D W. Hughs (Methodist); wife deceased,—of Oklahoma, Comanche Co

CHILDREN.

1 Herberta (9), b. at Cropper, O. T., 3 Feb., 1905.
2. Webster Aleander (9), b. 29 June, 1906, at Tecumsah, O. T

4. Francis James, b. near Denton, Texas, 7 Aug., 1882; m 7 Oct., 1901, to Bessie A. Vaughn, dau. of Samuel F. Vaughn and his first wife, of Drop, Denton Co, Texas Mr. Lobdell is engaged in the furniture business at Bowie, Texas

283

Simon Van Ness m as second wife Orinda Du Bois, b 6 Nov., 1819, at Norway, Herkimer Co, N Y, dau of Joel Du Bois. Had one child

Fred W., of Utica, N Y, b 31 Jan., 1857 at Annsville, Oneida Co, N Y., m. 5 Dec., 1883 to Martha M Baker, b 23 March, 1861 at Lee, Oneida Co, dau. of Martin and Margaret (Niess) Baker. Have on child, Lela M Lobdell (8), b. 25 June, 1885

Mr. Fred Lobdell was educated in the common schools and Whitestown Seminary. Was commercial traveler for Hollister and Noble, Auburn, N. Y for 18 years, wholesale rubber boots and shoes Is still in their employ during the busy season Is bookkeeper for the Utica Electric Light & Power Co Clerk of Board of Supervisors of Oneida Co five years Special deputy revenue collector 1898 under the special act of Congress to raise additional revenue to pay expenses of Spanish-American War. Clerk to the Dawes Commission 1899 in the Indian Territory, but obliged to resign on account of the climate. Republican in politics, in religion, Agnostic.

———

Taberg, April 2—At his home in Taberg at 11 30 p m. on Friday, March 30, occurred the death of Simon V. Lobdell, aged 88 years and 2 months He had been in poor health from asthmatic trouble but the immediate cause of his death was a paralytic stroke, which he received on Tuesday. He suffered very much for three days, when death came to his relief. Mr. Lobdell was born in Northville, Fulton Co, N. Y, in 1812, and, in 1853, moved to Taberg, where he had since resided with the exception of four years in Illinois and two years in Rome At the time of his death it is thought he was the oldest male resident in the town of Annsville. He was a tanner and currier by trade, but for many years was employed by the Taberg Furnace Company. He has been a member of the M E Church of Taberg for many years His memory and recollections of events occurring in Rome and the northern towns were good, and facts and statements he would relate that transpired in this section during a period of 47 years were reliable He had the respect and esteem of all in the village, and, as one of the old landmarks, will be greatly missed. Besides his widow, aged 80, he is survived by two sons, Sidney A of Drop,

284

Texas, and Fred W of Utica, and one stepson, Frank D. Smith of East Florence, two brothers, Garrett and John of Northville, N Y, three sisters, Mrs. Matilda Bowman of Northville, Mrs. Sarah Fielder and Mrs. Laura Hill of Albany. The funeral was held from his late residence today at 10 a m, Rev. W R Helms, pastor of the M. E Church, officiating. Timothy Campbell, B. F. Secor, E. C. Spinning, G. H Kilbourn, J. N. Abbott and James Bailey were bearers The remains were placed in the receiving vault.—(From Newspaper Clipping)

---

2   Lydia, b. 30 June, 1814; m. Benj. Scribner
3   Garrett, b. 23 April, 1816; m Kimma Eglin.
4.   Effie, b. 12 Feb, 1818, m. Edward Wood.
5.   Mary, b. 9 Aug, 1822; m. Clark Carpenter.
6.   Clorinda, b. 18 July, 1824; m Wm Lawton.
7.   Lany, b 29 July, 1826; m. Hamilton Mason.

8   Sarah, b 11 June, 1828, was adopted by her cousin, Matilda Lobdell and her husband Alexander Lobdell (James) of West Troy, N Y. She lived with them until she m., 12 Nov., 1856, John Ward Fidler, b. 31 July, 1825 at Watervliet, Albany Co, N. Y., son of John and Prudence (Hills) Fidler. Mr. and Mrs. Fidler have always since their marriage lived on a farm—at first, for 13 years, near Troy, then moved to Duanesburg, Schenectady Co, N. Y., where they have resided 31 years Their son and his family live with them.

CHILDREN.

1.   Emma Helen Fidler (7), b 10 Aug., 1857, d. 3 Jan., 1866.

2   George Lobdell Fidler (7), b. near Troy; m. 13 Oct., 1886, Frances Liddle. Children:

1.   John Ward Fidler (8), b 16 Feb., 1890.

2   Charles Myron Fidler (8), b. 28th Sept, 1894.

9.   John, b. 20 May, 1830; m. Ann Potter. They resided at Northville, where he d. in 1902.

10. Laura A., b. 22 July, 1832; m 20 Feb., 1852 at Northville, Fulton Co., N. Y., Augustus P Hull, b. 1 Nov, 1828 at West Stockbridge, Berkshire Co., Mass, son of Stephen and Sybil (Pomeroy) Hull. They reside at Albany, N. Y., where Mr. Hull is in the American Express Company as one of their chief men.

285

CHILDREN.

1. Louise G. Hull (7). 2. Ida A. Hull (7). 3. John E. Hull (7). 4. Augustus P. Hull, Jr. (7).

11. Samuel, b. 20 Aug. 1834, always lived with his Uncle Samuel Lobdell. He was killed by the fall of a broken limb from a tree, 14 April, 1851.

12. Matilda, b. 1 May, 1837; m. 8 April, 1857 at Northampton, N. Y., Julius Frary Bowman, b. 4 Jan., 1834 at Kinderhook, Columbia Co., N. Y. The family are Presbyterians and reside at Northville, N. Y., where Mrs. Bowman d. in 1901, of cancer.

CHILDREN.

1. Ward Myron Bowman (7), b. 4 July, 1859; m. Elizabeth Ames.

2. Isaac Elias Bowman (7), b. 4 June, 1861; m. first in 1883, Jennie McKnight; m. second in 1899, Margaret Shipman.

CHILDREN OF GEORGE RODNEY (5) AND ABIGAIL (DART) LOBDELL.

1. Harriet. 2. Emily. 3. Pliny. 4. Charlotte. 5. Albert W. 6. Marietta. 7. Merritt. 8. Emmet. 9. Melissa. 10. Emmons H.

SIXTH GENERATION.

(All born in Hamburg, Erie Co., N. Y.)

1. Harriet, b. 13 July, 1828, never married.
2. Emily, b. 6 Feb., 1834, m. Gilbert DeGraff.
3. Pliney, b. 27 July, 1835; never married.
4. Charlotte, b. 2 Jan., 1836; m. Isaac DeGraff.
5. *Albert W., a lumberman of Portland, Oregon, b. 19 March, 1838; m. 21 March, 1859 at Buffalo, Erie Co., N. Y., Emma Clark, b. 24 May, 1841 at Buffalo, d. 29 June, 1875 at Greenville, Montcalm Co., Mich., dau. of ——— Dart and Bernice Huff.

Mr. Lobdell remarried 31 Dec., 1879 to Widow Eliza Frazier. No children by second wife. Albert W. served in the War of the Rebellion under Sherman.

* Of this family of ten children, all have passed away excepting Albert W. Lobdell

CHILDREN.

1 Clara Isabel, b. 25 Jan., 1860; m. Jesse Walter Holt. Reside in St. Paul, Minn.

2. Burdella, b. 24 Jan., 1862, d. 7 Feb., 1883

3. Marietta, b. 17 April, 1868.

4. Mildred Emma, b. 14 July, 1874.

6. Marietta, b. 25 March, 1840; m. Finley McManus

7. Merritt, b. 29 June, 1842; never married.

8. Emmet, never married.

9. Melissa, b. 21 Oct, 1845; m. Andrew Swift.

10. Emmons H., b. 20 Jan., 1849, m. 28 Feb., 1869 at Greenville, Mich., Ellen Melissa Worden, b 4 July, 1850 at Greenville, Mich., dau. of Elijah E. and Amelia (Kendrick) Worden.

Mr. Lobdell d. 7 July, 1899 at Charlevoix, Mich. Widow Lobdell resides at Boyne Falls, Mich.

CHILDREN.

1. Edna (7), b. 3 June, 1871; m. Charles Glasier.

2. Bell (7), b. 26 March, 1874, d at the age of 7 months.

3 Edith (7), b. 6 Sept., 1875; m. Addison Shantz.

SEVENTH GENERATION.

CHILDREN OF MARY (6) LOBDELL AND BENJ. AUSTIN.

(All born in Norway, Herkimer Co., N. Y.)

1. Daniel Austin, b. 26 June, 1827; m Eliza Shepherd.

2 Martha Austin, b. 25 Aug., 1829, d. 15 July, 1830.

3. Adaline Austin, b. 9 April, 1831; m. Orren Clark

4. Mary Austin, b. 27 Feb., 1833; m. 20 Feb., 1862 at Norway, N. Y., Levi Crofoot, b. 10 Dec., 1817 at West Turin, Lewis Co., N. Y., d. 12 May, 1877, son of James and Clarissa (Burnam) Crofoot. Mrs. Crofoot has been an invalid for many years, rheumatism having crippled her joints so that she is unable to get around. She was an educated woman of a lovely, exemplary, Christian character, bearing with fortitude her suffering and patiently waiting for the call of the Master. She resided with her son Henry, at Little Falls, N. Y., where on March 11, 1904, she was released from suffering.

CHILDREN.

1. Henry Alex. Crofoot (8), resides at Little Falls, Herkimer Co, N. Y., b. 4 March, 1863; m. Marietta Kilts. Their children:

    1 Herman K. Crofoot (9). b. 18 May, 1886.

    2 Clarence Elijah Crofoot (9), b. 10 May, 1888.

    3. Harry Alex. Crofoot (9), b 21 Feb, 1893.

2. Mary Ella Crofoot (8), b 26 July, 1865; d 28 March, 1866.

3. Geo. Levi Crofoot (8), b. 30 Jan, 1870; m Mary A Thomas and resides in Forest City, Pa. One child

    1. Helen Elizabeth Crofoot (9), b. 29 May, 1900.

5. Benj. F. Austin, b. 6 June, 1834; m. Harriet Wells

6. Matilda Austin, b. 9 July, 1836, m Wilber Powers.

7. Martha Austin, b. 12 Sept., 1838, is unmarried and resides at Oneida Castle, Oneida Co., N. Y.

8. Lydia Austin, b 5 July, 1840; m Joseph Ellis

9. Emily Austin, b. 10 April, 1842, d 28 March, 1847.

10. Hiram Austin (deceased), b 23 June, 1847; m. Camilla J. Emhaugh

11. Geo Austin, b. 7 Aug, 1850, m Ruth Snell

CHILDREN OF ELIZA LOBDELL AND STEPHEN JUDSON GAGE.

(All born at Norway, N Y.)

1 Sarah Jane Gage, b 16 April, 1835, m. Samuel Henry Carpenter Mrs. Gage is dead, no date Had one daughter

    Mrs. Fred Johnson (8), Dolgeville, Herkimer Co., N Y.

2 Wilson Pennock Gage, b 12 March, 1840; m. Gertrude Pullman. He is dead One dau is living, Mrs C E Wood (8), Watertown, N Y.

3 George Moses Gage, b. 29 Jan, 1845; m Ella Willoughby. Resides at Little Falls, Herkimer Co, N Y

4. Emily Paulina Gage, b 16 Dec, 1848; m 3 March, 1869 at Newport, Herkimer Co, N. Y, James Morrow, b. 1 Jan., 1844 at Kiney, Leitrim Co, Ireland, son of John and Mary Ann (Conway) Morrow Mr. and Mrs Morrow reside at Middleville, Herkimer Co, N Y, where he has business as shipping clerk The family are Episcopalians Two children have been born to them

CHILDREN.

1. Stephen Arthur Morrow (8), b. 4 May, 1870, d. 25 Dec., 1893.
2. Alice May Morrow (8), b. 28 Feb , 1872.

CHILDREN OF DAVID CLARK AND MARTHA (SLY) LOBDELL.

1. Wm. Noble. 2. Daniel. 3. Rheuma. 4. Franklin 5. Charles. 6. Robert. 7. Herman 8. Alice. 9. Emm.a

1 Wm. Noble, b. 7 Nov., 1839 at Concord Hill, Erie Co., N. Y. Is one of the oldest passenger conductors on the C M & Ct. P. R. R. When two and one-half years of age his parents left New York State and settled at Milan, Ohio, afterward moving to Wisconsin He m. for his first wife, Isabel Amanda Hill, of Wonewoc, Wis , who d. leaving one dau , Harriet (8) He m. for his second wife, Julia E. Farnsworth, who had one dau., Maude, the wife of Henry G. Williams of Minneapolis. Mr. Lobdell resides at Minneapolis Was a soldier in the late Civil War. A member of Co. G, 1st Wis, Vol. Inf "A staunch Democrat "

2. Daniel, b. 1 May, 1842, d. 9 April, 1863, in the army, at Nashville, Tenn.; served three years, less three months; was bugler in 2nd Wis Cavalry.

3. Rheuma, b. 8 May, 1844, d. Jan. 1863, aged 18 years.

4. Franklin, b. 20 July, 1847. Was in Civil War until the end. No notice taken of my letter of inquiry. I am told that he is a farmer, living at Lavalle, Sauk Co , Wis. He m. Derinda Mallow.

5. Charles, b 31 Dec., 1850; m. Cora Fugate Is a blacksmith Resides at Medina Station, Wis.

6. Robert, b. 20 March, 1854; m. Philoma Ray. He was accidentally killed in Minneapolis, Minn

7. Herman, b. 10 March, 1857 at Genesee, Waukesha Co., Wis.; m. 20 March, 1881 at Wonewoc, Jeneau Co., Wis., Emma Lemon, b. 18 April, 1858, at Baraboo, Sauk Co., Wis., dau. of Wm. and Elvira (Keen) Lemon. Mr. and Mrs Lobdell reside at Puyallup, Wash. He is by occupation a cooper, but engaged in fraternal insurance, holding the position of State Deputy; in religion a Methodist; in politics a Republican. Children·

Raymond (8), b. 25 Jan., 1884, d. 31 Aug., 1887.

Lewis and Willis (8), twins, b. 27 May, 1889.

8 Alice, b 4 May, 1859 at Genesee, Wis.; m 16 March, 1878 at Woodland, Sauk Co, Wis., Jesse M. Mallow, son of Jesse and Jane (Porter) Mallow They reside at Wonewoc, Wis, where Mr Mallow is President of Geo W Bell Corp No. 3 and Vice Oracle in the Royal Neighbors Lodge.

CHILDREN.

1 Herbert L. Mallow (8)

2 Ethel Blanch Mallow (8)

3. Billy Mallow (8).

4. Emma Belle Mallow (8).

9. Emma, b. 5 May, 1863, m Geo Pollock. She d the second year after marriage

---

SEVENTH GENERATION.

CHILDREN OF MILES CLARK AND SARAH (LITTLE-FIELD) LOBDELL.

---

1. Marion Clark. 2. Dwight Baxter 3 Celia M. 4. Hamilton M 5. Eugene L 6 Wray O 7. Sarah Belle.

---

1 Marion Clark, b. Hamburg, Erie Co., N. Y., 8 March, 1845; m Morey Evans

2. Dwight Baxter, b Hamburg, N. Y., 12 Nov., 1846; m. 11 March, 1874 at Lemars, Plymouth Co, Iowa, Mercy Morrison, b. 11 March, 1855 in Portage Co, Wis., dau. of Hiram and Sarah (Felch) Morrison

Mr Lobdell and family reside at White Lake, South Dakota, where he is engaged in agriculture

CHILDREN.

1 Geo Whitmore (8), b 21 Oct., 1875, d. 16 July, 1876

2. Sarah Belle (8), b. 16 June, 1877, a teacher at White Lake, S. D.

3. Jay Clyde (8), b. 25 Aug., 1879, m. 18 Dec., 1901, Augusta M. Gardener. Born to them, a little daughter:

1. Lois (9), b 25 Aug, 1902.

4 Don Clemence (8), b. 10 March, 1884.

290

5. Ruby Sarah (8), b 12 Jan., 1887, a teacher at White Lake, S. D.

6. Dwight B (8), Jr, b 25 Aug., 1890

3. Celia M Lobdell (deceased), b 30 Nov., 1850; m. Wm. H. Thompson.

4. Hamilton M. Lobdell, b. 11 Dec., 1853; m. Ella Heely

5. Eugene L Lobdell, b. 2 Jan., 1859 at Mukwonago, near Milwaukee, Wis.; m 1880, Martha Wilmina Frazier, b. 11 Oct., 1856 at Mukwonago, dau of William Melville Frazier and his wife Martha Maria Chaffee. Mr Lobdell is a farmer at Mukwonago; a Prohibitionist, and a Universalist in religion.

CHILDREN—EIGHTH GENERATION.

1. Harvey Ross, b. 18 Sept, 1883.
2. Garth Leland, b. 20 April, 1885.
3. Pearl, b. 3 March, 1887.
4. Ruth Bernice, b 5 Nov., 1888
5. Orphia Morgan, b. 2 May, 1891.
6. Floyd Frazier, b. 31 July, 1893.
7. Frazier Miles, b 20 Nov., 1899.

6. Wray O, b. 8 Oct., 1862, m Clara Horn.

7. Sarah Belle, b 27 Jan., 1866, d 1872.

FIFTH GENERATION.

CHILDREN OF DANIEL (4) AND RACHEL (OSBORN) LOBDELL.

1. James.   2. Daniel Granbee   3. Nathan Bradley.

I James, b. 25 Oct., 1784 at Hudson, Columbia Co., N Y.; m. 18 Oct., 1807, Sally Van Arman, b. 27 Jan., 1787 at Pittstown, Rensselaer Co, N. Y., dau of Abraham Van Arman.

History tells us. "They resided in Northville, Fulton Co., N. Y, and built for their private residence what is now 'the Northville House.'" There his three oldest children were born

About 1812 or 13 he moved his family to Johnstown, Fulton Co., N. Y., where the remainder of his children were born.

The house in which they lived is still standing—a double brick house, in one half lived James Lobdell and his family, in the other half lived Abijah Lobdell and his family.

James Lobdell was a progressive and successful business man, dealing largely in real estate, as the records of Montgomery (afterward Fulton) Co. show

He was in Johnstown as late as 1826 or 7, when he moved to West Troy, Albany Co., N Y., where in 1829 he opened a drygoods store, which was successfully conducted as the principal establishment. He was one of the first members of Trinity Episcopal Church, of which he was Warden in 1834.

His death occurred in West Troy, 19 May, 1860, aged 75 y., 6 m, 24 d   His widow d in West Troy 19 Sept, 1867, aged 80 y., 8 m., 22 d.

II Daniel Granbee, b 1 March, 1788 at Fulton Co., N. Y, d 23 March, 1808; unmarried.

III. Nathan Bradley, b 15 July, 1791 at Broadalbin, Montgomery Co, N Y. being the first child b in that section, d. 13 Sept., 1878 at Northville, Fulton Co, N. Y. He m 27 Dec, 1812 at Providence, Saratoga Co, N. Y, Nancy Richardson, b 2 Oct, 1788 at Providence, d 4 Feb, 1834 at Northville., dau. of Wm. and ——? (Montgomery) Richardson

292

NATHAN BRADLEY LOBDELL (5)
(Daniel [4])
Aged 82 y. 6 m.
First white child born in North-
ville, N. Y.

BRADLEY NATHAN LOBDELL (6)
(Nathan Bradley [5])
of Northville, N. Y.
(Page 294)

Nathan Bradley Lobdell was early identified with the interests of Montgomery Co, before the present county of Fulton was set off from Montgomery, he having charge of the transcribing of the records belonging to the new county of Fulton, set off in 1838, also of the county of Hamilton, set off in 1837 from Montgomery Co. Politically, he was a Jeffersonian Democrat from start to finish. Was Postmaster of Northville for 8 or 10 years.

SIXTH GENERATION.

CHILDREN OF NATHAN BRADLEY LOBDELL AND FIRST WIFE, NANCY RICHARDSON.

1. Daniel Granbee. 2. Mary Ann 3 James Henry 4. Wm. Richardson. 5. Maria Rachel. 6. Emily Nancy 7 Hiram Wm. 8 Charles Nathan. 9. Bradley Nathan.

(All born in Montgomery Co.)

1. Daniel Granbee, b. 7 Dec., 1813 in Montgomery Co, N. Y., d. unmarried at Washington, D. C., 9 July, 1875. He studied law with Harry Adams at Fonda, Montgomery Co., N. Y., afterward became a partner of Judge Yost of Fort Plain, Montgomery Co., to whom he bequeathed his library. He entered government employ during Pierce's administration; was Supervising Special Agent of Treasury. After visiting the principal custom houses in the United States he went to Europe and investigated the methods in the custom houses of different countries. In politics he was a Democrat. Interred at Albany, N. Y. Character beyond reproach.

2. Mary Ann, b. 12 Jan., 1816; m. Gilbert Le Fevre, had one son, living in Albany, N. Y.—Arthur Le Fevre (7)

3. James Henry, b 14 Feb., 1818; m. first Maria N Greenfield in 1845; had one dau., Helen Lobdell (7), b 6 April, 1846, m on 22 Oct., 1864 to John Tobias Van Hoesen at Northville, N. Y., and moved to Durand, Pepin Co, Wis, where her husband d. 1 Jan., 1901. No children

James Henry m second Mary Stone. Children·

    2. Emma (7), b. 15 March, 1856
    3. James Edward (7), b 15 March, 1859.
    4. Mary Elizabeth (7), b 11 Oct, 1861.
    5. Charles E. (7), b 15 March, 1864.

4. Wm. Richardson, b. 15 Jan., 1820, d. 8 Dec., 1824.

5. Maria Rachel, b 10 Dec , 1821; m. Truman Gilbert. Had—

   1. Truman James Gilbert (7), m. Miss Cowle. Moved to Kansas.

   2. Wm. Nathan Gilbert (7)

   3. Virginia Gilbert (7) m. Mr. Taft. Moved to Centralia, Ill

   4 Elizabeth Gilbert (7), d young.

   There may be other children.

6 Emily Nancy, b 25 March, 1824, d. unmarried, of consumption, at Northampton, 17 May, 1849, aged 25 years.

7. Hiram Wm., b 20 April, 1826; m Phebe Eliza Hood, b. 24 July, 1837 He studied for a physician and located at Flat Rock, Mich., where he d 10 Jan , 1884.

CHILDREN.

1 John H (7), a physician of Flat Rock, Mich , where he was b 14 Aug., 1860, m. Alice Morey on 2 Nov , 1880, b 3 March, 1859, at Flat Rock, dau of Willet S and Ellen (Ransom) Morey. Children:

   1 Hope (8), b 22 Oct , 1883 , d 4 Jan., 1885.

   2. Don W. (8), b 25 Dec., 1885.

2 Dan'l Granbee (7), a farmer, b 24 March, 1861, at Flat Rock; m 14 April 1886, Emma A Miller, b 10 Dec., 1859, at East Troy, Walworth Co , Wis , dau of Charles S. and Eliza A (Bush) Miller Children

   1 Lealah (8); b 26 March, 1891

   2 Bradley (8), b 18 Aug , 1896

   Both reside at Flat Rock, Mich.

3. Mary E (7), b 10 Sept , 1868; m. Mr. Matthews. Resides at Ypsilanti, Mich. Children':

   1. Grace, b 15 Dec , 1883.

   2. Fred L. Matthews (8), b 18 Dec., 1885

   3. Ina M. Matthews (8), b 19 Oct , 1890

8. Charles Nathan, b 3 Jan , 1829, d. 7 Sept., 1830.

9. Bradley Nathan Lobdell was b. in old Montgomery Co , N Y. (now Hamilton Co), 20 June, 1832, his father owning lumber mills there at that time. They were the first mills built in the (now) Hamilton Co , which was noted for being the greatest lumber tract in the state of New York During the period of taking off the lumber in Hamilton Co , many farmers left their

farms near Northville for the more money-making chances in lumbering. In consequence, the land vacated soon grew up to small forest trees, such as pine and other trees. Mr. Lobdell conceived the idea of cultivating timber on the deserted tract. At different times, he bought several hundred acres of the old farms and with employed labor has been busy trimming and cleaning up the woods for the past fifteen years. Since 1899 he has planted chestnut, white oak and black walnut on the old meadow and pasture land. Will continue to plant until all vacant space is filled in with choice timber, and is so well pleased with results that he intends to add more territory to the plot upon which he has experimented. In 1902 he planted twenty-two bushels of black walnuts, besides oak and other kinds of timber. He also owns valuable tracts of land in Michigan and Wisconsin. He m. 7 Nov., 1854, at Ionia, Ionia Co., Mich., Sabrina E. Miller, b. 6 Nov., 1836, d. 5 June, 1890 at Northville, dau. of David M. and Mardula E. (Olmstead) Miller, of Northville, N. Y. Three children were born to them.

CHILDREN.

1. Emilie Maria (7), b. 26 May, 1856; m. Leander McLean. No children. Deceased.
2. Ida (7), b. 26 Aug., 1863, d. 5 March, 1864
3. Josephine (7), b. 24 June, 1866; m. Wm. Hollearn. They reside at Northville, N. Y. and have three daughters (8)

ITEMS COPIED FROM FULTON CO. CLERK'S OFFICE (JOHNSTOWN, N. Y. 1772—1839).

Warranty Deed. Dated July 28th, 1794. Caleb Lobdell of Broadalbin to Daniel Lobdell.

Consideration, 100 pounds.

Land lying in the then County of Montgomery (now Fulton), containing 91 acres.

Warranty Deed. Dated March 29th, 1802. Alex. St. John to James Lobdell.

Consideration, $200.

Land in town of Northampton.

Containing 1 acre of land.

Warranty Deed. Dated June 12th, 1812.

Ussil Crosby of Johnstown to Jas. Lobdell, merchant of North-ampton.

Consideration, $1,400.

Land in village of Johnstown, one-half acre.

Warranty Deed. Dated May 16th, 1814.

Daniel Cady to James Lobdell.

Consideration, $100.

Land in village of Johnstown

Quit Claim Deed. Dated May 16th, 1814.

Polly Crosby to Jas. Lobdell.

Consideration, $10

Land in village of Johnstown.

Warranty Deed Dated Sept. 19th, 1810.

Ussiel Crosby and wife to Abijah Lobdell of Johnstown. Land in Johnstown.

Consideration, $1,000.

Warranty Deed. Dated May 17th, 1814

Abijah Lobdell of Johnstown, blacksmith, and Mary, his wife, to Jas Lobdell of Johnstown.

Land in Johnstown.

Consideration, $25

Warranty Deed. Dated April 23d, 1814.

Daniel Lobdell of Northampton and Nathan Lobdell of same place.

Land in Northampton, containing 91 acres of land.

Consideration, $500.

Warranty Deed Dated May 2d, 1817.

Jas. Lobdell to Duncan McLaren of Johnstown.

Land in village of Johnstown.

Consideration, $700.

Warranty Deed Dated February 24th, 1813.

Jas. Lobdell of Northampton, and Sally his wife, to Samuel Maxwell of same place

Land in Northampton, containing 1 acre.
Consideration, 600

Warranty Deed. Dated August 23d, 1825.
Abraham Van Vechten of Johnstown and Jas. Lobdell of Johnstown
Land in Johnstown, containing one-half acre of land
Consideration, $50.

Warranty Deed. Dated Sept 6th, 1825.
Jas. Lobdell and Sally his wife of Johnstown, and Eli Pierson, same place
Land in Johnstown, containing one-half acre.
Consideration, $2,000

Warranty Deed Dated Dec 1st, 1825. Jas. Lobdell to Isiah Lounglove of Johnstown.
Land in Johnstown, containing 1 acre.
Consideration, $60.

Sheriff's Deed Dated Nov 26th, 1823.
Seth Wetmore. Sheriff of Montgomery Co, and Jas. Lobdell of Johnstown
Land in Johnstown, containing 3 acres
Consideration, $388 35.

Warranty Deed Dated Jan 18th, 1826
Jas. Lobdell to Marcellus Weston
Consideration, $10

Warranty Deed. Dated Nov, 24, 1827.
Edward Ellice of London in Great Britain and John R. Mitchell, Rufus Washburne, Nathan B Lobdell and Morgan Lewis, all of Montgomery
Land in Mayfield, containing 111 acres
Consideration, $333.

Warranty Deed. Dated April 3d, 1828. Ammon Hammond of Northampton and Samuel Lobdell, same place.
Land in Northampton, containing 2 acres.
Consideration, $600

Warranty Deed. Dated July 28, 1835.
John Stewart of Mayfield and Chas. S. Lobdell of Johnstown.
Land in Mayfield, containing 100 acres.
Consideration, $1,600.

Warranty Deed Dated Aug. 24th, 1836.
Chas. S. Lobdell and Henry M. Lobdell of Mayfield
Land in Mayfield, containing 50 acres.
Consideration, $1,700

Warranty Deed. Dated Nov. 23d, 1836
Henry M. Lobdell of Johnstown and John J. Warren.
Land in Kingsboro, containing 50 acres
Consideration, $1,900

Warranty Deed Dated Dec 1st, 1836
Susan R Lobdell of Johnstown, wife of Chas. S. Lobdell and
John J Warren
Land in Kingsboro, containing 50 acres
Consideration, $100.

The records of births, marriages and deaths were kept in this
office for two years (1848-49) and the Lobdells recorded during
that time are:
Mary Lobdell died at Johnstown, July 21, 1849; 78 years old;
unmarried. Disease, general debility.
Lydia Lobdell died at Northampton, Sept 20th, 1849, aged 56;
married.
Emily Lobdell died at Northampton May 17th, 1849, aged 25;
unmarried. Disease, consumption.

SIXTH GENERATION.

CHILDREN OF JAMES (5) AND SALLY (VAN ARMAN) LOBDELL.

1. Rachel 2. Alex. St. John 3. Maria. 4. Harriet 5
Helen Maxwell. 6 James Dow 7. Richard Sadler. 8. Wm
Henry

I Rachel. b 13 July, 1808 at Northampton, Fulton Co , N Y ,
d at West Troy 26 July, 1852, aged 44 y., 13 d.

298

II. Alex. St. John, b 18 May, 1810 at Northampton, N Y., d 14 Nov., 1865 at West Troy, N. Y.; m. 10 Jan., 1833 at Northville, Fulton Co., N. Y., to Matilda Lobdell (his second cousin), b. 17 June, 1813 at Penfield, Monroe Co., N. Y., dau. of Daniel and Polly (Sackett) Lobdell.

The village of West Troy was incorporated in 1836, at which time Alex S. Lobdell was appointed as inspector of election in fourth ward.

His name heads the list of those who on 21 Jan., 1846, petitioned for a charter for the first organized and chartered lodge of Independent Oddfellows in West Troy—"Laurel Lodge No. 4. '

He was also instrumental in organizing, in the spring of 1849, the Ohio St Methodist E Church (From History of Albany Co, N. Y)

III Maria, b. 17 July, 1812 at Northampton, N Y., d at West Troy, 29 July, 1843 aged 31 y., 12 d She m 22 Sept., 1842 at West Troy, Morgan Lewis Taylor, b. 18 May, 1806 at Ballston, Saratoga Co, N Y., son of Raymond and Sarah (Riggs) Taylor. They resided at West Troy, of which village Mr Taylor was President during the year 1852.

IV. Harriet, b. 10 June, 1815 at Johnstown, Fulton Co., N Y. d at West Troy 8 May, 1880, aged 64 y, 10 m., 28 d.

V Helen Maxwell, b 10 Dec, 1817 at Johnstown, m 26 May, 1839 at West Troy to Jonas V. Oothout, d. in West Troy, 25 Dec, 1856, aged 39 y, 15 d Jonas Volkert Oothout d in West Troy 13 July, 1860, aged 46 y., 4 m., 18 d

The only living descendant of Helen Lobdell Oothout is a grandson named William Volkert Oothout

VI James Dow, b 26 May, 1821 at Johnstown, N Y., d 18 Jan., 1879 at West Troy, m. 1 Sept., 1847 at Johnstown to Alice Permelia Pierson, b 22 March, 1828 at Johnstown, d 11 Dec, 1885 at West Troy, dau of Eli and Amanda (Mason) Pierson.

"The dry-goods and wall paper establishment of James Dow Lobdell's Sons was established by James D. in 1847 and he carried on the business until his decease, when his sons, Wm, James and Edward succeeded to the business and carried on the same under the above mentioned firm name On 1 Feb, 1884, Mr James Lobdell withdrew from the firm and it was carried on under the same name by Wm and Edward Wm and James both died, and Edward remained until 1901-2, when he moved to Schenectady and was manager of James Roy & Co., branch store at Schenectady, where he d. of heart trouble on Christmas day at 6:30 p m., 1903. The only living son of James Dow Lobdell is Pierson, residing at 58 Jay St., Albany, N. Y. Children of James D. Lobdell

    1. Wm. (7), b 29 June, 1848, deceased, m. Josephine Bernard.

    2. Harriet (7), b 16 Jan., 1850 at West Troy, m 6 June, 1872 at West Troy, Edward Howard Wiswall, b 6 Dec., 1848 at West Troy, son of John and Sarah (Mark) Wiswall. Reside at West Troy Have one child.

        1. Alice Wiswall (8), b 6 April, 1873; m 25 April, 1894, Dr. Geo S Haswell. Children·

            1. Mildred Haswell (9)

            2. Laura Haswell (9)

    3 Edward, b. 28 Dec, 1853 at West Troy, d 25 Dec, 1903 of heart trouble at Schenectady, N. Y, leaving a widow and a son 7 years of age His widow returned to her old home at Johnstown, where her relatives reside Edward m 18 Sept., 1889 at Johnstown, Katie Moore, b. 1 March, 1864, at Johnstown, dau. of Frederick J and Sarah Moore. Children:

        1. Infant (8), b 24 June, 1893, d in infancy

        2 Harold Edward, b. 3 Sept., 1896

    4 James, b 1 Feb., 1857.

    5. Pierson, b 9 Sept., 1859; m. Kittie Randerson.

(West Troy was a village until 1 Aug., 1886, then changed to city of Watervliet.)

VII Richard Sadler, b. 19 Oct, 1823 at Johnstown, N. Y, d. 9 July, 1886 at Utica, N. Y, aged 62 y, 8 m, 10 d; m at West Troy, N. Y., 17 May, 1847 to Romelia Marsh, who d 24 Jan, 1885 at Utica, N Y

"Richard S. Lobdell was one of the original incorporators of West Troy Gas Light Co, Jan., 1853; capital stock $100,000. He was superintendent of this company from the fall of 1864 to March, 1879" (Albany History.)

From a "Church paper" I copy·

"Entered into rest eternal on Saturday, Feb, 10, 1900 at Ozone Park, L I., Ella A., oldest dau. of the late Richard and Romelia

Lobdell, formely of West Troy, N. Y. Interment, Albany, Rural Cemetery.

" 'It is enough : earth s struggles soon shall cease,
And Jesus call us to heaven's perfect peace.' "   -

The second daughter. Eliza Lobdell (7), m. Carl Berry and resides at New London, Conn.

VIII.   Wm Henry, b 26 Sept., 1826, d. aged 2 y., 1 m., 21 d

SEVENTH GENERATION.

CHILDREN OF ALEXANDER ST. JOHN (6) AND MATILDA (LOBDELL) LOBDELL.

1   Edgar.   2   Henry   3   Maria.   4   Harriet.   5   Geo
(All born in West Troy.)

1.   Edgar, b. 22 Aug., 1835 in West Troy, d. 3 Jan., 1878.

2.   Henry, b 17 Aug , 1838, d. 9 April, 1891 at Northampton, N. Y.; m. 10 Jan., 1861 to Alice R. Tobias, b 28 June, 1838 at Hudson, N. Y., dau of Henry and Hepzibeth (Hermans) Tobias. Mrs. L. d. in 1905.

CHILDREN.

1   Archie S. (8), b. 16 Jan , 1862; m Florence A. Toy.

2.   Wm Maxwell (8), b 26 March, 1864, d. 4 May, 1865.

3   Matilda Alice (8), b. 4 Dec , 1866; m. Edward G. Benson.   Residence, Pawling Ave , Troy, N. Y

4.   Mary Pickett (8), b. 29 Sept , 1870, d 26 Feb., 1894.

5   Myron Vaughn (8), b 4 March, 1873, d. 9 May, 1891.

3.   Maria, b. 12 Sept , 1843 in West Troy, d 10 Jan , 1845

4.   Harriet, b 9 Feb., 1846 in West Troy, d. 18 March, 1848.

5.   George, b 19 July, 1849-50 in West Troy, d. 4 May, 1888.

1, 3, 4 and 5 died in West Troy

FIFTH GENERATION.

CHILDREN OF LEWIS (4) AND ELIZABETH (OSBORN) LOBDELL.

1. Orra. 2. Chloe. 3. Lucy. 4. Hannah. 5. Esther. 6. Betsey. 7. Osmond. 8. Hiram. 9. Sally.

All born in Brookfield, Conn.

301

I. Orra, b. 4 Feb., 1781, m. May, 1813, as his second wife, Jerry Hoyt, b 9 Oct., 1779 in Danbury. Orra died in Rochester, Monroe Co., N. Y., Aug., 1836

CHILDREN.

1 Caroline Hoyt (6), a maiden lady, b. 24 June, 1814.

2. Laura Hoyt (6).

3. Henry L. Hoyt (6).

4. L. Starr Hoyt (6), m Miss Heywood

All resided in Rochester, N. Y.

II. Chloe, b 23 Feb., 1783. Died.

III. Lucy, b. 3 Nov., 1784.

IV. Hannah, b. 23 April, 1786; m Wm Corning.

V. Esther, b 20 March, 1788, m Nathaniel Barnum

VI Betsey, b 18 Feb., 1790; m. Levi Bostwick, 30 Dec., 1810, son of Levi and Anna (Smith) Bostwick of Brookfield

CHILDREN.

1. Cynthia Bostwick (6), b in Brookfield, Conn., 4 March, 1812; m in Kingston, Ont., 21 Sept., 1836, Josiah W. Cloyes, b. in Paris Hill, Oneida Co., N. Y., 6 July, 1810.

2. Laura Emma Bostwick (6), m. John Morehouse

3. Nelson Bostwick (6), b in Sherman, Fairfield Co., Conn., 6 April, 1819, m. in Albion, N. Y. 30 May, 1848, Malvina A. F. Treadwell.

4 Lewis Bostwick (6), d. 1834.

5. Eliza Bostwick (6), m Wm May.

6 Frances Bostwick (6), b in Sherman, Conn., 11 Oct., 1831; m. in White Pigeon, Mich., 19 Dec., 1850, Leander D. Tompkins.

(From Bostwick Genealogy.)

VII. Capt. Ormond, b. 14 Feb., 1792, m. 15 June, 1814, Prudence Bostwick, a sister of Levi Bostwick, who m Ormond's sister Betsey. Both husband and wife are buried at Brookfield

Ormond Lobdell was Lieut. first, and then promoted to Captain of his company. Children.

(Born in Brookfield, Conn.)

1. Lucy Ann, b. 2 May, 1815; m. John C. Gray 1 Jan., 1843, son of Thaddeus and Huldah (Lobdell) Gray and grandson of John and Abigail (Barlow) Lobdell.

Thaddeus d 31 March, 1852 Lucy Ann re-married to Abel Gray She d in Brookfield 17 Dec., 1888.

By her first marriage she had one son:

      1. Henry C. Gray (7), b. 29 Feb., 1844; m. Henrietta Lessey.

    2. Lewis Starr, b. 13 Oct., 1824, d. at Danbury, 2 April, 1901; m. in Brookfield, 6 June, 1847, Jeanette Adkins, dau of Norris and Charlotte (Griffen) Adkins of Danbury. They had one dau.:

      1. Charlotte (7), b. 13 July, 1851; now (1903) living at Danbury, Conn.

"Lewis Lobdell, an old resident of Danbury, died Wednesday afternoon at the hospital, of Bright's disease, aged seventy-two years. Mr. Lobdell had been suffering for the past two years, but was able to continue at his employment until six months ago.

" Most of Mr. Lobdell's life was spent in Beaver Brook, where he was for years a foreman in the Sturdevant hat factory. After that factory changed hands Mr. Lobdell was, for a number of years, employed in the Rundle and Holley factories. He had many friends in this city as well as throughout the state, and had the respect of all who knew him.

"Of late years Mr. Lobdell had lived in the Beltaire block on White street, with his daughter, Miss Lottie Lobdell, who alone survives him."—(Local Paper.)

    3. Laura, died—20 years old.

    4. Levi, b. 10 Feb., 1846, d 30 Sept., 1847.

    5. Hiram Lee, b. 5 May, 1848, m. Nov., 1869 at Lanesville, Litchfield Co, Conn., Almira Beardsley, b. 17 Dec., 1847 at New Fairfield, Fairfield Co., Conn, dau of Legrand M. and Alta (Chase) Beardsley. Mr. Lobdell and his wife are living at Brookfield (1902). Have no children. He is Democrat. In religion, an Adventist.

VIII. Hiram, b. 8 Oct, 1798, a farmer; m. for his first wife, Dolly Grace Lyon. For his second wife he m. Julia Jeanette Ives, dau. of Thomas and Sarah Elizabeth (Gilbert) Ives of Bridgewater, Conn., at which place Mrs. Lobdell d 17 March, 1901 (aged 84 years), at the home of her dau, Mrs. Thos. Kane (6). Mr. Lobdell d. 1887, aged 88 years. Both are buried at Brookfield, Conn.

IX. Sally, b. 26 Aug., 1801; m. 7 Dec., 1826 at Brookfield, Byrum Botsford Buckingham, son of Joseph and Sarah (Lockwood) Buckingham of New Milford, Conn. (now called Brookfield).

CHILDREN.

1. Herman Buckingham (6), b. 1827.
2. Henry Buckingham (6), b 1832; m Grace Bristol.
3. Fred'k Buckingham (6), b. 1835.
4. Sally Elizabeth Buckingham (6), b. 1837; m. Charles Hamlin.
5. Salmon Buckingham (6). In California.

(Buckingham Genealogy.)

FIFTH GENERATION.

CHILDREN OF CHLOE (4) LOBDELL AND ELIJAH BALDWIN.

1. Betsey. 2. Polly. 3. Abel. 4. Sherman Smith. 5. Chlotilda. 6. Boyle V. B.

I. Betsey Baldwin, b. 30 Aug., 1783; m. Heth Griffen of Stamford, Delaware Co., N. Y. Newtown, Conn. records says Betsey was b. Saturday, 11 o'clock, forenoon. Baldwin Genealogy gives children:

1. John Griffen (6), who m. Betsey Foote.
2. Orrin Griffen (6) m. Laura Foote.
3. Charles Griffen (6) of Stamford m., in succession, two daughters of Abel Baldwin.
4 Betsey Maria Griffen (6), m. Joel Carrington.

II Polly Baldwin, b. 4 July, 1785, 1 o'clock in the morning; d. unmarried

III. Abel Baldwin, b. 7 Oct., 1787, Sunday morning; m. Betsey Real.

IV. Sherman Smith Baldwin, b. 20 April, 1789 at 11 o'clock Saturday forenoon.

The above children were b at Newtown, Conn. About 1790 Elijah and Chloe moved to Stamford, Delaware Co, N. Y., where the remaining children were born.

V. Chlotilda Baldwin m. Peter Grant.

VI. Boyle V. B. Baldwin m. Margaret Wolf. Moved to Broome Co, N. Y.

304

Children and Descendants of
Darius [3] Lobdell, (Joshua[2], Simon [1])
Wife, Mary Baldwin

FOURTH GENERATION.

CHILDREN OF DARIUS (3) AND MARY (BALDWIN) LOBDELL.

1. Mary. 2 Eunice 3. Darius. 4. Rev. Jared. 5. John.

I   Mary, b at Ridgefield, 17 Dec., 1752; no record.

II   Eunice, b at Derby, Conn., 20 Dec., 1754; no record.

III   Darius, Jr., b at 9 Partners, N. Y., 13 June, 1762; m Angeleek Secor, a dau. of a French soldier who came to the United States with La Fayette. She d 25 Aug., 1849 at Schuyler Falls, Clinton Co., N. Y. Darius, Jr., was a farmer, residing at Danby, Vt., where he died.

IV   "Rev Jared, b. 22 Aug., 1767 at 9 Partners, N. Y., came while young with his father to Danby, Vt., where he worked at blacksmithing and on the farm. On 1 Dec., 1787 he m. Betsey Signor, b. 12 Oct., 1769, dau of John and Hannah Signor. After preparing himself for the ministry, in 1794, he was licensed to preach He was the father of Methodism in Danby and the first Methodist church in that town was built chiefly through his labors. In 1796 he preached his father's funeral sermon and in 1798 he was ordained Deacon by Bishop Asbury. In 1800 his church numbered about 70 His piety and sincerity were so strongly marked that they won the entire confidence of the people and he did valiant service for God His tenacity of memory and fluency of speech were alike remarkable. His delivery was ardent and the tones of his voice well managed and pleasing. Many years have passed away since the period of his ministry here and yet I find some who still retain a vivid recollection of portions of his sermons and the effects produced upon the congregation by them As a citizen he was highly respected, his social qualities being of a high order, he gained in a great degree the confidence and affection of all classes. He was a man of noble purposes, generous impulses, genial spirit and active in every good work. Mr. L. continued his labors here until 1832, when he removed to Plattsburgh, N Y , where

306

he spent the remainder of his days. He died peacefully 28 Aug., 1846 at the good old age of 79, and in that day when God 'shall make up the number of his jewels,' many, no doubt, will be the 'stars in his crown of rejoicing.' She who had been a faithful and devoted wife and a sharer in all his trials died 8 Nov., 1858, aged 90 years." (History of Danby, Vt.)

V. John Lobdell, a farmer, b. 4 Dec., 1777 at 9 Partners, N. Y., d. 14 Dec., 1837 at Middletown, Vt.; m. in 1798, Hannah Hulett, b 8 Nov., 1780 at Pawlet, Vt., d. 20 Feb., 1868 at Tinmouth, Vt., dau. of Daniel and Abigail (Paul) Hulett.

FIFTH GENERATION.

CHILDREN OF DARIUS (4) AND ANGELEEK (SECOR) LOBDELL.

1 Lois 2 Henry 3. Lewis 4 Darius 5. Miranda.
(All born in Danby, Vt)

1. Lois m. first Moses Vail, second Edward Bromley.

2. Henry Lobdell, a farmer and blacksmith of Schuyler Falls, Clinton Co, N. Y., was one of the original settlers, coming from Danby, Vt., where he was b 4 Feb , 1784, and where he m. Eunice Hulett, b. at Danby, 25 March, 1787, dau. of Daniel and Abigail (Paul) Hulett. Both Mr. and Mrs. Lobdell d. at Schuyler Falls; he, 9 Nov., 1868; she, 6 Jan., 1843. They were early identified with that part of Plattsburg that was afterward set off as Schuyler Falls, in 1856. He owned 500 acres of land and in early times found a market for his products in Albany, N. Y , 169 miles south of Plattsburg, whither he took them by teams. He raised a large family and Mr Frank P. Lobdell, his grandson, tells me. "He m. my mother's mother for his third wife, so he m. both of my grandmothers." He was 86 years old when he died Was 6 feet, 3 inches tall. A good, genuine Christian man, who won the respect of all.

3. Lewis, a blacksmith and farmer, was b. 8 Sept., 1788, d 7 June, 1863 in Schuyler Falls, where the latter half of his life was spent; m 1 Nov., 1811 in Vermont, Annie Salisbury, b 3 Dec., 1790 at Timmouth, Vt , d 18 April, 1875, dau of Daniel and ——? (Percy) Salisbury.

4. Darius Lobdell m. Eliza Vogan.

5. Miranda Lobdell m Jesse Davis.

SIXTH GENERATION.

CHILDREN OF LOIS LOBDELL (5)

First Husband, Moses Vail.
Second Husband, Edward Bromley.

1. Lois Anna. 2. Miranda 3. Angeleek. 4. Edward. 5. Erastus. 6. Barton 7 Lewis. 8. Moses. 9 Almeda. 10. Lucinda.

By her first husband she had—
1. Lois Anna Vail, who m Ira Hill and had—
    1. Charlotte Hill (7).
    2. Albert Hill (7)
    3. Alfred Hill (7)
    4. Samantha Hill (7).
    5 Moses Hill (7).
2. Miranda Vail m. Sherman Bromley.
CHILDREN.
    1. Josephine Bromley (7), m. and had two children.
    2. Jeanette Bromley (7).
3 Angeleek Vail, m. Joshua Bates.
CHILDREN.
    1. Moses Bates (7).
    2. Edwin Bates (7).
    3. Melissa Bates (7)
    4. Lucy Bates (7).
4. Edward Vail, had no children.
5. Erastus Vail m.; had—
    1. Moses Vail (7).
    2 Adelaide Vail (7).
    3 Alfred Vail (7)
    4 Jennie Vail (7).
Lois (5) m second Edward Bromley about 1814. Had—
1. Barton Bromley (6) m and had—
    Melvin (7) Celestia (7). Rufus K. (7). Ella (7) Loren (7). Barton Henry (7). Earl Bromley (7), who resides in Plattsburgh.

308

2. Lewis Bromley m. and had—

    Silas W. (7), Jeanette (7), Charles B. (7), Alice (7) and Merton Bromley (7). Residence, Plattsburgh, N. Y., Route 3

3. Moses Bromley m Charity Bromley and had—

    Martin (7)

Moses m. second Sabra Hewitt; had—

    Phebe (7), Marcus (7), Gideon (7), Lucy (7), Agnes (7), Betsey (7) and Varnum Bromley (7).

4. Almeda Bromley m. Moses Felton; had—

    Edgar (7), Jason (7) and Charles (7) Felton.

5. Lucinda Bromley, deceased.

SIXTH GENERATION.

CHILDREN OF HENRY (5) AND EUNICE (HULETT) LOB-DELL.

---

1. Lovicy. 2 Darius 3. Angelcck 4. Eunice 5. Jefferson. 6 Diana. 7. Harriet. 8. Abigail. 9. Samantha. 10. Henry. 11. Albert

---

1. Lovicy, b. 19 Sept., 1806 at Danby, Vt., d 27 Dec., 1888 at Schuyler Falls, N. Y.; m. 19 Feb, 1829, Stukely Arnold, a farmer, b. 25 April, 1801 at Peru, Clinton Co, N. Y, d 2 May, 1879 at Schuyler Falls.

CHILDREN.

1. Amos S. Arnold (7), b. 20 Jan., 1831; m. Lora A. Johnson Went west, seven children.

2 Mary L. Arnold (7), b 5 Nov, 1832.

3. Samantha M. L Arnold (7), b 27 June, 1835.

4. Abigail E Arnold (7), b 8 May, 1838; m. Jehiel B. White. One dau, Mary Lovicy, m Hiram Heyworth; two children.

5. Harriet M Arnold (7), b. 17 Nov, 1840.

2. Darius, b. 1808 at Schuyler Falls, m. in 1834 at same place, Lucena Moxley, b 20 Feb, 1814 at Edon, Vt, dau. of John and Roxey (Terry) Moxley. About 1840 Mr. Lobdell with his wife and three children moved to Russell, St. Lawrence Co., N. Y., and in 1849 moved to the town of Wyocena, Wis., where he settled

on a farm of 160 acres, three miles west of the town, on 18 Sept. Darius d 20 Aug., 1852; Mrs. L. d. 17 Feb., 1880.

3. Angeleek, b 1809; m Richmond Reed.

CHILDREN.

1 Henrietta (7) m Frederick W Baker Children: Cassius (8) and Loren (8) Baker.

2. Cynthia Reed (7) m. Enoch Keet. Had one child: Wallace Keet (8), m Miss Hare, one child (8) He m second Miss Wright.

3 Henry Reed (7) m Miss Castlow; had— Albert (8), Hettie (8) and Cynthia May (8) Reed

4. Eunice Reed (7)

5. Elizabeth Reed (7) m. Elnathan Vaughn, had one child (8), Angeleek Vaughn.

5. Jefferson, a farmer, b. 10 Nov, 1811 at Plattsburgh, Clinton Co, N. Y., d 12 Jan. 1855 at Schuyler Falls, m at same place 12 March, 1835 to Jemima Moore, b. 10 Oct., 1818 at Plattsburgh, dau. of Jacob and Betsey Patchen Moore Children, b. at Schuyler Falls:

1. Jerome B. (7), b. 22 March, 1836, m Phileda Terry; had Geo. and Mary Lobdell (8).

2 Josephine (7), b 19 March, 1838, d. 21 Aug, 1853.

3 Juliette (7), b 2 Jan, 1841 Resides at Schuyler Falls.

4. James H (7) m. Carrie Day; one son, Wm. D (8).

5. Jane Ann (7), b 25 June, 1842.

6 Josiah R. (7), b 22 July, 1847; m Nettie C. Everett; two children, Howard (8) and Myra (8).

7 Jacob M. (7), b. 1 June, 1851, m. Carrie Everett. In this family, the given names of father, mother and children all commenced with J.

6. Diana, b 1817, m Matthew Tucker. No children. She was "the poet" of the family and very handsome

7. Harriet, b 1820; m. Norman Lewis; had— Albert (8), Ellen (8), Francillia (8), Norman (8) and Emma (8) Lewis

8. Abigail, b. 1822, d. aged 6 y.

9. Samantha, b 1826, d. aged 16 y.

10 Henry Jr., a farmer honored by all, was b. 19 Jan., 1828 at Plattsburgh, Clinton Co., N. Y, d at Schuyler Falls; m Mary

E. Baker in 1850 at Schuyler Falls; she, b 1 May, 1830 at Peru, Clinton Co., N. Y., dau of Wm. and Elizabeth (Reed) Baker Mrs. Henry Lobdell resides (1907) at Schuyler Falls.

11. Albert, b. 2 Sept., 1831; m Prudentia Baker. Has one son, Melvin (8) Baker.

SEVENTH GENERATION.

CHILDREN OF DARIUS (6) AUD LUCENA (MOXLEY) LOBDELL.

1. Nancy. 2. Augustus. 3 John Lucius. 4 Wm. H. 5. Darius. 6. Ellen. 7. Richard P. 8 Emma

1. Nancy, b. 17 March, 1835, m in 1856, C L. Farrington.

2 Augustus, b 22 Jan, 1837

3 John Lucius, b 3 Nov, 1839 at Schuyler Falls, N Y., m. 6 Feb, 1877, Alice Johns, b June, 1850 at East Boston, d. 4 July, 1879, dau. of Wm. Johns. Mr Lobdell remarried on 20 May, 1885 to Jennie T. Whitelaw, b. 22 July, 1850 at Caledonia, Columbia Co, Wis, d 14 May, 1889, dau. of Robert Whitelaw. Mr. Lobdell is a miller residing (1902) in Poynette, Wis., a Republican He has no children He is the only one of the children of Darius third who answered my letters of inquiry.

Nancy, Augustus and John Lucius were born at Schuyler Falls, N. Y.

4 Wm. H., b. 18 Jan., 1841.

5. Darius, b. 3 Aug, 1843.

6. Ellen, b 6 July, 1846.

4, 5 and 6 were b. at Russell, St Lawrence Co, N. Y.

7. Richard P., b 30 March, 1849 at Wyocena, Wis

8. Emma, b. 31 March, 1850 at Wyocena

From Biographical Sketches of Town of Wyocena, Wis.

"Darius Lobdell, b. 3 Aug, 1808 in Plattsburgh, Clinton Co., N. Y; m in 1832 Lucena Moxley, b in Eden, Vt, 20 Feb, 1814.

"They came to Wisconsin in 1849 and setlted on a farm three miles west of Wyocena, on Sept. 18.

"Darius d 20 Aug., 1852 and Mrs. L. d. 17 Feb., 1880, leaving eight children, viz. ·

311

"Nancy, now Mrs. C. L. Farrington, of Wyocena; Augustus, living in Benton Co., Minn., John Lucius, living in Wyocena; Wm H., living in Pardeeville; Darius, living in Wyocena; Ellen, now Mrs. David B. Johnson of Richmond, Ind., Richard, living in Wyocena, Emma, now Mrs Hiram King of Dorchester, Wis.

"Augustus was in the navy three years in the War of the Rebellion.

"Darius was in 16th W. V. I. about two years.

"Wm. H. was in the 3d Regulars, Co K. during the whole of the war.

"John L. m. 6 Feb., 1878 to Alice C. Johns, dau. of Wm. Johns. She d 4 July, 1879, aged 28 y., 6 m. and 24 d., leaving no children. He is a Republican and lives on 160 acres of land, on which his father first located."

SEVENTH GENERATION.

CHILDREN OF HENRY, JR. (6) AND MARY E. (BAKER) LOBDELL.

1. Frank P. 2. Frances E. 3. Jefferson H. 4. Geo. M. 5. Chastine W.   (All b. at Schuyler Falls, N. Y.)

1. Frank P., a merchant, residing at Plattsburgh, Clinton Co., N. Y., since 1871. After working for two different merchants he established himself in trade in 1876 and has since done a paying business of about $50,000 a year. The winter of 1903 he, with his estimable wife, spent in southern California, and on their way home stopped over in Chicago, where we held a little family reunion, being present Mr. and Mrs. Charles W. Lobdell, Mr. and Mrs Henry H. Lobdell, Dr. Effie Lobdell and Mr. and Mrs. James H. Lobdell, at the home of the latter named; all spent a most enjoyable evening. Mr. Lobdell was b. 4 May, 1852; m. 23 Nov., 1876 at Plattsburg, N. Y., Mary M. Platt, b. 8 June, 1853 at Plattsburg, dau. of Peter Mignault and Charlotte Creigh (Morgan) Platt. Mrs. Lobdell can boast Colonial descent and is a member of the society of D. A. R. Her great grandfather, Judge Zephaniah Platt, b 1735, d. 1807, served on the Committee of Safety and in the Provincial Congress. He was commissioned Colonel of associated exempts of Dutchess Co., N. Y., 1779, and his regiment

FRANK P. LOBDELL (7)
(Henry, Jr. [6])
of Plattsburgh, N. Y.
(Page 312)

GEO. M. LOBDELL (7)
(Henry, Jr. [6])
of Plattsburgh, N. Y.
(Page 313)

HON. CHARLES E. LOBDELL (7)
(Darius Jared [6])
of Larned, Kansas
(Page 318)

MRS. KATE LOBDELL BLISS (6)
(Jared [5])
of Saranac, N. Y.
(Page 319)

marched to Stony Point. He was founder of the town of Plattsburgh, N. Y., where he died.

Her great, great grandfather, Zepheniah Platt, b. 1704, died from the effects of confinement in a prison ship. His dau. Dorothea interceded with Sir Henry Clinton for his release, but he died in 1778, a few days after he reached home, aged 74 years

They have two children

 1. Ross P. (8), b. 16 March, 1879 at Plattsburgh; m. 26 June, 1906, at Brooklyn, N. Y., Mabel Irene Ebbets, b. 31 Dec., 1876 at Brooklyn, dau. of James and Margaret (McNurney) Ebbets. Mr. Lobdell is a bookkeeper, Democrat; Presbyterian, resides in Plattsburgh.

 2. Margaret E. (8), b. 4 Oct., 1882

2 Frances E., b. 1 Feb., 1855; m. 23 March, 1882 at Dannemora, Clinton Co., N. Y., Albert D. Hill, b. 18 Sept., 1832, son of Ira Hill. Reside at Schuyler Falls. Methodists. Have no children

3 Jefferson H., of Plattsburg. b. 10 Feb., 1859; m. 16 March, 1892 at Cumberland Head, Clinton Co., N. Y., Ida Viola Oliver, b. 1 Feb., 1866 at same place, dau. of Thomas L. and Temperance (Moore) Oliver. Mr. Lobdell is a Methodist and, in politics, Independent

CHILDREN.

 1 Raymond Oliver (8), b. 30 April, 1894

 2 Thomas Jefferson (8), b. 30 Oct., 1896

 3. Ellen Amelia (8). b. 21 Oct., 1901

 4. George M., b. 22 Sept., 1862; m. 1 June, 1892 at Plattsburg, N. Y., Addie Maria Treadway, b. 19 Sept., 1864 at Port Henry, Essex Co., N. Y., dau. of John W. and Harriet (Barker) Treadway. The family are Presbyterians; reside at Plattsburg. In politics Mr. L. is a Democrat

CHILDREN.

 1. Ruth Barker (8), b. 27 Feb., 1893.

 2. Arthur Treadway (8), b. 14 Nov., 1895

 3. Geo. Henry (8), b. 5 Dec., 1897

5 Chastine W., b. 10 April, 1866; m. 12 Jan., 1898 at Plattsburgh, where they reside, to Edwin Stanton Day, a farmer, b. 20 May, 1868 at Plattsburgh, son of Cyrus and Mary (Robinson) Day.

CHILDREN.

 1. Cyrus Lobdell (8) Day, b. 1 Dec., 1898

 2. Robert Stanton (8) Day, b. 28 Nov., 1901

SIXTH GENERATION.

CHILDREN OF LEWIS (5) AND ANNIE SALISBURY LOBDELL.

1 Daniel S. 2. Lois. 3. Mary. 4. Henry. 5 Miranda, 6. Elias. 7. Fanny. 8. Martha. 9. Nathan S.

1. Daniel S., b. 15 April, 1813 at Danby, Rutland Co., Vermont, d. 2 Jan., 1869 at Nicholville, St. Lawrence Co., N. Y.; m. 5 Jan., 1837 at Plattsburgh, Clinton Co, N. Y., Luretta Learned, b. 9 Aug., 1815 at Plattsburgh, N Y, d. 9 May, 1901 at Norwood, St. Lawrence Co, N. Y., dau. of Bela P and Statira (Hilliard) Learned. Mr. Lobdell was a farmer, Republican and Methodist. He d. 2 Jan., 1868.

2. Lois, d. single 26 Nov, 1885.

3. Mary m. James Davis; d. 24 Feb., 1885.

4. Henry, b. 1 April, 1819; m. Nancy Calkins 25 Oct., 1852

5. Miranda, b. 25 Oct., 1822, d. 17 June, 1896; m Charles Kirby.

6 Elias m. Caroline Kimball.

7. Fanny, b. 9 Sept., 1828, d. 23 Jan, 1891; m. James Robinson.

8 Martha m. Wm. Newton.

9. Nathan S., b. 26 Sept., 1831, d 11 March, 1893; m. Mary Barnard.

Records copied from the family Bible give Lewis, the first born: b. 18 Oct., 1812, d. 4 Sept., 1814. The sixth child is given: Lydia Ann, b. 15 Feb., 1821; m. Sidney Arnold, 10 Oct, 1842, d. 14 Oct., 1880. There is no Martha nor Elias given in Bible, but I will give it as given by descendants, also as found in family Bible.

SEVENTH GENERATION.

CHILDREN OF DANIEL S. AND LURETTA (LEARNED) LOBDELL.

1. Anna Statira, b. 27 Dec, 1837 at Schuyler Falls, N. Y.; m 18 Sept, 1860 at Hopkinton, St. Lawrence Co, N Y., Philo A. Davis, b at Stockholm, St Lawrence Co., N. Y., son of Francis and Betsey (Converse) Davis. They reside at Fort Jackson, N. Y.

314

CHILDREN.

1   Edith L. Davis (8), b. 11 June, 1861; m. Rev. John Bartholamew.

2.   Martha E. Davis (8), b. 13 March, 1863; m. True W. White.

3.   Francis E. Davis (8), b. 25 July, 1866; m. Evelyn Miller.

4   Harry D Davis (8), b 19 May, 1873, d. aged 9 years.

2.   Mary Jeanette K., b. 18 Sept., 1839, m. first Wm S Taggart, afterward marrying a Mr. Wilcox.   She d. at Elmira, N Y. 22 May, 1900

3.   Marie Antoinette, b. 1 Oct., 1841 at Plattsburgh, N. Y.; m 10 Oct., 1863 at Nicholville, N. Y., to Joseph W Brown, b. 9 Dec., 1837 at Peru, N Y., son of Willard and Sarah (Stoddard) Brown. The family reside in Denver, Colo.   Mr Brown is a produce dealer. In politics a Democrat

CHILDREN.

1.   Mary Emma Brown (8), b. 11 June, 1865; m Chas F. Fury, 14 April, 1894   Resides at San Francisco, Calif.

2   Maude Gertrude Brown (8), b 25 June, 1875; m. John M Daniel, 24 Dec., 1896.   Resides at Denver, Colo.

3.   Helen Cecil Brown (8), b 22 May, 1879.   Resides at Denver.

4   Bernice Luretta Brown (8), b 24 April, 1882.   Resides at Denver.

4.   Lewis Frederick, b. 29 Aug., 1845, d. in infancy.

5   Howard Salisbury, b 19 Feb., 1847 at Schuyler Falls, Clinton Co., N. Y.; m 18 Oct., 1892 at Mitchell, Davison Co., S D., Alvena C. Jacobs, b. 10 Aug, 1865 at Davenport, Scott Co., Iowa, dau. of John and Christina (Rochelle) Jacobs.   The family reside at Blair, Washington Co., Neb., where Mr L. is engaged in life insurance   In politics a Democrat; in religion, Agnostic.

CHILDREN.

1.   Ralph G. (8), b. 17 April, 1894.

2.   Helen L (8), b. 20 May, 1896.

3.   Emmett J. (8), b 26 April, 1900.

Children all born at Parkston, S D.

6.   Alice Luretta, b 22 May, 1851, m Frank Converse   Resided in Hopkinston, N. Y, where she d. 3 Nov, 1871

315

7. Rebecca Adelaide, b 5 July, 1853 at Canton, St. Lawrence Co., N. Y.; m 2 Oct., 1877 at Moira, Franklin Co., N. Y., to Homer H. Loveland, b. 20 Feb., 1844 at Grand Isle, Vermont, son of Charles A and Sarah Hyde Loveland

Mr Loveland is a transfer agent residing at Norwood. St. Lawrence Co , N. Y A Republican and Methodist. They have no children.

8. Ida Cornelia, b 22 Sept , 1855 at Canton. N. Y.; m 15 Jan., 1885 at Fort Jackson, St Lawrence Co., N. Y , to Seymour L. Reynolds, b at Grand Isle, Vt., 6 Aug., 1836, son of Wm. V. Reynolds and Sarah Brown, his wife. The family reside in Burlington, Vt. Mr. Reynolds is a commercial traveler, Republican ; religion, Congregationalist.

CHILDREN.
1. Ruth Winifred Reynolds (8), b. 31 May, 1886.
2. Mildred Jane Reynolds (8), b. 14 Nov., 1887.
3. Doris Fuller Reynolds (8), b. 18 Jan , 1890.

9. William Daniel, b. 4 Sept., 1858, at Hopkinton, N. Y.; unmarried Resides at Dickinson, N. D

10 Elsie Luella, b. 25 June, 1861; m. Robert Fuller, resided at Dickinson, N. D , d. 29 Aug., 1895, her death was caused by an operation for a tumor.

CHILDREN OF REV. JARED (4) AND BETSEY (SIGNOR) LOBDELL.

1 Sarah. 2 Jared, Jr 3 Cata. 4. Anna. 5. Wesley.
6 Dennis 7. Eunice 8. Mary. 9 Betsey.
(All born at Danby, Vt.)

I. Sarah, b. 3 Nov., 1788; m. Wm. Robinson, a weaver by trade, who d. soon after, leaving one dau , Olive Robinson (6), b. 18 Sept., 1818.

Sarah remarried to Peter Rhoda and lived in Potsdam, St Lawrence Co., N. Y., where she d. in 1868.

II. Jared, Jr , b. 10 Oct., 1792, m. 9 Jan., 1817. Huldah, b. 22 July, 1801, dau. of Daniel Parris, and settled on "Dutch Hill," where he resided a few years He removed to the west part of Pawlet, thence to Peru, Clinton Co., N. Y., and from there to Saranac, Clinton Co., N Y , where he d. 23 Jan., 1853 His widow d 5 Nov., 1888 They were both members of the M. E. church.

III. Cata, b. 18 June, 1795; m. Caleb Parris

IV. Anna, b. 28 Oct , 1797 , m Barnabas Kirby and lived in Plattsburgh

V. Wesley, b. 5 Aug., 1800, "d. in love with God and man" 15 April, 1813

VI. Dennis, b. 31 March, 1803, d. 16 Jan , 1804

VII. Eunice, b. 30 Sept., 1805; m Alura Jones and lived in Peru, N. Y.

VIII. Mary B., b 24 April, 1808; m. Benjamin Hustus, raised a nice moral family of sons and daughters. Finally made their home in the west

IX. Betsey, b 11 Nov., 1810; m Daniel Thew. She d. at Peru, N. Y. Her first child was a son, who took the name of his mother's family. I copy from Rev. Jared Lobdell's family records: "18 Sept., 1818, our granddaughter Olive Robinson was born. 20 Oct., 1838 our grandson Darius was b I will give him something that he may know that his grandfather named him Jared Lobdell."

317

Betsey's second child was a dau., Kate Thew, still living at Peru, but feeble. I am told that her home inherited from her parents, is a clean, old fashioned home, good to enter, very hospitable in old days.

The son who always retained the name of Darius Jared Lobdell, b. 20 Oct., 1838 at Peru, Clinton Co., N. Y., left home as a young lad and while yet in his teens went to the west, stopping in Wisconsin. In 1859 he went to Kansas and located at Osawatomie, Miama Co., where in 1860 he m. Roxana Crockett Godding, b. in 1837 in Rockland, Waldo Co., Maine, d. in Feb., 1890 at Eldorado, Kansas, dau. of Hugh K. and Thirza (Crockett) Godding. At Osawatomie he was a member of the home guards and took an active part in the border warfare. Enlisted in 1862 in the 15th Kansas Cavalry and served until the fall of 1865. After the close of the war he became a commercial traveler, representing a wholesale drygoods house. In 1879 moved to Butler Co., Kansas and established a general store at Plum Grove. Reverses followed and about the same time he was stricken with paralysis, never fully recovering from its effects, dying in June, 1889 at Eldorado, Kansas.

CHILDREN.

1. Charles E. (7), a man of worth whose honored name is widespread throughout Kansas and adjoining states, b. 21 Sept., 1861 at Osawatomie, Kansas, educated at common schools, taught country school 1878-9, studied law and was admitted to practice 22 Sept., 1881. Elected county attorney of Butler Co., 1884, served four terms in the Kansas House of Representatives, being Speaker of that body in 1895. Abandoned law practice (for a time) and located on a cattle ranch in 1898 at Dighton. Was appointed Judge of the 33d District 1 Jan., 1902 by Governor Stanley. Was elected in Nov., 1902 and re-elected in Nov., 1906 without opposition. Resides at Larned, Kansas. Mr. Lobdell m. for his first wife Anna B. Jones, by whom he had one dau., Maud Avis, b. 8 Nov., 1882.; m. for his second wife 12 Sept., 1900 at Kansas City, Kansas, Nellie E., b. 16 Sept., 1870 at Wyandotte, Kansas, dau. of David M. Ward and his wife, Ellen J. Hendricks. Children:

    1. Charles E., Jr. (8), b. 12 Sept, 1902.
    2. David Stanley (8), b. 14 Dec., 1903.
    3. Hugh Jared (8), b 26 Oct, 1906

318

2. Adda F., b in Oct., 1863, educated at Central Normal College, Great Bend, Kansas.

3 Frederick H., b. 3 Jan., 1866 at Osawatomie, Kansas; m. 26 May, 1894 at Dighton, Lane Co., Kansas, to Cora W. Green, b 23 Aug, 1872 at Oskaloosa, Iowa, dau. of Joseph G. and Lizzie (Bonsall) Green

Mr. Lobdell resides at Dighton, Kansas. Is editor of Dighton Herald Has one dau :

1 Helen (8, b 6 June, 1896.

4. Cora Myrtle, b. 8 Aug, 1868, m.H. D Parks, and resides at De Graff, Kansas.

SIXTH GENERATION.

CHILDREN OF JARED (5) AND HULDAH (PARRIS) LOBDELL.

1. Hannah. 2 Artemesia. 3. Abraham W 4. Samantha. 5. Eunice. 6 Wesley. 7. Caleb Parris. 8. Nancy. 9. Betsey Ann. 10. Jane M. 11 Polly Ann. 12. Harvey. 13. Kate. 14. Luretta. 15. Richard Parks.

1. Hannah, b 8 Sept., 1818; m. 21 May, 1840, Robert Thew. Settled in Saranac, N. Y, d. 8 June, 1852.

2. Artemesia, b. on Thursday, 30 Sept., 1819; m. Ira Cook, of Danby, Vt., 24 Feb, 1843, d 30 Nov, 1851.

3. Abraham W., b on Sunday, 24 Dec., 1820; m. Orrilla Bassett or Bresett. Settled in Saranac, where his son, Solon J. (7) was b. in 1866, who as he attained manhood moved to Pawlet, Vt., where in 1892 he m Ettie M Greene, b in 1871 at Danby., Vt., dau. of Harris and Charlotte Goodspeed) Greene. Has one son, Durward W. (8).

Abraham has a son, James W (7), residing near Saranac, who is the possessor of Rev. Jared Lobdell's Bible, from whose pages Mrs. Kate Lobdell Bliss (6) (Jared, Jr (5)) copied (verbatim) the family record.

4 Samantha, b on Monday, 23 Sept., 1822, m. James Clark, 3 July, 1842. Settled in Bloomingdale, N. Y.

319

5 Eunice, b. on Monday 26 July, 1824; m. Charles Collins, 28 Sept , 1843

6. Wesley, b. on Wednesday, 29 Nov., 1826, d unmarried, 10 Feb., 1848.

7 Caleb Parris, b. on Sunday, 7 Sept , 1828 at Peru, N. Y., d. 13 Jan , 1886 at Providence, R I , m 20 June, 1853 Charity S. Herrick, b at Danby, Vt., dau. of Edward and Sophia (Andruss) Herrick, and settled in Providence, R I Was a cutter and dealer in marble. A Republican and a Protestant

CHILDREN.

1. Jared Wesley (7), b. 7 April, 1857. Resides at Plattsburg, N. Y.

2. Charles P. (7), b 16 Nov , 1859

3. Alice S. (7), b. 25 May, 1862.

4. Minnie Eunice (7), b. 31 Dec., 1866.

8 Nancy, b. on Sunday, Sept., 1830; m. Thomas J Bunker, 20 Sept., 1849, and settled in Stevenson Co , Ill.

9. Betsey Ann, b. on Saturday, 2 June. 1832; m. Henry Moore, 5 July, 1858. They lived in Rupert, Vt. Betsey d. in Denver, Colo.

10. Jane M , b on Saturday, 1 Feb , 1834, m Sewell F. Bunker of Illinois on 23 Feb , 1856, a soldier of the Civil War, in the Army of the Potomac

11 Polly Ann, b. on Monday, 14 March, 1836, m John W. Cook of Vermont, 1 Sept., 1856.

12 Harvey, b on Wednesday, 6 Sept., 1837; m. Caroline Morrison, 1 June, 1860 Resided at Saranac, N. Y.

13. Kate, b on Saturday, 23 March. 1839; m. 7 Aug., 1865, Capt. Wm. Donald Bliss, b. 6 Feb , 1826, son of Leonard S and Hannah Pratt Clark Bliss of Newport, R. I. It is my desire to meet this Christian woman, and hope that it may be my pleasure to do so. I have asked her for a sketch of her life but in her modest way she tells me "I do not think it would pay, it is most interesting to myself Suffice it to say that God in His own way has led me very close to Himself and made me to greatly rejoice in the God of my salvation. My husband was a Newport, R I., man of Scotch descent—his grandfather was Parson Donald Bliss (Presbyterian). My husband went to sea when a boy and studied navigation with Capt. Seth W Macy of Newport, R I., on a four-year whaling volage. He became master of vessels and was a good navigator, a well informed, genial man Since his decease I have

secured my living by my own personal efforts. Am a missionary and farmer; no income only what my Father sends by His rain and His sunshine from year to year, but His promises are sure, so I am rich." No children. Resides at Saranac, N. Y.

14. Luretta, b. on Friday, 28 May, 1841; m. Cecil Wright of England, 13 Sept., 1866.

15. Richard Parks, b. on Wednesday, 14 Aug., 1844. Was a soldier in our Civil War; m. Eleanor Ann Manning. Resided in Saranac, N. Y.

FIFTH GENERATION.

CHILDREN OF JOHN (4) AND HANNAH (HULETT) LOBDELL.

1. Hannah. 2. John. 3. Abigail. 4. Daniel. 5. Hulett. 6. Anna. 7. Darius. 8. Hiram. 9 Eliza 10. Emily Jane.

---

1. Hannah, b. 13 April, 1799 at Pawlet, Rutland Co., Vt., d. June, 1877 at Wallingford, Rutland Co., Vt; m. in 1820, Norris Smith, a mason, b. in 1800 at Springfield. d. 1825, son of Ebenezer Smith.

Hannah m. for her second husband Noah Gifford, who d. in the spring of 1858 at Pawlet, Vt. Noah Gifford had two brothers, Warren and Charles, who served in the War of the Rebellion, then went west and both died.

2. John, Jr., b. 8 June, 1801 in Danby, Vt., d. 28 March, 1872 at Centralia; m. June, 1822 at Wells, Rutland Co., Vt., Olive Mosier, b. 17 April, 1804 at Wells, Vt., d. 1890 at Centralia, dau. of Aaron and Ruth (Richardson) Mosier. Mr. Lobdell was a lawyer, resided in Wells, Vt. In politics a Democrat; religion, Methodist.

3. Abigail, b. 16 Oct., 1803 at Danby, Vt.; m. Josiah Willard. She d. at Wells, Vt

4. Daniel, b. 15 June, 1806 at Danby, Vt., lived with his mother until she died, then m. 7 Dec., 1857, Elvira Ferguson Had two children

    1. Dollie (6), b 7 Jan., 1872, d. aged 11 days.

    2. Gertrude (6), Lobdell, b. 14 July, 1874. d 10 Oct., 1879.

Mr. Lobdell d. in Pawlet, Vt., and his widow m. Mr. Hulett. Resides (1902) in Pawlet.

5. Hulett, b. 21 Jan., 1809 at Danby, Vt., d. 25 Oct., 1848 at Hebron, Washington Co., N. Y.; m. Squce Smith, b. 19 May, 1817, d. 16 Feb., 1877. After the death of Hulett, the family moved to Massachusetts, to be near the relatives of the widow.

6. Anna, b. 29 June, 1811 at Pawlet, Vt., d. 18 April, 1873 at Middletown Spa., Rutland Co., Vermont, m. 20 May, 1841 at Middletown Spa. Franklin Ray, b. 19 Jan., 1818 at Tinmouth, Vt., d. 1 Sept., 1890, at Paultney, Rutland Co., Vt., son of ———? Ray and Glorianna (Williams) Ray.

7. Darius, b. in Pawlet, 28 May, 1814, d. 22 July, 1893 at Middletown Spa, Vt., m. 28 May, 1840, Delana Coy, b. 20 Aug., 1823, at Middletown Spa, where she also d. 14 Feb., 1891, dau. of Matthew and Lucinda (Sherman) Coy. Darius was a farmer of Middletown Spa, Vt. A Republican and in religion Non-denominational.

8. Hiram Lobdell, b. at Pawlet, 14 Feb., 1817, never married.

9. Eliza Lobdell, b. at Pawlet, Vt., 18 May, 1820, d. in Danby, Vt., 25 June, 1877; m. at Danby, Narges Clark, a farmer of Tinmouth, Vt., 18 April, 1850, who was b. at Pawlet 28 Feb., 1828, now (1902) living at Danby, Vt. A Republican and Universalist.

CHILDREN.

1. Charles May Clark (6), a farmer of Pawlet, b. 7 Sept., 1851 at Pawlet; m. for his first wife, Julia Harrington, dau. of Philander and Mary (Hawkins) Harrington, 18 April, 1872 at Middletown, Vt., who bore him a daughter:

    1. Helen Clark (7), 16 July, 1873.

Mr. Clark m. for his second wife, 29 Dec., 1880, Lois Greene, b. at Wallingford, Vt., 25 March, 1855, dau. of Job and Frances (Perkins) Greene. They have one son:

    1. Leon Job Clark (7), b. 19 June, 1882. Mr. Clark is a Republican, and a Universalist. Has resided in Danby, Vt., 28 years; was in Tinmouth, Vt., 19 years and in Wells, Vt., 4 years. Mr. Clark has given much valuable information of this branch of the Lobdell family, for which we all are grateful to him.

2. Emily Jane Clark (6), b. 21 Oct., 1855 at Pawlet; m. 7 Sept., 1881, Leonard J. Parris. One child:

    1. Sylvia Rebecca Parris (7), b. 19 June, 1891.

SIXTH GENERATION.

CHILDREN OF HANNAH (5) LOBDELL AND HER FIRST HUSBAND, NORRIS SMITH.

1. Abigail. 2 George. 3 Almira.

1. Abigail L. Smith, b 21 May, 1821; m. Charles Hulett She d in Pawlet, Vt., in the spring of 1884.

2. George Smith, a farmer, b 6 April, 1823 at Rupert, Bennington Co., Vt.; m. 2 June, 1852, Anna L. Thompson, b. 27 June, 1833 at Danby, Rutland Co., Vt., dau. of Israel and Frelove Nichols Thompson Mr. Smith is a resident of Wallingford, Vt., having lived in both Danby and Mount Holly, of the same state. Is a Universalist in religion; politically, a Republican.

CHILDREN.

1. Emily A Smith (7), b. 1 Nov., 1853.
2. Horace G. Smith (7), b. 9 Sept., 1857.
3. Frances A Smith (7), b. 3 July, 1860
4 Ann A. Smith (7), b 13 Feb, 1868
5 Jane A Smith (7), b 31 July, 1869; m. R M. Tracy Mr. and Mrs. Smith have passed through "deep waters of sorrow," their children all passing away. Jane left two little daughters and a son. The grandson lives with his grandparents. Let us hope that he may be a comfort to them in their declining years

3 Almira Smith, b 24 Jan, 1826, m. Charles Wallaston Resides at Anamosa, Iowa.

CHILDREN OF HANNAH LOBDELL AND HER SECOND HUSBAND, NOAH GIFFORD.

1 Noah 2 Anna. 3 Agnes. 4 George. 5. Charles.

1 Noah E. Gifford; m. Emily Johnson. Both dead.
2. Anna Gifford.
3. Agnes Gifford.
4. George Gifford
5. Charles Gifford m. Elizabeth Hulett. His widow and three children reside in Springfield, Vt.

323

CHILDREN OF JOHN, JR. (5) AND OLIVE (MOSIER) LOBDELL.

1. Emily V. 2 Anna. 3 Olive. 4 William F 5. Eliza

1 Emily Virginia, b. at Rupert, Vt., 28 Nov., 1824, m. Edwin C. Bullis. Both are dead.

2. Anna, b 24 Dec, 1827 at Rupert; m Samuel Thomas Cook, a farmer of Fort Ann, b 1 May, 1821 at Fort Ann, Washington Co., N Y., son of Samuel and Sarah (Brayton) Cook Republican. Religion, Baptist

CHILDREN.

1 Palmer Augustus Cook (7), b. 21 Feb, 1849, d. 1887; m. Harriet E. Lace.

2. Emma Cook (7), b 3 Sept, 1850; m. J. Quincy Edwards, who died.

3. Florence Cook (7), b. 28 March, 1853, d. 28 Oct., 1853.

4. Leonard Hatch Cook (7), b. 1 July, 1855; m. Edith Lawrence. Reside at Boston, Mass.

5. Wm Warren Cook (7), b 26 March, 1859; m. Inez Livingston. Reside at Whitehall, N. Y.

6. Anna Marion Cook (7), b. 31 Aug., 1867; m. Edwin C. North. Reside in New York City.

3. Olive, b 27 Nov, 1829; m. Wm Lake Both dead

3 Wm. Ferris, b 11 June, 1833 Resides at Jasper, Minn.

5 Eliza, b 26 Nov., 1837; m. Henry Lake, who d His widow resides at Madison, Wis.

CHILDREN OF ABIGAIL (5) LOBDELL AND JOSIAH WILLARD.

1. Nancy. 2. Merrett. 3. Myron

1. Nancy Willard, b at Pawlet, Vt, 18 Oct., 1829; m Augustus Gillman of Middletown, Vt, where all her children were born.

CHILDREN.

1. Nina I. Gillman (7), b 7 May, 1865
2. Leon C Gillman (7), b. 21 Aug., 1866.
3. George L. Gillman (7), b. 5 May, 1868
4 Emily A. Gillman (7), b 10 Nov., 1869

5. Esther A Gillman (7), b. 20 Jan., 1871.

2. Merrett Willard, b. at Pawlet, Vt, 18 April, 1833; m Caroline Fish of Moriah, Essex Co., N Y. They had one son, Herbert Willard (7).

3. Myron Willard, b at Sheffield, Ohio, 27 Nov. 1835, m. Lura Ann Pratt.

CHILDREN.

1. Frank B Willard (7), b. in Wells, Vt., 31 March, 1871.

2. Bert L. Willard (7), b. in Wells, Vt., 5 Jan., 1875, d. in same place 10 Jan., 1887.

CHILDREN OF HULETT (5) AND SQUCE (SMITH) LOBDELL.

1. Lydia. 2 Electa A 3. Edwin R 4. Joel. 5. Smith. 6. Emeline.

1. Lydia, b 17 May, 1835, m Daniel Neale.

2. Electa A., b 26 April, 1837; m. David Joyce Thorp of North Adams, Mass.

3 Edwin Ruthvin, b. 12 Jan., 1842, d. 20 March, 1898, at Hartford, Conn.; m. 27 Aug. 1866 at South Glastonbury, Conn., Isabella M Truscott, b. 8 May, 1844 at Davenport, England, dau. of Robert and Isabella (Parsons) Truscott

CHILDREN.
(All born at Adams, Mass.)

1. Eugene Smith (7), m. Agnes Russell

2. Helena Belle (7).

3. Bessie Frances (7), b 17 April, 1873. Is a kindergartner at Bristol, Conn (1902).

4 May Electa (7), m Arthur Gowdy.

4. Joel, b. 10 Jan, 1845, m Alvira Smith.

5. Smith (7), b 10 March, 1848

6. Emeline (7), b 11 July, 1850; m Henry G. Varns.

CHILDREN OF ANNA LOBDELL AND FRANKLIN RAY.

1. Eliza. 2 Mary. 3 John L, 4. Hiram. 5. Martha A.

1. Eliza Anita Ray, b. 18 May, 1844 at Middletown, Vt; m. 8 Dec, 1863 at Tinmouth, Vt., Geo Rounds Leonard, a farmer,

b. 3 Sept, 1832 at Tinmouth, son of Arnold and Freelove Buck Leonard. Republican; Methodist.

CHILDREN.

1. Edwin DeWitt Leonard (7), b. 11 Jan., 1865; m. Jennie Belle Stuart Hart.

2. Charles Ernest Leonard (7), b 23 Nov., 1870; single (1902).

3. Frank Arnold Leonard (7), b 6 Feb, 1877, m. Effie Marie Ellis.

2. Mary Anna Ray, b. 10 Nov., 1845, d. 25 Aug., 1901, m David Martin Stoddard.

3. John Lobdell Ray, b. 10 Aug., 1848 at Poultney, Vt.; m. 1 Jan., 1873 at Castleton, Vt, Emma Matilda Gates, b. 25 June, 1850 at Middletown Spa, Vt, d 26 Oct., 1877 at same place of birth, dau. of Amos and Matilda Ann (Seward) Gates

CHILDREN.

1. Ethel E. Ray (7), b. 16 July, 1874; m. James Bell

2. Flora Ray (7), b. 10 Oct, 1876, d. 21 April, 1877.

John L. Ray m for his second wife, 18 March, 1879, at Hampton, N. Y., Mattie M Gates. b. 10 Nov., 1857 at West Pawlet, Vt, dau. of Russell and Polly (Jones) Gates (no relative of first wife.) By second one child:

1. Fred A. Ray (7), b. 17 Aug, 1880; single (1902)

4 Hiram Ray, b 19 May, 1851, d Oct., 1854.

5. Martha Anna Ray, b. 18 Oct., 1856; m Arthur Herbert Flanders of Middletown Spa, Vt.

CHILDREN OF DARIUS AND DELANA (COY) LOBDELL.

---

1. Emily L 2. Alice E 3. George S. 4. Julia A. 5. Marion F. 6 John 7. Horace G.

(All born at Middletown Spa. Vt)

---

1. Emily Lucinda, b 14 Jan.. 1842; m. 28 Sept, 1880 at Middletown Spa, Isaac Stevers

2. Alice Eliza, b. 16 June, 1845, d. 28 March, 1859.

3. Geo. Smith, b. 1 March, 1848, d in Middletown Spa, 13 April, 1885; m first, Phoebe Kelley, second, Ella Greene

CHILDREN.

1 Lawrence J (7), b. 31 Aug., 1875; m. Eliza Odell, 18 Aug., 1898.

2 Ethel (7), b. 1 April, 1878, d. 23 March, 1882.

4. Julia Ann, b 2 June, 1850; m. 2 Sept., 1868 at Middletown Spa, Samuel Thompson Kelley, a farmer, b. 3 Aug., 1847 at Tinmouth, Rutland Co., Vt., son of Obediah and Sarah Ann (Greene) Kelley.

5. Marion Frances, b. 6 Aug., 1852, d. at Middletown Spa, 3 Sept., 1876, m. Charles Willard and had one son·

1. Burt Oscar Willard (7), b. 24 May, 1876; unmarried, 1902.

6. John, b. 6 Aug., 1854, d. at Sandwich. Ill., 21 Feb., 1900; m. first Minnie Marshall, second Johanna Gunderson.

CHILDREN.

1. Ella Delana (7), b. 27 June, 1876.

2 Delmar (7), b 24 Jan, 1878.

3 Burt J. (7), b 13 March, 1880, d. 12 May, 1896.

4. Hattie Marion 7), b 5 Nov, 1884

5. Baby (7), b. 2 Dec., 1887. d aged 10 days.

6 Bertha Johanna (7). b 13 July, 1888.

7. Ethel Viola (7), b 5 Jan., 1892

8. John Darius (7), b 26 June, 1894.

9 Lawrence Wm. (7), b. 20 Sept., 1896.

7. Horace Greeley, b 4 Aug, 1863; m first, Clara Case; second, Martha Wescott. Has one dau.

1. Irene Angeline (7). b 12 April, 1894.

SEVENTH GENERATION.

CHILDREN OF EMILY LUCINDA LOBDELL (6) AND ISAAC STEVERS.

1. Charles E. Stevers, b 3 Feb, 1866, d. 26 Jan, 1870.

2 Frank E. Stevers, b 11 April, 1869, d 6 Jan., 1870.

3. Allen D. Stevers, b. 14 Aug, 1871; m Laura Morgan.

CHILDREN.

1 Wm. (8), and 2 Frank (8) Stevers

3. Alice May Stevers (8), b. 4 Sept, 1874; m. Wm. Bursey.

4 Carl Stevers (8), b 16 March, 1876, d 20 Aug., 1876.

CHILDREN OF JULIA ANN LOBDELL (6) AND SAMUEL THOMPSON KELLEY.

1   Alice Sarah Kelley, b. 28 Oct , 1871; m. Marshall B. Fish.
CHILDREN.
  1. Leah Alice Fish (8), b. 7 March, 1892.
  2. Vera Hattie Fish (8), b. 25 July, 1894.
  3. Wallace Kelley Fish (8), b. 5 May, 1898.

2. Fred Fayette Kelley, b 12 June, 1875, m. Jessie M Greene. Have one dau.:
  1. Gertrude Marion Kelley (8), b. 24 April, 1900.

3. Bertha May Kelley, b. 10 Jan , 1879; m. Earl Ephraim Gates.

4. Arthur Seymour Kelley, b 13 April, 1885; unmarried, 1902.

5. Kirby Lobdell Kelley, b 30 June, 1891.

FOURTH GENERATION.

CHILDREN OF ELIZABETH (3) LOBDELL AND ISAAC NORTHRUP.

I. Isaac Northrup, b. 24 Dec., 1752; m Hannah Olmstead, who d. about 1790.

II. David Northrup, b. 20 March, 1754; m. 1 Feb., 1770, Abigail Wilson. (?)

III. Elizabeth Northrup, b. 28 Oct, 1755, m. 1 March, 1781, Daniel Smith. (?)

IV. Lois Northrup, b. 17 July, 1757.

V. Rebecca Northrup, b. 13 July, 1759.

VI. Eunice Northrup, b. 3 Feb, 1761.

VII Phalle Northrup.

VIII. Sarah Northrup.

IX Ruth Northrup

X. Mollie Northrup

XI. Jonah Northrup.

XII. Lewis Northrup.

XIII. Isaac Northrup.

(Northrup Genealogy.)

Child and Descendants of
David [3] Lobdell (Joshua [2], Simon [1])
Wife, Phoebe Burt

FOURTH GENERATION.

CHILD OF DAVID (3) AND PHOEBE (BURT) LOBDELL

1　Joshua.

The only child of whom I can find any record is

1. Joshua, probably b in Warwick, Orange Co., N Y., about 1766, and registered on the rolls of the early First Baptist Church of that town in 1791, about which time the family left Warwick and whether they went directly to McConnelstown, Pa., or went to Clarkstown, Rockland Co, I can not say. But "in the spring of 1808, he moved from McConnellstown, Pa., to St. Alban's township, Licking Co, Ohio, and is said to have been the second settler who came for a permanent settlement His father, David Lobdell, came with him and made his home with him He settled on the farm known as the Atwood or Fitch farm, erected a cabin on the knoll on which the present house of Wm Green now stands, in the fall of 1808. Joshua Lobdell set out the first orchard in the township in 1809. the trees being brought from Muskingum Co. He also set out a pear tree which was brought from Pennsylvania, probably by David Drake (his brother-in-law) in 1811, which is still standing (1873). a good bearer, the largest as well as the oldest in the township Joshua and his father were among the number that organized the Baptist church on the Welsh Hill in Sept, 1808. Joshua was their first clerk. They both remained on the farm until their death. Joshua was the only son of David, a carpenter by trade, hence, our first carpenter. He did not long survive his father, dying in 1812. aged about 46 years. (Joseph M. Scott's, St. Albans Township.) The name of his first wife I have been unable to find, but by her he had three daughters.

1.　Phoebe (5). It is said died unmarried

2.　Julia (5), b about 1792; m on 17 July, 1810 to Gideon Cornell, which was the first marriage ceremony performed in St Alban's township Julia d in Alexandria, Licking Co., Ohio.

3　Margaret (5), b. 1793-5, d. 19 Oct., 1865 at Fort Wayne, Ind.; m about 1816 at Licking Co, Ohio, to Joshua

Holmes, a farmer, b. 1793 at Hebron, Licking Co., Ohio, d. about 1857 at Bluffton, Allen Co., Ind., son of James and Nancy (Whitaker) Holmes.

Joshua Lobdell m. for his second wife, presumably at McConnelstown, Pa., or in Hunterdon Co., N. J., Jane Melick, b. 31 May, 1781, d. 21 Sept., 1846, dau. of John and Mary (Todd) Melick. Mary, b. 1778, a sister of Jane Melick, m. David Drake, who after marriage was also one of the early settlers of St. Albans township; and a descendant tells me that she has often heard her grandmother (Zenobia (Lobdell) Hummell) talk of her aunts, Polly (Mary) Wilson, Polly (Mary) Drake and of her uncle, Osmer Curtis.

Joshua's widow re-married to James Buley and had dau. Caroline. The widow after remarrying, left Licking Co., Ohio, and went to Perry Co., Ohio, and after the death of James Buley went to Blandesburg, Knox Co., Ohio to her people, and is buried in the Melick plot at that place.

Evidently the Todds and the Melicks were with David and Joshua Lobdell, residents of Warwick and Goshen, Orange Co., N. Y., but migrated in the late 1700's. I find Elizabeth Todd m. Wm. Lobdell (Samuel). They moved to Romulus, N. Y.

Mary Todd m. John Melick and moved to Hunterdon Co., N. J. Daughters:

Jane Melick, b. 1781; m. Joshua Lobdell (David) as his second wife

Mary Melick, b. 1778; m. David Drake.

Rebecca Melick, b. 1786, m. Mr. Wilson.

SIXTH GENERATION.

CHILDREN OF JULIA LOBDELL (5) AND GIDEON CORNELL.

---

1. Mary. 2. Lovina. 3. George. 4. Naomi A. 5. Elizabeth. 6. Ann P. 7. Artemas. 8. Gideon. 9. Jane. 10. Leander. 11. Almira.

Cornell by name—

1. Mary m. Lloyd Tracy
2. Lovina m. Stewart Wilson.

3. George m. Retta Barnes.

4. Naomi Angeline, b. 3 Jan., 1820 at Belleville, Richland Co., Ohio. Is (1904) living at Cambridge, Ohio with her dau., Mrs. C. B Wilson. She m. 26 May, 1846 at Granville, Ohio to George Spellman, a farmer, b 25 July, 1815 at Alexandria, Ohio, where he also d 15 Dec., 1855, son of Thomas and Mirriam (Clark) Spellman.

5. Elizabeth m. Elisha Wells.

6. Ann Phoebe m. Anthony Rhodes.

7 Artemas m. Sarah Wright.

8. Gideon m. Emily ——?.

9 Jane m. Joseph Sterling.

10. Leander.

11. Almira m. Aaron Beem.

CHILDREN OF NAOMI ANGELINE (CORNELL) SPELL-MAN (6).

1. Ella Spellman 2. Susan T Spellman. 3. Anna S Spellman.

1 Ella Spellman (7), b. 5 Aug., 1847, d. 24 Nov., 1865.

2 Susan Talbot Spellman (7), b. 26 June, 1850; m. Howard M. Sedgwick.

3. Anna Louise Spellman (7), b 15 Feb., 1854 at Granville, Ohio; m. 2 Sept., 1885 at Zanesville, Ohio, Cyrus Burt Wilson, b. 4 Aug., 1847 at Cambridge, Guernsey Co., Ohio, where he also d 5 Feb., 1900, son of Otho and Catharine (Burt) Wilson Resided at Cambridge, O. A real estate dealer. Republican and Methodist.

CHILDREN OF MARGARET LOBDELL (5) AND JOSHUA HOLMES.

1. Lemuel. 2. Alfred 3 Leander. 4. Eliza 5. Evaline. 6. Sarah. 7 Emily. 8 George. 9. Wm. 10. Caroline. 11. Nancy. 12. Mary.

1. Lemuel Holmes, a merchant, b in 1817 in Hebron, Licking Co., Ohio, d. in March. 1888 at Portland. Indiana. His widow (not knowing her maiden name) is living (1902), 84 years old,

334

with her son, Mr. L. G. Holmes, a prominent business man of Portland and Briant, Ind. Lemuel has a dau. (7) who m. Mr. B. F. Brown and resides at Los Angeles, Calif.

2. Alfred Holmes, a merchant tailor, b 1819 at Hebron, also d. at Hebron; m. Mary Turner.

3. Leander Holmes, a lawyer. b 1821 in Hebron, d. in Portland, Oregon.

4 Eliza Holmes, b 1823 in Hebron, Ohio; m Mr. Ewing. Has a dau., Minnie (7); m Judge Zollers of Fort Wayne, Ind.

5. Evaline Holmes, b 1825 in Hebron, where she also d.; m. James Richardson.

6 Sarah Holmes, b. 1827 in Hebron; m John Wells.

7 Emily Holmes, b. 13 March, 1832 at Hebron. In 1904 is living with her dau., Mrs. Malleby at Pueblo, Colo She can tell me nothing of her mother's family as her mother had only a dim recollection of her own mother, who d when she was a small child Emily m. 28 June, 1851 at Hebron, Daniel Beatty, a dentist, b. 3 Sept., 1821 at Penfield, Monroe Co, N Y., d in 1890 at Amite, Tangipaho Co, La., son of ——? Beatty and ——? Vosburg.

CHILDREN.

1. Charles H. Beatty (7), b. 11 April, 1852, living in Amite, La.; m. Helen Packer.

2 Frank W. Beatty (7), b. 14 April, 1854, living in Crowley, La ; m. Georgia E Moys.

3 Josephine Beatty (7), b. 9 July, 1856; m. Charles B. Whitaker, living at St. Louis, Mo.

4 Martha B Beatty (7), b. 28 March, 1862; m. Oliver W. Mallaby, living at Pueblo, Colo.

8. George Holmes, b. 1831 in Hebron, Ohio, d. at same place; m Jemima Taylor

9 William Holmes, b 1834 at Hebron, d. unmarried at Toledo, Ohio.

10. Caroline Holmes, b 1838 at Hebron, d. at Portland, Ore., 1898; m. Joseph Misner.

11. Nancy Holmes, b 1841 at Hebron, where she d. in infancy.

12. Mary Holmes, b. ——?, d. at Hebron in infancy.

Of the granddaughters of Margaret (Lobdell) Holmes, one, Olive Holmes (7) m. Mr. A. J. Wells, in Fort Wayne, Ind., and now lives in San Francisco, Calif. She lived in her young days with her grandmother in Fort Wayne. She writes: "I know that grandmother's maiden name was Lobdell and that she had pride of family, but know nothing of her ancestors."

Another granddaughter (7), Mrs. Emma Studebaker. Address given, Bluffton, Wells Co, Ind

FIFTH GENERATION.

CHILDREN OF JOSHUA (4) LOBDELL AND SECOND WIFE, JANE MELICK.

(Not given in order of birth.)

1. Nathan M , b 23 Aug, 1808; no record (This is the Nathan Lobdell who went south and of whom a letter of inquiry to Mr John Little Lobdell of Louisiana, was written in 1859.)

2 Sarah m John Matthews. Had—
Julius (6) of Dubuque, Iowa.
Amos (6).
John (6), went to California
Amanda (6), m Mr Pettingill of Lyons, Iowa.
Elizabeth (6) m Mr Cole of Iowa or Kansas.

3. John Burt, b. 11 Oct , 1809 in St. Albans township, Licking Co , Ohio, d 13 Nov , 1890 in Washington township, Ind., aged 81 y ; m 4 June, 1835 near Summerset, Perry Co , Ohio, to Pleasant Ann Watson, b. 14 March, 1818 at Summerset, Ohio, d 15 Dec., 1897 in Washington township, Ind , aged 79 y , dau. of Thomas and Elizabeth (Havenner) Watson. (This was the author of the letter written to Mr. John Little Lobdell of Louisiana.)

4. Zenobia, b 12 May, 1811 in St. Albans township, Ohio Must have been an infant when her father d in 1812 She d 18 Oct., 1874 in Grant Co , Ind ; m. 3 April, 1831 in Perry Co , Ohio, to Charles Hummel, b 21 Sept , 1804 in Muskingum Co , Ohio, d 16 Dec., 1882 in Grant Co., Ind., son of Henry Hummell from Virginia and his wife, Eleanor McNaughton They came to Grant Co , Ind in 1831, where he d about 55 years ago (1907)

5 Samuel, while living in St Albans township, Ohio, was drafted during the war with Great Britain, but was under age When the heavy draft of 1813 came the lot again fell on him; he entered the army and d in the service at or near Detroit, but a few months after leaving home, being the first from our township to give his life for his country (St. Albans History.)

336

AARON THOMAS LOBDELL (6)
(John Burt)
of Marion, Ind.
(Page 337)

MRS. AARON THOMAS LOBDELL
of Marion, Ind.
(Page 337)

MR. AND MRS. J. B. BRUNER
Eleanor Jane (6) (Zenobia [5])
of La Fontaine, Ind.
(Page 338)

6. Hiram d. in St. Louis, Mo.; unmarried

7 and 8. Caleb and Lydia, probably d. young, as no descendant has any recollection of them.

SIXTH GENERATION.

CHILDREN OF JOHN BURT (5) LOBDELL AND HIS WIFE, PLEASANT ANN WATSON.

---

1. Aaron Thomas. 2. Robert. 3. Martha. 4. Eliza. 5. Harriet. 6. Alfred. 7. Frank. 8. Eleanor. 9. Melissa. 10. Amanda. 11. Sarah Jane. 12. William.

1. Aaron Thomas, b. 7 May, 1836 in Perry Co., Ohio; m. 23 Oct., 1856, Catherine Ann, dau. of John and Catherine (Coon) McDaniel, b. in 1842.

2. Robert, b. 10 Nov., 1837 in Perry Co., Ohio; m. Mary Eliza Brady.

3. Martha, b. 3 Oct., 1839 in Perry Co., Ohio, d. 3 June, 1894; m. first to Henry Curtis on 4 March, 1860 and had one dau., Lillie C. Curtis. Mr. Curtis d. from a kick of a colt, the year of his marriage, on 23 Aug., 1860. The widow remarried to Joseph Armstrong, who d. in 1896. Twins (Bertie and Mertie) were born to them, but both d. in childhood.

4. Eliza, b. 18 Sept., 1841 in Grant Co., Ind.; m. 11 April, 1872, James Otis. No children

5. Sarah Jane, b. 28 Aug., 1843 in Grant Co., Ind., d. 17 Feb., 1859.

6. William, b. 29 June, 1845 in Grant Co., Ind., d. 3 March, 1846.

7. Amanda, b. 23 Jan., 1847, d. 26 Sept., 1854.

8. Harriet, b. 23 April, 1849 near La Fontaine, Wabash Co., Ind.; m. 5 Sept., 1867, Geo. Flemm Johnson, a blacksmith, b. 9 July, 1843 at Marion, Ind., son of Wm. Elliot and Melissa (Dunn) Johnson. They reside at La Fontaine, Ind.

CHILDREN.

1. John Lobdell Johnson (7), b. 30 June, 1868.

2. Willie E. Johnson (7), b. 11 Dec., 1869, d. 8 May, 1870.

3. Henry Burt Johnson (7), b. 9 Sept., 1871, d. 29 June, 1872.

337

4   Geo Zenas Johnson (7), b. 15 April, 1873. Resides in Chicago. Is a telegraph operator for C. R. I. & P. R. R. Co.

5.   Albert Verne (7), b. 30 April, 1877, d. 7 Dec., 1881.

6.   Kenneth Carl (7), b. 22 April, 1883

7.   Jerre Luin (7), b. 18 March, 1885.

8.   Whitelaw Reed Johnson (7), b 20 June, 1892, d 29 Aug., 1893

9.   Melissa, b. 23 May, 1851, d 22 Sept., 1854

10.   Alfred, b. 3 March, 1854; m first Miranda Williams. Has two children, Charles (7) and Cora (7).

He m. second Amanda Dicken Has Chester (7) and Walter (7) by this marriage   (I have been unable to locate Mr L.)

11.   Ella, b. 7 Oct, 1857; m 21 Feb, 1885 to Albert Hummel

CHILDREN.

1.   Elmer and 2.   Edith (7), deceased

3   Wilber (7).

12.   Frank, b. 23 July, 1863; m Althea Hummel in May, 1887.

CHILDREN.

1.   Harry (7), deceased.

2   Alvah (7).

3   Eva (7).

CHILDREN OF ZENOBIA (5) LOBDELL AND CHARLES HUMMEL.

1   Henry

2.   Leander.

3.   John Lobdell Hummel resides at Pomona, Franklin Co, Kansas

4   Charles

5.   Constantine resides at Fox, Grant Co., Ind.

6   Eleanor Jane, b 14 April, 1848 in Grant Co., Ind., m 24 Oct, 1871, James B Bruner, b in Aug., 1834 at Montgomery, Va., son of Henry Bruner of La Fontaine, Ind. (a native of Virginia) and Eleanor Michael of Virginia No children. Reside at La Fontaine, Ind. Mrs. Eleanore Hummel Bruner is the possessor of the original letter written to John Burt Lobdell by John Little Lobdell in 1859 It was given to her by her cousin, Mrs. Harriet (Lobdell) Johnson and is greatly prized.

In 1842 the parents of Aaron Thomas Lobdell with their family, then consisting of three children, migrated from their old home in Ohio, hoping to better their condition farther west. The father secured the northwest quarter section of land in Washington township, Indiana. Here the remainder of their lives was passed. At that time the tract was new, with but a small clearing. With the help of his sons he made a most desirable farm, adding some two hundred acres, nearly all of which he gave to his sons during his lifetime. After a most honored and useful life, this respected couple passed to their reward, he being eighty-one and she seventy-nine, having survived him about seven years.

Soon after their coming to the county they rendered material assistance in the building of the well-known Range Line Christian Church, which stood on a corner of his farm, the land being donated by him. During the course of a long and useful life, he was recognized as the most ardent and influential member of the above society, never flagging in his observance of Christian duty and upright living, never lacking in the necessary financial support, in a thousand ways contributing to the life and vigor of the church.

After marriage, Aaron and his bride settled on their present farm, which was then owned by his father. Some four years later he was given one thousand dollars by his father, still however, assuming an indebtedness of $400 on the land. This gift was in lieu of further claims on his father's estate, preferring to have this when most needed, rather than a greater amount several years later. The tract was wild and covered with heavy timber, of which but twenty acres had been cleared. He placed upwards of fifty acres under cultivation, and added until the farm now contains one hundred and sixty-four acres.

Five children have been born to them. Josephine, wife of Henry C. Creviston, of Van Buren township; Francis Marion, who became a teacher in his eighteenth year and assumed an enviable position among the successful teachers of the county When nearing the close of his fourth term he was stricken with disease that had undermined his constitution, and which terminated in death. The loss of this talented young man was keenly felt by pupils, friends and relatives, all of whom had felt that for him a brilliant future was in store; Emma Catherine, wife of Henry L Bradford, of Washington township; Laura Ellen, wife of Albert Feighner, also of the same township; and John Thomas, who

339

remains at home assisting in the operation of the farm. Mr Lobdell and wife have ever indicated the greatest interest in the education and training of their children, few parents having done more for the advancement of their families than they.—(Grant County Representative Men.)

Since the above was written Mr. and Mrs. Lobdell have moved (in Dec., 1902) from the home farm into the town of Marion, the county seat of Grant Co., Ind., where they built a residence, fitted with all modern conveniences, hoping to enoy—with less care—the remaining days of their lives.

Bayous, Parish West Baton Rouge, La.,
Saturday, 18th June, 1859.

Mr. John Lobdell,

My Dear Sir:—Yours mailed May 23d last, reached me at this place some few days ago. You state that your only brother (whose name was Nathan), after he had grown to manhood went to the South, came back several times, and went back again, and understood that he was married there, but as you have not heard from him for many years, you, and your family supposed he was dead—and not having come across or heard the name of Lobdell in the course of a long life (nearly half a century) before that day, when you noticed in reading of the rise and overflow of the Mississippi, causing a crevass at Lobdell's plantation in West Baton Rouge, 16 miles above the town of Baton Rouge, which naturally made my sisters and myself very anxious to learn whether you were our lost brother or any connection. We have been anxious for years to hear from our brother or his wife, or family, if he had any. You state that you were born in the state of Ohio, and that your father's name was Joshua. The designation of the location of your brother is so vague and uncertain that I cannot assist you in the inquiry, as the South comprehends many states of our Union.

I am a native of the state of New York, born in the village of Johnstown (formerly Montgomery Co., now Fulton Co.), 40 miles west of the city of Albany. I left there in Oct., 1821, arrived in New Orleans in November of that year, and have remained in this state as a resident ever since, now nearly 38 years, living six years of that time in New Orleans, about sixteen years in the Parish of West Feliciana and sixteen years in this Parish. My father's name was Abijah. He is dead. He had three brothers (Joshua 1752, Isaac 1755, and Simon 1762), living at Westerloo, Albany Co., N. Y., one brother in this state and one in the state of Mississippi, all of whom are dead. He had cousins, of different families of the same name, residing in Fulton, Herkimer, Essex, Chenango and Westchester Counties, N. Y., some of whom I know, as well as many of my uncles and cousins in Albany Co. I know my Uncle Abraham and all his family, who resided in this state. My Uncle James was dead before I came south, but

341

most of his children and grandchildren I know, all of whom resided in the state of Mississippi. My uncles' two families, James and Abraham of Mississippi and Louisiana are the only persons of our name that I have known in the South, except my own three brothers who lived with or near me. I am satisfied that we are relations and descended from the same Welsh stock. The name is formed of two Welsh words, Lob (round or oblong) and Dell (valley)—round or oblong valley, where our ancestors originally resided in Wales. The tradition of our branch of the family is that three brothers of the name came over from Wales, and settled in some part of Massachusetts, from whom those of the name in this country have descended. On further search and reading I am convinced that those of our ancestors who came to this country were among the non-conformists in England and Wales, though believing in almost all the distinctive principles and articles of faith of the Church of England; and from an article published in Household Words that they attended the preaching of a Welsh clergyman of the Established Church, by the name of Clifton, who was silenced from preaching for not conforming to all the requisitions of the rules of the church, and went over with a considerable portion of his flock to Holland for protection and to enjoy the teachings of their pastor unmolested—among whom was William Bradford, of an influential family and one of the gentry; that this flock found Smith and Robertson with their flocks of Pilgrims in Holland, but did not settle with them, in consequence of contentions among themselves, but settled in another part of Holland—and I have good reason to believe that they followed the Pilgrims to Plymouth Rock and settled with them, as I found that Nicholas Lobdin (spelled wrong) in 1630 received a lot and outlot at Plymouth with other settlers, and when the old town got full several years after the first settlement, that the Bradfords, Lazells and Lobdells (spelling the name right), evidently Welsh families, with others, settled the town of Plympton in Plymouth Co. (This information I obtained from a book called "The Antiquities of the New England Towns." I have seen gentlemen who say there is a Lobdell House now standing in Plympton, and that one of the family is now residing in Hartford, Conn There have been late publications of the "History of the Pilgrim Families," and I presume full information can be obtained of the first settlers of our name, and of their descendants, for

342

some generations, from these publications, from the records of Plympton and Plymouth and from the descendants of the family.

The information derived from my own branch commences from Salem, Mass., with Joshua Lobdell as the root, not fixing the date of their settlement at Salem nor the name of his wife. He had six sons and three daughters, viz.: Joshua, James, Simon, Sarah, Hannah, Ebenezer, Daniel, John and Rachel. A portion of this family probably removed from Salem to Newtown, Conn., as I find six of the name, viz.: Joshua, Samuel, Joshua, Jr., John, Caleb and Ebenezer, formed part of the Church of England congregation of the Rev. Mr. John Beach of Newtown, Conn., and with other Episcopalians of that state in the year 1738 signed a memorial and address to the Governor, Council and Representatives of the Colony of Connecticut for their proportion of the public monies toward the support of their ministers and schools, which was refused them. (This you will find in the Church Review and Ecclesiastical Register, Vol. 10, No. 1, April, 1857, published at New Haven, Conn., by Rev. N. S. Richardson.

If they were part of the Salem family, then Joshua, Sr., was my great grandfather and Joshua, Jr., my grandfather Our branch appears to be the oldest branch—the oldest son bearing the name of Joshua—at least it was so for three generations. This traces the family back within something less than 100 years of the first settlement in this country, which can be filled up by referring to late publications—the records of Plymouth, Plympton, Salem and Newtown—and the consulation with branches of the family still residing at those places. Following down the pedigree from Salem, in our branch, say, from about 1720 to 1730, in Joshua 1st (gt. gr. f.) we find that Joshua (2) (gr. ft.) the oldest son, married Sarah Scott, lived first in Salem and afterward in Newtown, (or maybe) removed to Stephentown, Rensselaer Co., N. Y., and that they had issue, viz.· Joshua 1752, Isaac 1755, James, Sarah, Hannah, Simon 1762, Huldah, Mary, Abraham, Abijah, Rachel and Rebecca.

Joshua, born 1752, married Jane Pouce, and removed from Stephentown to Rensselaerville, Albany Co., N. Y., and had ten children, viz.. Joel, Joshua, Abraham, Sarah, Abijah, Philip, Hannah, Daniel, Electa, John. I believe these children married and had large families. Some of them removed to Otsego Co., and others to western counties of N. Y., and some probably to the western states.

343

Isaac, born 1855, married first William Pomeroy of Berkshire Co., Mass, and second, Jerusha Lobdell, his cousin (daughter of John Lobdell, born March 10, 1743, and Elizabeth, his wife, from Westchester Co., N. Y.). He also removed from Stephentown to Rensselaerville and had, by first wife:

Lois; married Joshua Tompkins.
Mirriam; married James Jacox.
Anna, married Knight Bennett.
Isaac, married Nancy Udell.
Joshua Pomeroy, married Phebe Ruland
Olive; married John Meyers.
Princess; married Asa Jackson.

By second wife:

Jerusha, married Fred'k Slater
Levisa; marrier first Francis Atkins, second, Silas B. Martin.

James Harvey, married Harriet Crawford.

James, brother of Joshua, 1752, married Miss Vernor, and removed from Stephentown, a short time after Shay's rebellion in Mass. with his brother Abraham, his sister Hannah and her husband, Jerry Goodrich, and several cousins by the name of Rundell, etc., etc., with others, to the western country, intending to settle on the Lyman or Putnam purchases on the Ohio—but after arriving there they saw the proclamation of the King of Spain, through the Governor of Louisiana, offering lands to settlers on favorable terms. His family, his brother Abraham (a very young man) and several cousins, with others, came down the river, took up lands on the border of the Mississippi River, at a place called Palmira, and having been drowned out three years, sold their lands and moved back into the Gulf hills in Warren Co., Miss. (Mr. Goodrich and his family, with other of the relations, remained on the Ohio and settled on the Miama Valley, where their descendants still remain.)

James and Miss Vernor or Vernon had six children, viz.: Gilbert, John, Sarah, Mary, ——, ——.

John (2) married —— Conger and left three children, viz.:

1. Lewellyn, married, died; left 2 sons.
2. Jonathan Conger, married —— Stowers, dead; left 4 children

344

3. John Venable, married —— Coffee, is now living in Bolivar Co., Miss. Several children.

3 Sarah, married Seth Rundell, her cousin; is living in Warren Co., Miss. Several children.

4 Mary, married first John Walker and second, John Gorman I know nothing of her family, nor of 1 Gilbert, nor Nos. 5 and 6, except that one of them, a daughter, married a Stotts, and the family are living in Texas

Sarah, sister of Joshua, 1752, married first —— Sprague and had children (particulars not known); married second Daniel Hubbard of Lenox, Berkshire Co., Mass, by whom she had two children:

1 Daniel, married ——, and had children living on the Onondago River, Broome Co, N. Y

2. Sarah, married —— Seymour. Children also living in Broome Co.

Hannah, sister of Joshua, 1752, married first Jerry Goodrich and settled in the great bend of the Ohio or the Miama Valley She had five children by Goodrich, viz Abijah, Jacob, Jerry, Hannah and Lucy Who the second husband was, or whether they had children, I do not know

Simon, brother of Joshua, 1752, married Grace Pomeroy of Berkshire Co, Mass ; moved from Stephentown to Rensselaerville, and had 8 children, viz. Rebecca Simon, Jacob, Gideon, Lydia, James, Isaac, Grace. Probably some of them removed west.

Huldah, sister of Joshua, 1752, married John Hamlin, and removed from Stephentown to the county of Chenango or Otsego, N. Y She had 3 children, Gilbert, John, Marcia. I know nothing of their descendants.

Mary, sister of Joshua, 1752, married Peleg Allyn, and moved from Stephentown, first, to the Owasco Lake, Cayuga Co., N Y, and afterward to, or near, the Wabash Valley, Indiana. They had several children, among whom was a son Abijah, who visited me a few years ago He raised a family of 14 or 15 children, some of whom are living in the state of Missouri.

Abraham, brother of Joshua, 1752, moved as before stated, with his brother James and other relatives, into the state of Mississippi, there married Sarah Kennard and moved first to the Parish of East Baton Rouge, and afterward to the Parish of West Baton Rouge, state of Louisiana. Had six children. Polly married Asa

345

Conner and died, without issue Abraham married Caroline Broussard, has four children living, is a sugar-planter and lives in this
Parish. Sarah married first —— Watson, second ——. is living
in the Parish of East Baton Rouge, and has three children by first
marriage James Alexander married Celestine Allains; is a cotton
broker living at New Orleans; has two sons, James A and Albert
Gallatin Lobdell Wm. Carter is living in this Parish, has no
children Lydia, died young.

Abijah, brother of Joshua, 1752, moved from Stephentown to
Johnstown (then Montgomery Co., afterward Fulton Co., N Y.),
where he married Mary Little, daughter of John Little and Leah
Crawford; had seven children, Abijah, John Little, Sarah, James
Alexander, Wm Scott, Henry Milton, Charles Sidney. Abijah,
Jr, married Sarah Burget of Oxford, Chenango Co., N. Y. He
was a merchant, residing in Oxford, afterward moved to Utica,
Oneida Co, subsequently returned to Chenango Co., purchased
a farm on the Chenango River, a short distance from Oxford,
where he resided with his family, when he died. They had five
children: Mary Ann, single, living with her mother at Oxford;
Jane, single, and living with her mother; Sarah, married Geo. W
Godfrey, has children, is a widow, James Henry, unmarried; Helen,
single; John Little, myself, was a merchant at Oxford and Johnstown, afterward studied law and was admitted to practice Moved
from Johnstown first to New Orleans, then to the Parish of West
Feliciana, and afterward to West Baton Rouge (this Parish, where
I still reside.) On the 18th of Dec., 1828, in the Parish of West
Feliciana, I married Ann Matilda Sterling of W Feliciana, La.,
daughter of Lewis Sterling and Sarah Turnbull. Have seven
children: Lewis Sterling, still unmarried; Mary, died Oct, 1855
of yellow fever, unmarried; Catherine Hereford, died at eight
months; Catherine Hereford 2d, 19 years old, Sarah Turnbull, 14
years old; John Little, 12 years old; Annie Alston, 9 years old
I have been planting cane, corn and cotton for many years, and
am still planting cane and corn in this Parish.

Sarah, my sister, married Dr. Oren Johnson of Johnstown,
where they resided and had eight children, viz.: Wm. Henry,
married Harriet McCarty, is a practicing physician living at Johnstown, has several children; Charles Weeb, died unmarried, Mary,
lives with her mother; John Lobdell, died young; Sarah and Elizabeth are twins; Sarah married John Young and has a large

family of children living at Johnstown. Elizabeth died young; James Oren, married and has several children. Ann Frances married Lucien Bertrand, has no children.

James Aleander, my brother, died at Johnstown, unmarried.

Wm. Scott, my brother, moved from Johnstown, first to West Feliciana, and afterward to this Parish, where he pursued his profession of a physician, and went into the business of planting and where he still continues planting in company with our brother, Charles Sidney. He is unmarried.

Charles Sidney, my brother, married Susan Coffin of Johnstown and moved to this Parish in 1847, where he still resides in partnership with his brother William, in planting. His wife has no children.

Rachel, sister of Joshua, 1752, married James Dixon, and removed to Ontario Co., N. Y. Children were James, John, De Witt, Harry, 5 and 6. Do not know particulars.

Rebecca, the other sister, died young.

James, son of Joshua (1) of Salem. I have no account of his history. He probably remained in Salem or removed to Westchester Co. or Northampton, Fulton Co., N. Y., where there were other families of Lobdells residing.

Simon, Sarah and Hannah, children of Joshua (1), died young.

Ebenezer, son of Joshua (1) of Salem, probably removed with his father to Newtown, Conn., as I find that name on the memorial with Joshua (1) and (2), John, Samuel and Caleb in the year 1738. His descendants are probably at Newtown still.

Daniel, son of Joshua (1) of Salem, moved to the Royal Grant, Herkimer Co., N. Y.; married and had a large family of children. He visited my father at Johnstown when I was a child. I have heard of his daughters, one of whom married an Episcopal clergyman named Lounsburg or Lounsbury,, and in 1822 saw a lady on the Big Black, Warren Co., Miss., married to a Mr. Rundell, who told me that she was a daughter of Mr. Lobdell of the Royal Grant, and had been a captive among the Indians.

John, son of Joshua (1) of Salem, must have moved with his father to Newtown, as I also find the name of John to the memorial of 1738. He married and afterward removed to Sherburne, Chenango Co., N. Y., where he raised a large family. I have heard of this family, but never became acquainted with any of them.

347

Rachel, the daughter of Joshua (1) of Salem, I have no history of her, probably married, and raised a family. Residing either at Salem or Newtown. There is now remaining two names of the memorial—Samuel and Caleb They must have belonged to other branches of the Plymouth or Plympton stock, and possibly Joshua, Sr. and Jr. John and Ebenezer of the Newtown memorial may be from the same stock, but I think they were part of the Salem branch, as the Joshua, Jr., who moved to Stephentown, was an Episcopalian, as those of Newtown were. We find others of the same name at Plymouth, Mass , Plympton, Mass., Newtown, Conn. and Westchester, Fulton and Essex Counties, N. Y., who must have been branches of the original stock, and from these sources we will be able to fill up the family tree from the first settlers among the Pilgrims, until the present time, and ascertain what branch your own family belong to, and I must beg your assistance, as well as others of the name, in obtaining this full information.

The Mississippi on June 22d was confined within its banks, and the water of the crevasse on my place ceased running a few days thereafter. The water has left the fields, and we hope to save a portion of the cane. I fear it is too late to expect a certain crop of corn. My neighbors below have been badly injured by the crevasse, but will probably have cane enough for seed for next crop, and some of them to make some sugar this year. I had about 175 acres under water. Expect to get seed for another crop from my drowned lands, and hope to make from my other lands from 350 to 400 hhds. sugar and 700 bbls. of molasses, although the crop is very backward, not half of it layed by yet. My corn crop is very unpromising.

Truly Yours,

JOHN L. LOBDELL,

(A true copy.)

NICHOLAS LOBDEN (LOBDELL).

I have never been able to trace the relationship between Nicholas Lobden (or Lobdell) who was of Hingham, Mass., in 1635, and Simon, who had a house lot given him in Milford, Conn., in 1646, but it hardly seems probable that Ann and Elizabeth, with their young brother Simon, would have come to the new country unless some of their kindred had preceded them. Nicholas and Simon were the only Lobdells in New England at that time; indeed, I have never found one bearing the name of Lobdell who could not be traced to one of these two. The descendants of Nicholas, with only a few exceptions, have their homes in the eastern states.

I assume that Nicholas Lobden came from Hastings, Kent County, England.

"Nicholas Lobden, a retainer of Capt. James Lasher, Baron to Parliament, arrested on a plea of debt, prayed to be discharged, 22 Sept., 1621. Letters from Sir Thomas Richardson secured his pardon 3 Oct., 1621.

"James Lasher was Mayor of the ville and port of Hastings, Kent, England." (This was copied at Boston Library, but I have mislaid name of book from which it was taken.)

From Parish Records of All Saints', Maidstrom in Kent, England· "James Sargis and Annis Lobdell m. 25 Aug., 1600."

The name has different spellings, viz.: Lobdale, Lobden, Lobdle, Lobdel, Lobdill, and Lopdell. (In Boston Library in Burke's Landed Gentry, Vols. 2, 3, 4, 5 and 6, the Lopdells of Ireland are quoted.)

Some of the descendants claim French ancestry but I differ with them. Kent County is a maritime county in the southeast of England, including the angle next to France, from which its nearest point is about 24 miles distant. Hastings is a parish of Kent. If Nicholas came from Kent Co. it may be possible that some of his family—brothers or sisters, may have crossed the short distance over into France and that the descendants may keep up a friendly correspondence (as I am told that the Plympton Lobdells have correspondents in France.) Nothing more can

349

be found on early New England records to give assistance than is placed before you. I have made every effort through able workers, over the entire ground, with the following results:

I have not made so extended a search for the descendants of Nicholas as for Simon, as I feared the infirmities of age might cause me to lay the work aside and deemed it for the best to publish what I have secured.

Yours sincerely,
Julia Harrison Lobdell.
(Mrs. James H. Lobdell.)

Nicholas Lobden (Lobdell) 1635

Of Hingham, Mass.

and some of His Descendants

"One generation comes,
Another goes and mingles with the dust;
    And thus we come and go,
Each for a brief moment filling up
Some little space; and thus we disappear
In quick succession. And it shall be so
Till time in one vast perpetuity
    Be swallowed up."

FIRST GENERATION.

Spelled Lobden in all of the early records.

"Nicholas Lobden had grants of land in Hingham, Mass., in 1635 and 36, but whether he was a resident of the town for any time appears doubtful " (History of Hingham.) "Goodman Lobdell's wife d. 1641." (Hobart's Diary.)

After much research my idea of the family of Nicholas Lobden differs from any I have found and I give "my version," to be accepted or denied by descendants First wife died 1641.

I assume that the Pierce family with the Lobdells came from England as friends Now, did Michael Pierce of Hingham, Mass., have a sister Bridget Pierce, who m. Nicholas Lobden as his second wife, and did Nicholas die about 1645-6 and his widow as Mrs. Bridget Lobdell re-marry in 1647 or 8 to Nathaniel Bosworth, who came with his parents in the "Elizabeth Dorcas" in 1634, and was in Hingham as early as 1635 (afterward in Hull and later in Bristol)?

From copy of his will of 15 March, 1689 or 90: "I, Nathaniel Bosworth of Bristol in the County of Bristol in ye colony of New Plymouth, in New England," etc., he mentions his wife Bridget (he m. Mrs. Bridget Lobdell) and his children, each, by name, etc. "Fifthly, moreover, I will that at my wife's decease then out of my cattle and movables Mary Lobdell shall have five pounds, Sarah Lobdell, one pound; John and Nathan Lobdell shall be given ten shillings apiece. (Isaac is not mentioned, but he was probably a son of Nicholas. In 1681 Isaac Lobdell in behalf of the selectmen of Hull, petitioned that Serg't Nathaniel Bosworth, of Hull, be empowered to administer oaths and to marry persons)

From this point of view, I give—

SECOND GENERATION.

1. Isaac 2. John. 3. Nathan 4 Mary. 5. Sarah

I. Isaac of Hull, Mass, m. Martha Ward, dau. of Samuel Ward, a wealthy citizen, first of Charlestown, then of Hingham, pro-

353

prietor of large tracts of land at these towns and at Hull Copy of a deed of land in Hull is given by Isaac Lobdell and Martha his wife to John Lobdell, 17 May, 1670, is found in Suffolk deeds, 314 p. The land is bounded on the southeast by the land of Richard Stubbs, Sr. Isaac and John were admitted Freemen in 1673 and Isaac Lobdell was one of the grand jurymen at Plymouth in 1686

Suffolk County deeds, 24-17: "Isaac Lobdell of Hull (yoeman) and wife Martha, for love and affection to son Joseph of Boston (mariner)—messuage in Hull and balance of lease for 18 years in Bumpus Island, also his negro slave, Sambo, etc.; in consideration of support for life and sundry payments (yearly rent). 15 March, 1702."

WILL OF ISAAC LOBDELL.

Will dated 22 May, 1710; proved 5 May, 1718.

"Well stricken in years. To son Joseph my dwelling house I now dwell in, great chest, £5, etc.

"To dau. Perry, £15, silver spoon, cupboard, etc.; to her husband my black suit.

"To dau. Marah Pierce, bed, gray rug, silver spoon, £15, etc.; to her husband, my next wearing suit and a great coat.

"To dau. Abigail Street, £10 and the £10 her husband borrowed of me long since, and a silver spoon, etc.

"To dau. Rebecca Stubbs, the bed I lie on, green rug, chest of drawers, silver baker, £15.

"Grand children, Ann and Lydia Lendall, each, £5.

"Four children of son Isaac, deceased, each £5.

"£5 to Zachariah Whitman

"My five children, viz. Joseph, Elizabeth, Marah, Abigail, Rebecca. Son Joseph executor with son Perry." Suffolk Probate 20-412.)

II John m. in Himgham on 19 July, 1659, Hannah, dau. of Dea. John Leverett. Hannah d. 23 April, 1662. Children by Hannah (bapt. at Hingham):

    1. Hannah (3), b. 27 May, 1660, d Jan., 1681 or 2.

    2. Elizabeth (3), b 23 April, 1662, d. in 7 days

John re-married on 21 Feb., 1664 or 5 to Mary ——? (Hingham

records say to Mary Bosworth). John d. in 1673 and in the same year Nathaniel Bosworth, called his father-in-law, had administration upon his estate. (In early days a father-in-law meant a father by law, or what we call a step-father.) Bosworth genealogist tells us that John Lobdell did not m. Mary Bosworth, as Mary, dau. of Nathaniel was a school-dame, d aged 78 years on 21 April, 1735 (town record) Nathaniel Bosworth in his will gives: "Fourthly. I give and bequeath to Mary, my dau.," etc. And from Bristol copy (original copy is in Taunton Book 8, p 134): "30 April, 1709, Mary Bosworth sells land, etc , to Eleazer Cary."

Will of John Lobdell, who d. 1673 (Suffolk Co., Mass., 7-339 Probate Records) dated 26 Oct , 1673:

"House and land and all 'sollid" estate to my two sons, John and Nathaniel when of age. The eldest to have three-fifths. They are to be brought up at trades at the disposal of father Bosworth. Eldest dau Hannah to be brought up with the rent of the house and after my sons are of age they are to care for her. To two youngest daughters, Sarah and Mercy, all movable estate. Father Bosworth and my father Leverett to be executors

"Witnessed by Isaac Lobdell, Samuel Shore. Proved 7-9 mo , 1673 by Shore Dea John Leverett renounces exec't'ship 28 Jan.. 1673 Inventory, real estate £156; total, £229 19s I have paid in money for my son's burial £1 12s. signed Nathaniel Bosworth. Inventory taken 3 Nov., 1673 "

The above will is of John numbered 3 in History of Hingham It adds to the account there.

III. Nathan was in the Colony of New Plymouth in 1686. Further than this I have not been able to trace him.

IV. Mary; no record.

V Sarah , no record.

.   ———

THIRD GENERATION.

CHILDREN OF JOHN (2) LOBDELL BY SECOND WIFE, MARY ——.

1. John   2. Nathaniel   3. Sarah   4. Mercy.

1 John, probably m. Hannah Vickers, 23 May, 1704; had dau. Hannah, b. 19 June, 1706.

6. Joseph, b 21 July, 1743. Resided in Boston.

7 Mary, b. 1 July, 1745; m. Joseph Sprague of Hingham, son of Benj. and Deborah (Corthell) Sprague

8. Cromwell, b 11 May, 1747, d. 1754.

9. Celia, b. 11 April, 1749; m. Peter Sigourney of Boston.

WILL OF JOSEPH LOBDELL OF HULL (HUSBANDMAN.)

Dated 21 Jan., 1724. Proved by relict Elizabeth, 3 June, 1725. Wife Elizabeth whole of estate for life, if she marry not again; if she marry, my negro slaves Cose and Kate and £200 in full of her dower. Children, Benjamin, Rebecca and Elizabeth each £200 at age or marriage, in four payments of £50 per annum. Residue of estate to sons Cromwell and Joseph, but eldest son Joseph to have £80 more than the other.

Wife Executor. (Suffolk Probate 24-88.)

V. Mary, b 1663, d. 18 Dec, 1744, buried at Copp's Hill, Boston; m. 4 Dec., 1683, Jonathan Pierce, b 1661. They resided in Charlestown, where he d. 14 July, 1722.

CHILDREN.

1 Mary Pierce (4), b. 4 Sept., 1686; m. 22 Nov., 1707, Isaac Smith of Reading. She d 1740.

2. Samuel Pierce (4), b 19 Feb., 1687, m. 5 Feb., 1711, Mehitable Harrise.

3. Jonathan Pierce (4), b. 18 Oct., 1689, "dead born."

4. Jonathan Pierce (4), b. 24 Jan., 1690; m. Mary Webb.

5. Thomas Pierce (4), b. 29 March, 1693, d. young.

6. Joseph Pierce (4), b. 27 Jan., 1694; m. 17 May, 1715, Mary Mellens.

7 Martha Pierce (4), b. 5 Jan., 1696; m. John Steele of Boston.

8. Benj. Pierce (4), b 30 Sept, 1698; m. Mary ——.

9 Sarah Pierce (4), bapt. at Cambridge, 28 July, 1699

10. Elizabeth Pierce (4), b. 29 June, 1700; m. 5 Nov., 1720, Abraham Smith.

11. Isaac Pierce (4), b. 27 June, 1702; m. Agnes Kent

12. John Pierce (4), b. 23 Dec., 1703; m. first Elizabeth, second Mary Hoppins.

ALBERT ROSCOE STUBBS (9)
(Charles Ramsdell [8])
Librarian of the Maine Genealogi-
cal Society, Portland, Maine
(Pages 359, 363)

JOSEPH WESCOTT LORDELL (9)
(Isaac [8])
of Boston, Mass.
(Page 370)

13. Jacob Pierce (4), b. 24 Aug., 1705, d. 24 Aug., 1705.

14. Stephen Pierce (4), b. 24 Jan., 1706; m. 20 May, 1728, Elizabeth Rand.

Benj. Pierce (the 8th child) m. Mary ——. He was a housewright They lived in Stratford, Conn. Children:

     1. Mary (5), b. 4 April, 1727.

     2. Bettee (5), b. 12 June, 1728; m. Ephraim Beers.

     3. John (5), bapt March, 1730.

     4 Ruth (5), b. May, 1735.

     5. Charity (5), b April, 1742.

     6. Tabitha (5), b. Aug., 1744.

     (Given by a descendant, H H. B.)

VI. Abigail m. Mr. Street; no record.

VII. Rebecca m. in Hull, Mass., Richard Stubbs, b. about 1660 in Hull, son of Richard (1) Stubbs of Hull and Margaret, dau. of Wm Read of Boston

Mr. Albert Roscoe Stubbs, a director, also Librarian of the Maine Genealogical Society, has kindly given for the work his line of descent from Nicholas Lobden through Rebecca (Lobdell) Stubbs.

Richard and Rebecca had—

     Son, Richard (4) Stubbs, b. in Hull, 10 Jan., 1692, d. in North Yarmouth, Maine, about 1751; m. 16 Feb., 1716, Jael Tower, dau. of Benjamin and Deborah Tower of Hingham.
     Had—

          Dau., Hannah (5) Stubbs; m. Philip Greely.
          Had—
          Son, Eliphalet (6) Greely; m. Sarah Prince.
          Had—
          Son, Philip (7) Greely; m. Dorcas Blanchard.
          Had—
          Dau, Ann Matilda (8) Greely, b. 13 March, 1808 at Portland, Me., d. 18 June, 1901 at Portland; m. 30 Sept., 1830 at Portland to John Bundy Brown, b. 31 May, 1805 at Lancaster, N. H, d 10 Jan, 1881 at Portland, Me. (son of Titus Alcott Brown, a farmer, b. 25 Aug., 1764 at Tolland, Conn, d. 23 Feb., 1855 at Norway, Oxford Co., Me., m. 16 June, 1794 at Walpole, N. H., Susanna Bundy, b 19 Dec., 1771 at Walpole, N. H., d. 30 Oct, 1851 at Norway, Me., dau.

of Isaac and Sarah (Johnson) Bundy.)

Had—

John Marshall (9) Brown, "Trustee," of Portland, Me., b. in Portland; m. in Washington, D. C., Alida Catherine Carroll, dau. of Wm. Thomas and Sally (Sprigg) Carroll.

Had—

Sally Carroll (10) Brown m. Herbert Payson

Had—

John Brown (11) Payson.

(Given by Mr. John Marshall Brown.)

VIII. "Elizabeth, m. Wm. Perry in 1681 (son of Thomas and Sarah (Stedman) Perry). They settled at Scituate, east of the church hill; his home stood in what is now Howland's field. He had twelve children, one of whom was Amos who lived near Cornet's dam. Elizabeth, his dau., was the wife of Bezaleel Palmer and m. secondly Capt. Benj. Tolman and was the grandmother of the respectable family of Copeland. There are descendants in Hanover. Wm. Perry also was owner of a half share in Conihassett with Wm Holmes in 1646. He left no family on record." (Deane's History of Scituate.)

On page 121 of same work. "In 1678 ordered that Wm. Perry of Scituate be released from military duty on account of great wounds received in late war (Narragansett fight). The next year he was allowed £10 from the County Treasury on the same account."

IX. A dau. who m. Mr. Lendall, deceased at the time that her father made his will.

LINE OF DESCENT OF MR. ALBERT ROSCOE STUBBS
OF PORTLAND, MAINE.

Nicholas (1) Lobden of Hingham. Mass , 1635, m ——.

Isaac (2) Lobdell of Hull, m Martha Ward, dau. of Samuel Ward of Hull.

Rebecca (3) Lobdell, seventh child of Isaac and Martha (Ward) Lobden of Hull, m Richard (2) Stubbs, b in Hull about 1660, son of Richard (1) and Margaret (Read) Stubbs, who was m. 3 March 1658-9 (dau of Wm Read of Boston, Mass.

Richard (4) Stubbs. b in Hull 10 Jan., 1692, d. in N. Yarmouth, Maine, about 1751, m 16 Feb , 1716. Jael Tower. dau. of Benjamin and Deborah Tower of Hingham

Richard (5) Stubbs. b 19 July, 1717 at Hull. Suffolk Co., Mass., d 5 July, 1785 at N. Yarmouth. Cumberland Co , Me.; m. 13 Oct , 1739 at N Yarmouth, Mary Brown, b 26 Dec., 1718 at Salisbury, Essex Co , Mass . d at N Yarmouth , dau. of Abner and Mary (Morse) Brown Mr Stubbs was a farmer, resided at North Yarmouth In religion a Congregationalist

CHILDREN—SIXTH GENERATION.
1. William, bapt. 11 Oct., 1741.
2. Susannah, bapt 23 Jan., 1743; m. first Bradley, second True.
3. Richard, bapt 21 Oct., 1744, m. first Nabby Kought, second Ruth Allen
4. Samuel, bapt. 15 April, 1750; m —— True.
5. John, bapt. 18 July, 1756
6. Moses, bapt. 28 May, 1758, m. Betsey Noyes.
7 Mercy, bapt. 3 Aug., 1760.
8. Ann, bapt., 7 Nov., 1762; m. Wm. Goff.
9. Benjamin m. Rebecca Dunbar.
10. Jeremiah m. Jane Bradley True.
11 Abigail.
12. Abner

13. Jonathan m. Joanna Merrill.

14 Jedidiah m. —— True.

15 Jael m. Thomas Prince.

Benj. (6) Stubbs, b. at N. Yarmouth, d. at N. Yarmouth; m. at N. Yarmouth, Rebecca Dunbar, b. at Falmouth, Me., d at N. Yarmouth, dau. of Peter and Rebecca (Stubbs) Dunbar. Mr Stubbs was a sea captain; his residence N Yarmouth, and in religion, a Congregationalist.

CHILDREN—SEVENTH GENERATION.

1. John, bapt. 9 Aug., 1778; m. Abigail Grover.
2. Benjamin, bapt. 6 Nov., 1783; m. Nisy Grover.
3. Charles, bapt 13 Sept., 1787; m. Nancy Ramsdell.
4 Hipsebah, bapt 18 July, 1779, m. —— Titcombe.
5. Phebe, bapt 8 Aug., 1790, m. William Noyes.
6 Rebecca.

Charles (7) Stubbs, b. 30 June, 1787 at N Yarmouth, d. 3 Feb., 1858 at Portland, Cumberland Co., Maine; m 18 Feb., 1809 at Marblehead, Essex Co., Mass., to Nancy Ramsdell, b. 1 Sept., 1790 at Marblehead, Mass., d 25 Jan., 1874 at Portland, Me., a dau. of James and Margaret (Reddan) Ramsdell. Mr. Stubbs was a blockmaker; resided in N. Yarmouth and Portland. In religion a Baptist, in politics a Democrat.

CHILDREN—EIGHTH GENERATION.

1 Octavia Ann, b. 16 March, 1810, d. single, 1 Jan., 1896.
2. Rebecca Dunbar, b. 3 May, 1812; m. James Bryant
3 Charles Ramsdell, b 2 April, 1813; m. Almira Sanborn.
4. Margaret, b. 30 Aug., 1815; m. Wm. Kelly
5. Annis, b 25 Aug., 1818, d. 15 March, 1825.
6. Caroline Leah, b 7 Jan., 1823, d. single, 22 May, 1891
7 Olive, b. 12 May, 1827, d. 15 Sept., 1836.

Charles Ramsdell (8) Stubbs, b. 2 April, 1813 at N. Yarmouth, d. 15 Nov., 1883 at Portland, Me., m. in June, 1840 at Portland, Me., to Almira Sanborn. b 3 Aug., 1815 at Harrison, Cumberland Co., Me., d 3 Jan., 1879 at Portland, Me., dau. of Benjamin and Abigail (Hobbs) Sanborn.

Mr. Stubbs was a block-maker, resided at Portland, in religion a Baptist; in politics, a Democrat.

CHILDREN—NINTH GENERATION.

1. Albert Roscoe, b. 15 May, 1841 at Portland, Me. unmarried.
2. Mary Augusta, b. 1 June, 1843; unmarried.
3. Olive Amanda, b. 20 Oct., 1846, d. young.
4. Geo. Ramsdell, b. 21 July, 1848, d. young.
5. Francis Jay, b. 17 Oct., 1852; m. Elizabeth Courtney

FIFTH GENERATION.

CHILDREN OF EBENEZER (4) LOBDELL.
FIRST WIFE, LYDIA SHAW.
SECOND WIFE, MERCY STANDISH.

1. Isaac 2. Sarah. 3. Lydia. 4. Ezekiel.

1. Isaac, b. 26 Dec., 1716, m. 24 Feb., 1741, Ruth Clark, dau. of Thomas and Alice (Rogers) Clark

2. Sarah, b 4 July, 1719, m. 24 Feb., 1741, Thomas Loring of Plympton (Caleb). Thomas was Captain in Revolutionary War of a company of minute men, and afterward joined the Continental army. His son Ezekial m. Hannah Stetson. He was a member of the same company as his father

3. Lydia, b. 4 June, 1733, m. Samuel Elles of Plymouth, 4 Nov., 1752

4. Ezekiel, no record

SIXTH GENERATION.

CHILDREN OF ISAAC (5) AND RUTH (CLARK) LOBDELL.

1. Samuel. 2. Sarah. 3. Deborah. 4. Hannah. 5. Ebenezer. 6. Isaac.

Born at Plympton

1. Samuel, b. 2 May, 1742, d unmarried 19 Feb., 1784.

2. Sarah, b. 2 March, 1744; m. first George Bryant, 15 Dec., 1763, m. second Mr. Hamlin

3. Deborah, b 6 Jan., 1746; m. first Seth Bryant, second Wm. Waterman

4. Hannah, b. 16 Dec., 1748; m. Job Randall, 15 Feb., 1770.

5. Ebenezer, b. 4 July, 1752, d. 18 Jan., 1805 at Norfolk, Va.; m. Judith Bumpus, b. 20 June at Wareham, Plymouth Co., Mass., d. 16 Aug., 1818 at Plympton, dau. of Jeremiah and Judith (Randall) Bumpus.

Capt. Ebenezer was captain of a vessel and resided at Plympton.

6. Isaac (Captain), b. 5 Oct., 1755, d. 18 June, 1806. Is buried in Stroudwater, Maine, cemetery. He m. 21 Sept., 1776, Polly Stetson, b. 7 Sept., 1759, d. 26 Nov., 1797, dau of Caleb and Abigail (Bradford) Stetson. of Scituate, Mass

SEVENTH GENERATION.

CHILDREN OF EBENEZER (6) AND JUDITH (BUMPUS) LOBDELL.

1. Mercy, b. 23 July, 1777, d 8 Sept., 1831; m. Pelham Holmes, Esq. They had a son Pelham who lived in Fall River.

2. Sally, b. 12 Aug., 1779, d 10 Feb., 1820; unmarried

3. Judith, b 13 Oct., 1781, m. 23 Sept., 1800, Wm Sturtevant, who d 23 June, 1802 Left one child, Judith Lobdell Sturtevant; m Zenas Bryant. Jr., who had a dau.—d. young—and two sons, Zenas Francis (9) and Wm. Sturtevant Bryant (9), both married and had children but Wm. S is the only one living of the two sons. He lives in Middleboro, Mass

4. Ruth, b. 10 April, 1784, m. 18 Oct., 1804, Zabdiel Sampson, Esq., of Plympton and Plymouth

CHILDREN.

1. Milton Sampson, b 1805.

2 Eudora Rowland Sampson, b 1807; m., 1828, Francis L. Alden of New Bedford.

3. Algernon Sydney Sampson, b. 1809

4. Marcia Lobdell Sampson, b. 1811, m. 1st John H. Coggshall of New Bedford, 2nd John Hornby of Poughkeepsie

5. Maria Louise Sampson, m. Daniel Rickertson of New Bedford.

6 Algernon Sydney Sampson, b. 1815; m. Adeline Lombard of New Bedford.

7. Ruth Lobdell Sampson, b. 1819; m. Daniel Hathaway of Fairhaven.

8. Dr. Zabdiel Silsbee Sampson, b. 1821; m. Helen Bird of Dorchester. His widow and married dau. (Mrs. Parkhurst) resided in or near Providence, R. I.

9. Judith Lobdell Sampson was a twin to

10. Nancy Ripley Sampson, who m James L Baker of Hingham, son of John and Sarah Lobdell (Loring) Baker. (From Hingham History)

5. Ebenezer, b 4 March, 1786, at Plympton; m Elizabeth (Fuller) Thomas of Kingston, Mass. They had three sons b. in the old homestead at Plympton where Mr Lobdell d. after a long illness.

1. Charles H., b. 20 Oct , 1817; d 22 Dec., 1874, settled in New Bedford, Mass.; m. Mary Ann Dunbar Bates 28 Nov., 1846

2 Ebenezer Thomas, b. at Plympton, d in 1870 at Hartford, Conn, m Agnes Susan Bennock, dau. of John Bennock, b. 1825 at Orono, Maine, d 1875 at Bangor, Me.

Mr Lobdell was a merchant at Boston, before settling at Hartford, Conn In 1844 the firm was Lobdell and Howe, doing business at 30 India St About that time he was also Lieutenant of Artillery at Boston.

CHILDREN—EIGHTH GENERATION.

1. James Francis, b. 18 March, 1847 at Boston, Mass.; m Clara Linabury, b. 29 Dec., 1853, at Pontiac, Mich., dau. of Henry and Frances (Mattison) Linabury. Had one dau , b 6 June, 1874 at Pontiac, Mich., d 26 April, 1893. Mr. Lobdell is manager of Arcade Hotel at Newton, Kansas. Has a residence at Helper, Utah

2. John, b. 1849, d in infancy.

3. Clarence H., b. 1852.

4 Edith, b. 1857, m Edward Stetson of Bangor, Me.

5. Arthur, b. 1859, d. 1861.

6 Agnes, d. 1863

7. May, b 1864, d 1898

3. Geo Walter, settled in Mattapoisett, Mass ·

6. Jeremiah, b 9 May, 1788 at Plympton, d. 21 Nov., 1818 at Plymouth, North Carolina , m 30 Nov., 1816 at Kingston, Plymouth Co., Mass., Maria Drew, b 7 June, 1795 at Kingston, Mass , d. 17 May, 1831 at Kingston, dau of Stephen Nye and Sylvia (Prince) Drew. They had one son .

1. George Granville. b. 1 Oct., 1817; m. Adeline Wheeler

7. George Bryant, b. 25 Feb., 1791; m Nancy Pease of New

Bedford, and he has descendants living in Plympton, but no answer came to me after writing to those whose names and addresses were given to me

8. Thomas Jenkins, a twin of Geo Bryant, d. 8 Dec., 1796.

9. Hannah, b. 8 March, 1794, d. 17 July, 1820.

10. Thomas Jenkins, b 27 June, 1797; m. first in 1817 Hannah, dau. of Wm. Sturtevant, she d at Boston 3 Oct, 1818, aged 22 years. Is buried in Burial Hill, Plymouth, Mass. Mr. Lobdell m. for his second wife in 1821, Sophia Prentiss, b at Leominster, Mass, 1 Sept., 1796, d 27 Oct, 1864, dau. of Charles and Sophia (Gardner) Prentiss Thomas J Lobdell was, in 1821, Major of Artillery at Boston, Mass., and manufactured the first calico prints made in this country and later a merchant in the East India trade. Children, b in Boston:

1. Sophia. b. 1822, d unmarried 29 May, 1852.

2, 3, 4, 5, 6, 7 died young

8. Elizabeth Salesbury, b. 1835, d 1881 single.

9. Annie Louise, b. 1837; m. 1863, Lieut. Ellis Loring Motte of Boston, a lawyer—graduate of Harvard College, 1859. Was a soldier in the Civil War; enlisted 13 Dec., 1862 and mustered 3 Jan., 1863, First Lt., 13th battery Mass. light artillery; resigned 9 March, 1864.

CHILDREN.

1. Margaret Berrion Motte, b. Boston, 1866; m. 1894, Russell Sargeant of New Haven

2. Mellish Irving Motte of Boston (b. 1868), electrical engineer, graduate of Harvard College, 1892.

(John Gibson and his descendants.)

NINTH GENERATION.

CHILDREN OF GEORGE GRANVILLE (8) AND ADELINE (WHEELER) LOBDELL.

---

1. Maria Drew 2. Wm. Wheeler. 3. Anna Prince. 4. Elizabeth Prince. 5. Geo Granville 6. Carolyn Wheeler. 7. Florence Delano. 8. Alice Dike. 9. Howard White. 10. Addie Wheeler.

1. Maria Drew, b 15 Dec., 1842; m. John Wagstaff Huxley.

2. Wm. Wheeler, manufacturer of car wheels at Wilmington,

Delaware, was b. 25 Feb, 1844 at Wilmington; m. 8 Nov., 1866 at Wilmington, Emma Deane Jones, b 24 April, 1842 at Wilmington, dau. of Washington and Margaret W. (Rice) Jones.

CHILDREN—TENTH GENERATION.

1. Margaret Jones, b. 20 July, 1868.
2. Emma Delano, b. 13 Oct., 1870; m. Dr Charles M. Allmond.
   3. Wm. Wheeler, Jr, b. 23 Aug , 1873, d. 14 Aug., 1874.
   4. Howard White, b 3 Feb., 1876, d. 14 Dec , 1879.
   5 Herbert Drew, b. 17 Oct, 1878, d. 3 Jan , 1880.
   6 Carolyn Wheeler, b 23 March, 1882.
3. Anna Prince, b 19 Sept , 1845, d. 31 July, 1847
4. Elizabeth Prince, b. 24 Aug., 1847, d 28 Aug., 1855.
5. Geo. Granville, b. 16 July, 1850, m Eva Wollaston.
6. Carolyn Wheeler, b. 17 Dec., 1851; m. Wm Gideon Jones.
7. Florence Delano, b. 5 Feb., 1854; m. Harry Degan Zeigler.
8. Alice Dike, b. 19 Jan , 1856; unmarried
9. Howard White, b. 25 Dec., 1857, d 1 Dec , 1867.
10 Addie Wheeler, b 5 Oct , 1860; m. Wm. Seawan.

SEVENTH GENERATION.

CHILDREN OF ISAAC (6) AND POLLY (STETSON) LOBDELL.

---

1. Abigail 2. Nancy. 3. Stetson. 4. Mary Gray. 5. Deborah. 6 Isaac. 7. Marcia. 8 Charles. 9 Edward Gray.

1. Abigail, b. 26 July, 1777, d 29 April, 1828 at Minot, Maine; m. Oakes Sampson of Plympton.

2. Nancy, b. 20 Nov., 1779, d. 11 Dec., 1846; m Rev Elisha Moseley of New Gloucester by Caleb Bradley, 27 Oct , 1812

3. Stetson, b 1 April, 1782; m. 3 Sept , 1815, Betsey Gordon of Portland   Settled in Philadelphia   He d 15 Dec , 1854.

4. Mary Gray, b 16 Aug , 1784, m. 22 Aug., 1803 by Caleb Bradley to Joshua Shaw   He was a hat maker at Stroudwater, Maine; removed with his family to Philadelphia in 1814, where he continued the same business. He d 27 July, 1820, in his 40th year. She d. 13 Dec., 1833.

5. Deborah, b. 27 Sept , 1786; m. 25 May, 1813 by Caleb Bradley to Godfrey Malbone, son of Seth and Abigail (Keyes) Gros-

venor of New Gloucester Had a settlement in Minot, Maine, where a dau. Lucia Williams was b. 1821, m. Mr. Humphrey and d. in Buffalo, N. Y., 1877.

6. Isaac, b. 17 May, 1789; m. Charlotte Pratt, b. 1791 or 3 at Cape Elizabeth, dau. of Zenas and Nancy (Thomas) Pratt of Cape E. They resided at Westbrook, Me., or at Stroudwater village Both are buried in the cemetery at Stroudwater. He d. 31 July, 1832, aged 44. She, 27 Feb, 1840, aged 47 or 49.

CHILDREN—EIGHTH GENERATION.

1. Theodore, b. Oct., 1807. Was killed in the Civil War.

2. Ann m Vernon Dunbar of Virginia.

3 Isaac, b. 25 May, 1811 at Westbrook, Me., d. 12 Nov., 1890 at Pownal, Me ; m. 7 Oct., 1834 at Cape Elizabeth to Sarah Jordon Wescott, b. 30 Jan., 1812 at Cape E., d. 15 Nov., 1898 at Pownal, dau. of Col. Joseph Wescott and his wife Betsey Jordon

4. Charles, b. 12 Feb., 1815 ; m. Lucinda Waterhouse.

5. Mary m Morton Jennings.

6. Edward, b 26 May, 1817, d. unmarried 187—.

7. Elizabeth Gordon m Samuel M. Brown.

7. Marcia, b. 12 April, 1797; m. 21 Nov., 1816, Jacob Hill, admitted to the bar at Augusta, Me ; settled in Minot, being the first lawyer to take residence in that town. She d. 11 April, 1830.

8 and 9. Twins, Charles and Edward Gray, b. 27 Oct., 1799. Charles d. 9 Aug., 1801. Edward d. 3 days old.

(For part of the record of the line of Capt. Isaac and Polly (Stetson) Lobdell I have had assistance from the Maine Historial and Genealogical Recorder. Also I copy the following from same: "Capt. Lobdell d. 18 June, 1806; his wife continued to occupy the homestead at Stroudwater for several years, but before 1820 she removed to Minot, where her home was the mecca of children and grandchildren until her death, 3 Sept., 1843."

CHILDREN OF ISAAC AND SARAH J. (WESCOTT) LOBDELL.

---

1. Marcia H. 2. Lydia C 3. Charlotte. 4. Prentiss. 5. Clara B. 6. Joseph W. 7. Grosvenor. 8. Frank.

1. Marcia Hill, b. 19 Aug., 1835, d. 10 Feb., 1861.

2. Lydia Cummings, b. 13 April, 1839; m. Charles B. Deane.

3. Charlotte, b. 4 June, 1841, d. 19 July, 1898.

4. Prentiss, b. 22 Sept., 1844 at Durham, Maine, d. 30 Sept., 1898 at Chelsea, Mass.; m. 20 Oct., 1869 at Newberryport, Essex Co., Mass , Elizabeth Cone Bartlett, b. 5 Aug., 1846 at Newberryport, dau of Jonathan and Sarah (Shute) Bartlett. Mr. Lobdell was a direct descendant of Gov. Bradford and had an honorable army record, having volunteered in Co. A first battalion 17th U. S. regulars, early in 1861, served through all the campaigns of the army of the Potomac, and was mustered out in 1865. Is buried at Pownel, Me. Children ·

> 1 Horace Mannard, b 7 Aug., 1870 at Chelsea, Mass ; m ——. Resides at Chelsea. Is an electrical engineer. Has one little son, Roger Wescott, b. Feb., 25, 1906.
>
> 2. Sarah Bartlett, b. 4 Feb , 1872; m. Charles Danforth Ilsley.
>
> 3. Samuel, b 23 Sept , 1873.
>
> 4. Jessie, b. 12 Oct., 1874. Is the violinist of the Boston Ladies' Symphony Orchestra.
>
> 5. Geo. Stetson, b 22 Feb., 1879.
>
> 6 Hazel Agnes, b 11 July, 1882.
>
> 7. Elizabeth Plummer, b. 18 July, 1889.

5. Clara Bliss. b. 30 March, 1847.

6. Joseph Wescott, b. 7 May, 1850 at Pawnel, Me.; m. 27 April, 1891. Harriet E. Dennis, b. 17 Dec., 1860 at Salem, Mass., d. 22 April, 1892 at Boston, Mass , dau. of Devereaux and Harriet Ellen (West) Dennis. One little son was b. 13 April, 1892, who d. an infant. Mr Lobdell was educated with the intention of following the law, but came to Boston and entered into business when 19 years of age After 17 years of commercial life, desiring to see the world, travelled extensively in foreign countries. After returning to his native land he entered business as stock broker on State St., Boston.

7. Grosvenor, b. 6 May, 1855 at Pawnal, Me ; unmarried. Resides at 41 Pinckney St., Boston, Mass.

8 Frank, b. 13 Jan., 1858.

ISAAC LOBDELL (8)
(Isaac [7])   (1811-1890)
of Pownal, Maine
(Page 369)

PRENTISS LOBDELL (9)
(Isaac [8])   (1844-1898)
of Chelsea, Mass.
(Page 370)

HORACE MAYNARD LOBDELL (10)
(Prentiss [9])
of Chelsea, Mass.

ROGER WESCOTT LOBDELL (11)
(Horace M. [10])
(Page 370)

COPY OF ITEMS FOUND IN SUFFOLK CO., MASS., PROBATE RECORDS, AND ALSO BOSTON RECORDS.

Administration on estate of Joseph Lobdell of Hull, gent, 28 May, 1773, granted to Nicholas Lobdell of Boston, mariner, who gave as sureties Benjamin Loring of Boston, silversmith, and Caleb Loring of Boston, feltmaker. Suff. Probate 72-584.

Administration on estate of Nicholas Lobdell of Boston, innholder 30 Mar., 1789, to his widow Agnes, who gave as sureties, Isaac and Erasmus Pierce Suff. Probate 88-119.

Dower set off to the widow of Nicholas Lobdell 12 Aug., 1790. Committee all of Hull and apparently the lands there located. Suff. Probate 89-670.

Nicholas m. Agnes Pierce, Boston 1764. Kept tavern at Minot's Wharf.

Rebecca L. m. Caleb Loring of Hull, 1732.

John Loring (son of John and Elizabeth (Baker) Loring of Hull), b. 15 Jan, 1707: m. 18 Sept., 1729, Elizabeth or Experience Lobdell and was afterward of North Yarmouth, Maine. (History of Hingham.)

Administration of estate of Joseph Lobdell, late of Boston, innholder, granted to widow Sarah, who gave as surety Simon Hall, joiner, and Erasmus Peirce, distiller, both of Boston, 1 Aug., 1787. Suff. Probate 86-410.

John, son of Isaac and Mirriam (James) Pierce. m Mrs. Sarah Lobdell, Boston, Dec. 29, 1791, by Rev. Sam'l Stillman. (Boston Records.)

Daniel, son of Joseph and Content (Tower) Souther of Hingham, b 13 Aug., 1737; m. Judith Lobdell. He was known as Captain. Was town treasurer several years and a man of prominence, especially during the War of the Revolution. He d. 1797 aged 70 years. (History of Hingham.)

Guardianship of Sarah and Joseph Lobdell, children under fourteen, children of Joseph Lobdell, late of Boston, mariner, to Joshua Eaton, of Boston. 13 Sept., 1790. 89-605.

WORCESTER PROBATE—Hannah Lobdell, late of Boston, now resident in Sutton, will dated 1 Nov., 1775. Effects in Boston to be divided between my cousins, viz Lydia Snowdon and Mehitable Greenleaf both of Boston, except my chair with wheels, which to cousin Mary Nothe of Lynn. Kindness of Mary, wife of Rev. Eben. Chaplin of Sutton and her children, Mary, Sarah, Aaron, Morse. Filed 28 May. 1778 Statement by Rev. Mr. Chaplin that the estate is insolvent (No 37599.)

81103 Indenture between Benj Lobdell of Hull, laborer, and Cromwell Lobdell of Hull, said Benj. for £13-6-8 gives receipt in full of one-half of two-thirds of £200 given by his grandfather, Joseph Lobdell of Hull in his will to his father Benj, deceased, and all my rights in 22 acres in Hull as given me by will of my father. 2 Sept., 1752

81103 Same to Joseph Lobdell; same date.

118-150. Indenture—Joseph Lobdell of Hull, yeo., to Nicholas Lobdell of Boston, innholder; mtg. of land in Hull Joseph is indebted £200 to Nicholas 16 Jan., 1771.

103-170. Thomas, John, Jona., Wm., and Moses Collier, John and Jane Doane. Thomas and Susanna Copeland, Mary Spear, Cromwell and Judith Lobdell, all the true heirs of Gershom Collier of Hull, gent, deceased; division of two-thirds his estate 21 March. 1753.

(Cromwell and Judith Collier married 1726.)

85-176. Henry Price of Boston, gent, for £18-13-0 sells to Jos. Lobdell, gent., a house there 14 May, 1754 Wife Mary Price releases

125-261. Mary Lobdell, widow of Hull for £12 sells to David Louther of Hull, gent., all right and dower in estate which my late husband, Cromwell Lobdell, died seized of. 2 May, 1774 (Mary Harris married Cromwell Lobdell 1741.) (Daniel Louther b 1727, m. at Hull, Judith Lobdell.)

73-191. Whereas Joseph Lobdell of Hull dec'd by his last will, etc., left to Joseph Lobdell of Hull, one-half his estate and one-half to Cromwell Lobdell, both of Hull, they paying the legacies. Division between sd Jos and Cromwell. Jos. has the home lot. 14 Apr., 1747.

73-193 Cromwell Lobdell and wife Mary, to Jos 15 Apr. 1747 See above.

73-195 Joseph Lobdell of Hull; division between him and Cromwell as in 73-191. Cromwell has mansion house. 15 Apr, 1747.

95-37. Judith Lobdell of Hull, "sempstriss," for £19 sells to Ephraim Bosworth of same, gent., 2½ common rights, it being five-ninths of all the undivided lands belonging to one allotment. Mary Lobdell, widow, surrenders right of dower in same. 6 May, 1757.

95-36. Cromwell Lobdell of Hull, yeo , for £31-10-0 sells to Ephraim Bosworth, malster of Hull, land on Great Brewster Is , being 1½ lots of the 34 on the island 18 Apr., 1740.

26-242. Joseph Lobdell, mariner, and w Ely'b., Sam'l Binney, husbandman, and w. Rebecca, Benj. Loring, husbandman, and w. Anna, all of Hull, and sd Ely'b , Rebecca and Anna being daughters of Ely'b. Vickre sometime Ely'b Price, dau. of Capt Thomas Cromwell, to Wm. Brown of Boston. Mch., 1712.

186-78 Sarah Lobdell's estate to Dan. Loring. 1797.

125-261. Mary Lobdell to Dan Louther, right of dower in estate of Cromwell Lobdell. 1774.

188-137. Caleb Clapp of Boston, mtg. to Agnes Lobdell. 1797.

67-216/7. Cromwell Lobdell surety for bail of Thos. Gains, from Gaines and wife. 1749.

22-44 Martha Ballard, widow, of Boston, daughter of Robert Knight, whose widow Anne m John Jolliffe, release of dower to Jos and Ely'b Lobdell, Binney et als., heirs of Capt. Cromwell, in estate sold by them. 1704.

85-176. Henry Price, to Jos. Lobdell, land in Hull 1754.

137-232. Benj Loring and w. Eunice, to Nicholas Lobdell, mariner of Hull, land in Hull. 1782.

138-31. Caleb Loring of Hull to Nicholas Lobdell, mariner of Hull, land in Hull, 1783.

21-304 Isaac Lobdell et als., proprietors of Further's Hill at Hull, to Israel Nicolo. 1696.

21-307. John Lobdell et als., proprietors of Further's Hill. 1697.

9-314 Estate of John Lobdell to S Shore-Hull.

23-98. John Lobdell to John Benny, Cartway. Hull, 1706.

92-46. Judah or Judeth Lobdell, single woman, to Jos. Andrews, State Island, Hull. 1757.

She also sells to John Loring and Ephraim Bosworth. 1757 and 1760.

Above shows the genealogical material in the deeds

Boston marriages to 1800: 29 Dec., 1791, John Pierce to Sarah Lobdell, by Rev. Sam Stillman.

Intentions—John Gaines and Martha Lobdell, 22 Dec., 1745.
Intentions—John Milton and Rebecca Lobdell, 20 May, 1746.
Intentions—Lawrence Clee and Sarah Lobdell, 21 May, 1736.
Intentions—John Steele and Abigail Lobdell, 15 May, 1696.
Intentions—Joseph Smith and Mary Lobdell, 23 Jan., 1700.
1710 Agnes Lobdell was innholder on Congress St.
1764-8 Capt. Nicholas Lobdell was approbated by the selectmen as an innholder, he having hired the tavern at Minot's Wharf.
Joseph Lobdell lived in Boston 1695.
Born—Sarah to Samuel and Sarah Lobdell, 19 Nov., 1710.
Born—Isaac to Samuel and Sarah Lobdell, 6 July, 1715.
Nicholas Lobden was burned out in the great Boston fire, 1760. (Boston Records.)
Copied: "John Lobden of the parish of Harley in Devonshire and Ann Hetton of London, both of Great Britain, will marry, 1716."

INDEX

Embracing Christian names of descendants of " Simon Lobdell," of Milford, Conn.

Also names of others, than Lobdell.

The figures after the names refer to the page.

A

D

E

G

K

L

M

N

O

T

U

V

W

Descendants of
Nicholas Lobden (Lobdell)
of Hingham, Mass. 1635

INDEX

Embracing Christian names of descendants of "Nicholas Lobden" of Hingham, Mass. 1635.

Also names of others, than Lobdell.

The figures after the names refer to the page.

A

B

C

CPSIA information can be obtained
at www.ICGtesting.com
Printed in the USA
BVHW012332280322
632215BV00001BA/118